HISTORICAL
MATERIALISM

A SYSTEM OF SOCIOLOGY

BY

NIKOLAI BUKHARIN

1921

British Library Cataloguing-in-Publication Data
A catalogue record for this book is available from
the British Library

CONTENTS

3

NIKOLAI BUKHARIN

Nikolai Ivanovich Bukharin was born in Moscow, Russia in 1888. He joined the Russian Social Democratic Labour Party in 1906, becoming a member of the Bolshevik faction. By age twenty, he was a member of the Moscow Committee of the party. In 1911, Bukharin was exiled by the authorities. While living in Hanover, Kraków and Vienna, he met all the leading Russian revolutionaries – including Vladimir Lenin, Lev Kamenev, Gregory Zinoviev, and Leon Trotsky – and wrote for *Pravda*, *Die Neue Zeit* and *Novy Mir*. He also published his economic study, *Imperialism and World Economy* (1915). Lenin would freely borrow from the work in his *Imperialism: The Highest Stage of Capitalism* (1917).

After the Bolsheviks seized power in 1917, Bukharin became the editor of the party newspaper *Pravda*. At this point, according to Lenin, Bukharin was "rightly considered the favourite of the whole Party." He had an extremely productive three years, publishing the popular primer *The ABC of Communism* (1919), the more academic *Economics of the Transitional Period* (1920) and *Historical Materialism* (1921).

However, in the years after Lenin's death in 1924, party factionalism saw Bukharin increasingly clashing with Joseph Stalin, and in February of 1937 he was arrested and charged with conspiring to overthrow the Soviet state. While in prison, Bukharin wrote at least four book-length manuscripts including a lyrical autobiographical novel, *How It All Began*, a philosophical treatise entitled *Philosophical Arabesques*, and a collection of poems, *Socialism and Its Culture*.

In 1938, Bukharin was a defendant in the last of the public Great Purge trials. Despite sending thirty-four letters to Stalin, protesting his innocence and professing his loyalty, he was found guilty of counter-revolutionary activities and espionage, and was executed on 14th March, 1938.

INTRODUCTION:
THE PRACTICAL IMPORTANCE
OF THE SOCIAL SCIENCES

---

a. The Social Sciences and the Demands of the Struggle of the Working Class

Bourgeois scholars speak of any branch of learning with mysterious awe, as if it were a thing produced in heaven, not on earth. But as a matter of fact any science, whatever it be, grows out of the demands of society or its classes. No one takes the trouble to count the number of flies on a window-pane, or the number of sparrows in the street, but one does count the number of horned cattle. The former figures are useful to no one; it is very useful to know the latter. But it is not only useful to have a knowledge of nature, from whose various parts we obtain all our substances, instruments, raw materials, etc,; it is just as necessary, in practice, to have information concerning society. The working class, at each step in its struggle, is brought face to face with the necessity of possessing such information. In order to be able to conduct its struggle with other classes properly, it is necessary for the working class to foresee how these classes will behave. For this it must know on what circumstances the conduct of the various classes, under varying conditions, depends. Before the working class obtains power, it is obliged to live under the yoke of capital and to bear in mind constantly, in its struggle for liberation, what will be the behavior of all the given classes. It must know on what this behavior depends, and by what such behavior is determined. This question may be answered only by social science. If the working class has conquered power, it is under the necessity of struggling against the capitalist governments of other countries, as well as against the remnants of counter-revolution at home; and 'it is also obliged to reckon with the extremely difficult tasks. of the organization of production and distribution. What is to be the nature of the economic plan; how is the intelligentsia to be utilized; how are the peasantry and the petty bourgeoisie to be trained to communism. how shall experienced administrators be raised from the ranks of the workers; how shall the broad masses of the working class itself, as yet only slightly class-conscious, be reached; etc., etc., - all these questions require a knowledge of society in order to answer them properly, a knowledge of its classes, of their peculiarities, of their behavior in this case or that; they require a knowledge also of political economy and the social currents of thought of the various groups in society. These questions show the need for the social sciences. The practical task of a reconstruction of society may be correctly solved by the application of a scientific policy of the working class, *i.e.,* a policy based on scientific theory; this scientific theory, in the case of the proletarian, is the theory founded by Karl Marx.

b. The Bourgeoisie and the Social Sciences

The bourgeoisie also has created its own social sciences, based on its own practical requirements.

When the bourgeoisie is the ruling class, it must solve a great number of questions: how to maintain the capitalist order of things; how to secure the so called "normal development" of capitalist society, which means a regular influx of profits; how to organize for this purpose its economic institutions; how to conduct its policy with regard to other countries; how to maintain its rule over the working class; how to eliminate disagreements in its own ranks; how to train its staffs of officials: priests, police, scholars; how to carry on the business of instruction so that the working class may not become savage and destroy the machinery, but may continue to be obedient to its oppressors, etc.

For this purpose the bourgeoisie needs the social sciences; these sciences aid it in its adaptation to the complicated social life and in choosing a proper course in the solution of the practical problems of life. It is interesting, for example, to note that the first bourgeois economists were great practical merchants and government leaders, while the greatest theoretician of the bourgeoisie, Ricardo, was a very able banker.

c. The Class Character of the Social Sciences

Bourgeois scholars always maintain that they are the representatives of so called "pure science", that all earthly sufferings, all conflicting interests, all the ups and downs of life, the hunt for profit, and other earthly and vulgar things have no relation whatever with their science. Their conception of the matter is approximately the following: the scholar is a god, seated on a sublime eminence, observing dispassionately the life of society in all its varying forms; they think (and yet more loudly proclaim) that vile "practice" has no relation whatever with pure "theory". This conception is of course a false one; quite the contrary is true: all learning arises from practice. This being the case, it is perfectly clear that the social sciences have a class character. Each class has its own practice, its special tasks, its interests and therefore its view of things. The bourgeoisie is concerned chiefly with safeguarding, perpetuating, solidifying, extending the rule of capital. The working class is concerned in the first place with the task of overthrowing the capitalist system and safeguarding the rule of the working class in order to reconstruct life. It is not difficult to see that bourgeois practice will demand one thing, and proletarian practice another; that the bourgeoisie will have one view of things, and the working class another; that the social science of the bourgeoisie will be of one type, and that of the proletariat unquestionably of a different type.

d. Why is Proletarian Science Superior to Bourgeois Science?

This is the question we have now to answer. If the social sciences have a class character, in what way is proletarian science superior to bourgeois science, for the working class also has its interests, its aspirations, its practice, while the bourgeoisie has a practice of its own. Both classes must be considered as interested parties. It is not sufficient to say that one class is good, highminded, concerned with the welfare of humanity, while the other is greedy, eager for profits, etc. One of these two classes has one kind of eye-glasses, red ones, the other class has a different kind, white ones. Why are red glasses better than white ones? Why is it better to look at reality through red ones? Why is there superior visibility through red ones?

We must approach the answer to this question rather carefully.

We have seen that the bourgeoisie is interested in preserving the capitalist system. Yet it is a well-known fact that there is nothing permanent under the sun. There was a slavery system; there was a feudal system; there was, and still is, the capitalist system; there also have been other forms of human society. It is evident - and incontrovertibly so - that we must infer the following: he who would understand social life on its present basis must also understand, at the outset, that all is changing, that one form of society follows upon another. Let us picture to ourselves, for example, the feudal serf-owner, who lived in the period before the liberation of the peasants from serfdom. Such a man in many cases could not even imagine that there might exist an order of society in which it would be impossible to sell peasants or exchange them for greyhounds. Could such a serf-owner really understand the evolution of society correctly? Of course not. Why not? For the reason that his eyes were covered not by glasses, but with blinders. He could not see further than his nose, and therefore was unable to understand even the things going on right under his nose.

The bourgeoisie also wears such blinders. The bourgeoisie is interested in the preservation of capitalism and believes in its permanence and indestructibility. It is therefore blind to such phenomena and such traits in the evolution of capitalist society as point to its temporary nature, to its approaching ruin (even to the possibility of its destruction), to its being succeeded by any other organization of life. This is made most clear by the example of the World War and the revolution. Did any one of the more or less prominent bourgeois scholars foresee the consequences of the world slaughter? Not one! Did any one of them foresee the outbreak of revolution? Not one! They were all busily occupied in supporting their bourgeois governments and predicting victory for the capitalists of their own country. And yet, these phenomena, namely, the general destruction by warfare, and the unprecedented revolution of the proletariat, are deciding the destinies of mankind, are changing the face of the entire earth. But of all this, bourgeois science had not a single premonition. But the communists-the representatives of proletarian science-did foresee all this. The difference is due to the fact that the proletariat is not interested in the preservation of the old and is therefore more farsighted.

It is not difficult to understand now why proletarian social science is superior to bourgeois social science. It is superior because it has a deeper and wider vision of the phenomena of social life, because it is capable of seeing further and of observing facts that lie beyond the vision of bourgeois social science. It is therefore clear that Marxists have a perfect right to regard proletarian science as true and to demand that it be generally recognized.

e. The Various Social Sciences and Sociology

Human society is a very complicated thing; in fact, all social phenomena are quite complicated and varied. We have for

11

instance the economic phenomena, the economic structure of society and its national organization; and the fields of morality, religion, art, learning, philosophy; and the domain of family relations, etc. These are often interwoven into very peculiar patterns, constituting the current of social life. It is of course clear that for an understanding of this complicated social life it is necessary to approach it from various starting points, to divide science into a group of sciences. One will study the economic life of society (science of economics) or even the special universal laws of capitalist economy (political economy) ; another will study law and the state and will go into special matters of detail; a third will study - let us say- morality, etc.

And each of these branches of learning, in its turn, can be divided into two classes: one group of these sciences will investigate the past, a certain time in a certain place-this is historical science. For example, in the field of law: it is possible to investigate, and to describe precisely, how law and the state have developed, and how their forms have changed. This will be the *history* of law. But it is also possible to investigate and solve certain questions: what is law; under what conditions does it grow, or die out; on what do its forms depend; etc. This will be the *theory* of law. Such branches of learning are the *theoretical* branches.

Among the social sciences there are two important branches which consider not only a single field of social life, but the entire social life in all its fulness; in other words, they are concerned not with any single set of phenomena (such as, economic, or legal, or religious phenomena, etc.), but take up the entire life of society, as a whole, concerning themselves with all the groups of social phenomena. One of these sciences is history; the other is sociology. In view of what has been said above it will not be difficult to grasp the difference between them. History investigates and describes how the current of social life flowed at a certain time and in a certain place (for example, how economy and law and morality and science, and a great number of other things, developed in Russia, beginning in 1700 and going down to 1800 ; or, in China, from 2000 B.C. to 1000 A.D.; or, in Germany, after the Franco-Prussian War in 1871; or in any other epoch and in any other country or group of countries). Sociology takes up the answer to general questions, such as: what is society? On what does its growth or decay depend? What is the relation of the various groups of social phenomena (economic, legal, scientific, etc.), with each other; how is their evolution to be explained; what are the historical forms of society; how shall we explain the fact that one such form follows upon another; etc., etc.? Sociology is the most general (abstract) of the social sciences. It is often referred to under other names, such as: "the philosophy of history", "the theory of the historical process", etc.

It is evident from the above what relation exists between history and sociology. Since sociology explains the general laws of human evolution, it serves as a *method* for history. If, for example, sociology establishes the general doctrine that the forms of government depend on the forms of economy, the historian must seek and find, in any given epoch, precisely what are the relations, and must show what is their concrete, specific expression. History furnishes the material for drawing sociological conclusions and making sociological generalizations, for these conclusions are not made up of whole cloth, but are derived from the actual facts of history. Sociology in its turn formulates a definite point of view, a means of investigation, or, as we now say, a *method* for history.

f. The Theory of Historical Materialism as a Marxian Sociology

The working class has its own proletarian sociology, known as *historical materialism*. In its main outlines this theory was elaborated by Marx and Engels. It is also called "the materialist method in history", or simply "economic materialism". This profound and brilliant theory is the most powerful instrument of human thought and understanding. With its aid, the proletariat finds its bearings in the most complicated questions in social life and in the class struggle. With its aid, communists correctly predicted the war and the revolution and the dictatorship of the proletariat, as well as the conduct of the various parties, groups, and classes in the great transformation through which humanity is now passing. This book is devoted to expounding and developing this theory.

Some persons imagine that the theory of historical materialism should under no circumstances be considered a Marxian sociology, and that it should not be expounded systematically; they believe that it is only a living *method* of historical knowledge, that its truths may only be applied in the case of concrete and historical events. In addition, there is the argument that the conception of sociology itself is rather vague, that "sociology" signifies sometimes the science of primitive culture and the origin of the primitive forms of the human community (for instance, the family), and at other times extremely vague observations on the most varied social phenomena "in general", and at still other times, an uncritical comparison of society with an organism (the organic, biological school of sociology), etc.

All such arguments are in error. In the first place, the confusion prevailing in the bourgeois camp should not induce us to create still more confusion in our ranks. For the theory of historical materialism has a definite place, it is not political economy, nor is it history; it is the general theory of society and the laws of its evolution, *i.e.*, sociology. In the second place, the fact that the theory of historical materialism is a method of history, by no means destroys its significance as a sociological theory. Very often a more abstract science may furnish a point of view (method) for the less abstract sciences. This is the case here also, as the matter in large type has shown.

1: CAUSE AND PURPOSE IN THE SOCIAL SCIENCES (CAUSATION AND TELEOLOGY)

---

a. The Uniformity of Phenomena in General and of Social Phenomena in Particular

If we regard the phenomena of nature which surround us, as well as those of social life, we shall observe that these phenomena by no means constitute a confused mass in which nothing may be distinguished or understood or predicted. On the other hand, we may everywhere ascertain, by attentive observation, a certain regularity in these phenomena. Night is followed by day; and, just as inevitably, day is followed by night. The seasons regularly follow one upon the other, accompanied by a great number of concomitant phenomena, repeating themselves year after year; the trees put forth their leaves and shed them; various kinds of birds of passage fly into our country and out again; men sow or reap; etc. Whenever a warm rain falls, mushrooms grow up in profusion, and we even have a saying, "to grow like mushrooms after a rain." A grain of rye, falling upon the ground, will strike root and the plant under certain circumstances will ultimately produce an ear of grain. But we have never observed that any such ear grew - let us say - out of frogs' eggs or from bits of sandstone. Everything in nature, therefore, from the movements of the planets down to the little grain or mushroom, is subject to a certain uniformity or, as it is generally put, to a certain *natural law.*

We observe the same condition in social life also, i.e., in the life of human society. However complicated and varied this society may be, we nevertheless observe and discover in it a

15

certain natural law. For example, wherever capitalism develops (in America or in Japan, in Africa or in Australia), the working class also grows and expands, likewise the socialist movement; the theory of Marxism is spread. Together with the growth of production there is a growth in "mental culture": in the number of persons able to read and write, for example. In capitalist society, crises arise at definite intervals of time, which follow upon industrial booms in as precise a succession as the succession of day and night. The bringing out of any great invention which revolutionizes technology also speedily alters the entire social life. Or, let us take another example; let us count the number of persons born every year in a certain country: we shall see that in the following year the increase in the population by percentage will be approximately the same. Let us calculate the quantity of beer consumed each year in Bavaria; we shall find that this quantity is more or less constant, increasing with the increase in population. If there were no uniformity, no natural law, it is of course clear that nothing could be predicted, nothing could be done. Day might follow upon night today, and then there might be daylight for a whole year. This year, snow might fall in winter, while next winter oranges might grow. In England, the working class might grow up by the side of capitalism, while in Japan the number of landowners might perhaps increase. Now we bake bread in an oven but then - why not? - perhaps loaves of bread will grow on pine trees instead of cones.

As a matter of fact, however, no one has any such thoughts, every one well knows that loaves of bread will not grow on pine-trees. Every one has observed that in nature and society there is a *definite* regularity, a *fixed* natural law. The determination of this natural law is the first task of science.

This causality in nature and society is objective; it exists whether men are aware of it or not. The first step of science is to reveal this causality and free it from the surrounding chaos of phenomena. Marx considered the earmark of scientific knowledge to be its character as "a sum of many determinations and relations", as opposed to a "chaotic conception". (Introduction to *A Critique of Political Economy*, Chicago, 1913.) This character of science of "systematizing", "coordinating", "organizing", etc., is recognized by all Thus Mach (in *Erkenntnis und Irrtum)* defines the process of scientific thinking as an adaptation of thoughts to facts and of thoughts to thoughts. Karl Pearson, an English professor, writes: "Not the facts themselves constitute science, but the method of elaborating them." The original method of science is the "classification" of facts, which does not mean a mere collection of facts, but their "systematic connection". (Karl Pearson, *Grammar of Science,* London, 1892, p.15 and 92.) Yet, the great majority of present-day bourgeois philosophers find the function of science to be not the discovery of those causalities that exist objectively, but the invention of such causalities by the human person. But it is clear that the succession of day and night, of the seasons, the uniform sequence of natural and social phenomena, are independent of whether the mind of the learned bourgeois will have it so or not. The causality of phenomena is an objective causality.

b. The Nature of Causation, Formulation of the Question

If uniformity, as stated above, may be observed in the phenomena of nature and society, we may well ask what is this uniformity? When we examine the mechanism of a watch and note its precise operation, when we observe how beautifully the little wheels have been adjusted one with regard to the other, each tooth meshing with another, we are fully aware why the mechanism works as it does. Watches are made on a *definite plan*; this instrument has been constructed for a definite end; each screw has been put in its place precisely for the attainment of this end. Similarly, in the great universe, the planets move regularly and smoothly in their courses; nature wisely preserves the specially developed forms of life. We have only to regard the construction of the eye of any animal in order to observe at once how cunningly and skilfully, with what practical *planfulness* this eye has been constructed. And everything in nature seems informed with a plan: the mole, living under the surface of the ground, has little blind eyes, but very excellent hearing; while the deep-sea fish against whose body the weight of the water is pressing, resists this pressure by an equal pressure from within (if taken out of the water, the fish will burst), etc. And how is it in human society? Does not humanity propose a great goal for itself; namely, communism? Does not the entire evolution of history move toward this great goal? Therefore, if everything in nature and in society has an object, which may not in every case be known to us, but which consists in an eternal process of perfection, should we not consider all things from the point of view of these goals? In this case, the natural law condition of which we have spoken will appear to be a condition of *purposeful* natural law (or of *teleological* natural law; from the Greek *telos*, "goal", "purpose"). This is one of two possibilities, one of the ways in which the question as to the character of natural law may be formulated.

Another formulation of the question starts with the fact that every phenomenon has its *cause*. Humanity moves toward communism for the reason that the proletariat has grown up within capitalist society and this proletariat cannot be accommodated in the framework of this society: the mole has poor sight and excellent hearing because in the course of thousands of years the natural circumstances have been exerting their influence on these animals, and the changes called forth by these circumstances have been handed down to their offspring; those animals which were more adapted to these circumstances finding it easier to continue to live, to reproduce and to multiply, than those less adapted to the changes. Day is followed by night, and vice-versa, because the earth revolves about its axis and turns to the sun now one side and now the other. In all these cases we do not ask for the *purpose* ("for what end?"), but we ask for the *cause* ("why?"). This is the *causal* (from Latin *causa*, "cause") formulation of the question. The natural law of phenomena is here represented as a law of *cause and effect*.

Such is the nature of the conflict between causality and teleology. We must dispose of this conflict at once.

c. Teleology and Objections to Teleology, Immanent Teleology

If we consider teleology as a general principle, *i.e.*, if we closely examine this view, according to which everything in the world is subject to certain purposes, it will not be difficult to grasp its complete absurdity. After all, what is a goal? The conception of a goal presupposes the conception of some one who sets this goal as a *goal, i.e.*, who sets it *consciously*. There is no such thing as a purpose apart from him who conceives the purpose. A stone does not set any goals for itself, any more than does the sun, or any of the planets, or the entire solar system, or the Milky Way. A purpose is an idea which can be associated only with conscious living creatures, having desires, representing these desires to them selves as goals, and aspiring to the realization of these desires (in other words, to "approach" a certain "goal"). Only a savage may ask the purpose pursued by a stone lying by the wayside. The savage imputes a soul to nature and to the stone. Therefore, "teleology" is dominant in his mind, and the stone acts in the manner of a conscious human being. The advocates of teleology are similar to this savage, for in their minds the entire world has a purpose, this purpose having been set by some unknown being. It is clear from the above that the *conception of purpose, of planfulness, etc., is absolutely inapplicable to the world as a whole, and that the natural law of phenomena is not a teleological natural law.*

It is not difficult to trace the roots of the conflict between the adherents of teleology and those of causality. Ever since human society has been divided into groups, some of which (the minority) rule, command, control, while the others are ruled, and obey, them, men have been disposed to measure the entire world by this standard. As the earth holds kings, judges, rulers, etc., who make laws, pronounce judgments, impose punishments, so the universe has a celestial king, a celestial judge, his heavenly host, generals (arch-strategists). The universe has been conceived as a product of the creative will which- appropriately enough gives serious attention to fixing the goals it has in mind, its "divine plan". The causality in phenomena has been taken to be an expression of this divine will. Aristotle went so far as to say: "Nature is the goal" (ἡ δέ Φῦσις τέλος ἐστιν). Greek nomos (νόμος "*law*") meant both a "natural law" and a "moral law" (commandment, standard of conduct), as well as order, planfulness, harmony.

As the omnipotence of the emperors was extended, the jurisprudence of ancient Rome also was transformed into a worldly study of divinity. Its further development proceeded hand in hand with dogmatic theology. Law now simply meant a standard (rule of conduct: - *N.B.),* emanating from the supreme power - the celestial imperator, in theology; the terrestrial God, in jurisprudence - and prescribing a certain conduct for its creatures. (E. Spektorsky: *Sketches on the Philosophy of the Social Sciences,* Series I, *The Social Sciences and Theoretical Philosophy,* in Russian, Warsaw, 1907, p. 158.) The system of causalities in nature began to be regarded as a system of divine legislation. The famous Kepler thought the corporeal universe had its pandects (Emperor Justinian's codes of law were called *pandects*). Such conceptions are also found at later periods, for instance, the French physiocrats in the Eighteenth Century furnished the first masterful outline of capitalist society and confused the causality of natural and social phenomena with the laws of the state and the decrees of the divine powers. Thus, François Quesnay writes: "The fundamental social laws are the laws of the natural order, which are most *advantageous* for the human race . . . . These laws were *fixed* by the creator for all time. Obedience to these . . . (*i.e.,* `divine', `immutable'. *N. B.)* laws must be maintained by the tutelary authority *(autorité tutélaire)."* (F. Quesnay:*Despotisme de la Chine,* chap. viii, par. 1, 2, *Oeuvres,* Francfort, 1888, p.637). Obviously, the laws of the tutelary authority (*i.e.,* the bourgeois policeman) are here skilfully made to depend on the "divine creator" for the support of whom they were created.

Numerous other examples might be adduced, all going to show the same thing, namely, that the teleological standpoint is based on religion. In its origin, this standpoint is a crude and barbarous transfer of the earthly relations of slavery and submission, on the one hand, and domination on the other, to the universe as a whole. It fundamentally contradicts a scientific explanation, and is based on faith alone. No matter what fragrant sauce may be served with it, it remains a priestly point of view.

But how shall we then explain a number of phenomena in which the "purpose" is obvious to the naked eye (the "planfulness" of the construction of certain organs, social progress, the perfection of animal forms, of the human form, etc.)? If we assume a crudely teleological point of view and invoke God Almighty and his "plan", the folly of this "explanation" will become at once apparent. Therefore, the teleological point of view assumes a more attenuated form in certain persons - he form of the doctrine of the so called "immanent teleology" (a purposefulness inherent in the phenomena of nature and society).

Before investigating this question, it is worth while to devote a few words to religious explanations. An intelligent bourgeois economist, Böhm-Bawerk, gives the following example. Let us assume, he says, that I have set up a theory to explain the universe, according to which it consists of a countless number of little devils, whose writhings and contortions produce all the phenomena in nature. These little devils, I add, are invisible and inaudible, may not be detected by the sense of smell nor seized by their tails. I defy anyone to refute this "theory". It cannot be refuted outright, for I have fortified it by assuming the invisibility

21

and intangibility of these little devils; yet everyone will recognize that it is humbug, for the simple reason that there is no proof of the correctness of such a conception.

Of like nature are all the religious pseudo-explanations. They are intrenched behind the intangibility of mysterious powers, or the essential insufficiency of our reason. A father of the Church has set up the following principle: "I believe, because it is absurd" *(Credo quid absurdum).* According to the Christian doctrine, God is one, but also three, which contradicts the rudiments of the multiplication table. But it is declared that "our weak reason cannot comprehend this mystery." Obviously, the most ridiculous absurdities can be covered by such considerations.

This doctrine rejects the idea of a mysterious power, in the crude sense of the word. It speaks only of goals which are constantly being revealed by the course of events, of goals inherent in the very process of evolution. Let us clarify this conception by means of an example. Let us consider a certain type of animal. In the course of time, this type, by reason of a number of causes, alters and adapts itself to nature more and more. Its organs are constantly being perfected, *i.e.,* they are progressing. Or, let us consider human society. No matter how we imagine the future of this society to be (whether this future will be socialism, or any other form of society), is it not apparent that the human type is growing, that man is becoming more "cultivated", that he is "perfecting himself", and that we, the lords of creation, are advancing on the road of civilization and progress? Precisely as the structure of the animal is becoming better adapted to its purpose, so also is society becoming more perfected in its structure, *i.e.,* more adapted to plan. Here the goal (perfection) is revealed in the course of evolution. It is not designed in advance by divinity, but blows forth like the rose from its blossom, simultaneously the development of this blossom into the rose, by virtue of certain causes.

Is this theory a correct one? No, it is not. It is merely a disguised and attenuated form of the teleological fallacy.

First, we must oppose the conception of a goal that is set by no one. This would be equivalent to speaking of thoughts without assuming a thinking means, or to speaking of wind in a region in which there is no air, or of moisture in a place where there is no fluid. As a matter of fact, when people speak of purposes that are "inherent" in something, they are often simultaneously and tacitly assuming the existence of an extremely delicate and inscrutable internal force, to which the setting of the purpose must be assigned. This mysterious force has on the surface but little similarity with the god who is crudely represented as a gray-haired old man with a beard and mustaches; but at bottom the god is again invisibly present, completely enveloped, however, by the most ingenious instruments of thought. We are again dealing with the same teleological theory which we discussed above. Teleology (the doctrine of purpose) leads straight into Theology (the doctrine of God).

But let us return now to immanent teleology in its pure form. For this purpose it is best to discuss the idea of a general progress (a general perfection), on which the advocates of immanent teleology chiefly lean for their support.

Every one will recognize that it is more difficult to overthrow the teleological point of view in this case, for the "divine" element is here hidden in the background, as it were. However, it is not difficult to ascertain the facts of the case if we regard the entire process of evolution as a whole, i.e., if we consider not only those forms and types (animals, plants, peoples, inorganic portions of nature), which have survived, but also those which have been destroyed, and those which are being destroyed. Is it true that this much vaunted progress is being accomplished in the case of all the forms? It is not true. There were once mammoths, now there are none; within our own memories the buffalo has died out; and, in general, we may say that an endless multitude of living types of all kinds have perished forever. With human groups, the tale is the same; where are now the Incas and the Aztecs, who once lived in America? Where is the Assyro-Babylonian system of society? the Cretan civilization? the ancient Greek? Where is ancient Rome, ruler of the world? All these societies have perished; their existence is a thing of the past. But a few of the countless multitude have survived and "perfected" themselves. "Progress" then simply means that-let us say-against ten thousand combinations, which were unfavorable for development, we have one or two combinations that were favorable to development.

If we bear in mind only the favorable conditions and the favorable results, everything will of course impress us as being highly planful and marvelous ("How wondrously this world is made!"). But our friends the immanent teleologists do not look on the reverse side of the coin; they do not consider the countless instances of destruction. The whole matter reduces itself to the fact that there are conditions that are favorable and others that are unfavorable for survival, that under favorable conditions we obtain also favorable results, while under unfavorable conditions (which is much more frequently the case) we have unfavorable results; the whole picture at once loses its divinely planful halo, and the teleological fallacy falls of its own weight.

One of the Russian teleologists, once a Marxist, later an orthodox priest and preacher of pogroms under General Wrangel (Sergey Bulgakov) writes, in the volume of collected essays called *Problems of Idealism* (in Russian, Moscow, 1902, pp.8, 9): "By the side of the conception of evolution, as a *colossal and directionless evolution* (our italics, N.B.), there arises the conception of progress, of teleological evolution, in which causality and the gradual unfolding of the goal of this evolution overlap to the point of complete identity, precisely as in metaphysical systems." This clearly shows us the psychological roots of the seeking after a *Weltanschauung* that shows purpose. The soul of the discontented bourgeois, feeling insecure, longs for consolation. The course of evolution actually operative displeases him because it is not guided by a saving reason, a goal of deliverance. It is so much more pleasant to take a nap after a

24

good meal, and to know that there is one who watches over us.

It is unnecessary to point out that the apparently teleological elements in the formulations of Marx and Engels are to be understood merely as a metaphoric, esthetic mode of expression; when Marx speaks of *value* as congealed muscle, nerves, etc., only malicious opponents of the workers, like P. Struve, will take this figure of speech literally, and look for real muscles.

d. Teleology in the Social Sciences

When we speak of the teleological point of view in its application to inanimate nature, or to animals aside from man, the incorrectness and folly of this point of view are evident. How can there be a purposeful law of nature, when there is no purpose! But the matter is quite different when we speak of society and of human beings. The stone sets no goal for itself; the giraffe is doubtful on this point; but man differs from the other portions of nature precisely by virtue of the fact that he does pursue definite purposes. Marx formulates this difference as follows: "A spider conducts operations that resemble those of a weaver, and a bee puts to shame many an architect in the construction of her cells. But what distinguishes the worst architect from the best of bees is this, that the architect raises his structure in imagination before he erects it in reality. At the end of every labor-process, we get a result that already existed in the imagination of the laborer at its commencement. He not only effects a change of form in the material on which he works, but he also realizes a purpose of his own that gives the law to his modus operandi, and to which he must subordinate his will. And this subordination is no mere momentary act. Besides the exertion of the bodily organs, the process demands that, during the whole operation, the workman's will be steadily in consonance with his purpose. This means close attention."[1] Marx here draws a sharp line between man and the rest of nature, and he is right in doing this, for the thesis that man sets himself goals. Let us no one can deny see what are the inferences drawn from this fact by the adherents of the "teleological method" in social science.

For this purpose let us consider the views of our most prominent opponent, the German scholar Rudolf Stammler, who some time ago published a large book in opposition to Marxism under the title: "Economics and Law from the Standpoint of the Materialistic Interpretation of History"(*Wirtschaft and Recht nach der materiulistischen Geschichtsauffassung,* second edition).

What, asks Stammler, is the substance of the social sciences? He answers: The social sciences concern themselves with social phenomena. And social phenomena are distinguished by certain peculiarities which are not present in phenomena of any other kind. For this reason special (social) sciences are necessary. Now, what is the special characteristic, the special token, of social phenomena? Stammler answers as follows: the earmark of the social phenomenon is in the fact that it is regulated from an external standpoint, or, more definitely, by the norms of law (laws, decrees ordinances, regulations, etc.). Where there is no such regulation, no practice of law, there is no society. But where there is a society, this means that the life of such a society is conducted within a certain framework, and adapts itself to this framework as molten metal adapts itself to the mould.

Stammler's precise words are: "This (determining. - N. B.) factor is the regulation by men of their intercourse and their life together. The *external* regulation of human conduct in mutual relations is the necessary prerequisite of a social life as a specific goal. It is the *ultimate factor,* to which all *social* thought must formally be traced back in its peculiarities as such" (p. 83).

But if it is the distinguishing characteristic of social phenomena that they are subject to regulation, says Stammler, it is perfectly clear that the law of nature in social life is a *purposeful* law of nature. As a matter of fact, who "regulates", and what is the meaning of "regulation"? *Men* regulate, by creating definite norms (rules of conduct) for the attainment of definite *purposes,* which are also consciously formulated by *men*. It follows, according to Stammler, that there is a tremendous difference between nature and society, between social evolution and evolution in nature (social life, according to Stammler, is something that is directly "opposed to nature")[2] and consequently also between the natural sciences (*Naturwissenschaften*) and the sciences concerned with society. The social sciences are *sciences with a purpose* (*Zweckwissenschaften*); the natural sciences consider all things from the standpoint of *cause and effect*.

Is this point of view a correct one? Is it true that there are two kinds of sciences, some of which are as remote from the others as the heavens from the earth? No, it is not true. And now for the reason.

Let us agree for a moment that the fundamental characteristic of society actually is the fact that men consciously regulate their relations with each other by means of law. Would it follow that we may never ask ourselves why people regulate these relations at a certain time and in a certain place in one way, while they order them quite differently in another place and at another time? For example, the bourgeois German Republic in 1919 and 1920 regulated social relations by shooting the workers; the Soviet Proletarian Republic regulates these relations by shooting counter-revolutionary capitalists; the legislation of bourgeois governments pursues the goal of strengthening, extending, perpetuating the rule of capital; the decrees of the proletarian state pursue the goal of overthrowing the rule of capital and safeguarding the rule of labor. Now, if we should wish to understand scientifically, *i.e.*, to explain these phenomena, would it be sufficient simply to say that the purposes are different? Everyone will at once see that this would not be sufficient, for everyone will ask: but why, why should "men" in one case set themselves one goal, and in another case a different goal? This brings us face to face with the answer: because in the one case the proletariat is in power, in the other case the bourgeoisie; the bourgeoisie desires one thing, because the conditions of its life cause it to have one set of desires; but the conditions of the life of the workers cause them to have a different set of wishes, etc. In a word, as soon as we wish really to understand social phenomena, we immediately find ourselves asking the question: "why?" i.e., we ask concerning the *causes* of these phenomena, in spite of the fact that these phenomena may be the expressions of certain human purposes. In other words, even if men should regulate everything consciously, and even if everything should be accomplished in society just as these men desire, we should still need an explanation of social phenomena, not teleology, but a consideration of the causes of the phenomena, i.e., the determination of a cause and effect relation, as their law. And for this reason. there is no difference at all in this regard between the social sciences and the sciences concerned with nature.

If we consider the matter well, it is at once apparent that it could not be otherwise. As a matter of fact is not man himself, is not any specific human society, a portion of nature? Is not the human race a portion of the animal world? Anyone denying this is ignorant of the very rudiments of present-day science. But if man and human society are portions of nature as a whole, it would really be very remarkable to find that this portion is in complete contradiction with the rest of nature. It is not difficult to see that the advocates of teleology here again display the thought of the divine nature of man, *i.e.,* the naive thought already discussed above.

We have thus become aware of the complete fallacy of the teleological standpoint, even if we should admit that the basic characteristic of society is its external regulation (law). Even here teleology does not "hold water". Besides, in the last analysis, "external regulation" is not the most fundamental trait of society. Almost all the societies that have existed, to the present day (particularly capitalist society) have been distinguished precisely by the absence of any regulation, by their anarchy. In the great mass of social phenomena, any regulation that positively regulates in the manner desired by the law-givers, has never played a very decisive part. And how about the future (communist) society? In that society, there will be no "external" (legal) regulation at all. For the class-conscious population that has been trained in the spirit of workers' solidarity will not be in need of any external pressure (we shall discuss these questions in detail in the following chapter). In other words, even from this point of view Stammler's theory is of no avail, and the sole correct method for a scientific consideration of social phenomena remains that based on the law of cause and effect.

Stammler's theory clearly shows the ideology of the capitalist state official, which seeks to perpetuate essentially temporary conditions. State and law are in reality products of class society, whose parts are in constant, sometimes very bitter, struggle with each other. Doubtless the legal standards and the state organization of the ruling class were a condition for the existence of this society. But it is precisely in a classless society that the picture changes completely. We may not therefore regard a relation of historically changeable nature (state, law) as a permanent attribute of all society.

Furthermore, Stammler overlooks the following condition. Very frequently it happens that the laws and standards of the state power, whereby the ruling class seeks to attain certain results, in reality by reason of a blind evolution, and the social anarchy lead to entirely different results than those originally aimed at. The World War is an excellent example; with the aid of state measures (mobilization of army and navy, military actions under the leadership of the state authority, etc.), the bourgeoisie of the various countries imagined it would attain certain definite goals. But the actual outcome was the revolution of the proletariat against the bourgeoisie. Apparently, Stammler's pious teleological point of view will not work here. His basic error is in overestimating the element of "regulation", and under estimating the elemental course of evolution, and all his lucubrations are therefore devoid of any foundation.

e. Causality and Teleology; Scientific Explanations are Causal Explanations

It follows from the above that whenever we wish to explain a certain phenomenon - and this includes any phenomenon of social life - we must inevitably seek its cause. All the efforts of the teleological pseudo-explanation are at bottom only expressions of religious belief and cannot explain anything. We may therefore answer the fundamental question as to whether the inherent law in the phenomena of nature and society, the uniformity which we observe in these fields, is teleological or causal: *Both in nature and in society there exists objectively* (i.e., *regardless of whether we wish it or not, whether we are conscious of it or not) a law of nature that is causal in character.*

What constitutes such a law of cause and effect? Such a law is a necessary, inevitable, invariable and universal relation between phenomena; if, for example, the temperature of a body rises, its volume will increase; if fluids are heated to a sufficient extent, they will be transformed into vapors; if immense quantities of paper money are issued, far exceeding normal requirements, they will become worthless; if capitalism exists, there will necessarily be wars from time to time; if in any country there is a small-scale production by the side of a large-scale production, the large-scale production will ultimately be the victor; if the proletariat launches an attack on capital, capital will defend itself with all its might; if the productivity of labor increases, prices will fall; if a certain amount of poison be introduced into the human organism, it will die, etc., etc. In a word it may be said that any law of cause and effect may be expressed by the following formula: *If certain phenomena are actually present, there must necessarily be also present certain other phenomena corresponding to them.* The explanation of any phenomenon means the finding of its cause, in other words, the finding of a certain other phenomenon on which it depends, *i.e.,* the explanation of the *cause and effect relation* between the phenomena. As long as this relation is not determined, the phenomenon has not been explained. Once this relation has been found, once it has been discovered and verified that this relation is really a constant one, we are dealing with a scientific (causal) explanation. This mode of explanation is the sole explanation that is scientific, both in the phenomena of nature and in those of social life. This method of explanation completely rejects divinity; it completely rejects any use of supernatural forces, any appeal to the time-worn trumpery of the past, and opens up the road for man to obtain a true control both over the forces of nature and his own social forces.

Many oppose the conception of causality and law in nature with the argument that (as we have seen) this conception is itself the result of an erroneous assumption of a celestial lawgiver. No doubt that is the origin of the idea, but the idea has left its origin far behind. Language presents many cases of such evolution. When we say, for example, "the sun has come up", "the sun has gone down", of course we do not believe that the sun has actually "come", or "gone", as a man comes or goes, on two legs, but that was probably the original conception. Similarly, in the case of the word "law", we may say that "a law prevails", or "applies", which by no means signifies that the two phenomena (cause and effect) involve any third invisible little god, lodged in the cause, reins in hand. The causal relation is merely the constantly observable connection between phenomena. This conception of causality is perfectly in accord with science.

BIBLIOGRAPHY

G. Plekhanov: *Grundprobleme des Marxismus* (translated from the Russian, published by Dietz, Stuttgart). *Criticism of our Critics* (in Russian). Korsak: *Society of Law and Society of Labor* (in the Russian collection: *Sketches of a Realistic Conception of the Universe*). Stammler: *Wirtschaft und Recht*. A. Bogdanov: *On the Psychology of Society* (in Russian).

Max Adler: *Kausalität and Teleologie im Streite um die Wissenschaft.* Max Adler: *Marxistische Probleme* chap. vii: *Zur Erkenntniskritik der Sozialwissenschaften.* Friedrich Engels: *Anti-Dühring.* Friedrich Engels: *Feuerbach* (translated into English by Austin Lewis, Chicago, 1906). N. Lenin: *Materialism and Empirio-Criticism* (Russian edition, pp.151-167, 187-194; for English translation see Volume XIII, Lenin's *Collected Works).* *Problems of Idealism* (a collection of essays against Marxism, in Russian).

Notes

[1] *Capital*, Chicago, 1915, vol. I, p.198.
[2] In German: *Gegenstück zur Natur..*

2: DETERMINISM AND INDETERMINISM (NECESSITY AND FREE WILL)

a. The Question of Freedom or Lack of Freedom of the Individual

WE have seen that in social life as well as in the life of nature there is a certain regularity of law, yet one may have doubts on this point. As a matter of fact, social phenomena are created by persons. Society consists of persons who think, cogitate, feel, pursue purposes, act. One does one thing; another for example, may do the same thing; a third, another thing; etc. The result of all these actions is a social phenomenon. Without people there would be no society, there would be no social phenomena. If social phenomena follow a uniform law and if they are nevertheless the result of the actions of men, it follows that the actions of each individual also depend on something. It thus follows that man and his will are not free, but bound, being subject also to certain laws. If this were not the case, if each man and his will did not depend on anything, where would we get any regularity in social phenomena? There would be no such thing. This is clear to everyone. If everybody were lame, it follows that the whole of society would be a society of lame persons: there would be nothing with which to form a society of my other kind.

But, on the other hand, what is this question of the dependence of human will? Does not man himself decide what he wishes to do? I decided to drink water, and I am drinking water; I decided then go to the meeting, and I made up my mind to go. On a free evening, my comrades proposed that we go to the Proletkult Theatre, while others wanted to go to the Comedy Theatre; I decided to go to the Proletkult; I myself decided it. Has not man therefore the freedom of *choice?* Is he not free in his actions, in his wishes, in his desires, his aspirations? Is he a puppet, a mere chessman moved by forces outside of himself? Does not every man know from his own experience that he may freely resolve, choose, act?

This question is called in philosophy the question of freedom or of freedom of the human will. The doctrine which maintains that the human will is free (independent) is called *indeterminism* (the doctrine of the unconditioned, independent will). The doctrine which maintains that the human will is dependent, conditioned, unfree, is called *determinism* (the doctrine of the dependence or conditioning of the will). We must therefore decide which of these two points of view is the correct one.

First of all let us consider to what the doctrine of indeterminism would lead us if we should pursue it to its logical conclusion. If the human will is free and depends on nothing at all, this would mean that it is without cause. But this being the case, what would be the result? The result would be the good Old Testament religious theory. As a matter of fact we should then have the following condition: Everything in the world is accomplished according to certain laws. Everything, from the multiplication of fleas to the motions of the solar system has its causes; only the human will is not subject to this rule. It constitutes the sole exception. Here man is already no longer a part of nature, he is a sort of god standing above the world. Consequently the doctrine of freedom of the will leads straight to religion, which explains nothing, for in religion there is no knowledge but only blind belief in the practices of the devil, in the mysterious, in the supernatural, in bugbears of all kinds.

Of course this is unreasonable. In order to crack this little nut, we must dwell on this point for a bit. Often - almost always - there is a confusion between the *feeling* of independence, and *real objective* independence. Let us take an example. Let us suppose that at a meeting you are looking at the speaker. He takes a glass of water from the table and empties it thirstily. What does he feel when he reaches for the glass? He is fully conscious of his freedom. He *himself* has decided that he should drink the water and not - let us say - dance a jig. He *feels* his freedom. But does this mean that he is really acting without cause, and that his will is truly independent? By no means. Every sensible man will at once recognize the nature of the case. He will say: "The speaker's throat is dry." What does this mean? Simply, that the exertion of speaking has brought about such changes in the speaker's throat as to call forth in him a desire to drink water. That is the cause. An alteration in his organism (physiological cause) has brought about a certain desire. It therefore follows that we must not confuse a sense of freedom of the will, the *feeling* of independence, with causelessness, with an independence of human desires and actions. These are two entirely different things. And yet, the confusion of these two things is very frequent in all the reasonings of the indeterminists, who wish at any price to rescue the special "divinity" of the human spirit.

One of the greatest philosophers, Baruch Spinoza (1632-1677) wrote concerning most of these philosophers: "They obviously think of man in nature as of a state within the state, for they believe that man disturbs nature more than he complies with it; and that he has unconditional power over his actions, being determined from within himself and not from elsewhere." *(Ethics,* German translation by Otto Baensch, Leipzig, 1919, p.98). This erroneous conception arises only because men are not yet conscious of the external causes of their own actions. "Thus, a child believes it desires milk of its own volition, likewise, the angry boy believes he desires revenge, voluntarily, while the timid man believes he voluntarily desires to flee" *(ibid.,* p.105). Leibnitz (1646-1716) likewise speaks of men as losing sight of the causes of their actions *(causas . . . fugientes),* which gives them the illusion of absolute freedom; he mentions the example of the magnetic needle, which, if it were able to think, would surely rejoice *(laetaretur)* in its constantly pointing to the north pole (G. G.

Leibnitz*Opera omnia*, Tomus I, Genevae, 1768, p.155).

The thought was expressed by D. Merezhkovsky, before he was attacked by his apocalyptic anti-bolshevik insanity

> Each drop of rain,
> If minded as you,
> Descending from on high,
> A blessing from heaven,
> Would surely have surmised:
> "No aimless power
> Controlleth me,
> For of my own free will
> Upon the thirsting fields below
> Swiftly I fall."

At bottom, people completely contradict in their actions the theory of the freedom of the will. For, if the human will were entirely independent of everything, it would be impossible to act at all, since there would be no possibility of reckoning or of predicting. Let us suppose that a speculator is going to the market. He knows there will be trading and haggling there, that each seller will ask too much, and that the purchasers will attempt to obtain lower prices, etc. But he does not expect that people will be walking about on all fours in the market, like cats, because it is contrary their nature. What does that mean? Simply, that their organism is constituted in a certain way. But do not clowns go about on all fours? Yes, for the reason that their will is determined other conditions, and when the speculator goes to the circus he expects that people will go about on all fours, at the circus, "contrary to nature". Why do the buyers wish to buy cheap? For the simple reason that they are buyers. Their position as buyers "obliges" them to secure cheap goods; their wish, their will, their action is determined in this direction. But suppose this man is a seller? He will then act in the contrary direction. He will seek to sell as high as possible. It follows, in consequence, that the will is not at all independent, that it is determined by a number of causes, and that persons could not act at all if this were not the case.

Let us now approach the subject from another standpoint. Everyone knows that a drunken man will develop "stupid" desires and that he will perform "stupid" actions. His will acts in a different manner from that of the sober man; the reason is to be found in alcoholic poisoning. Simply introduce a certain quantity of alcohol into the human organism, and the "divine will" begins to indulge in pranks that will surprise the saints. The reason is obvious. Or, let us take another example; feed salt to a man; he will necessarily begin "freely" to desire to drink much more than usual; the cause is quite obvious And suppose we feed the man "normally"? He will then drink a "normal" quantity of water; he will "feel like" drinking as any other man would "feel like" drinking. In other words, in this case also, the will is precisely as dependent as in the unusual cases.

Man will fall in love when his organism has developed to that point. Man in a condition of extreme exhaustion surrenders to "black despair". In a word, man's feeling and will are dependent on the condition of his organism and on the circumstances in which on he finds himself. His will, like all the rest of nature, is conditioned by certain causes, and man does not constitute an exception to all the rest of the world: whether he desire to scratch his ear, or accomplish heroic deeds, all his actions have their causes. To be sure, in some cases these causes are very difficult to ascertain. But that is another matter. We have by no means succeeded in ascertaining all the causes in the domain of inanimate nature. But this does not mean that these things cannot be explained at all. We must bear in mind that, as we have seen, not only the "normal" cases are subject to the law of cause and effect. All phenomena are subject to this law. The mental diseases may serve as the clearest example. Is it possible that the incoherent, stupid, strange and peculiar desires and actions of the mentally deranged, the insan, can have any law of cause and effect, any "order"? Even these have their causes. Under the influence of certain causes the insane behave in a certain way; under certain other influences, they will behave in another way, under a third set of causes, in still another way; etc. In other words, even in the case of the insane, law of cause and effect remains in full force.

This is the basis of the classification of mental diseases, all of which play be traced back along certain lines: 1. Heredity (syphilis, tuberculosis, etc.); 2. Lesions (traumata); 3. Intoxications (poisons); 4. Various destructive influences and commotions (cf. "Mental Diseases" in Granat's Russian Encyclopedia). For example, the dementia of dipsomania is described as follows: "The patients believe that evil things are planned against them, that all those around them are in a plot, not only neighbors, but even domestic animals and inanimate objects" etc. (A. Bernstein, same article). Dipsomania is a result of alcoholic intoxication. In progressive paralysis (due to syphilis) we have different "symptoms": *first stage,* mental disturbance, levity, coarse actions, credulity; *second stage,* hallucinations (ideas of grandeur; the patient becomes a millionaire, a king, etc.); *third stage,* general collapse (P. Rosenbach: "Progressive Paralysis," in Brockhaus Russian Encyclopedia, vol. 49). In the case of certain lesions diseased condition of certain portions of the brain or nervous system), the will is determined in certain directions; in other lesions, in other directions, etc. The entire practice of medicine in nervous diseases is based on the dependence of the mental life on certain causes.

We have purposely chosen examples of the most varied kind. A consideration of these examples has shown that under all conditions, both usual and unusual, both normal and abnormal, the will, the feeling, the actions, of the individual man always have a definite cause; they are always conditioned ("determined"), defined. The doctrine of freedom of the will (indeterminism) is at bottom an attenuated form of a semi-religious view which explains nothing at all, contradicts all the facts of life, and constitutes an obstacle to scientific development. The only correct point of view is that of determinism.

b. The Resultant of the Individual Wills in Unorganized Society

There is no doubt that society consists of individual persons, and that a social phenomenon is composed of a numerous aggregation of individual feelings, moods, wills, actions. A social phenomenon is, in other words, the result (or, as is sometimes said, the "resultant", the sum total) of the individual phenomena. Prices are an excellent example. Buyers and sellers go to market. The sellers have the goods, the buyers have the money. Each of the sellers and buyers is aiming at a certain object: each of them makes a certain estimate of goods and money, ponders, calculates, scratches and bites. The result of all this commotion in the market is the market price. This price may not represent the idea of any individual buyer or seller; it is a social phenomenon arising as a result of a struggle of the various wills. The same phenomenon as in price-fixing is also observable in all other social relations. Let us take, for example, the epoch of the revolution Some persons proceed more energetically, others less so; some are pushing in one direction; others in another. From this struggle *between persons* there finally, after the "victory of the revolution", arises a new social structure, a new order of things. A certain order of social relations, wrote Marx, "is as much a product of human beings as is canvas, linen, etc." (Karl Marx: *The Poverty of Philosophy,* French edition, Giard and Brière, 1908, page 155).

We may consider in this connection two different cases, each of which has peculiarities of its own. These two cases are: that of unorganized society, or a simple commodities or capitalistic society; and that of organized communist society. In the former case, let us take the extremely typical example mentioned above, namely the example of price fixing. What will be the *relation of the price* which is fixed on the market, *with the desires,* with the estimates and intentions which were present in the mind of each individual who came to market? It is obvious that the price will not coincide with these wishes. For many persons this price will be outright ruinous; namely, for those who simply cannot buy anything "at such prices," and who leave the spot, their pennies in their pockets and their stomachs empty; also for those who are *wiped out* by the, fact that the price is too low for them. Everyone knows that a great number of tradesmen, petty merchants and petty peasants are destroyed by the fact that the great factory owners flood the market with their cheap wares, which ruin the petty trader, unable to maintain the struggle, unable to meet prices at the low points to which they may go, when depressed under the weight of the great mass of goods thrown on the market by the great capitalists.

We mentioned above another characteristic example, the example of the imperialist war, in which many capitalists in the various countries desired to make seizures, with great resulting impoverishment; from this impoverishment was born the revolution against the capitalists; although, of course, these capitalists had not desired such a revolution at all.

What does this mean? It means that an unorganized society, where there is no planful production where classes are fighting each other, where nothing is done according to plan, but in an elemental natural manner, the result obtained (social phenomenon) does not coincide with the wishes of many persons. Or, as Marx and Engels frequently said, social phenomena are independent of the consciousness, the feeling and the will of individuals. This "independence of the will of persons" consists not in the fact that the events of social life proceed outside of the persons concerned, but in the fact that in unorganized society, in chaotic, elemental evolution, the social product of this will (or wills) does not coincide with the objects that are proposed by many persons, but sometimes is in direct contradiction with these objects (a man wishing to make profit finds himself ruined).

A great many objections against Marxism are based on the misunderstanding of the phrase "independence of the will", as used by Marx and Engels. A few lines from Engels will be in place here:

"Nothing appears without an intentional purpose, without an end desired . . . . That which is willed but rarely happens. In the majority of cases the desired ends cross and interfere with each other. So, the innumerable conflicts of individual wills and individual agents in the realm of history reach a conclusion which is on the whole analogous to that in the realm of nature, which is without definite purpose. The ends of the actions are intended, but the results which follow from the actions are not intended, or in so far as they appear to correspond with the end desired, in their final results are quite different from the conclusion wished" *(Feuerbach,* translated by Austin Lewis, Chicago 1906, pp.104, 105)

"Men make their own history, in that each follows his own desired ends independent of results, and the results of these many wills acting in different directions and their manifold effects upon the world constitute history . . . . But ... we have seen in history that the results of many individual wills produce effects, for the most part quite other than what is wished - often, in fact, the very opposite" *(Feuerbach,* p.105, 106).

From the above it follows that in unorganized society, as well as in any other society, events are accomplished not outside of the will of the individuals, but through this will. In this case the individual man is subject to an unconscious natural process which is the product of the individual wills.

Let us now turn our attention to another circumstance. Once a certain social result of the individual wills has been obtained, this social result determines the conduct of the individual. We must emphasize this point, for it is very important.

Let us begin with the example that has already been mentioned twice, namely, that of price fixing. Let us assume that a pound of carrots costs so much on the market. It is obvious that both the new purchasers and the new sellers already have had this price in mind in advance, that they have already been approximately assuming this price in their reckonings. In other words, the social phenomenon (price) has a determining influence on the individual phenomena (offers and demands). The same thing takes place in all the other phases of life. The incipient painter bases his activity on all the preceding evolution of his art and on the social feelings and social tendencies with which he is surrounded. On what are the actions of the statesman based? On the circumstances under which he acts: he may desire either to strengthen a certain order or destroy it. This will depend in turn on the side on which he stands, on the environment in which he lives, on the social class and on the social aspirations from which he draws his strength. In other words, his will also is determined by social conditions.

We have seen above that in unorganized society the final consequence very often is different - sometimes quite different - from the original desires of the persons involved. It may here be said that the "social product" (social phenomenon) *dominates* the persons. And this, not only in the sense that it determines the conducts of these persons, but even in the sense that it directly contradicts their desires. Thus, in *unorganized* society we may set up the following laws

1. *Social phenomena are the resultant of the conflict of individual wills, feelings, actions, etc.*

2. *Social phenomena determine at any given moment the will of the various individuals.*

3. *Social phenomena do not express the will of individual persons, but frequently are a direct contradiction of this will; they prevail over it by force, with the result that the individual often feels the pressure of social forces on his actions* (example: the ruined merchant, the capitalist, who has stood for war, is disestablished by the revolution, etc.).

c. The Collectively Organized Will (the Resultant of Individual Wills in Organized Communist Society)

Let us now consider the state of affairs in organized society. In such a society there is no anarchy in production; there are no classes, no class struggles, no oppositions of class interests, etc. There are not even contradictions between personal and social interests. We are now dealing with a friendly brotherhood of workers with a common plan for production.

What now is the situation of the individual will? Of course, society will continue to consist of persons, and social phenomena will continue to be the product of the individual wills. But the *character* of this aggregation, the *method* by which this resultant is obtained, are completely different from those obtaining in unorganized society. In order to grasp this difference clearly, let us take a little preliminary example. Let us suppose that we have a little society or circle of persons who have organized to sing together. All propose the same goal for themselves, propose to solve the questions involved, to evaluate the difficulties with which they are faced, in short, they make resolutions in common and carry them out in common. Their common action, their common resolution - these are already a collective "product". But this product is not an external, crude, elemental force flying in the face of the individual desires; on the contrary, it constitutes an enhanced possibility of each individual's attaining his desire. Five men resolve to lift a stone together. Alone, none of them could lift it; together, they do so without difficulty. The general resolution does not differ by a hair's breadth from the desire of each individual. On the contrary, it aids in the realization of this desire.

The case will be the same - but on a more magnificent scale, and in more intricate form - in communist society (by which we mean not the period of proletarian dictatorship, nor the first steps of communism, but the fully developed communist society in which there are no remnants of classes, no state, and no external legal norms). In such a society, all the relations between men will be obvious to each, and the social volition will be the*organization* of all their wills. It will not be a resultant obtained by elemental accident, "independent" of the will of the individual, but a consciously organized social decision. We therefore cannot have the same result as in capitalist society. Under communism, the "social product" will, not dominate over men, but men will control their own decisions, for the very reason that it is they who make the resolve, and who make it consciously. It will be impossible to observe social phenomena whose effect on the majority of the population will be harmful and ruinous.

But it by no means follows from the above that in a communist society the social will and the will of the individual will be independent of everything, or that there will be freedom of the will under communism, with man suddenly becoming a supernatural creature who is not subject in any way to the law of cause and effect. Under communism, man will remain a portion of nature, subject to the general law of cause and effect. Will not each individual continue to depend on the circumstances surrounding him? He will; he will not act as a savage in Central Africa or as a banker belonging to the trading firm of J. Pierpont, Morgan and Company, or as a hussar in the period of the imperialist war. He will act as a member of the *communist* society. The circumstances of life will determine man's will. Everyone, for example, understands that it will be necessary for a communist society to struggle with nature, and consequently the conditions of this struggle will of themselves define the conduct of men, etc. In a word, the deterministic theory will remain in full force in communist society also.

Therefore, we may set up the following laws in the case of *organized* society

1 *Social phenomena are the resultant of the conflict of individual wills, feelings, actions, etc.* But here this process does not proceed with elemental confusion, but - in the decisive instances - in an

organized manner.

2 *Social phenomena determine at any given moment the will of the various individuals.*

3 *Social phenomena are an expression of the will of men and usually do not fly in the face of this will; men control their own decisions and do not feel any pressure of blind social forces upon them, since these forces have been replaced by a national social organization.*

Engels wrote that humanity, in its transition to communism, makes a "leap" from the realm of necessity into the realm of freedom. Some bourgeois scholars inferred that Engels meant that determinism would lose its validity in communist society. This view is based on a crude distortion of Marxism. Engels meant - and rightly that in the communist society evolution would assume a consciously organized character, as opposed to the unconscious, blind, elemental stage. Men will know what they are doing and how they must operate under the given circumstances. "Freedom is the recognition of necessity."

d. Accidentalism in General

In order to understand fully the general interdependence of phenomena, we must continue to dwell here on the discussion of so called "accidentalism". As a matter of fact, we very frequently encounter accident in every-day life, as well as in social life. Certain scholars have even taken up special investigations of the rôle of accident in history". We very frequently speak of accident: persons "chanced" to be walking in the street; a brick, falling from the roof, killed a man; by chance I purchased an extremely rare book; accidentally, in a strange city, I met a man I had not seen for twenty years, etc. Further examples: playing "heads or tails", or dice. By accident, "heads" came out: I won; by accident, it was "tails": I lost. How shall we explain this accident in terms of natural law, or, in other words, where does *causal necessity* enter here?

Let us examine this question. Let us first consider the case of "heads" and "tails". Why, for example, should "heads" come out on top? Is it true that there were no reasons, no causes? There must have been causes. Heads came out on top, because, with a coin of given shape, I made certain motions with my hand, with a certain force, in a certain direction; result: the coin fell with a certain surface down, etc. If all these conditions should be repeated, inevitably "heads" would again appear. And if the experiment should be made a third time, the result would be the same. But the fact is that in tossing the coin, it is simply impossible to discount all the circumstances in advance. A slight inclination of the hand, a flip of a finger, a change of the force with which the coin is tossed, all these will influence the result. The causes leading to the result (obverse or reverse appearing on top) cannot there be calculated in practice. They exist, but we cannot reckon with them, because we do not know them. In this case we term our ignorance "accident".

Let us now take another example: my accidental meeting with an acquaintance whom I had not seen for twenty years. It is not difficult to see that there are causes for this meeting; impelled by certain causes I left at a certain time and went by a certain route a certain speed; impelled by another set of causes, my acquaintance at a certain time began his journey on a certain road, with a certain speed. It is quite evident that the combined action of all these causes necessarily brought about our meeting. Why should this meeting appear accidental to me? Why should it seem me that no causal necessity was present? For the very simple that I am ignorant of the causes governing my friend's that I am ignorant even of the fact that he is living in the same city, and consequently am unable to foresee our meeting.

If, of two or more causal chains (series) of intersecting actions, we know only one, the phenomenon obtained by their intersection will appear accidental to us, though in reality it is in accordance with law. I know one of the chains (one series) of causes, those resulting in my own passing through the street; of the other chain (series) of causes, those impelling my friend, I am ignorant. For this reason, this intersection strikes me as an "accidental" phenomenon. Strictly speaking, therefore, there are no accidental, *i.e.,* causeless phenomena. But phenomena may impress us as "accidental" when their causes are insufficiently clear to us.

Spinoza already knew this: he states that "a thing is called accidental merely through lack of inner understanding because the series of causes is concealed from us" *(Ethics,*translation by Baensch, Leipzig, 1919, p.*30).* John Stuart Mill, in his *System of Logic,* Book iii., chap. *xvii,* par. 2, after making a correct analysis, writes as follows: "It is incorrect, then, to say that any phenomenon is produced by chance; but we may say that two or more phenomena are conjoined by chance, that they coexist or succeed one another only *by chance;* meaning that they are in no way related through causation; that they are neither cause and effect, nor effects of the same cause, nor effects of causes between which there subsists any law of coexistence, *nor even effects of the same original collocation of primeval causes."* We have italicized the incorrect statements. The fact is (in the example of my meeting a friend) that I did not leave my house because my friend had gone away, and my friend did not set out because I had gone away. But if there is given a certain "distribution of causes", *i.e.,* if we assume as given that I went away at a certain time, on a given path, with given speed, and if we assume the same details to be given in the case of my friend, we are in possession of the causes of our meeting; there is as little of accident and independence in this "distribution of causes" as in the case of eclipses of the sun or moon, which are determined by a certain situation ("meeting") of celestial bodies.

e. Historical "Accident'"

After what has been said above, the question of so called "historical accident" is a relatively simple matter.

If at bottom all things proceed in accordance with law, and if there is nothing that is accidental - causeless - it is clear there can be no such thing as accident in history. Each historical event, however accidental it may appear, is absolutely and completely conditioned by certain causes; historical accidentalism also simply means the intersection of certain causal series of which only one series is known.

Sometimes, however, the term *historical accident is* used in another sense. For instance, when we say that the imperialist war was a *necessary* result of the evolution of world capitalism, we are also in the habit of adding that the murder of the Austrian Archduke was an *accidental*phenomenon; but here "accident" is something different. When we speak of the necessity (causal necessity, inevitability) of the imperialist war, we infer this inevitability from the immense power of certain causes in the evolution of society, causes leading to war. Similarly, the war in its turn is also an event of immense importance, an event exerting a decisive influence on the further destinies of society. Therefore, the expression "historical accident" as used here, signifies a circumstance that does not play an important part in the chain of social events: even if this "accident" had not come to pass, the subsequent evolution would have been altered so little as not to be essentially changed in any way. In the given case: the war would have come if the Archduke had not been killed, for the "crux of the matter" was not in this slaying, but in the sharpening of the between the imperialist powers, growing fiercer day by day with the evolution of capitalist society.

May we say that such "accidental" phenomena play no part at all in social life, that they have no effect on the destinies of society, that they are equivalent to zero? A truly correct answer could deny the importance even of "accidental" events, for each event, "insignificant" though it may be, actually has an influence on all of subsequent history.

The important point is the magnitude of the effect of such an event on the evolution of the future. When we speak of phenomena that are "accidental" in the sense above indicated, their practical influence is unimportant, insignificant, infinitely small. This influence may be infinitesimal, but it is not zero. We shall understand this if we consider the *combined* aggregate action of such "accidental" facts. For example: let us consider the fixing of prices. The market price is fixed by the conflict of a great mass of guesses on the part of buyers and sellers. If we consider a single case, a single price-estimate, the meeting of a single buyer and a single seller, such an instance may be considered "accidental". Merchant John Brown fleeces old man Smith. This act, from the point of view of the *market-price, i.e.,* of a *social* phenomenon, the resultant of a multitude of meetings between various estimates, accidental. What does it matter what happened to John Brown in any given case? What we want is the final result, the social phenomenon, the *typical* fact in the matter. We often hear such statements, and they are quite reasonable. For the individual case is of negligible importance. But just combine a great number of such "accidents", and you will at once see that their "accidental nature" begins to disappear. The function and significance of many actions, their combined action, is at once felt in the sequel. So the individual cases are by no means zero quantities, for zero, however frequently multiplied, will never give more than zero.

We therefore observe that, strictly speaking, there is no such thing as an accidental phenomenon in the historical evolution of society; the fact that Karl Kautsky could not sleep one night because he was dreaming of the terrors of the Bolshevik Revolution; the fact that the Austrian Archduke was killed shortly before the war; the fact that England was pursuing a colonial policy; the fact that the world war was brought about; in a word, *all* events, from the most petty and insignificant to the most epoch-making events of our times, are *equally not accidental,* are equally conditioned by causes, i.e., are equally the result of causal necessity.

f. Historical Necessity

It follows from the above that the conception of "accident" must also be banished from the social sciences. Society and its evolution are as much subject to natural law as is everything else in the universe.

Characteristically enough, the doctrine of accident, when it seriously admits accidentalism as a fact, leads directly into a faith in the supernatural, a faith in God. This is the basis of the so called "cosmological proof" of the existence of God; if the cosmos is not subject to the law of cause and effect, it is evident that there must be a special cause for its existence and evolution. This alleged reasoning is also designated as a "proof of the accidental nature of the universe" (*e contingentia mundi*), and may be found in Aristotle, Cicero, Leibnitz, Christian Wolff, etc. In the present period of decline and disintegration of bourgeois society, the doctrine of accident is again being widely accepted (for instance, by the French philosophers Boutroux, Bergson, etc.).

The conception of accidentalism is directly opposed to that of necessity (causal necessity).

"A thing is necessary when it follows inevitably from certain causes." When we say that a certain phenomenon was a historical necessity, we mean that it necessarily had to follow, without regard to whether it would be good or bad. When we speak of causal necessity, we are not giving the slightest indication of our opinion of the event, of its desirability or undesirability; we are considering only its inevitability. But we must not - as is often done - conuse two entirely different conceptions: *necessity* in the sense of "great desirability", and *causal necessity.* No two things could farther apart. And when we speak of historical necessity, we not mean "desirability" from the standpoint of - let us say - progress, but *the inevitable result* of the course of social evolution. In this sense, we may speak of the historical necessity of the rapid growth of the productive forces at the end of the Nineteenth Century, or of the disappearance of the so called Cretan civilization. *Necessary* means only: *conditioned by cause.*

We now are brought to a rather difficult question, still connected with this difficult matter of necessity.

Let us suppose that we have before us a human society which has doubled in population in the course of twenty years. We may rightly infer that production has grown in this society. If it had not grown, the society could not have doubled its population. If this society has increased in numbers, production must also have increased. This example would not seem to require further explanation. But what does it involve? We are here seeking by a special method the *cause* of social growth, the cause that constitutes the necessary condition of this growth. If this condition is not present, there will be no growth; if there is a growth, *as a consequence,* this condition must also be present.

This example might lead to conflicts of the following nature. At the beginning of this book we mercilessly cast out teleology. Now it looks as if we were ourselves restoring it: "Drive nature out by the door, and she will fly in through the window." But does our formulation of this question permit this inference? For the growth of society, for the doubling of its numbers, it was necessary that production should increase. The growth and increase of society is the goal, the "telos". The increase of production is the *means* for realizing this goal. The natural law of growth is therefore a teleological natural law. But this would be equivalent to a violation of scientific method, and to falling into the open arms of the priests

As a matter of fact, we are dealing with an entirely different at all teleological in its nature. We are here proceeding from the assumption that society has grown (in a concrete case, we may proceed from the *fact* that society has grown). But then, society

51

may *not* grow. And if it should *not* grow, but - let us say - should decrease by one-half, and if, furthermore, the decrease should be due to insufficient food, it is clear that production must have been curtailed. No man can be prevailed upon to behold "purpose" in the destruction of society. No one can be induced, in this case, to reason as follows: the goal is the decrease in the numbers of society by insufficient food; the means for realizing this goal is a curtailment of production. Here we cannot see teleology at all. We are simply seeking the condition (cause) leading to the result (effect). The necessary condition for further evolution is also frequently called *historical necessity*. In this sense of the term "historical necessity", we may speak of the "necessity" of the French Revolution, without which capitalism could not have continued to grow; or of the "necessity" of the so called "Liberation of the Serfs" in Russia in 1861, without which Russian capitalism could not have developed. In this sense we may also speak of the historical necessity of socialism, since *without it* human society cannot continue to develop. If society is to continue to develop, socialism will inevitably come. This is the sense in which Marx and Engels speak of "social necessity".

The method of finding the *necessary conditions* from the given or accepted facts was very often used by Marx and Engels, although but little attention has been given to their use of this method. The whole of *Capital* is built up on it. Given: a commodities-producing society with all its elements; how explain its existence? *Answer:* it can exist only under the condition that the law of value exists; countless commodities are exchanged against each other; how may we explain this? It is possible only if we assume the existence of a money system (social necessity of money). Capital is accumulated on the basis of the laws of commodities circulation. This is possible only because the value of the labor power is lower than that of the product turned out, etc.

g. Are the Social Sciences Possible? Is Prediction Possible in this Field?

From what has been said above it follows that prediction is possible in the domain of the social sciences as well as in that of the natural sciences. Such prediction is not of the kind practiced by the charlatan or faker, but is of scientific nature. We know, for example, that astronomers are able to predict with the utmost precision the time of an eclipse of the sun or moon; they can predict the appearance of comets or of great numbers of "falling stars"; meteorologists can predict the weather - sunshine, wind, storm rain. There is nothing mysterious about these predictions, as we may see from the example of the astronomer, who knows the laws of motion of the planets; the path followed by sun, moon, earth; and also, the velocities with which they move, and at what points they will be in their paths at a certain time. There is nothing miraculous in the fact that under these conditions it can be precisely calculated when the moon will come between the earth and the sun and hide the "light of heaven" from our sight. Now, let us ask whether there is anything similar to this in the social sciences; the answer is in the affirmative. If we know the laws of social growth, the paths along which society necessarily travels, the direction of this evolution, it will not be difficult for us to define the future society. In social science we have had many instances of such predictions which have been fully justified by the outcome. On the basis of our knowledge of the laws of social evolution, we predicted economic crises, the devaluation of paper money, the world war, the social revolution as a result of the war; we predicted the behavior of the various groups, classes and parties in the time of the Russian Revolution; we predicted, for example, that the Social-Revolutionists would be transformed, after the proletarian coup *d'etat,* into a counter-revolutionary party of rich peasants, of Whites, of lawless bands; long before the revolution, as early as the nineties of the last century, Russian Marxists were predicting the inevitable growth of capitalism in Russia and with it the inevitable growth of the workers' movement. We might give hundreds of examples of such predictions, in none of which is there anything miraculous, once we know the laws of the social-historical process.

We cannot predict the *time* of the appearance of any such phenomenon, for we do not yet possess sufficient information regarding the laws of social evolution to be able to express them in, precise figures. We do not know the velocity of the social processes but we are already in a position to ascertain their *direction*.

Bulgakov, in his *Capitalism and Agriculture* (in Russian, 1900, vol. pp.457-458) says: "Marx considered it possible to measure and predict the future in accordance with past and present, whereas each epoch furnishes new facts and new forces of historical evolution - the creative power of history never runs dry. Therefore, any prognosis with regard to the future, which is based on the results of the present, must necessarily (!!!) be in error. . . The veil of the future is impenetrable." The same author, in his *Philosophy of Economy* (in Russian, Moscow, 1972, p.272): "But even much more modest predictions may be admitted, in the case of social science, only with a grain of salt. The 'tendencies of evolution' determined by science and favorable to socialism, have very little in common with the 'laws of natural science', that Marx takes them to be. They are merely 'empirical' . . . they have an entirely different logical nature from that of the laws of mechanics." These quotations from Professor Bulgakov will serve as a very characteristic example of the "refutation" of Marxism; needless to say, they will not hold water. Bulgakov thinks that the laws of capitalist evolution, for example, are "empirical laws". "Empirical" is the term given to such causal relations as have not yet been unraveled. For instance, it has been observed that more boys are born than girls, but the reasons for the phenomenon are unknown. Such "laws" are truly different in their "logical nature". But this is not the case with the laws of evolution of socialism, which have a causal thread. The law of the centralization of capital, for instance, is not an "empirical law", but a real law of natural science. If small production units are competing with large ones, the victory of the latter is inevitable. We know the causal connections; we may predict the victory of large-scale production in Japan or in Central Africa.

Our first quotation from Bulgakov is merely superficial literary drivel. History "furnishes new facts", the creative power of history does not run dry, etc. But the evolution of nature also furnishes "new facts"; such new facts are not unknown to the natural sciences, or to mathematics, with their different "logical nature". Bulgakov is right only in his statement that we never know everything, but that is no reason for inferring that science is an insufficient instrument.

It is also quite characteristic that Bulgakov, in his *Philosophy of* Economy, dwells frequently and very seriously on angels, the lust of the flesh, man's fall from grace, Saint Sophia, etc. This stuff, to be sure, is of a "different logical nature", one that much resembles the charlatanry and quackery attacked by Bulgakov.

The theory of determinism in the field of social phenomena, and of the possibility of scientific prediction, has called forth a number of replies, of which we shall consider one, from the mouth of R. Stammler. Stammler asks the Marxists - who maintain that socialism must come with the same degree of certainty as does an eclipse of the sun - why the Marxists should attempt to *bring about* socialism in that case. One of two things is true, says Stammler, either socialism will come, like an eclipse of the sun, in which case there is no reason for effort, for struggle, for a party organization of the working class, etc.; for no one would think of organizing a party to support an eclipse of the sun; for, in organizing a party, in conducting the struggle, etc., you are admitting that it is possible that socialism may not come; but you *desire* it, and consequently are struggling for it.

But such is not the nature of the necessity of socialism. It is easy, in view of our foregoing exposition, to detect Stammler's error. An eclipse of the sun does not depend either directly or 'indirectly on human desires; in fact, it does not depend on *men* at all. All humans might die, without distinction of class, sex, nationality, and age, and yet the sun would be eclipsed at a certain moment. The case with social phenomena is entirely different, for they are accomplished *through* the will of men. Social phenomena *without* humans, without society, would be something like a round square or burning ice. Socialism will come inevitably because it is inevitable that men, definite classes of men, will stand for its realization, and they will do so under circumstances that will make their victory certain. Marxism does not *deny the will, but explains it.* When Marxists organize the Communist Party and lead it into battle, this action is also an expression of historical necessity, which finds its form precisely through the will and the r actions of men.

Social determinism, i.e., the doctrine that all social phenomena are conditioned, have causes from which they necessarily flow, must not be confused with *fatalism,* which is a belief in a blind, inevitable destiny, a "fate", weighing down upon everything, and to which everything is subjected. Man's will is nothing. Man is not a quantity to be considered among causes; he is simply a passive substance. This teaching denies the human will as a factor in evolution, which determinism does not.

This "Fate" is often embodied in godlike creatures, as the Moira of the ancient Greeks, the Parcae of the Romans; in a number of Fathers of the Church (for instance, Saint Augustine), the doctrine of pre-destination plays the same role; the Reformer Calvin illustrates the same phenomenon (cf. R. Wipper: *Church and State in Geneva in the Sixteenth Century,* in Russian); we have a particularly striking expression of fatalism in Islam. But we cannot help calling attention to this fatalistic tendency among the Social-Democrats. Precisely in that section of the Social-Democracy which has allied itself with the bourgeoisie, Marxism has degenerated into a fatalistic notion. Cunow, whose whole "philosophy" is expressed in the thesis that "history is always right", and that therefore no one should oppose either the

World War or imperialism, is the best example of this fatalistic distortion of Marxism. This distorted view would represent any communist uprising of the workers as a senseless effort to violate the laws of historical evolution from without, and not as an outcome of historical necessity.

BIBLIOGRAPHY

Karl Marx: *A Contribution to a Critique of Political Economy, Introduction.* Friedrich Engels: *Anti-Dühring.* Friedrich Engels: *Feuerbach*(translation by Austin Lewis, Chicago, 1906). Plekhanov (Beltov): On *the Question of the Development of the Monistic Standpoint in History.* Plekhanov: *Criticism of Our Critics.* Plekhanov: *Fundamental Problems of Marxism* (all three in Russian). N. Lenin: *Materialism and Empirio-Criticism* (translated). V. Bazarov: *Authoritarian Metaphysics and the Autonomous Personality* (in Russian; sketches contributing to a realistic *Weltanschauung*). A Labriola: *Aufsätze.*

3: DIALECTICAL MATERIALISM

---

a. Materialism and Idealism in Philosophy; the Problem of the Objective

In our consideration of the question of the human will, the question whether it is free, or determined by certain causes, like everything else in the world, we arrived at the conclusion that we must adopt the point of view of determinism. We found that the will of man is not divine in character, that it depends on external causes and on the conditions of the human organism. This brought us face to face with the most important question that has troubled the human mind for thousands of years - the question as to the relation between matter and mind, which in simple parlance is often spoken of as the relation between "soul" and "body". In general, we distinguish between two kinds of phenomena. Phenomena of the one kind have *extension,* occupy space, are observed through our external senses: we may see them, hear them, feel them, taste them, etc.; such we call material phenomena. Others have no place in space and cannot be felt or seen. Such, for example, are the human mind, or will, or feeling. But no one can doubt their existence. The philosopher Descartes considered just `` this circumstance to be the proof of man's existence; Descartes said *"Cogito, ergo* sum" - I think, therefore I am. Yet, man's thought cannot be felt or smelt; it has no color and cannot be directly measured in yards or meters. Such phenomena are called *psychical;* in simple language, "spiritual". We have now to consider the question of the relation between these two kinds of phenomena. Is the mind "the beginning of all things", or is it matter? Which comes first; which is the basis; does matter produce mind or does mind produce matter? What is the relation between the two? This question involves the fundamental conception of philosophy, on the answer to which dePend the answers to many other questions in the domain of the social sciences.

Let us try to consider it from as many standpoints as possible. First of all, we must bear in mind that man is a part of nature. We cannot know for certain whether other more highly organized creatures exist on other planets, although it is probable that such do exist, for the number of planets seems endless. But it is clearly apparent to us that the being called "man" is not a divine creature, standing outside of the world, projected from some other, unknown, mysterious universe, but, as we know from the natural sciences, he is a product and a portion of nature, subject to its general laws. From the example of the world as we know it, we find that psychic phenomena, the phenomena of the so called "spirit", are an infinitesimal portion of the sum of all phenomena. In the second place, we know that man has sprung from other animals, and that, after all, "living creatures" have been in existence on earth only for a time. When the earth was still a flaming sphere, resembling the sun today, long before it had cooled, there was no life on its surface, nor thinking creatures of any kind. Organic nature grew out of dead nature; living nature produced a form capable of thought. First, we had matter, incapable of thought; out of which developed thinking matter, man. If this is the case - and we know it is, from natural science - it is plain that matter is the mother of mind; mind is not the mother of matter. Children are never older than their parents. "Mind" comes later, and we must therefore consider it the offspring, and not the parent, as the immoderately partisan worshipers of everything "spiritual" would make it.

In the third place: "mind" does not appear until we already have *matter organized in a certain manner.*

A zero cannot think; nor can a doughnut - or the hole in it - think; nor can "mind" think without matter. Man's brain, a part of man's organism, thinks. And man's organism is matter organized in a highly intricate form.

In the fourth place: it is quite clear from the above why matter may exist without mind, while "mind" may not exist without matter. Matter existed before the appearance of a thinking human; the earth existed long before the appearance of any kind of "mind" on its surface. In other words, matter exists objectively, independently of "mind". But the psychic phenomena, the so called "mind", never and nowhere existed without matter, were never independent of matter. Thought does not exist without a brain; desires are impossible unless there is a desiring organism. "Mind" is *always* closely connected with "matter" (only in the Bible do we find the "spirit" hovering unaided over the waters). In other words: psychic phenomena, the phenomena of consciousness, are simply *a property of matter organized in a certain manner, a "function" of such master* (a function of a certain quantity is a second quantity depending on the first). Now man is a very delicately organized creature. Destroy this organization, disorganize it, take it apart, cut it up, and the "mind" at once disappears. If men were able to put together this system again, to assemble the human organism, in other words, if it were possible to take a human body apart and put it together again just as one may do with the parts of a clock, consciousness would also at once return; once the clock has been reassembled it will operate and start to tick; put together the human organism, and it will start to think. Of course, we are not yet able to do this. But we have already seen, in our discussion of determinism, that the state of "mind" of the consciousness, depends on the state of the organism. Intoxicate the organism with alcohol, the consciousness will become confused, the mind is befuddled. Restore the organism to its normal state (for instance, administer antidotes for toxic substances) and the mind will again begin to work in the normal manner. The above clearly shows the dependence of consciousness on matter, or in other words, "of thought on life".

We have seen that psychical phenomena are a property of matter organized in a certain manner. We may therefore have various fluctuations, various forms of material organization, and also various forms of mental life. *Man,* with his brain, is organized in one manner - he has the most perfect psychical life on earth - a true consciousness; the *dog* is organized in a different manner and the psyche of the dog therefore differs from that of man; the *worm* is also organized in a special manner, and the "mind" of the worm is consequently extremely poor, by no means comparable with that of man; the organization of the *stone* places it with inanimate matter, and it therefore has no psychic life at all. A special and intricate organization of matter is required for the appearance of a psyche. An extremely intricate organization of matter is the necessary presupposition for the appearance of an intricate psychic life, which we call a consciousness. On earth, this consciousness appears only when matter has been organized, as in the case of man, with his most complicated instrument, the brain in his head.

Thus, mind cannot exist without matter, while matter may very well exist without mind; matter existed before mind; mind is a special property of matter organized in a special manner.

It is not difficult to discern that idealism (the doctrine based on a fundamental idea underlying all things, a "spirit"), is simply a diluted form of the religious conception according to which a divine mysterious power is placed *above* nature, the human consciousness being considered a little spark emanating from this divine power, and man himself a creature chosen by God. The idealistic point of view, if pursued to its conclusion, leads to a number of absurdities, which are often defined with a serious face by the philosophers of the ruling classes. Particularly, we find associated with idealism such views as deny the external world, i.e., the existence of things objectively, independently of the human consciousness, sometimes also the existence of other persons. The extreme and most consistent form of idealism is the so called solipsism (Latin solos, "alone", "only"; *ipse,* "self").

The solipsist reasons as follows: "What data do I possess? My consciousness, nothing more; the house in which I live is present only in my sensations; the man with whom I speak, also only a sensation. In a word, nothing exists outside of myself, there is only my ego, my consciousness, my mental existence; there is no external world apart from me; it is simply a creature of my mind. For I am aware of only my own internal life, from which I have no means of escaping. Everything I see, hear, taste, everything about which I think and reason, is a sensation, a conception, a thought, of mine."

This insane philosophy, concerning which Schopenhauer wrote that genuine supporters of it could be found only in the insane asylum (which did not prevent Schopenhauer, however, from considering the world *als Wille and Vorstellung,* "as volition and concept", in other words, from being an idealist of the purest water), is contradicted by human experience at every step. When we eat, conduct the class struggle, put on our shoes, pluck flowers, write books, take a wife or a husband, none of us ever thinks of doubting the existence of the external world, *i.e.,* the existence - let us say - of the food we eat, the shoes we wear, the women we marry. None the less, this fallacy is based on the fundamental position of idealism. As a matter of fact, if "mind" is the basis of all things, what was the state of the case before man existed? There are two possible answers: either we must assume the existence of a certain extra-human, divine spirit of the variety mentioned in the ancient Biblical stories; or, we must assume that the events of ages long past are also the product of my imagination. The first solution leads us to so called objective idealism, which recognizes the existence of an external world independent of "my" consciousness. The essence of this world is found in its spiritual origin, in God, or in a "supreme mind" which here takes the place of God, in a "world will", or in some other such hocus pocus. The second solution leads us straight into solipsism, through subjective idealism, which recognizes the existence only of spiritual beings, of a number of thinking subjects. It is easy to recognize solipsism as the most consistent form of idealism. But where does idealism find its basis as a matter of fact? Why does it consider the mental beginning to be more primitive and fundamental? For the reason, in the last analysis, that it assumes "my" data to consist of my sensations only. But if this is the case, I may doubt equally well the existence of a post in the yard, and of any other human being but myself, including my own parents. Thus solipsism commits suicide, for it destroys not only all of idealism in philosophy, but, in the consistent pursuit of its idealistic views, leads to a complete absurdity, to complete insanity, contradicted at every step by the actual practice of men.

Theoretical materialism and idealism must not be confused with "practical idealism" and "materialism", for the latter have nothing to do with the former. A man who remains faithful to his ideal is called an "idealist" in the practical sense; he may be an outspoken opponent of philosophical idealism, of theoretical idealism. A communist who sacrifices his life is an idealist in practice, and yet a materalist through and through. The philistine who sobs to his Lord may have very idealistic notions, which do not prevent him, however, from being a base, stupid, selfish and narrow-minded creature.

Plato is commonly considered the founder of philosophical idealism: Plato believed that only "ideas" exist objectively, i.e., in reality. Men, pears, wagons, do not exist; the idea of a man, of a pear, of a wagon, does exist. These ideal patterns, existing from the beginning of time, dwell in a special supermundane resort of "reason". What men consider to be pears, wagons, etc., are merely wretched shadows of the corresponding idea. Above all these ideas there hovers, like the spirit of God, the supreme idea, the "idea of the Good". A tendency to subjective idealism is usually found in those Greek philosophers known as Sophists (Protagoras, Gorgias, etc.), who set up the principle that "man is the measure of all things". In the Middle Ages, the Platonic "ideas" began to be interpreted as models and patterns according to which the Lord shapes visible things. For instance, the louse that we see is created by God according to his "louse-idea", which dwells in a supersensual world. More recently, Bishop Berkeley developed the view of subjective idealism, maintaining that only the spirit exists, the rest being mere imagination. Fichte believed that without a subject (a cognizing spirit) there could be no object (external world), and that matter is an expression of the idea. Schelling held ideas to be the essences of things, based on a divine eternity. All being, according to Hegel, is merely an effluvium of objective reason in the course of its unfolding.

Schopenhauer regards the world as will and conception *(Wille and Vorstellung)*. Kant recognizes the existence of the objective universe *(Ding an sich)*, but it is not subject to cognition and is immaterial in its nature. Idealism, with its many subdivisions, has become very strong in modern philosophy, by reason of the predilection of the bourgeoisie for everything that is mystical, an indication of its low morale, now full of despair, eager for mental solace.

We first find tendencies to materialist philosophy in the ancient Greek philosophers of the so called Ionic school, who considered matter to be the basis of all being, but likewise believed that all matter was capable of more or less feeling. These philosophers were therefore called *Hylozoists* (those who put life into matter; from Greek *hyle*, ὕλη, matter; and *zoe*, ἐωή, life).

Of course these first steps were rather unsatisfactory in their result. Thus, Thales sought the basis of all being in water; Anaximenes, in air; Heraclitus, in fire, Anaximander, in a certain substance of indefinite nature and embracing all things, called by him *apeiron*, the "infinite", "unlimited". The Hylozoists also included the Stoics, who considered all existing things to be material. Materialism was further developed by the Greeks Democritus and Epicurus, later by the Roman Lucretius Carus. Democritus magnificently expounded the basis of the atomistic theory. According to his doctrine the world consists of moving, falling material particles, atoms, whose combinations constitute the invisible universe. In the Middle Ages, the idealistic claptrap prevailed on the whole. The brilliant and profound intellect of Baruch Spinoza developed the idea of the Hylozoist materialists. In England, the materialist standpoint was defended by Thomas Hobbes (1588-1679). Materialism was much encouraged in the period preliminary to the French revolution, which produced a number of excellent materialist philosophers: Diderot, Helvetius, Holbach (whose chief work, *Système de la nature,* appeared in 1770), Lamettrie *(Man a Machine,* 1785).. This group of philosophers of the then revolutionary bourgeoisie has furnished us with excellent formulations of the materialistic theory (*cf.* N. Beltov: On *the Question of Evolution of the Monistic View of History,*and N. Lenin: *Materialism and Empirio-Criticism,* pp. 26 et seq.). Diderot ingeniously derided the idealists of the type of Berkeley: "In a moment of madness, the sentient piano imagined it was the only piano existing in the world, and that the entire harmony of the universe was accomplished within itself" (*Oeuvres complètes de Diderot,* Paris, 1875, vol. ii, p. 118) In Germany, in the Nineteenth Century, this cause was advanced by Ludwig Feuerbach, who had a great influence on Marx and Engels, and they, in turn, furnished the most complete theory of materialism, by combining it with the dialectic method (see below), and extended the materialistic theory to the social sciences, banishing idealism from its last place of refuge. Of course, the senile bourgeoisie, now drooling about God like a soft-brained old man, regards materialism with hatred. It is easy to understand that materialism necessarily will be the revolutionary theory of the young revolutionary class, the proletariat.

b. The Materialist Attitude in the Social Sciences

Everyone will understand that this dispute between materialism and idealism cannot possibly fail to be expressed in the social sciences also. In fact, human society presents a number of phenomena of various kinds. For instance, we find "exalted matters" such as religion, philosophy and morality; we also find innumerable ideas held by men, in various fields; we find an exchange of goods or a distribution of products; we find a struggle between various classes among themselves; there is a production of products, wheat, rye, shoes, machinery, varying with the time and place. How shall we proceed to explain this society? From what angle shall we approach it? What shall we consider its fundamental element, and what its secondary, or resulting element? All these are obviously the same questions that have been faced by philosophy and that have necessarily divided the philosophers into two great camps-that of the materialists and that of the idealists. On the one hand, we may imagine persons approaching society in approximately the following manner: society consists of persons, who think, act, desire, are dominated by ideas, thoughts, "opinions", from which they infer: "opinion dominates the world"; an alteration of "opinion", a change in the views of men is the fundamental cause of everything that goes on in society; in other words, social science must in the first place investigate precisely this phase of the matter, namely, the "social consciousness", the "mind of society". Such would be the idealist standpoint in the social sciences. But we have seen above that idealism involves an admission of the independence of ideas from the material, and of the dependence of these ideas on divine and mysterious springs. It is therefore obvious that the idealist point of view involves a downright mysticism, or other tomfoolery, in the social sciences, and consequently leads to a destruction of these *sciences,* to their substitution by *faith* in the acts of God or in some other such conception. Thus, the French writer Bossuet (in his *Reflections on Universal History,* 1682) declares that history reveals a "divine guidance of the human race"; the German idealist philosopher Lessing declares that history is an "education of the human race by God"; Fichte states that reason is manifest in history; Schelling, that history is a "constant and progressively discovered revelation of the Absolute", in other words, of God. Hegel, the greatest philosopher of idealism, defined the history of the world as a "rational, necessary evolution (*Gang*) of the world spirit". Many other such examples could be given, but the above will suffice to show how close is the connection between philosophical views and those prevailing in the social sciences.

The idealist forms of the social sciences and the idealist sociologists therefore behold in society, first of all, "the idea" of this society; they consider society itself as something psychical, immaterial; society in their opinion is a great mass of human desires, feelings, thoughts, wills, confused in endless combinations; in other words, society is social psychology and the social consciousness is the "mind" of society.

But society may also be approached from an entirely different standpoint. In our discussion of determinism, we found that man's will is not free, that it is determined by the external conditions of man's existence. Is not society also subject to these laws? How shall we explain the social consciousness? On what does it depend? The mere formulation of these questions brings to mind the materialist standpoint in social science. Human society is a product of nature. Like the human race itself, it depends on nature and may exist only by obtaining its necessities from nature. This it does by the process of production. It may not always do so consciously; a conscious process is possible only in an organized society, in which everything proceeds according to a plan. In unorganized society, the process goes on unconsciously: for example, under capitalism, the manufacturer wishes to obtain more profits and therefore increases his production (but not for the purpose of affording assistance to human society). The peasant produces, in order to provide himself with food, and to sell a portion of his production to pay his taxes; the tradesman, in order to keep himself above water and establish himself in society; the worker, in order not to starve. As a result, the entire society in some way continues to muddle along, for better or for worse. *Material production and its means* ("the material productive forces") are the foundation of the existence of human society. Without it, there cannot be a "social consciousness", "mental culture", just as there cannot be a thought without a thinking brain. We shall take up this question in detail later on; for the present let us consider only the following; let us imagine two human societies; one, a society of savages; the other, a society in the final stage of capitalism. In the former society, all activities are devoted to the immediate securing of foodstuffs, hunting, fishing, the gathering of roots, primitive agriculture; of "ideas", of "mental culture", etc., there is very little; we are dealing here with men that are hardly more than monkeys, tribal animals. In the second example, we have a sublime "mental culture", a great Babylonian confusion of morality; justice, with its countless laws; highly evolved, endless sciences, philosophies, religions, and arts, from architecture down to fashion plates. And yet, this Babylonian confusion is of one type where the bourgeoisie rules; it is quite different where proletarians rule; different again for the peasants, etc. In a word, in this case, as we usually put it, the sublime "mental culture", the "mind" of society, the sum of "ideas", is extremely developed. How was it possible for this mind to develop? What were the conditions of its growth? The growth of *material production,* the increase in the power of man over nature, the increase in the *productivity of human labor.* For, when not all the available time is consumed in exhausting material labor, people are free a portion of the time, which affords them an opportunity to think, reason, work with a plan, create a "mental culture". As everywhere else, so in society also, matter is the mother of mind and not mind the mother of matter; it is not the social "mental culture" ("social consciousness") that produces the substance of society, *i.e.,* above all, material production, the obtaining of all kinds of useful objects from nature by society, but it is the evolution of this social substance, *i.e.,* the evolution of material production, that creates the foundation for the growth of the so called "mental culture". In other words, the spiritual life of society must necessarily depend on the conditions of material production, on the stage that has been attained in the growth of the productive forces in human society. *The mental life of society is a function of the forces of production.* What this function is, just how the mental life of society grows out of the productive forces: that is a subject that will be discussed later. For the present we may only observe that this view of society naturally makes us consider it *not* as an aggregate of all possible kinds of opinions, particularly in the domain of the "sublime and beautiful", the "elevated and pure", but first of all as a *working organization* (Marx sometimes called it a "productive organism").

Such is the materialist point of view in the domain of sociology. This point of view, as we know, by no means denies that "ideas" have their effects. Marx even said distinctly, in discussing the highest stage of consciousness, which is scientific *theory*: *"Every* theory becomes a force when it secures control over masses." But materialists cannot be satisfied with a mere reference to the fact that "people thought so". They ask: why did people in a certain place, at a certain time, "think" so, and "think" otherwise under other conditions? In fact, why do people think such an awful lot anyway in "civilized" society, producing whole mountains of books and other things, while the savage does not "think" at all? We shall find the explanation in the material conditions of the life of society. Materialism is therefore in a position to explain the phenomena of "mental life" in society, which idealism cannot, for idealism imagines "ideas" developing out of themselves, independently of the base earth. For this very reason the idealists, whenever they wish to construct any real explanation, are forced to resorting to the divine: "This Good", wrote, Hegel in his *Philosophy of History,* "this Reason in its most concrete conception, is God; God rules the world ; the content of his government *Regierung),* the execution of his plan, is universal history:[1] To drag in this poor old man who constitutes perfection, according to his worshipers, and who is obliged to create, together with Adam, lice and prostitutes, murderers and lepers, hunger and poverty syphilis and vodka, as a punishment for sinners whom he created and who commit sins by his desire, and to continue playing this comedy forever in the eyes of a delighted universe - to drag in God is a necessary step for idealist theory. But from the point of view of science it means reducing this "theory" to an absurdity.

In other words, in the social sciences also, the materialist point of view is the correct one.

The consistent application of the materialist point of view to the *social* sciences is the work of Marx and Engels. In the year (1859) in which Marx's book, *A Contribution to the Critique of political Economy,* which presents an outline of his sociological theory (the theory of historical materialism) appeared, there also appeared the principal work of Charles Darwin (*Origin of Species*), whose author maintained and proved that changes in the animal and vegetable kingdoms are influenced by the material conditions of existence. But it by no means follows that the Darwinian laws may be applied without further ado to society. We have first to prove the peculiar form in which the general laws of natural science are applicable in human society, a form characteristic of human society only. Marx bitterly derided anyone who failed to understand this; thus he wrote, concerning the German scholar F. A. Lange: "Herr Lange, it seems, has made a great discovery : all history must be sublimated under a single great law of nature. This law of nature is the *phrase* (for in this use, Darwin's expression is a mere phrase), the 'struggle for life'. Instead of analyzing this 'struggle for life , which expresses itself historically in distinct and varied forms of society, all you need do is to re-christen any concrete struggle with the phrase struggle for life'.' (Letters to Kugelmann, June 27, 1870, *Die Neue Zeit,* 1902, vol. 20, pp. 541, 542)

Of course, Marx had his forerunners, particularly the so called Utopian socialists (Saint Simon). But before Marx, the materialist standpoint had not been consistently carried out by anyone in a form capable of creating a truly scientific sociology.

c. The Dynamic point of View and the Relation Between Phenomena

There are two possible ways of regarding everything in nature and in society; in the eyes of some, everything is constantly at rest, immutable ; "things ever were and ever will be thus" ; "there is nothing new under the sun." To others, however, it appears that there is nothing unchanging in nature or in society; "all earthly things have passed away"; "there is no going back to the past." This second point of view is called the *dynamic* point of view (Greek *dynamis*, "force", "motion"); the former point of view is called static. Which is the correct position? Is the world an immovable and permanent thing, or is it constantly changing, constantly in motion, different today from yesterday? Even a hasty glance at nature will at once convince us that there is nothing immutable about it. People formerly considered the moon and the stars to be motionless, like golden nails driven into the sky; likewise, the earth was motionless, etc. But we now know that the stars, the moon, and the earth are dashing through space, covering enormous distances. And we also know that the smallest particles of matter, the atoms, consist of still smaller particles, electrons, flying about and revolving within the atom, as the heavenly bodies of the solar system revolve around the sun. But the whole world consists of such particles, and how can anything be considered constant in a universe whose component parts gyrate with whirlwind speed? It was formerly also believed that plants and animals were as God created them: ass and asafoetida, bedbug and leprosy bacillus, plant-louse and elephant, cuttlefish and nettle, all were created by God, in the first days of creation, in their present form. We now know that such was not the case. The forms of animals and plants are not such as the Lord of creation deigned to make them. And the animals and plants now living on earth are quite different from those of other days; we still find skeletons or impressions in the rock, or remnants in the ice, of the huge beasts and plants of bygone ages: gigantic flying beasts covered with scales (pterodactyls), huge horse-tails and ferns (whole forests, later petrified into anthracite coal, a remnant of the primeval forests of prehistoric days), veritable monsters, such as ichthyosauri, brontosauri, iguanadons, etc. All these once existed and are now extinct. But we then had no fir-trees, birches, cows, or sheep, in a word, "all is changing under our zodiac". What is more, there were no humans, for the latter developed from hairy semi-apes not very long ago. We no longer marvel at the changes that have taken place in the forms of animals and plants. But it should surprise us still less that we ourselves may outdo the Almighty in this field: any good swine-herd, by an appropriate choice of food and an appropriate mating of male and female can continue to produce new races; the Yorkshire hog, which is so fat that it cannot walk, is a creature of human effort, as is also the pineapple-strawberry, the black rose, and many a variety of domestic animals and cultivated plants. Is not man himself constantly changing under our very eyes? Does the Russian worker of the revolutionary epoch even externally resemble the Slavic savage and hunter of bygone days? The race and appearance of men are subject to change with everything else in the world.

What is the inference? Evidently, that there is nothing immutable and rigid in the universe. We are not dealing with rigid things, but with a process. The table at which I am writing at this moment cannot be considered an immutable thing: it is changing from second to second. To be sure, these changes may be imperceptible to the human eye or ear. But the table, if it should continue to stand for many years would rot away and be transformed into dust and this would merely be a repetition of all that has gone before. Nor would the particles of the table be lost. They would assume another form, would be carried away by the wind, would become a portion of the soil, serving as a nourishment for plants, thus being transformed, for instance, into plant tissue, etc.; there is therefore a constant change, a constant journey, a constant succession of new forms. Matter in motion: such is the stuff of this world. It is therefore necessary for the understanding of any phenomenon to study it in its process of origination (how, whence, why it came to be), its evolution, its destruction, in a word, its motion, and not its seeming state of rest. This dynamic point of view is also called the *dialectic* point of view (other traits of dialectics will be treated below).

The difference between the dynamic and static point of view is already found in the ancient Greek philosophers. The so called Eleatic School, headed by Parmenides, taught that everything was immovable. According to Parmenides, being is eternal, constant, unchanged, unique, uniform, indivisible, homogeneous, immutable, like a round sphere at rest. Zeno, an Eleatic philosopher, sought to prove, by means of very ingenious observations, that motion was impossible at all. Heraclitus, on the other hand, taught that there was nothing that did not move; he maintained that "everything flows", nothing rests (*panta rei, pauta rei*); according to Heraclitus, it was impossible to descend twice into the same river, for the second time the river would already be a different river. His associate, Kratylos, was of the opinion that it was impossible to bathe even once in the same river, since the latter was constantly changing. Democritus also assumed motion to be the basis of all things, specifically, a straight-line motion of atoms. Among modern philosophers, Hegel, of whom Marx was a disciple, defended *motion* and *becoming* (origin, transformation from not-being into being) with particular persistence. But, for Hegel, the basis of the universe was the movement of mind, while Marx-to use the latter's own words - turned Hegel's dialectics upside down, replacing the movement of mind by the movement of matter. In the natural sciences, the view still prevailed at the beginning of the Nineteenth Century which was expressed by the famous scientist Linnaeus : "There are as .many species as the Supreme Being has created." (Theory of the persistence of species.) The most important advocate of the opposite view was Lamarck and later, as already indicated, Charles Darwin, who finally refuted the old conceptions.

The world being in constant motion, we must consider phenomena in their mutual relations, and not as isolated cases. All portions of the universe are actually related to each other and exert an influence on each other. The slightest motion, the slightest alteration in one place, simultaneously changes everything else. The change may be great or small - that is another matter - at any rate, there is a change. For example: let us say the Volga forests have been cut down by men. The result is that less water is retained by the soil, with a resulting partial change in climate; the Volga "runs dry," navigation on its waters becomes more difficult, making necessary the use, and therefore the production, of dredging machinery; more persons are employed in the manufacture of such machinery; on the other hand, the animals formerly living in the forests disappear; new animals, formerly not dwelling in these regions, put in their appearance; the former animals have either died out or migrated to forest areas, etc.; and we may go even further: with a change in climate, it is clear that the condition of the entire planet has been changed, and therefore an alteration in the Volga climate to a certain extent changes the universal climate. Further, if the map of the world is changed to the slightest extent, this involves also a change - we must even suppose - in the relations between the earth and the moon or sun, etc., etc. I am now writing on paper with a pen. I thus impart pressures to the table; the table presses upon the earth, calling forth a number of further changes. I move my hand, vibrate as I breathe, and these motions pass on in slight impulses ending Lord knows where. The fact that these may be but small changes, does not change the essential nature of the matter. All things in the universe are connected with an indissoluble bond nothing exists as an isolated object, independent of its surroundings. Of course, we are not obliged at every moment to pay attention to the universal concatenation of phenomena: a discussion of poultry- raising need not always lead us into a discussion of everything else same time, the sun, the moon, for instance; which would be folly, for in this case the universal bond of all phenomena would not help us. But in a discussion of theoretical questions it is very often necessary for us to bear this relation in mind; even in practice it cannot always be ignored. We are in the habit of saying that a certain man cannot "see further than his nose", which means that he considers his environment as isolated, as having no relation with what lies beyond it. Thus, the peasant brings his product to the market, thinking he will make a handsome profit, but suddenly finds prices so low that he hardly recovers his outlay. The market *binds* him together with the other producers, it transpires that so much grain has been produced and thrown on the market that only a low price can be obtained. How could our peasant make such a mistake? Simply because he did not (and could not from his out-of-the-way home) observe his own relations with the world market. The bourgeoisie, instead of becoming richer after the war, found itself facing a revolution of the workers, for the reason that this war was connected with a number of other things which the bourgeoisie did not understand. The Mensheviks and the Social-Revolutionaries, the Social patriots in all countries, declared that the Bolshevik power in Russia could not maintain itself for long; the root of their error was in the fact that they regarded Russia as an isolated case, having no relation with all of Western Europe or with the growth of the world revolution, which lends assistance to the Bolsheviks. When, in simple parlance, we rightly say that "all the circumstances must be taken into consideration , what we really mean is that a given phenomenon or a given question must be considered with regard to its connections with other phenomena, indissoluble union with "all the circumstances".

In the first place, therefore, the dialectic method of interpretation demands that all phenomena be considered in their indissoluble relations; in the second place, that they be considered in their state of motion.

d. The Historical Interpretation of the Social Sciences

Since everything in the world is in a state of change, and indissolubly connected with everything else, we must draw the necessary conclusions for the social sciences.

Let us consider human society, which has by no means been always the same. A number of very different forms of human society are known to us. For instance, in Russia, the working class has held power since November, 1917, supported by a portion of the peasantry, while the bourgeoisie is being kept within bounds, although a part of it (about 2,000,000) has emigrated. The workers' state controls the factories, machine shops, railroads. Before 1917, the bourgeoisie and the landowners were in power, controlling everything, and the workers and peasants labored for them. At a still earlier period, before the so called Liberation of the Peasants, in 1861, the bourgeoisie was for the greater part a trading class; there were few factories; the landholders ruled the peasants like cattle, and had the right to whip them, sell them, or exchange them. If we trace the course of bygone centuries, we shall find semi-savage nomadic tribes. So slight is the similarity between these various forms of society that if we should be able by a miracle to resuscitate a robust feudal landowner, given to whippings and greyhounds, and to bring him - let us say - into a meeting of a factory or works committee, or Soviet, the poor fellow would probably die of heart-failure at once.

We are also acquainted with other forms of society. In ancient Greece, for example, when Plato and Heraclitus were constructing their philosophies, everything was built up on the labor of slaves, who were the property of the great slaveholders. In the ancient American state of the Incas, there was a regulated and organized society dominated by a class of priestly nobles, a sort of intelligentsia, which controlled and managed everything, and guided the national economy, a ruling class superior to all other classes. We might give many other examples as evidence of the constant flux in the social structure. Nor does this necessarily mean that the human race has constantly improved, *i.e.*, gradually approached perfection. We have already pointed out that there have been many cases of the destruction of very highly developed human societies. Thus, for example, the land of the Greek sages and slaveholders passed away. But Greece and Rome at least had an enormous influence on the later course of history; they served as a fertilizer for history. But it has sometimes happened that entire civilizations have disappeared without a trace in other peoples and other times. For example, Professor Eduard Meyer writes concerning the evidences of an ancient civilization discovered in France by means of excavations: "We are here dealing with a highly developed civilization of primitive men ..... which was subsequently destroyed by a tremendous catastrophe and had *no influence* whatever on future ages. There is *no historical relation* between this Palaeolithic culture and the beginnings of the neolithic epoch:[2] But *while we may not always observe growth, there is always motion and alteration, though it may end in destruction or dissolution.*

Such motion is observed not only in the fact that the social system is in process of change; for social life as such is constantly changing *decisively in all its expressions.* The technology of society is changing: we need only to compare the stone hatchets and spear-heads of ancient times with the steam-hammer; manners and customs change: for instance, we know that certain races of man take pleasure in eating the captives they have taken, which even a French imperialist of the present day would not do himself (but he will have his black troops, in the process of serving civilization, cut the ears off dead bodies); certain tribes had the habit of killing their old men or young girls, and this practice was considered highly moral and holy. The political system is changing: we have seen with our own eyes how the autocracy yielded to a democratic republic, then to a Soviet republic; scientific views, religion, every-day life and all the relations between these, change; even the things we consider essential, fundamental, were by no means always as they are, we have not always had newspapers, soap, clothing; we have not even always had a state, faith in God, capital, firearms. Even the conception of what is beautiful and not beautiful is subject to change. The forms of family life are not immutable: we are aware of the existence of polygamy, polyandry, monogamy, and "promiscuous cohabitation". In other words, social life suffers constant change together with everything else in nature.

Human society therefore passes through different stages, different forms, in its evolution or decline.

It follows, in the first place, that *we must consider and investigate each form of society in its own peculiar terms.* We cannot throw into a single pot all epochs, periods, social forms. We cannot consider under a single head, and recognize no differences between, the feudal, the slaveholding, and the proletarian workers' systems of society. We cannot afford to overlook the differences between the Greek slaveholder, the Russian feudal landowner, the capitalist manufacturer. The slaveholding system is one thing; it has its special traits, its earmarks, its special growth. Feudalism is another type; capitalism, a third, etc. And communism - the communism of the future - also has its special structure. The transition period preceding it - the period of proletarian dictatorship, is also a special system. Each such system has peculiar traits that require special study. By this means only, can we grasp the process of change. For, since each form has its special traits, it also must have its special laws of growth, its special laws of motion. For instance, Marx says, in *Capital,* concerning the capitalist system, that the main object of his study is to discover "the laws of motion of capitalist society". For this purpose, Marx had to explain all the peculiarities of capitalism, all its characteristic traits; only thus could he discover its "law of motion" and *predict* the inevitable absorption of petty production by largescale production, the growth of the proletariat, its collision with the bourgeoisie, the revolution of the working class, and, together with this, the transition to the dictatorship of the proletariat. Most bourgeois historians do not proceed thus. They are inclined to confuse the merchants of ancient times with the present-day capitalists, the parasite *lumpenproletariat* of Greece and Rome with the proletariat of the present day. This confusion is useful to the bourgeoisie in its effort to demonstrate the enduring power of capitalism and the futility of the slave uprisings in Rome, from which it augurs the futility of present-day proletarian uprisings. And yet, the Roman "proletarians" had nothing in common with the present-day workers, and the Roman merchants had very little similarity with the capitalists of our time. The whole structure of life was different. It is therefore easy to see that the course of change must then have been different. Marx says : "Every historical period has laws of its own . . . . As soon as society has outlived a given period of development, and is passing over from one given stage to another, it begins to be subject also to other laws."[2] For sociology, which is social science in its most general form, dealing not with the individual forms of society, but with society in general, this law is very important as a guide for the specific social sciences, for all of which sociology, as we have seen, constitutes a method.

In the second place, each form must be studied in its internal process of change. We are not dealing, first, with a single form of social structure, perfect and immutable, and succeeded by another equal immutable form. In society, it is untrue - for instance - that capitalism continues throughout its entire period in unchanged form, to be succeeded by an equal unchanging socialism. As a matter of fact, each specific form is constantly undergoing change throughout the period of its existence. It has passed through a number of stages in its development: trading capitalism, industrial, financial capitalism with its imperialist policy, state capitalism during the world war. Nor did the nature of the case remain uniform within each of these stages; it would then have been impossible for one stage to yield place to another. Indeed, each preceding stage was a preparation for the following stage; during the period of industrial capitalism, for example, the process of concentration of capital was going on. On this foundation financial capital with its trusts and banks was built up.

In the third place, each form of society must be considered in its growth and in its necessary disappearance, i.e., *in its relation with other forms.* No form of society descends from heaven; each is a necessary consequence of the preceding social state; often it is difficult to discern the boundaries between them, the termination of one, the beginning of the other; one period overlaps the other. Historical epochs are not rigid and immovable units, like physical objects; they are processes, current forms of life, subject to constant change. In order to trace properly any such form of society we must go back to its roots in the past, follow the causes of its growth, all the conditions of its formation, the motive forces of its development. And it is also necessary to study the causes of its inevitable destruction, the tendencies which necessarily involve the disappearance of this form and prepare the introduction of the next form. Each stage is thus a link in the chain; it is connected with a link behind it and a link ahead of it. Even though bourgeois scholars may admit this fact as far as the past is concerned, it is impossible for them to grant it with regard to the present: capitalism will not perish. They are willing to go so far as to trace the roots of capitalism, but they are afraid to think of the conditions that lead capitalism to its destruction. "This blindness constitutes all the wisdom of present-day economists, who teach the permanence and harmony of the existing social relations."[4] Capitalism evolved from medieval feudal conditions owing to the growth of the commodities system. Capitalism is passing into communism through the dictatorship of the proletariat. Only by tracing the connections of capitalism with the preceding system, and its necessary transformation into communism, can we understand this form of society. Every other form of society must be studied from the same point of view; this is one of the demands of the dialectic method, which may also be called "the historical point of view", since it regards each form of society *not as permanent,* but *as an historical stage,* appearing at a certain moment in history, and similarly disappearing.

This historicism of Marx has nothing in common with the so called "historical school" in jurisprudence and political economy. This reactionary school finds its principal task in proving the slowness of all changes, and in defending any bit of antiquated gossip that is "hallowed by age". Heinrich Heine already said concerning this school:

> Beware of that king in Thule, avoid
> The North and its lurking dangers;
> Police, gendarmes, whole historic school
> You and they are better strangers.

(Heinrich Heine, *Germany: A Winter's Tale,* Caput xxvi, in Collected Works, translated by Margaret Armour, London 1905, vol. xi, p.89).

To guard the "sacred traditions" is an imperative necessity for the bourgeoisie. It is for this reason, particularly, that phenomena that owe their origin to a specific historical stage are considered to be eternal, to have been handed down by God, and therefore insurmountable. We shall take three examples.

I. *The State.* We now know that the state is a class organization, that there cannot be a state without classes, that a classless state is a round square, that the state could not arise until a certain stage in human evolution had been reached. But listen to the bourgeois historians, even the best of them! Eduard Meyer says: "How far the formation of organic groups can proceed in the case of animals, I often had occasion to observe, thirty years ago, in Constantinople, in the case of the street dogs; they were organized in sharply distinct quarters, into which they would admit no outside dogs, and every evening all the dogs of each quarter gather in an empty lot for a meeting of about half an hour, in which they bark loudly. We may therefore actually speak of dog *states* of definite outline in space." (Eduard

Meyer: *Geschichte des Altertums*, vol. i, first half, 3d ed., p.7,) It will therefore not surprise us to find Meyer accepting the state as a necessary property of human society. If even dogs have states (and therefore, of course, laws, justice, etc.), how could men get along without one?

II. *Capital.* On this subject the bourgeois economists show the same idiosyncrasies. It is well known that capital has not always existed, nor capitalism either. Capitalists and workers are a phenomenon of historical growth, by no means eternal. But the bourgeois scholars always defined capital as if it - and also the capitalist regime - had existed from all time. Thus, Torrens wrote: "In the first stone which he (the savage) flings at the wild animal he pursues, in the stick that he seizes to strike down the fruit which hangs beyond his reach, we see the appropriation of one article for the purpose of aiding in the acquisition of another, and thus discover the origin of capital." (Marx *Capital*, vol. i, Chicago, 1915, p.205, footnote.) The monkey beating nuts out of a tree is therefore a capitalist (but without workers !). Modern economists are not much better; in order to prove the eternity of the state power, these poor wretches are obliged to endow their dogs with the capacities of Lloyd George and their monkeys with those of the Rothschilds!

III. *Imperialism.* Bourgeois scholars who take up this question often define imperialism as the effort at expansion in any form of life. Of course, imperialism is the policy of financial capital, and financial capital itself did not arise as a dominating economic form until the end of the Nineteenth Century. Little the bourgeois scholars care about that! In order to show that "things have ever been thus", they elevate the chicken which picks up kernels into an imperialist, since it "annexes" these kernels! The dog state, the capitalist ape and the imperialist chicken are an excellent indication of the level of modern bourgeois science.

e. The Use of Contradictions in the Historical Process

The basis of all things is therefore the law of change, the law of constant motion. Two philosophers particularly (the ancient Heraclitus and the modern Hegel, as we have already seen) formulated this law of change, but they did not stop there. They also set up the question of the manner in which the process operates. The answer they discovered was that changes are produced by constant internal contradictions, internal struggle. Thus, Heraclitus declared: "Conflict is the mother of all happenings," while Hegel said: "Contradiction is the power that moves things."

There is no doubt of the correctness of this law. A moment's thought will convince the reader. For, if there were no conflict, no clash of forces, the world would be in a condition of unchanging, stable equilibrium, *i.e.,* complete and absolute permanence, a state of rest precluding all motion. Such a state of rest would be conceivable only in a system whose component parts and forces would be so related as not to permit of the introduction of any conflicts, as to preclude all mutual interaction, all disturbances. As we already know that all things change, all things are "in flux", it is certain that such an absolute state of rest cannot possibly exist. We must therefore reject a condition in which there is no "contradiction between opposing and colliding forces", no disturbance of equilibrium, but only an absolute immutability. Let us take up this matter somewhat more in detail.

In biology, when we speak of adaptation, we mean that process by which one thing assumes a relation toward another thing that enables the two to exist simultaneously. An animal that is "adapted" to its environment is an animal that has achieved the means of living in that environment. It is suited to its surroundings, its qualities are such as to enable it to continue to live. The mole is "adapted" to conditions prevailing under the earth's surface; the fish, to conditions in the water; either animal transferred to the other's environment will perish at once.

A similar phenomenon may be observed also in so called "inanimate" nature: the earth does not fall into the sun, but revolves around it "without mishap". The relation between the solar system: and the universe which surrounds it, enabling both to exist side by side, is a similar relation. In the latter case we commonly speak, not of the adaptation, but of the equilibrium between bodies, or systems of such bodies, etc. We may observe the same state of things in society. Whether we like it or not, society lives within nature: is therefore in one way or another in equilibrium with nature. And the various parts of society, if the latter is capable of surviving, are so adapted to each other as to enable them to exist side by side: capitalism, which included both capitalists and workers, had a very long existence!

In all these examples it is clear that we are dealing with one phenomenon, that of *equilibrium*. This being the case, where do the contradictions come in? For there is no doubt that conflict is a *disturbance* of equilibrium. It must be recalled that such equilibrium as we observe in nature and in society is *not* an absolute, unchanging equilibrium, but an equilibrium in flux, which means that the equilibrium may be established and destroyed, may be reestablished on a new basis, and again disturbed.

The precise conception of equilibrium is about as follows: "We say of a system that it is in a state of equilibrium when the system cannot of itself, *i.e.*, without supplying energy to it from without, emerge from this state." If - let us say - forces are at work on a body, neutralizing each other, that body is in a state of equilibrium; an increase or decrease in one of these forces will disturb the equilibrium.

If the disturbance of equilibrium is of short duration and the body returns to its former position, the equilibrium is termed *stable*; if this does not ensue, the equilibrium is *unstable*. In the natural sciences we have mechanical equilibrium, chemical equilibrium, biological equilibrium. (Cf. H. von Halban: *Chemisches Gleichgewicht,* in *Handwörterbuch der Naturwissenschaften,* vol. ii, Jena, 1912, pp.470-519, from which we take the above quotation.)

In other words, the world consists of forces, acting in many ways, opposing each other. These forces are balanced for a moment in exceptional cases only. We then have a state of "rest", *i.e.,* their actual "conflict" is concealed. But if we change only one of these forces, immediately the "internal contradictions" will be revealed, equilibrium will be disturbed, and if a new equilibrium is again established, it will be on a new basis, *i.e.,* with a new combination of forces, etc. It follows that the "conflict", the "contradiction", i.e., the antagonism of forces acting in various directions, determines the motion of the system.

On the other hand, we have here also the form of this process: in the first place, the condition of equilibrium; in the second place, a disturbance of this, equilibrium; in the third place, the reestablishment of equilibrium on a *new* basis. And then the story begins all over again: the new equilibrium is the point of departure for a new disturbance, which in turn is followed by another state of equilibrium, etc., *ad infinitum.* Taken all together, we are dealing with a process of motion based on the development of internal contradictions.

Hegel observed this characteristic of motion and expressed it in the following manner: he called the original condition of equilibrium the *thesis,*the disturbance of equilibrium the *antith*esis, the reestablishment of equilibrium on a new basis the synthesis (the unifying proposition reconciling the contradictions). The characteristic of motion present in all things, expressing itself *in* this tripartite formula (or triad) he called *dialectic.*

The word "dialectics" among the ancient Greeks meant the art of eloquence, of disputation. The course of a discussion is as follows: one man says one thing, another the opposite ("negates" what the first man said); finally, "truth is born from the struggle", and includes a part of the first man's statement and a part of the second man's (synthesis). Similarly, in the process of thought. Since Hegel, being an idealist, regards everything as a self-evolution of the spirit, he of course did not have any disturbances of equilibrium in mind, and the properties of thought as a spiritual and original thing were therefore, in his mind, properties also of being. Marx wrote in this connection: "My dialectic method is not only different from the Hegelian, but is its direct opposite. To Hegel, the life-process of the human brain, i.e., the process of thinking, which, under the name of 'the Idea', he even transforms into an independent subject, is the demiurgos of the real world, and the real world is only the external phenomenal form of 'the Idea'. With me, on the contrary, the ideal is nothing else than the material world reflected by the human mind, and translated into forms of thought . . . . With him (Hegel) it (dialectics) is standing on its head. It must be turned right side up again, if you would discover the rational kernel within the mystical shell" (*Capital*, Chicago, 1915, vol. i, p.25). For Marx, dialectics means evolution by means of contradictions, particularly, a law of "being", a law of the movement of matter, a law of motion in nature and society. It finds its expression in the process of thought. It is necessary to use the dialectic method, the dialectic mode of thought, because the dialectics of nature may thus be grasped.

It is quite possible to transcribe the "mystical" (as Marx put it) language of the Hegelian dialectics into the language of modern mechanics. Not so long ago, almost all Marxians objected to the mechanical terminology, owing to the persistence of the ancient conception of the atom as a detached isolated particle. But now that we have the Electron Theory, which represents atoms as complete solar systems, we have no reason to shun this mechanical terminology. The most advanced tendencies of scientific thought in all fields accept this point of view. Marx already gives hints of such a formulation (the doctrine of equilibrium between the various branches of production, the theory of labor value based thereon, etc.).

Any object, a stone, a living thing, a human society, etc., may be considered as a whole consisting of parts (elements) related with each other; in other words, this whole may be regarded as a *system*. And no such system exists in empty space; it is surrounded by other natural objects, which, with reference to it, may be called the *environment*. For the tree in the forest, the environment means all the other trees, the brook, the earth, the ferns, the grass, the bushes, together with all their properties. Man's environment is society, in the midst of which he lives; the environment of human society is external nature. There is a constant relation between environment and system, and the latter, in turn, acts upon the environment. We must first of all investigate the fundamental question as to the nature of the relations between the environment and the system; how are they to be defined; what are their forms; what is their significance for their system. Three chief types of such relations may be distinguished.

1. *Stable equilibrium.* This is present when the mutual action of the environment and the system results in an unaltered condition, or in a disturbance of the first condition which is again reestablished in the original state. For example, let us consider a certain type of animals living in the steppes. The environment remains unchanged. The quantity of food available for this type of beast neither increases nor decreases; the number of animals preying upon them also remains the same; all the diseases, all the microbes (for all must be included in the "environment"), continue to exist in the original proportions. What will be the result? Viewed as a whole, the number of our animals will remain the same; some of them will die or be destroyed by beasts of prey, others will be born, but the given type and the given conditions of the environment will remain the same as they were before. This means a condition of rest due to an unchanged *relation* between the system (the given type of animals) and the environment, which is equivalent to stable equilibrium. Stable equilibrium is not always a complete absence of motion; there may be motion, but the resulting disturbance is followed by a reestablishment of

equilibrium on the former basis. The contradiction between the environment and the system is constantly being reproduced *in the same quantitative relation.*

We shall find the case the same in a society of the stagnant type (we shall go into this question more in detail later). If the relation between society and nature remains the same; *i.e.,* if society extracts from nature, by the process of production, precisely as much energy as it consumes, the contradiction between society and nature will again be reproduced in the former shape; the society will mark time, and there results a state of stable equilibrium.

2. *Unstable equilibrium with positive (favorable) indication (an expanding system).* In actual fact, however, stable equilibrium does not exist. It constitutes merely an imaginary, sometimes termed the "ideal", case. As a matter of fact, the relation between environment and the system is never reproduced in precisely the same proportions; the disturbance of equilibrium never actually leads to its reestablishment on exactly the same basis as before, but a new equilibrium is created on a new basis. For example, in the case of the animals mentioned above, let us assume that the number of beasts of prey opposing them decreases for some reason, while the available food increases. There is no doubt that the number of our animals would then also increase; our "system" will then grow; a new equilibrium is established on a better basis; this means *growth*. In other words, the contradiction between the environment and the system has become quantitatively different.

If we consider human society, instead of these animals, and assume that the relation between it and nature is altered in such manner that society - by means of production - extracts more energy from nature than is consumed by society (either the soil becomes more fruitful, or new tools are devised, or both), this society will *grow* and not merely mark time. The new equilibrium will in each case be actually new. The contradiction between society and nature will in each case be reproduced on a new and "higher" basis, a basis on which society will increase and develop. This is a case of unstable equilibrium with positive indication.

3. *Unstable equilibrium with negative indication (a declining system)*. Now let us consider the quite different case of a new equilibrium being established on a "lower" basis. Let us suppose, for example, that the quantity of food available to our beasts has decreased, or that the number of beasts of prey has for some reason increased. Our animals will die out. The equilibrium between the system and the environment will in each case be established on the basis of the extinction of a portion of this system. The contradiction will be reestablished on a new basis, with a negative indication. Or, in the case of society, let us assume that the relation between it and nature has been altered in such manner that society is obliged to consume more and more and obtain less and less (the soil is exhausted, technical methods become poorer, etc.). New equilibrium will here be established in each case on a lowered basis, by reason of the destruction of a portion of society. We are now dealing with a declining society, a disappearing system, in other words, with motion having a negative indication.

Every conceivable case will fall under one of these three heads. At the basis of the motion, as we have seen, there is in fact the contradiction between the environment and the system, which is constantly being reestablished.

But the matter has another phase also. Thus far we have spoken only of the contradictions between the environment and the system, *i.e.,* the *external* contradictions. But there are also internal contradictions, those that are within the system. Each system consists of its component parts (elements), united with each other in one way or another. Human society consists of people; the forests, of trees and bushes; the pile of stones, of the various stones; the herd of animals, of the individual animals, etc. Between them there are a number of contradictions, differences, imperfect adaptations, etc. In other words, here also there is no absolute equilibrium. If there can be, strictly speaking, no absolute equilibrium between the environment and the system, there can also be no such equilibrium between the elements of the system itself.

This may be seen best by the example of the most complicated system, namely, human society. Here we encounter an endless number of contradictions; we find the struggle between classes, which is the sharpest expression of "social contradictions", and we know that "the struggle between classes is the motive force of history". The contradictions between the classes, between groups, between ideals, between the quantity of labor performed by individuals and the quantity of goods distributed to them, the planlessness in production (the capitalist "anarchy" in production), all these constitute an endless chain of contradictions, all of which are within the system and grow out of its contradictory *structure* ("structural contradictions"). But these contradictions do not of themselves destroy society. They *may* destroy it (if, for example, both opposing classes in a civil war destroy each other), but it is also possible they may at times not destroy it.

In the latter case, there will be an unstable equilibrium between the various elements of society. We shall later discuss the nature of this equilibrium; for the present we need not go into it. But we must not regard society stupidly, as do so many bourgeois scholars, who overlook its internal contradictions. On the contrary, a scientific consideration of society requires that we consider it from the point of view of the contradictions present within it. *Historical "growth" is the development of contradictions.*

We must again point out a fact with which we shall have to deal more than once in this book. We have said that these contradictions are of two kinds: between the environment and this system, and between the elements of the system and the system itself. Is there any relation between these two phenomena? A moment's thought will show us that such a relation exists.

It is quite clear that the internal structure of the system (its internal equilibrium) must change together with the relation existing between the system and its environment. The latter relation is the decisive factor; for the entire situation of the system, the fundamental forms of its motion (decline, prosperity, or stagnation) are determined by this relation only.

Let us consider the question in the following form: we have seen above that the character of the equilibrium between society and nature determines the fundamental course of the motion of society. Under these circumstances, could the internal structure continue for long to develop in the opposite direction? Of course not. In the case of a growing society, it would not be possible for the internal structure of society to continue *constantly* to grow worse. If, in *a condition of growth,* the structure of society should become poorer, *i.e.,* its internal disorders grow worse, this would be equivalent to the appearance of a new contradiction: a contradiction between the external and the internal equilibrium, which would require the society, if it is to continue growing, to undertake a reconstruction, *i.e.,* its internal structure must adapt itself to the character of the external equilibrium. Consequently, *the internal (structural) equilibrium is a quantity which depends on the external equilibrium (is a "function" of this external equilibrium).*

f. The Theory of Cataclysmic Changes anal the Theory of Revolutionary Transformations in the Social Sciences

We have now to consider the final phase of the dialectic method, namely, the theory of sudden changes. No doubt it is a widespread notion that "nature makes no sudden jumps" *(natura non facit saltus)*. This wise saying is often applied in order to demonstrate "irrefutably" the impossibility of revolution, although revolutions have a habit of occurring in spite of the moderation of our friends the professors. Now, is nature really so moderate and considerate as they pretend?

In his *Science of Logic* (*Wissenschaft der Logik*)[5], Hegel says: "It is said that there are no sudden changes in nature, and the common view has it *(meint)* that when we speak of a growth or a destruction *(Entstehen oder Vergehen)*, we always imagine a *gradual* growth *(Hervorgehen)* or disappearance *(Verschwinden)*. Yet we have seen cases in which the alteration of existence *(des Seins)* involves not only a transition from one proportion to other, but also a transition, by a sudden leap, into a *quantitatively*, and, on the other hand, also *qualitatively* different thing *(Anderswerden.)*; an interruption of the gradual process *(ein Abbrechen des Allmählichen)*, differing qualitatively from the preceding, the former, state" (the italics are mine. - N. B.).

Hegel speaks of a transition of quantity into quality; there is very simple illustration of such a transition. If we should heat w ater, we should find that throughout the process of heating, before a temperature of 100 C. is reached, the water will not boil and turn into steam. Portions of the water will move faster and faster, but they will not bubble on the surface in the form of steam. The change thus far is merely *quantitative*; the water moves faster, the temperature rises, but the water remains water, having all the properties of water. Its quantity is changing having its quality remains the same. But when we have heated it to 100 C, we have brought it to the "boiling-point". At once it begins to boil, at once the particles that have been madly in motion burst apart and leap from the surface in the form of little explosions of *steam*. The water has ceased to be water; it becomes *steam*, a gas. The former quality is lost; we now have a new quality, with new properties. We have thus learned two important peculiarities in the process of change.

In the first place, having reached a certain stage in motion, the quantitative changes call forth qualitative changes (or, in more abbreviated form, "quantity becomes quality") ; in the second place, this transition from quantity to quality is accomplished in a sudden leap, which constitutes an interruption in the gradual continuous process. The water was not constantly changing, with gradual deliberateness, into a little steam at a time, with the quantity of steam *constantly* increasing. For a long time it did not boil at all. But having reached the "boiling-point", it began to boil. We must consider this a *sudden* change.

The transformation of quantity into quality is one of the fundamental laws in the motion of matter ; it may be traced literally at every step both in nature and society. Hang a weight at the end of a string, and gradually add slight additional weights, each being as small as you like; up to a certain limit, the string will hold". But once this limit has been exceeded, it will suddenly break. Force steam into a boiler; all will go well for a while; only the pressure indicator will show increases in the pressure of the steam against the walls of the boiler. But when the dial has exceeded a certain limit, the boiler will explode. The pressure of the steam exceeded perhaps by a very little the power of resistance offered by the walls of the boiler. Before this moment, the quantitative changes had not led to a "cataclysm", to a *qualitative* change, but at that "point" the boiler exploded.

Several men are unable to lift a stone. Another joins them; they are still unable to do it. A weak old woman joins them - and their united strength raises the stone. Here, but a slight additional force was needed, and as soon as this force was added the job was done. Let us take another example. Leo Tolstoi wrote a story called "Three Rolls and a Cookie". The point of the story is the following: a man, to appease his hunger, ate one roll after another, for each still left him hungry; in fact, after his third roll, he was still hungry; then he ate a little cookie, and his hunger was appeased. He then cursed his folly for not having eaten the cookie first: for then he would not have had to eat the rolls. Of course, we are aware of his mistake; we are dealing here with a *qualitative* change, the transition from the feeling of hunger to that of satiation, which transition was accomplished in one bound (after eating the cookie). But this qualitative difference *ensued after the quantitative differences:* the cookie would have been of no use without the rolls.

We thus find that it is foolish to deny the existence changes, and to admit only a deliberate gradual process. Sudden leaps are often found in nature, and the notion that nature permits of no such violent alterations is merely a reflection of the fear of such shifts in society, *i.e.,* of the fear of revolution.

It is a characteristic fact that the earlier theories of the bourgeoisie, touching the question of the creation of the universe, were catastrophic theories, though naive and wrong ones. Such, for instance, was Cuvier's theory. This was displaced by the evolution theory, which introduced many new elements, but one-sidedly denied cataclysmic changes. Of such nature are the works of Lyell (*Principles of Geology*), in the field of geology. But at the end of the last century there again arose a theory which recognized the importance of sudden changes. For instance, the botanist De Vries (the so called *mutation* theory) maintained that from time to time, on the basis of previous changes, sudden alterations of form ensue, which later fortify themselves and become the starting paints of new courses of evolution. The older views, which were hostile to "sudden changes", are now no longer sufficient. Such notions (Leibnitz, for instance, says: "Everything in nature goes step by step, never by leaps and bounds" - *tout va par degrés dans la nature et rien par saut*) evidently arose on a conservative social soil.

The denial of the contradictory character of evolution by bourgeois scholars is based on their fear of the class struggle and on their concealment of social contradictions. Their fear of sudden changes is based on their fear of revolution; all their wisdom is contained in the following reasoning: there are no violent changes in nature, there cannot be any such violent changes anywhere; therefore, you proletarians, do not dare make a revolution! Yet here it becomes exceptionally evident that bourgeois science is in contradiction with the most fundamental requirements of all science. Everybody knows that there have been many revolutions in human society. Will anyone deny that there was an English Revolution, or a French Revolution, or a

Revolution of 1848, or the Revolution of 1917? If these violent changes have taken place in society, and are still taking place, science should not "deny" them, refusing to recognize facts, but should *understand* these sudden shifts, and *explain* them.

Revolutions in society are of the same character as the violent changes in nature. They do not suddenly "fall from the sky". They are prepared by the entire preceding course of development, as the boiling of water is prepared by the preceding process of heating or as the explosion of a steam-boiler is prepared by the increasing pressure of the steam against its walls. A revolution in society means its reconstruction, "a structural alteration of the system". Such a revolution is an inevitable consequence of the contradictions between the structure of society and the demands for its development. We shall discuss the nature of this process below. For the present we need only to know the following: in society, as in nature, violent changes do take place; in society, as in nature, these sudden changes are prepared by the preceding course of things; in other words, in society as in nature, evolution (gradual development) leads to revolution (sudden change) : "The violent changes presuppose a preceding evolution, and the gradual changes lead to violent changes. These are two necessary factors in a single process."[6]

The contradictory nature of evolution, the question of cataclysmic changes, is one of the most essential theoretical questions. Though a great number of bourgeois schools and tendencies oppose teleology and favor determinism, etc., they nevertheless stumble on these questions. The Marxian theory is not a theory of evolution but of revolution. For this very reason it is inacceptable to the ideologists of the bourgeoisie, and they are therefore ready to "accept" the whole theory except its revolutionary dialectics. Objections to Marxism usually assume the same form. Thus, Werner Sombart, a German professor, treats Marx with great respect where evolution is involved, but at once attacks him as soon as he scents theoretically the revolutionary elements of Marxism. Entire theories are even built up, showing that Marx was a scholar in his evolutionary point of view, but ceased to be a scholar when he became - even theoretically - a revolutionist; he then leaves the sphere of science and gives himself up to revolutionary passions. P. Struve, once a Marxian, author of the first manifesto of the Russian Social-Democracy, a man later metamorphosized into a protagonist of pogroms and a prime counter-revolutionary ideologist, also began by attacking Marxism in its theory of cataclysmic changes. Plekhanov, then a revolutionist, wrote- "Mr. Struve wants to show us that nature makes no sudden leaps, and that the intellect (reason) will not bear such leaps. The fact is, Struve means his own intellect, which indeed *tolerates no leaps,* for the simple reason, as is said, that he *cannot bear a certain dictatorship:"*(The italics are Plekhanov's; *Criticism of Our* Critics, p.99.) The so called "organic school", the Positivists, Spencerians, evolutionists, etc., all oppose cataclysmic changes because they cannot bear a "certain dictatorship".

BIBLIOGRAPHY

As with chapters i and ii, adding the following: Deborin : *Introduction to the philosophy of Dialectic Materialism* (in Russian). G. Plekhanov (N. Beltov) : *Criticisyia of Our Critics* (in Russian). Karl Marx: *Introduction to a Critique of Political Economy,* Chicago, 1913. G. Plekhanov: *Fundamental Problems of Marxism* (translated). J. Berman: *Dialectics in the Light of the Modern. Theory of Cognition* (in Russian; not orthodox, but critical). A. Bogdanov: *General Science of Organization* (in Russian; an ingenious attempt to dispense with philosophy). L. Orthodox (Axelrod): *Philosophical Sketches* (in Russian). Karl Kautsky: *Anti-Bernstein* (in German). N. Bukharin: *The Economic Theory of the Leisure Class* (chapter one). The critical literature written in opposition to dialectic materialism is exceedingly voluminous. The most important Russian writers in this field are Kareyev and Tugan-Baranovsky (*The Theoretical Foundations of Marxism*)

NOTES

[1]*Philosophie der Geschichte,* Reclam edition, page 74

[2]Eduard Meyer *Geschichte des Altertums,* I, i, second edition, 1910, page 247.

[3]Karl Marx: *Capital,* vol. i, pp.22, 23. Chicago, 1915. TRANSLATOR'S NOTE: This quotation is taken by Marx from a paraphrase of his position in the words of Professor A. Sieber, of the University of Kiev.]

[4]Karl Marx: *Introduction to a Critique of Political Economy,*Stuttgart, German edition, 1921, p.xvi.

[5]*Hegels Werke,* 2d ed., vol. iii, p.434 (German original).

[6]Plekhanov: *Criticism of Our Critics* (in Russian), 1906 edition, p.104.

4: SOCIETY

a. Concept of Aggregates; Logical and Real Aggregates

We encounter not only simple bodies, which at once impress us as constituting units (for example, a sheet of paper, a cow, John Smith), but also meet with compound units, intricate quantities. When considering the movement of the population, we may say the number of male infants born within a certain interval of time has increased so much. We then regard this "number of male infants" as a total quantity, existing apart from the various units, and considered as a unit in itself (a "statistical aggregate"). We also speak of a forest, a class, human society, and at once find that we are dealing with compound quantities: we regard these quantities as individual quantities, but we likewise know that these wholes consist of elements having a certain degree of independence the forest consists of trees, bushes, etc.; the class, of the various persons constituting it, etc. Such composite quantities are called aggregates.

From the examples given above we may learn, however, that aggregates may be of various kinds: when we speak of the male infants born in a certain year, and when we speak of the town forest, it is clear that there is a difference between the two. In the one case, that of the male infants, we know that these individuals are not found together in life, in actual reality: one is in one place and another in another; none has any influence on another; each is for himself. It is *we* who are combining them when we add them up. It is *we* who make the aggregation: this is a mental aggregate, a paper aggregate, not a living or real aggregate. Such artificial aggregates may be called imaginary or logical aggregates. But when we speak of society, or of a forest, or of a class, the case is quite different; here the union of the component elements is not only a mental (logical) union. For we have before us the forest, with its trees, bushes, grass, etc., which surely constitutes an actual living whole. The forest is not merely a summation of its various elements. All these elements are continually interacting one upon the other, in other words, they are in a state of constant mutual interaction. Cut down some of the trees, and perhaps the others will wither by reason of the subsequent decrease in moisture, or perhaps they will grow better because they can get more sun. We are here clearly dealing with an interaction of the parts making up "the forest", and the interaction here is a perfectly real one, existing in fact, not imagined by us for one purpose or another. Furthermore: this interaction is of long duration and constant, being present as long as the whole continues to exist. Such aggregates are called *real aggregates*.

All these differences are conditional. Strictly speaking, there are no simple units. John Smith is in reality a whole colony of cells, i.e., he is a highly complicated body. We have seen that even the atom may be subdivided. And as (in principle) there are no limits of divisibility, so there are ultimately no uniform units. Nevertheless, our distinctions may hold within certain limits: an individual human is an individual body and not a totality, when compared with society; but he is a composite body, a real aggregate, when compared with the cell, etc. If we wish to speak in a non-comparative way, we make use of the term system. *System* and *real aggregate* are identical terms. The conditional nature of all these distinctions may be shown in another way also: strictly speaking, the entire universe is an infinite real aggregate, all the particles of which are in process of constant and uninterrupted interaction. We thus have an interaction between all the objects and elements of the universe, but this interaction is in some cases more or less direct, in some cases more or less indirect. Hence our distinctions, as made above; they hold good - as we have said - when understood dialectically, i.e., within certain bounds, conditionally, according to circumstances.

b. Society as a Real Aggregate or a System

Let us now view society from this standpoint. There is no doubt that society constitutes a real aggregate, for there is a constant uninterrupted process of mutual interaction between its various parts. Mr. Smith went to the market; there he traded, exerted an influence on the formation of the market price, which in turn influenced the world market, perhaps in an infinitesimal degree, but nevertheless it was an influence on world prices; the latter, in turn, influence the market of the country in which Mr. Smith lives, and the little market which he frequents; on the other hand, let us say he buys a herring at the market; this will have an influence on his budget, for it will make him spend the rest of his money in a certain way, etc., etc. Thousands of such little influences be enumerated. Mr. Smith gets married for this purpose he has bought a number of presents and thus has exerted economic influence on other persons. Being an orthodox Christian, and not a Bolshevik, he calls in the priest and thus strengthens the Church organization, and this act will have its effect in little waves on the influence of the Church, and on the entire system of feelings and tendencies in the given society; he has paid money to the priest, and thus has increased the demand for the commodities demanded by priests, etc. His wife bears him children, and this in turn produces thousands of consequences. It is easy to see that many persons are influenced, in however slight a degree, by the fact of John Smith's marriage. Mr. Smith enters the Liberal Party in order to do his "duty as a citizen". He begins to attend meetings, together with hundreds like him, to experience the same feelings of hatred for the cursed rascals who loaf about the streets and support those children of Satan, the Bolsheviks. Their influence at the meetings, touches and moves, either directly or indirectly, a great number of persons. To be sure, this influence may be difficult to ascertain but, no matter how small it may be, it yet exists. And no matter what branch of activity our Mr. Smith might enter, you would always observe that he had an influence on others; as well as others on him. For in society, all things are united by millions of little threads.

We have begun with the individual man, and shown his influence on others. But we might just as well begin with the manner in which society acts *on him*. There is a great industrial boom, and the concern for which Smith is working as chief bookkeeper is making more profits; Mr. Smith gets a little "raise". War breaks out; Mr. Smith is enlisted, defends the fatherland of his employers (he is convinced he is defending civilization) and is killed in the war. Such is the power of social relations.

If we picture to ourselves the immense number of mutual interactions existing in human society, if only in our day, we shall find a magnificent picture taking shape before us. Some of these relations are of crude elemental force; they are not regulated in any way, or by any person; the interactions of persons on one another are countless in their expressions. But there are also many more or less regulated and organized forms, from government authority down to the chess club and the bald-headed men's society. If we consider that all these countless interactions are constantly intersecting each other, we shall understand how truly tremendous is the Babylonian confusion of influences and mutual interactions in social life.

Wherever there is a mutual interaction of long duration, we have a real aggregate, a "system". But we must point out the fact that a real aggregate or system is by no means necessarily characterized by a *conscious organization* of the parts of this system, and this statement is true both of animate nature and of inanimate nature, both of "mechanisms" and of "organisms". Some persons go so far as to deny the very existence of society because there are other systems existing within society (classes, groups, parties, circles, organizations of various kinds, etc., etc.).

But there is no doubt of the mutual interaction of these systems and groups within society (struggles between classes and parties, moments of cooperation, etc.); furthermore, the persons constituting these groups may be influencing the remaining persons in *other* connections in an entirely different way (the capitalist and the worker, who purchases from the same capitalist goods for his own consumption). Furthermore, these groups-in the mutual interactions between them-are not organized; we here have an elemental social product; a "social resultant" (see our discussion of determinism, in chapter ii) is nevertheless obtained in this unorganized and elemental process (which will continue until a communist society is realized). Yet, there is such a social "product". It exists; it is an irrefutable fact of reality; world prices are a definite fact; so are world literature, or world routes of commerce, or world war; these facts are - sufficient to show that human society, embodied in the systems of the various nations, really does exist at the present time.

In general, whenever we have a sphere of constant mutual interaction, we also have a special system, a special real aggregate. *The broadest system of mutual interactions, embracing all the more permanent interactions between persons, is society.*

We define society as a real aggregate, or as a system of interactions, rejecting all the attempts of the so called "organic school" to interpret society in terms of an organism.

The official object of the "organic" theory is perfectly expressed in the fable of Menenius Agrippa, a Roman patrician who used the following "organic" arguments to conciliate the rebellious Plebeians: the hands may not rebel against the head, for otherwise the entire human body would be ruined. The social interpretation of the organic theory is the following: the ruling class is the head; the workers, or slaves, are the arms and legs; as arms and legs may not in nature replace the head, it is well for subordinates to hold their peace!

This wise humility on the part of the organic theory has made it quite popular among the bourgeoisie. The "founder" of sociology, Auguste Comte, considered society as a collective organism (*organisme collectif*); Herbert Spencer, the most popular of bourgeois sociologists, considered society to be something self-organic, without consciousness to be sure, but possessing organs, tissues, etc. René Worms even endows society with consciousness, as in the case of the individual, and Lilienfeld declares outright that society is an organism as much as a crocodile or the inventor of this theory. No doubt society has much in common with an organism; but it also has much in common with a mechanism. These traits, precisely, are the traits of any true totality, any system. But as we have no intention to take up such childish problems as to what constitutes the liver or the vermiform appendix of society, or what social phenomena are equivalent to ulcers, we shall not dwell on this point at all, the more since the adherents of the organic theory seem themselves to be ready to fall into the arms of mysticism, and to reconstruct society as a huge fabulous beast.

Society thus exists as a true aggregate of the persons composing it, as a system of mutually interacting elements. As we have seen, the number of mutual interactions in this system is endless. But the very existence of society suggests that all these numberless forces, acting in the most various directions, do not constitute a mere insane whirl, but move, as it were, through certain channels, in obedience to an internal law. If there were an outright and complete chaos, there would be no possibility of even an unstable equilibrium in society, in other words, there would be no society at all. We have discussed above the question as to the law of human actions, from the point of view of the individual (see chapter ii). We now take up the question from the other side, from the point of view of society and the conditions of its equilibrium. The result, however, is the same; we are brought to recognize the *regularity* of the social process. It is easiest to discover this uniformity. in the social process by an investigation of the conditions of social equilibrium. But before proceeding to this subject, we must dwell more in detail on the nature of society itself. It is not enough to say that it is a system of mutually interacting persons, or that this system is in force over a long period. It is necessary to explain the nature of this system, how it is distinguished from other systems, what is its necessary condition of life, and its necessary condition of equilibrium.

c. The Character of the Social Relations

The mutual interaction between persons, which constitutes social phenomena, is quite various. What is the *condition* for the permanence of these relations? In other words, where is the basic condition of equilibrium for the whole system, among all these interactions? What is the *basic* type of social relation without which all other types would be inconceivable?

The basic social relation is that of *labor,* as expressed chiefly in *social labor, i.e.,* in the conscious or unconscious work performed by people for each other. This becomes clear at once from an assumption of the opposite. Let us assume for a moment that the labor relation between persons should be destroyed, that products (goods) should not be transmitted from one place to another, that people should cease working for each other, that social labor should lose its social character. The result would be the disappearance of society, which would fly into a thousand pieces. Or, to take another example: Christian missionaries are sent to tropical countries to preach a knowledge of God and the Devil. These missionaries thus establish the so called higher intellectual relations. Would it be possible for these relations to endure between the country from which these gentlemen have set forth and the "savages" to whom they are sent, if there were no frequent steamers, no *regular* (as opposed to *casual)* exchange, *i.e.,* if no working relations should be established between the "civilized" countries and the home of the "savages"? All such relations can only be permanent when they are of the nature of *working* relations. The bond of labor is the fundamental condition for the possibility of an internal equilibrium in the system of human society.

We may also approach this question from another side. No system, including that of human society, can exist in empty space; it is surrounded by an "environment", on which all its conditions ultimately depend. If human society is not adapted to its environment, it is not meant for this world; all its culture will inevitably pass away; society itself will be reduced to dust. Thinking as hard as they can, none of the idealist professors can offer the slightest proof in opposition to our assertion that all the life of society, the very question of its life or death, depends on the relation between society and its environment, i.e., nature. We have spoken of this above, and may consider the subject disposed of. The social relation between men which most clearly and directly expresses this relation to nature is the relation of work. Work is the process of contact between society and nature. By work, energy is transferred from nature to society; and it is on this energy that society lives and develops (if it develops at all). Labor is also an active adaptation to nature. In other words, the process of production is a fundamental living process. of society. Consequently, the labor relation is a fundamental social relation. Or, in the words of Marx, "we must seek the anatomy of society in its economy",[1] *i.e.,* the structure of society is its *labor* structure ("its economic structure"). Consequently, our definition of society will read: *society is the broadest system of mutually interacting persons, embracing all their permanent mutual interactions, and based upon their labor relations.*

We have thus arrived at a completely *materialist* view of society. The basis of its structure is a working relation, just as the basis of life is the material process of production.

The following objection is often raised: "If things are as you say, how are the labor relations established? Do not people speak together, think together, in the process of labor? Is the labor relation then not a psychic, a spiritual relation? Where is your materialism now? What do all your labor and your labor relations amount to, if not to psychological relations?"

This question is worth going into, in order that future misunderstandings may be avoided. Let us begin with a simple example, that of a factory at work. In the factory there are unskilled workers and various types of skilled workers; some are working at certain machines, some at others; in addition, there are foremen, engineers, etc. Marx describes the condition as follows in his *Capital*: [2] "The essential division is, into workmen who are actually employed on machines (among whom are included a few who look after the engine) and into mere attendants (almost exclusively children) of these workmen. Among the attendants are reckoned, more or less, `feeders' who supply the machines with the material to be worked. In addition to these two principal classes, there is a numerically unimportant class of persons, whose occupation it is to look after the whole machinery and repair it from time to time; such as engineers, mechanics, joiners, etc." Such are the labor relations between the people in the factory. What is the prime nature of these relations? In the fact that each person is occupied with "his own job", but his job is only a part of the whole. The individual worker is therefore stationed at a *certain* place, goes through a certain motion, has a certain *material* contact with things and with other workers, uses up a certain quantity of *material* energy. All these relations are material, physical relations. Of course, they may have their "psychological" side; people think, exchange thoughts, converse, etc. But these activities will be determined by their distribution in the factory building, by the machines at which they are stationed, etc. In other words, they are distributed through the factory as distinct physical bodies; they are therefore in certain physical, material relations in time and in space. Such is the material, working organization of the workers in a factory, which Marx calls the "collective worker"; we are now dealing with a material human working system. When in operation, we have the process of material labor; men give out energy, and turn out a material product. This is also a material process, also having its "psychological" aspect.

What we have just observed in the factory is also applicable on a more intricate and far vaster scale in human society as a whole. For all of society constitutes a peculiar human working apparatus, in which the overwhelming majority of persons or groups of persons occupy a certain place in the working process. For instance, in present-day society, which includes all of so called "civilized mankind", and perhaps even more, wheat, as we have seen, is chiefly produced in certain countries; cacao, in certain other countries; metal products, in still another group of countries, etc. And within the various countries, certain factories produce one group of products, other factories other products. All these workers, peasants, colonial slaves, and even the engineers, overseers, foremen, organizers, etc., who are placed in the various corners of the earth, distributed over the various quarters of the globe, are all actually, although perhaps not consciously, working for each other. And when masses of commodities pass #rom one country to another, from factory to market, from market through tradesman to consumer, all this constitutes a material bond between all these persons. They are a part of the material skeleton, the working apparatus of a single social life. When we read of the life of the bees, we do not consider it remarkable to find the writer beginning with the discussion of the kinds of bees, the work they perform, the relations between them, both in time and in space, in a word, the material working apparatus of the "society of the bees". No one would think of considering the bees as a *psychical* aggregate, a "spiritual brotherhood", although he might speak of the instincts and the psychic life of the bees, of their "manners and customs", etc. But man, with his divine nature, must not be subjected to the same treatment as the bees!

It is self-evident that psychical interactions of the most varied kinds are inestimably more numerous in human society than even in a herd of the most highly developed apes. The "mind" of human society, i.e., all its psychic interactions, are as far superior to the "mind" of the herd of apes, as the mind of the individual man is superior to the mind of the individual ape. But the infinitely varied, complicated, exceptionally rich patterns of these mental and spiritual inter-relations, presenting all the colors of the rainbow, and constituting the "mind" of present-day society, also have their "body", without which they cannot exist, any more than the mind of the individual man can exist without his sinful earthly body. This "body" is the labor skeleton, the system of material relations between persons in the process of labor, or, as Marx puts it, the *production relations.*

Sentimental petty bourgeois dames may think it "terrible" to explain the divine fragrance of the narcissus as due to an excitation of so prosaic an organ as the nasal mucous membrane; and these ladies are not much different from most bourgeois scholars. Some of the latter will venture to deride the "organic theory", as does an Italian professor. A. Loria, who plagiarized Marx and could not digest him: "The German scholar Schäffle goes to grotesque lengths in his enumeration of social strata, organs, segments, blood vessels, motor centers, nerves, and ganglia; but the other sociologists of the same school are not much more moderate than he. They have already gone so far as to describe the social thigh, the social solar plexus, the social lungs. They already point to the vascular system of society, represented by the savings banks. A professor at the Sorbonne describes the clergy as a fatty nervous tissue. Another sociologist compares the nerve fibers with telegraph wires, and the human brain with a central telegraph office. One writer .goes so far as to distinguish male nations from female nations. In his opinion, the conquering states are males, who subjugate the defeated nations; while the defeated nations "are female nations." (Achille Loria: *Die Soziologie*, Jena, 1901, p.39.) This is all very well, but even the best of the bourgeois scholars become quite timid when they reach the confines of materialism. Professor E. Durkheim, in his book "On the Division of Labor", having emphasized the conception of "moral density" (by which he means the frequency and intensity of psychical interactions between men), goes on to say: The moral density cannot become greater unless the material density simultaneously becomes greater" (la densité morale me peut done s'accroître sans que la densité materielle s'accroisse en même temps . . .). This simply means that the "mental turnover" between men is based on the "material turnover", i.e., the density and frequency of the material, physical interactions is the condition for the corresponding density and frequency of their mental interactions. After making this correct statement, M. Durkheim is frightened at having expressed so materialist a thought and beats a retreat: "But it is useless (!!) to attempt to show which of the two phenomena determines the other; it is sufficient to have stated that they are indissoluble." (E. Durkheim: *De la division du travail social*, Paris 1893: p.283.) Useless, I suppose, because people are afraid to appear in decent bourgeois society as materialists.

Most modern bourgeois sociologists consider society to be a certain psychical system, a psychical "organism", or the like, which is quite in accord with the idealist view of the universe. The fundamental error of these theories is in their separating "mind" from "matter", and then declaring this "mind" to be incapable of explanation, i.e., their deifying it. In some societies, the psychical interactions are different from those of other societies. For instance, in the reign of Nicholas I, there was a "spirit" of police violence, of subjection under the Czar's might, love of the traditional, while Soviet Russia presents something quite different, i.e., the psychical interrelations have become altogether different. Psychological theories of society cannot explain this difference; here again the only scientific conception is that of materialism (Marx speaks of an "organism of production"; cf. *Capital*, vol. iii).

d. Society and Personality; Precedence of Society over the Individual

Society consists of individual persons; it could not exist without them, as we may assume without further discussion. But society is not merely an aggregate of persons, constituting their sum. Society is more than a mere summation of its various Jacks and Jills. We have already seen that society is a real aggregate, a "system"; we have seen that it is a very complicated system of mutual interactions between the various persons, which interactions are extremely varied in quality and quantity. This means that society, as a whole, is greater than the sum of its parts. It cannot in any way be reduced to these parts, which is also true of many systems of various kinds, both living organisms and dead mechanisms. For instance, let us take the case of any machine, a simple watch, let us say. Take any such machine apart and lay its component parts in a heap. This heap will constitute their sum; but it will not be the machine; it will not be the watch; for the heap lacks the definite relation, the definite *mutual interaction*. of the parts which transforms them into a mechanism. What makes these parts a *whole*? A certain arrangement of them. The same is true in society; society consists of people; but if these people, in the labor process, should not be at their posts at each given moment, if they were not connected by the labor bond between them, there would be no society.

We must here point out another phenomenon observed in society; namely, society consists not only of various persons mutually interacting, either directly or indirectly; it also consists of mutually interacting groups of persons, also constituting "real aggregates", standing as it were *between* society and the individual. For instance, present-day society is exceedingly large; already people in the most remote countries have been brought into relation, are being drawn in further and further, by a labor bond; there is practically a world *society*. But this society of almost 1,500,000,000 persons mutually interacting, united by the fundamental tie (of labor), as well as countless other ties, includes within it partial systems of persons united in some way or other; classes, states, church organizations, parties, etc. This subject will be discussed in detail later. For the present, we must observe that within society there are a great number of groups of men; these groups, in turn, also consist of individual persons; the mutual interrelations between these persons usually become more frequent and intimate "in their own circle" than between men in general; the German philosopher and sociologist, G. Simmel, rightly observes that the narrower the circle of mutually interacting persons, the more intimate the relations between them, in general; besides, all these groups come into contact among themselves. In other words, the various individuals constituting society do not always influence each other directly, but through groups, through partial systems within the single great system of human society. Let us consider, for instance, an individual worker in capitalist society. Whom does he meet most frequently, with whom does he talk, discuss questions, etc.? Most often, it is with workers; very rarely does he meet artisans, or peasants, or bourgeois. This is an illustration of the existence of the class relation. This worker most frequently comes into contact with other classes, not simply as an individual personality, but as a member of his class, sometimes even as a member of a consciously organized body, a party, a trade union, etc. The same case applies also to the other groups in society, not only to classes: scholars associate mostly with scholars; journalists, with journalists; priests with priests, etc.

In the material field, we find that society is not a mere aggregate of persons, that it is more than their sum, that their grouping and definite "disposition" (Marx calls it their "distribution") in the labor process amounts to something new, something greater than their "sum" or "aggregate". The same holds good also in the psychological ("mental") life, which plays a very important part. We have already several times made use of the example of the fixing of a market price as a result of various individual guesses. The price is a social phenomenon, a social "resultant", a product of the mutual interactions of persons. The price is not an average of the guesses, nor does it in every case approximate the individual guesses, for the individual guesses are a personal matter, concerning one man only, existing only in his mind, while the actual price is something that influences all; it is an independent fact which all must count on; an objective fact though it be immaterial (see chapter ii of this book); the price, in other words, is something new, something that leads its own social life, is independent more or less of individual persons, although it is created by them. The case with the remaining evidences of the psychical life is the same. Languages, the political system, science, art, religion, philosophy, and a great number of less important phenomena and subdivisions, such as fashions, customs, "good behavior", etc., etc., all are products of social life, a result of the mutual interaction of persons, of their constant association with each other.

Just as society is not merely a sum of the persons composing it, so the mental life of society is not merely a sum of the ideas and feelings of the individual persons composing it, but is a product of the association with each other, is to a certain extent something apart, new, not to be explained as a mere arithmetical sum; it is a new element resulting from the mutual interactions of persons.

We can thus explain the necessity of special social sciences; Wundt correctly remarks: "It is rather the uniting and interacting of individuals which produces this community as such, and thereby also awakens in the individual, performances specifically appertaining to the common life." (W. Wundt: *Völkeypsychologie*, vol. i, part i, Leipzig,. 1911, p.21.)

Individual men are inconceivable outside of society, without society. Nor can we imagine society's having been established by the various persons, living, as it were, in their "natural state", coming together and uniting in order to form a society. This conception was at one time quite widespread, but it is entirely erroneous. If we trace the development of human society, we shall find that it was originally composed of a herd, and not at all of individual creatures of human shape, living in various places, who suddenly discovered, one fine day, that it would be a fine thing (bright savages that they were!) to live together; and, having talked the thing over to the general satisfaction in their meetings, got together for the construction of a society. "The starting point (of science, N. B.)," wrote Karl Marx, "is the individual, producing in society, and thence comes the socially conditioned production of these individuals. The individual and isolated hunter and fisher . . . belongs to the insipid illusions of the Eighteenth Century "Production by isolated individual sons outside of society . . . is as great an absurdity (*Unding*) as would be the growth of language without the assumption of persons living together and talking with each other."[3]

The doctrine of the individual man entering into contractual relations with others was expressed with particular crassness in J. J. Rousseau's work, *Le Contrat social* (1762); man is born free in a "state of nature"; to assure his liberty, he enters into relations with others; society, as a state form, arises on the basis of the "social contract" (Rousseau draws no distinction between state and society). "The object of the social contract," writes Rousseau (Book ii, chap. 5), "is to protect the signatory parties." As a matter of fact, Rousseau does not investigate the true origin of the society or the state, but merely states what must be, what is the conception of society from the standpoint of "reason", *i.e.,* how a decent society should be constructed. Anyone violating the "contract" is subject to punishment. It followed logically that kings abusing their power must be deposed. Therefore, Rousseau's doctrine, in spite of its entirely erroneous conceptions, played an important revolutionary role during the French Revolution.

Man's social qualities could develop only in society. It is an absurdity to suppose that man (in the savage state) could have recognized the advantages of society without ever having seen a society. This would really be equivalent to assuming the growth of language among persons not in contact with each other, and distributed in various places. Man always was, as Aristotle puts it, "a social animal", i.e., an animal living in society, never out of society. We cannot imagine that human society was "established" (a merchant, who has himself established a corporation, may imagine that human society was brought about in the same way). Human society has existed as long as there have been humans; humans have never existed outside of society. Man is a social animal "by his nature"; his "nature" is a social nature, changing with society; he lives in society "by his nature", and not by agreement or contract with other persons.

Man having always lived in society, i.e., having always been social man, it follows that the individual has always had society as his environment. Since society has always constituted this environment for the individual, it is natural to infer that this environment has also determined the various individuals: one society, or environment, has produced one kind of individual; another society, another kind of individual; "a man is known by the company he keeps".

An interesting question which has been a source of many disputes, is that of *the role of the individual in history.*

This question is not as difficult as it may seem. Does the individual play a part, or is he a mere zero in the course of events? Of course, since society consists of individuals, the action of any individual will have its influence on social phenomena. The individual does play a "part"; his actions, feelings, desires enter into the social phenomenon as a component part; "men make history". Social phenomena are composed of the mutual interactions of the forces of the various individuals, as we have seen.

Furthermore, if the various individuals influence society, is it possible to determine how the actions of the various individuals are brought about? Yes; for we know that the will of man is not free, that it is determined by external circumstances. Since the external circumstances, in the case of the individual, are social circumstances (the conditions of life of the family, the group, the given occupation, the class, the situation of the entire society at a certain moment), his volition will be determined by external conditions; from them he will draw the motives of his activity. For instance, the soldier in the Russian army at the time of Kerensky observed that his peasant farm was going to pieces, that life was getting harder, that there was no end of the war in sight, that the capitalists were becoming more impudent, and were not giving the land to the peasants. Thence arose the motives of his action: to put a stop to the war, seize the land, and, for this purpose, overthrow the government. Social circumstances therefore determine the individual's motives.

These circumstances set the limits for the realization of the goals proposed by the individual person. Milyukov, in 1917, wished to strengthen the influence of the bourgeoisie and to lean for support on the Allies; but his desire was not realized; circumstances shifted so that Milyukov obtained nothing of what he wished.

Furthermore, if we examine each individual in his development, we shall find that at bottom he is filled with the influences of his environment, as the skin of a sausage is filled with sausage-meat. Man "is trained" in the family, in the street, in the school. He speaks a language which is the product of social evolution; he thinks thoughts that have been devised by a whole series of preceding generations; he is surrounded by other persons with all their modes of life; he has before his eyes an entire system of life, which influences him second by second. Like a sponge he constantly absorbs new impressions. And thus he is "formed" as an individual. Each individual at bottom is filled with a social content. The individual himself is a collection of concentrated social influences, united in a small unit.

Another circumstance is worthy of attention. Often the role of the individual is quite large by virtue of his specific place and the specific work which he performs. For instance, the general staff of an army consists of a small number of persons only, while the army itself counts hundreds of thousands, perhaps millions of persons. It is apparent to anyone that the significance of the few persons in the general staff far exceeds that of the great number in the army (soldiers or officers). If the enemy should succeed in taking the general staff, this might be equivalent, under certain circumstances, to a defeat of the entire army. The importance of these few persons is therefore very great. But what would the general staff amount to without its telephone system, its reports, its announcements, its maps, its opportunities to issue orders, the discipline in the army, etc.? Very little. The persons constituting the general staff might be no more than the rest of the army; their strength, their significance is the result of a special social connection, of the organization within which these persons are working. To be sure, they may be capable of discharging their duties (they may have sufficient training or natural aptitude, the latter developed by experience, as was the case with many of Napoleon's generals, or with the commanders of the Red Army). But apart from this special connection, they lose their significance entirely. The opportunity on the part of the general staff to exert a powerful influence on the army is conditioned by the army itself, by its structure, its dispositions, by the aggregate of mutual interactions that have here been brought together.

In society the case is the same. The role of political leaders, for instance, is much larger than the role of the average man of a certain class or party. Of course, it is necessary to have certain aptitudes, mental qualities, experience, etc., in order to become a political leader. But it is also clear that in the absence of the necessary organizations (parties, unions, a proper approach to the masses, etc.) the "leaders" could not play such an important part. It is the strength of the social bonds that gives strength to the individual persons of prominence. Quite similar is the case in other relations also, let us say with regard to inventors, scholars, etc. They can "develop" only under certain circumstances. Suppose an inventor, talented by nature, has had no opportunity to "push himself", has learned nothing, read nothing, has been obliged to take up an entirely different activity, for instance, selling rags. His "talent" would go to pot; no one would ever hear of him. Just as the military leader is inconceivable without an army, so the technical inventor is inconceivable without machinery, apparatus and the people that go with them. And, on the other hand, if our rag-dealer should succeed in "making his way in the world", i.e., in occupying a certain place in the system of social relations, he might become a second Edison. We might give any number of such examples, but it is self-evident that in all these cases society has a certain influence, and that it is impossible to "develop" except on the basis of this influence within which the social (class, group, general) demand is felt.

Thus, the social relations themselves impart importance to the various individuals.

This point of view has made very slow headway, for the reasons so brilliantly revealed by M. N. Pokrovsky (*Outlines of the History of Russian Culture*, vol. i, p.3, in Russian). The historian, by reason of his personal situation, is a mental worker, an intellectual; proceeding to a consideration of his more specific earmarks, he is a man who does work in writing, a literary worker. What is more natural for him than to consider mental work as the chief substance of history, and literary works, from poems and romances to philosophical treatises and scientific publications, as the fundamental facts of civilization?" Furthermore, "men who do mental work - quite naturally " were seized with the pride that dictated the hymns of praise to the Pharaohs. They began to believe that they were making history." It should be added that this professional standpoint fully coincided with the class standpoint of the ruling classes, the minority that dominated the great majority. It is not difficult to see that this emphasis and preference for leaders, particularly kings, princes, etc., and also for so called geniuses - is closely allied with the religious point of view; for here the *social* power is overlooked, the power which is conferred by society on the individual; in its stead, the historian visualizes the inscrutable, i.e., actually, "divine" power of the individual person. This is excellently expressed by the Russian philosopher, V. S. Solovyov, in his *Justification of the Good,* chap. iv: "The providential persons who have enabled us to share the heights of religion and of human enlightenment were originally by no means the creators of these possessions. That which they gave us was taken by them from earlier world-historic geniuses, heroes and martyrs, all of whom we must bear gratefully in mind. We must attempt to restore the full line of our mental ancestors, the men through whom *Providence* has been impelling mankind forward on the path to perfection. " In these *'chosen vessels,' we worship that which He (the Heavenly Father) has imbued them with; in these visible counterfeits of invisible divinity, the divinity itself is recognized and worshiped.*" This balderdash speaks for itself - it requires no refutation.

It follows from the above that the "individual" always acts as a social individual, as a component part of a group, a class, a society. The "individual" is always filled with a social content, for which reason it is necessary, in an effort to understand the growth of society, to begin with a consideration of the social conditions, and to proceed from them, if that be necessary, to the individual; the contrary process is worthless. By means of the social relations - by an investigation of the conditions of the entire social life, the life of a class, of a trade group, the family, the school, etc.- we may more or less explain the development of the individual; but we could never explain the development of society by means of the development of the "individual". For each individual, whatever be his activity, always has in mind what has already taken place in society; for example, when the buyer goes to market to buy shoes or bread, his price estimates are based on his personal approximation to prices now prevalent or formerly prevalent on the market. When the inventor devises a new machine, he proceeds on the basis of what is already in existence, on the basis of existing technique or existing science, on the problems presented by this science, on the demands of practical work, etc. In a word, if we should attempt - as do certain bourgeois scholars - to explain social phenomena on the basis of individual phenomena (on the individual psychology), we should have not an explanation, but an absurdity; the social phenomenon (for instance, the price) cannot be explained by the individual phenomenon (for instance, the value put upon the goods by Smith, Jones, or Robinson), but their estimates can be explained by the price which Smith, Jones, or Robinson had in mind from some previous occasion. We have therefore seen that the individual draws his motives from the generality, the social environment; the conditions under which the social environment develops provide the limits for the individual's activity; the individual's role is determined by social conditions. Society takes precedence over the individual.

e. Societies in Process of Formation

The fact that man has always existed in society by no means signifies that *new* societies may not be formed or that old societies may not grow.

Let us assume that at a certain time various human groups are in existence at various points on the earth's surface, and that these human organizations have no relation whatever with each other; they are divided by mountains, rivers and oceans, and have not yet attained a stage of "cultural development" that would enable them to overcome these obstacles. If they succeed in coming into contact with each other at all, it is only at the rarest intervals, and with no regularity; a permanent relation does not exist between them.

Under these circumstances, we cannot speak of a single great society embracing these various groups. Instead of a universal society, we have as many societies as there are groups of the kind mentioned, for the basis of society, its most outstanding characteristic, is a permanent *labor bond,* a series of "production relations", constituting a skeleton for the entire system. In the case above described there is no such relation between the groups, no universal society, but a number of petty societies, each with its own special history.

We cannot therefore speak of a union of "men" in a single society, but may only group them as "men", as opposed to other animals; in other words, we may consider them as united in a biological group (as distinct from fleas, giraffes, elephants); but not in a social group from the standpoint of social science, of sociology; we are dealing with a single type of animal, but not with a single society. From the standpoint of biological unity, it is sufficient that these animals should have the same morphology, the same organs, etc. But sociological unity would require that these animals should *work together* in some way or other, not simultaneously, not merely in parallel activities, but together.

Some go so far as to deny that society exists as a unit. For example, Professor Wipper says:[4] "A completely closed system of natural economy has perhaps never existed from the beginning of civilization. We have always had commercial relations, colonization, migrations, propaganda. Doubtless, independent work has been done in certain places, much has been simultaneously accomplished within various geographical limits and conditions by independent effort, but perhaps the next following stage in evolution has in most cases been attained by a sudden bound, as a sort of premature lesson, crudely and imperfectly taught, but nevertheless repeated by others and later learned." But while there may never have been an *absolute,* complete system, there is no doubt whatever that the exchange relations existing between various human societies were once extremely slight. For instance, what relations existed between the European peoples and America. before Columbus? Even among the European peoples themselves - let us say - in the Middle Ages, relations were very weak. It is therefore impossible in such cases to speak of a single human society; humanity was then a unit only from the biological standpoint.

Let us now suppose that contacts begin between our various

societies, first, military contacts, then commercial relations. These commercial relations become more and more permanent; finally a time comes when one society cannot exist without the other; certain societies produce chiefly one thing, while others produce another thing; these products are exchanged and thus the societies work upon each other, this work now having a regular and not merely accidental character, which is necessary far the existence of both groups of societies. We now already have a *single society* on a large scale, formed by the union of societies once distinct from each other.

The opposite process may also take place; under certain conditions, society may dissolve into a number of societies (usually under conditions of decline).

It follows that society is not a permanent thing, existing from time immemorial for we may trace, the process of its formation. For example, we have seen such a process going on in the second half of the Nineteenth Century and the beginning of the Twentieth Century. In various ways (through colonial wars, the increase in exchanges of goods, export and import of capital, movement of population from one country to another, and the like) closet and closer mutual relations have been built up between countries. All countries have been joined by permanent economic bond, which means, in the last analysis, labor bond. A world economic system has resulted, world capitalism has grown up, all of whose parts are interrelated with each other. Together with the international movement of things and people: commodities, capital, workers, merchants, engineers, traveling salesmen, etc., a tremendous current of ideas has also been moving from country to country: scientific ideas, artistic ideas, philosophical ideas, religious ideas, political ideas, etc., etc. The world trade in ma terial things has brought with it a world exchange of mental products. A single human society has begun to exist, having a single history.

BIBLIOGRAPHY

K. Marx: *A Contribution to a Critique of Political Economy*, Chicago, 1913. K. Marx: *Capital, vol. i*, Chicago, 1915; F. Engels: *Anti-Dühring*; F. Engels: *Feuerbach* (translated into English by Austin Lewis, Chicago, 1906; H. Cunow: *Soziologie, Ethnologie and materialistische Geschichtsauffassung*. H. Cunow: *Die Marxsche Geschichts-, Gesellschafts- and Staatslehre; Grundziige der Marxschen Soziologie*, vol.i; Plekhanov: *Twenty Years* (in Russian); N. Bukharin: *The Economic Theory of the Leisure Class*. On the subject of production relations, cf. N. Bukharin: *Imperialism and World Economy*.

NOTES

[1]*Contribution to a Critique of Political Economy.*

[2]Chicago, Charles H. Kerr Company, 1915, vol. i, p.459.

[3]Karl Marx: *Introduction to the Critique of Political Economy*, printed with *A Contribution to the Critique of Political Economy*, Chicago, 1913, pp.265-261.

[4]KIn his article, "New Horizons in the Science History" (in Russian), of in the periodical *Sovremenny Mir*, November, 1906.

5: THE EQUILIBRIUM BETWEEN SOCIETY AND NATURE

a. Nature as the Environment of Society

A consideration of society as a system involves the recognition of "external nature" as its environment, i.e., chiefly the terrestrial globe with all its natural properties. Human society is unthinkable without its environment. Nature is the source of foodstuffs for human society, thus determining the latter's living conditions. But nothing could be more incorrect than to regard nature from the teleological point of view: man, the lord of creation, with nature created for his use, and all things adapted to human needs. As a matter of fact, nature often falls upon the "lord of creation" in such a savage manner that he is obliged to admit her superiority. It has taken man centuries of bitter struggle to place his iron bit in nature's mouth.

Now man, as an animal form, as well as human society, are products of nature, parts of this great, endless whole. Man can never escape from nature, and even when he "controls" nature, he is merely making use of the laws *of nature* for his own ends. It is therefore clear how great must be the influence of nature on the whole development of human society. Before proceeding to a study of the relations existing between nature and man, or of the forms in which nature operates on human society, we must consider first of all with what phases of nature man comes chiefly in contact. We have only to look about us in order to perceive the dependence of society on nature: "The soil (and this, economically speaking, includes water) in the virgin state in which it supplies man with necessaries or the means of subsistence ready to hand, exists independently of him, and is the universal subject of human labor. All those things which labor merely separates from immediate connection with their environment, are subjects of labor spontaneously provided by nature. Such are fish which we catch and take from their element water, timber which we fell in the virgin forest, and ores which we extract from their veins " As the earth is his original larder, so too it is his original tool house. It supplies him, for instance, with stones for throwing, grinding, pressing, cutting, etc."[1] Nature is the *immediate* object of labor in the acquisitive industries (mining, hunting, portions of agriculture, etc.). In other words, nature determines what raw materials are to be manipulated. Man, as we have seen above, is constantly making use of the laws of nature in his struggle with her. "He makes use of the mechanical, physical and chemical properties of some bodies in order to make other substances subservient with his aims:" [2] Man makes use of the power of steam, electricity, etc., the attraction of the earth for bodies (law of gravitation), etc. It is impossible, therefore, for the *state of nature* at a certain place and at a certain time not to act upon human society. Climate (quantity of moisture, winds, temperature, etc.), configuration of surface (hills or valleys, distribution of water, character of rivers, presence of metals, minerals, all the resources buried in the earth), the character of the shore (in the case of a maritime community), the distribution of land and water, the presence of various animals and plants, etc., such are the chief elements of nature that influence human society. Whales and fish may not be caught on land; agriculture may not be pursued on rocky mountains; deserts are a poor place for forestry; you cannot live in tents in cold countries during the winter, nor do you heat your but in hot weather ... if no metals are in the ground, you cannot conjure them down from heaven or suck them out of your finger-tips, etc.

In detail, the influence of nature is found expressed in the following conditions:

Distribution of land and water. In general, man is a land animal; the ocean therefore has a double influence: it divides: and, on the other hand, furnishes a transportation route. The former influence is earlier than the latter. The influence of the coast-line is chiefly in its possessing - or not possessing - good harbors. With few exceptions (Cherbourg, for instance), modern seaports are established where the natural curves of the seacoast provide natural harbors. The surface of the earth, whose influence on man is felt through the animal and vegetable kingdoms, has also a more direct influence - varying greatly in accordance with the stage in evolution - by determining the nature and direction of transportation routes (paths, highways, railroads, tunnels, etc.).

Stones and minerals. Construction work depends on the nature of the available stone quarries. In mountainous regions, the hard varieties (for instance, porphyry, basalt, etc.) predominate; in valleys, softer varieties. The importance of minerals and metals has increased particularly in recent days (iron, coal). Certain minerals furnish the principal reason for the migration of nations, as well as colonization. (The presence of tin lured the Phoenicians northward; gold drew them to South Africa and East India; gold and silver brought the Spaniards to America.) The centers of modern heavy industry are determined by the location of deposits of iron ore and coal. The character of the soil, together with the climate, have their influence on the vegetable kingdom.

Continental bodies of water. Water is of value, in the first place, for drinking purposes (therefore it is so precious in the desert); second, we have its significance for agriculture (the soil - depending on the amount of water in it - must be drained or irrigated). It is well known how significant are the inundations of the great rivers (Nile, Ganges, etc.) for agriculture, and how great was the influence of this circumstance on the ancient Egyptians and East Indians. Water is also important as motive power (water-mills are among the earliest inventions; therefore, cities arose in close proximity to regions rich in water; more recently, the utilization of water power in electrification may be mentioned, the so called 'white coal," now widely exploited in America, Germany, Norway, Sweden and Italy). Finally, there is the fact that water furnishes transportation routes, which some scholars consider its most important function.

The Climate's influence is chiefly through its effect on production. The species of plants to be cultivated depend on the climate, which also determines the length of the agricultural season (very short in Russia; lasting nearly a year in southern countries); labor forces are therefore liberated in northern climates, becoming available for industry, etc. Climate also has an influence on transportation (traffic by sleigh in winter; harbors frozen up or open in winter, also rivers, etc.). A cold climate requires a greater quantity of labor devoted to nourishment, clothing, housing, artificial heating, etc.; in the north, more time is spent indoors; in the south, more in the open air.

The Flora has a varying influence: at lower levels of culture, the paths depended on the nature of the forests (inaccessible primeval forests), the species of trees determine the character of construction, fuel, etc., also the chase, agriculture, even the specific variety of agriculture. The same is true of cattle breeding. The *fauna,* for primitive tribes, constitutes a powerful hostile element, serving chiefly for nutrition, in other words, as the object of the chase and of fishery; later, there came the taming of beasts, with a further effect on production and transportation (draught animals).

The Ocean has always been of great importance; travel and freight are cheaper by sea; the ocean also furnishes the theater for many branches of production (fisheries, whaling, sealing, etc.). (*Cf. A.* Hettner: *Die geographischen Bedingungen der menschlichen Wirtschaft* in *Grundriss der Nationalökonomik,* Tübingen 1914.) The influence of climatic conditions may be illustrated as follows: in the matter of average annual temperatures (so called *isotherms* on the charts), "it may be observed that the greatest populations have congregated between the isotherms of + 16· C. and + 4· C. The isotherm + 10· C. coincides pretty closely with the central axis of this climatic and cultural zone, and on this isotherm lie the richest and most populous cities of the globe: Chicago, New York, Philadelphia, London, Vienna, Odessa, Peking; on isotherm + 16· we find: St. Louis, Lisbon, Rome, Constantinople, Osaka, Kioto, Tokio; on isotherm + 4·, we have: Quebec, Oslo, Stockholm, Leningrad, Moscow. Very few cities of more than 100,000 inhabitants are found south of isotherm + 16·: Mexico, New Orleans, Cairo, Alexandria, Teheran, Calcutta, Bombay, Madras, Canton. The northern limit - isotherm + 4· - is more sharply drawn; north of it, the only important cities are Winnipeg (Canada) and the administrative centers of Siberia." (L. I. Mechnikov: *Civilization and the Great Historical Rivers,* quoted from the Russian edition, Petersburg, 1898, pp.38, 39.)

b. Relations between Society and Nature; the Process of Production and Reproduction

We already know that in any system the cause for alterations in the system must be sought in its relations with its environment; also, that the fundamental direction of growth (progress, rest, or destruction of the system), depends precisely on what the relation is between the given system and its environment. An alteration in this relation impels us to seek a cause producing a change in the system itself. Where shall we seek the constantly changing relations between society and nature?

We have already seen that this changing relation is in the field of social labor. As a matter of fact, how does the process of adaptation of human society to nature express itself? What is the character of the unstable equilibrium between society and nature?

Human society, ever since it began, has had to abstract material energy from external nature; without these loans it could not exist. Society best adapts itself to nature by abstracting (and appropriating to itself) more energy from nature; only by increasing this quantity of energy does society succeed in growing. Let us suppose, for example, that on a certain day all labor should stop-in factories, machine-shops, mines, on railroads, in the forests and fields, by land and sea. Society would not be able to maintain itself for a single week, for even in order to live on the existing supplies, it would have to transport, forward, and distribute them. "Every child knows that any nation would perish of hunger if it should stop work, I shall not say for a year, but only for a few weeks."[3] Men cultivate the ground, raise wheat, rye, maize; they breed and graze animals; they raise cotton, hemp and flax; they cut down trees, break stone in quarries, and thus satisfy their demands for food, clothing, and shelter. They seize coal and iron-ore in the bowels of the earth and create great machines of steel, with the aid of which they dig down into nature in various directions, changing the entire earth into a gigantic workshop, in which men beat with hammers, work at the benches, dig holes underground, see to it that the great engines run smoothly, cut tunnels through the mountains, cross the oceans in huge ships, bear burdens through the air, trace a great network of rails over the earth, lay cables at the bottom of the sea-and everywhere, from the noisy city centers to the remote country nooks on the earth's surface, they work like beavers for their "daily bread", always by adapting themselves to nature and adapting nature to themselves. One part of nature, *external* nature, the part that we are calling the "environment", is opposed to another part, which is human society. And the form of contact between these two parts of a single whole is the process of human labor. "Labor is, in the first place, a process in which both man and nature participate, and in which man of his own accord, starts, regulates, and controls the *material reactions* between *himself and nature.* He opposes himself to nature as one of her own forces."[4] The immediate contact between society and nature, *i.e.,* the abstraction of energy from nature, is a *material* process. "Man sets in motion his arms and legs, head and hands, the natural forces of his body, in order to appropriate nature's productions in a form adapted to his own wants."[5]

This material process of "metabolism" between society and nature is the fundamental relation between environment and system, between "external conditions" and human society.

In order that society may continue to live, the process of production must be constantly renewed. If we assume that at any moment a certain amount of wheat, shoes, shirts, etc., have been produced, and that all these are eaten, worn, used up, in the same period, it is clear that production must at once repeat its cycle; in fact, it must be constantly repeated, each cycle following immediately upon the other. The process of production, viewed from the point of view of a repetition of these productive cycles, is called the *reproductive process.* For a realization of the reproductive process it is necessary that all its material conditions be repeated, for example: for the production of textile fabrics, we need looms; for looms we need steel; for steel we need iron ore and coal; for transporting the latter substances we need rail, roads, and therefore also rails, locomotives, etc., also highways, steamers, etc.; warehouses, factory buildings, etc.; in other words, we need a long series of material products of the most varied nature. Of course, all these material products deteriorate - some faster than others - in the process of production; the foodstuffs obtained by the weavers are eaten up; the weaving looms wear out; the warehouses become old, need overhauling; locomotives get out of repair, cars, the ties, must be replaced. In fact, a constant replacement (by new *production)* of worn-out, used up, consumed objects, in all their various material forms, is a necessary condition of the process of reproduction. At any given moment, human society requires for continuing the progress of reproduction a certain quantity of foodstuffs, buildings, mining products, finished industrial products, replacement parts for transportation units, etc. All these things must be produced if society is not to lower its standard of living, beginning with wheat and rye, coal and steel, and ending with microscopes and chalk for schools, book-bindings, and news-print paper. All these things are a necessary part of the material turnover of society; they are the material components of the social process of reproduction.

We therefore regard the metabolism between society and nature as a *material* process, for it deals with material things (objects of labor, instruments of labor, and products obtained as a consequence-all are material things); on the other hand, the process of labor itself is an expenditure of physiological energy, nerve energy, muscular energy, whose material expression is in the physical motions of those engaged at work. "If we examine the whole process from the point of view of its result, of the product, it is plain that both the instruments and the subject of labor, are means of production, and that the labor itself is productive labor".[6]

Even bourgeois professors, sticking to their "specialty", reluctantly recognize the material character of the process of production. Thus, Professor Herkner (*Arbeit und Arbeitsteilung,* in *Grundriss der Sozialökonomie,* vol. ii, p.170) writes: "An investigation of the essence of labor requires the understanding of two types of processes " In the first place, bodily labor is expressed in certain external movements. The smith's left hand, for instance, seizes the red-hot iron with a pair of tongs, placing it on the anvil, while his right imparts form to it through blows with the hammer ". The number, variety and size of the results of labor may be determined " It is possible to describe the entire labor process, as well as the instruments of labor used in it," etc. Herkner calls this labor in the objective sense". On the other hand, the same process may be regarded from the point of view of the thoughts and feelings produced in the worker; this is labor "in the subjective sense". Since we are concerned with the mutual relation between society and nature, and since this mutual relation happens to coincide with *objective* (material) labor, we may now ignore the subjective phase of this process. It is therefore important for us to examine the material production of all the material elements necessary for the process of reproduction.

But the fact that instruments of precision, for instance, are material things, and that their production is a part of material production, necessary in the process of reproduction, does not justify the conclusion drawn by Kautsky (Die Neue Zeit, vol. 15, p.233) or Cunow (Die Neue Zeit, vol. 39, p. 408) namely, that mathematics and its study are a portion of production, merely because they are necessary for this production. However, if all persons should suddenly lose the faculty of speech, and if there should be no other means of communication aside from this lost faculty, it would at once transpire that production also would cease. Language therefore is also "necessary" for reproduction, like many other elements in any society. Yet it would be ridiculous to consider language as a part of production. Nor need we here cudgel our brains with another allegedly troublesome question: which came first, the chicken or the egg; society or production? This question is an absurd one; society is inconceivable without production; production is inconceivable without society. But it is important to determine whether the alteration in a system is conditioned by the alterations taking place between the system and its environment. If so, we must next ask: wherein is this alteration to be sought? The answer is: in *material* labor. This mode of formulating the question disposes of most of the "profound" objections to historical materialism, and it becomes evident that the "first cause" of social evolution is to be found precisely here. But more of this later.

The metabolism between man and nature consists, as we have seen, in the transfer of material energy from external nature to society; the expenditure of human energy (production) is an extraction of energy from nature, energy which is to be *added* to society (distribution of products between the members of society) and *appropriated* by society (consumption) ;this appropriation is the basis for further expenditure, etc., the wheel of reproduction being thus constantly in motion. Taken as a whole, the process of reproduction therefore includes various phases, together constituting a unit, at the bottom of which is again the same productive process. It is obvious that human society comes most directly into contact with external nature in the process of production; it rubs elbows with nature at this point; therefore, within the process of reproduction, the productive phase determines also that of distribution and consumption.

The process of social production is an adaptation of human society to external nature. The process is an active one. When any type of animal adapts itself to nature, this type is subject, at bottom, to the constant action of its environment. When human society adapts itself to its environment, it also adapts the environment to itself, not only becoming subject to the action of nature, as a material, but also simultaneously transforming nature into a material for human action. For example, when certain forms of insects or birds have a coloring similar to that of their environment (mimicry), this phenomenon is not a result of any effort on the part of these organisms, and certainly not a result of their action on external nature. This result was obtained at the price of the destruction of countless myriads of individual animals, in the course of many thousands of years, with those best adapted surviving and multiplying. Human society struggles with nature; man plows the ground, constructs roads through impassable forests, conquers the forces of nature, uses them for his own ends, changes the whole face of the earth; this is an active, not a passive, adaptation, and constitutes one of the basic differences between human society and the other types of animals.

This was already well understood by the French Physiocrats in the Eighteenth Century. Thus, we find in Nicolas Baudeau (*Première introduction de la philosophie èconomomique, ou analyse des états poliées*, 1767, *Collection des Economistes et des Réformateurs sociaux de France*, published by Dubois, Paris, 1910, p.2): "All animals are daily attempting to find products produced by nature, *i.e.,* food furnished by the earth itself. Certain species . . . collect these commodities and preserve them . . . . Man only, destined (this thought is expressed teleologically. N.B.) to investigate the mysteries of nature and its fruitfulness, can obtain more useful products than he finds on the surface of the earth in its wild and unworked condition. This activity (*cet art*) is perhaps one of man's noblest traits on earth."

"Man," writes the geographer L. Mechnikov (op. *cit.*, p.44), "who shares with all other organisms the valuable property of adaptation to his environment, dominates all by reason of the more precious ability - peculiar to him - of adapting the environment to his needs.

Strictly speaking, active adaptation (by means of labor) is found in elementary outline among certain types of so called social animals (beavers, who build dams; ants, who erect large hills; plant-lice, who exploit certain plants; bees, etc.); the primitive forms of human labor were also animal-like, instinctive forms of labor.

c. The Productive Forces; the Productive Forces as an Indicator of the Relations between Society and Nature

Thus, the interrelation between society and nature is a process of social reproduction. In this process, society applies its human labor energy and obtains a certain quantity of energy from nature ("nature's material", in the words of Marx). The *balance* between expenditure and receipts is here obviously the decisive element for the growth of society. If what is obtained exceeds the loss by labor, important consequences obviously follow for society, which vary with the amount of this excess.

Let us suppose a certain society must devote all its working time to covering its most rudimentary needs. It is obvious that the products obtained will be consumed as rapidly as new products are produced. This society will therefore not have enough time to produce an additional quantity of products, to extend its requirements, to introduce new products; it will hardly be able to make ends meet, will live from hand to mouth, will eat up what it produces, consuming just enough to keep on working; all its time will be spent in the production of an unvarying quantity of products. This society will remain at the same low level of existence. It will be impossible for its demands to increase; it will have to suit its wants to its resources and both will remain unchanged.

Now let us suppose that for some reason the same quantity of necessary products is obtained with an expenditure, not of all of society's time, but of only one-half of this time (for example, the primitive tribe has migrated to a place where there is twice as much game, twice as many beasts of all kinds, or where the earth is twice as fruitful; or, the tribe has improved its method of working the soil, or devised new tools, etc.).

In such a case, society will be free for one-half of its former working time. It may devote this free time to new branches of production: to the manufacture of new tools; to the obtaining of new raw materials, etc., and also to certain forms of mental labor. Here the growth of new demands becomes possible, for the first time we have an opportunity for the birth and development of so called "mental culture". If the free time now available is used only partly in perfecting the former types of labor, it follows that in the future the former demands may be satisfied by devoting to them even less than one-half the entire labor time (new perfections in the labor process arise); in the next cycle of reproduction, still less time is required, etc., and the time thus rendered available will be devoted in greater and greater measure to the manufacture of more and more improved tools, instruments, machines, on the one hand, and, on the other hand, to new branches of production, satisfying new wants; and, in the third place, to "mental culture", beginning with those phases that are more or less connected with the process of production.

Let us now suppose that the same quantity of necessary

objects which formerly demanded the expenditure of the entire labor time, now require not one-half this time, but twice the time (for instance, owing to an exhaustion of the soil); it is clear that unless new modes of labor are resorted to, or new lands settled, this society will decline, a portion of its numbers will die out. Let us further suppose that a highly developed society, with a rich "mental culture", with the most varied wants, an infinite number of different branches of production, with "arts and sciences" in full bloom, suddenly finds difficulty in satisfying its needs; perhaps, owing to certain reasons, the society is not able to manipulate its technical apparatus (for example, there may be constant class war, with no class gaining the upper hand, and the productive process, with its highly developed technique, dies out); it is then necessary to return to an older stage of labor, in which, for covering the former demands, a much greater period of time would be required, at present an impossibility; production will be curtailed, the standard of living will go down, the flourishing "arts and sciences" will wither; mental life will be impoverished; society, unless this lowering of its standard is the result of merely temporary causes, will be "barbarianized", will go to sleep.

The most noteworthy feature in all these cases is the fact that the growth of society is determined by the yield or *productivity of social labor;* the productivity of labor means the relation between the quantity of product obtained and the quantity of labor expended; in other words, the productivity of labor is the quantity of product per unit of working time, for example, the amount of product turned out in one day, or in one hour, or in one year. If this amount of product obtained per working hour is doubled, we say the productivity of labor has increased 200 per cent., if it is halved, we say it has gone down 50 per cent.

Obviously, the productivity of labor is a precise measure of the "balance" between society and nature; it is a measure of the mutual interaction between the environment and the system by which the position of the system in the environment is determined, and an alteration of which will indicate inevitable changes throughout the internal life of society.

In considering the productivity of social labor, we must also consider among labor expenditures the amount of human labor which is devoted to the production of suitable instruments of labor. If, for example, a certain product has hitherto been manufactured by human hands only, practically without tools, and now begins to be made with the aid of complicated machinery, and if the application of this machinery makes possible the manufacture of twice the quantity of products in the same time as formerly, this will not mean that the productivity of labor of the entire society will be doubled. For we have not counted the expenditure of human labor that went into the manufacture of the machines (or, more correctly, we have not counted the labor that *is indirectly* involved in the product because it went *directly* into the machines). The total productivity of labor will therefore be found to have somewhat less than doubled.

Those who love to harp on petty things may object to the conception of the productivity of social labor, and its adaptation to society as a whole, as does P. P. Maslov (*Capitalism*, in Russian). For example, one may raise the objection that the conception of the productivity of labor is valid only as applied to single branches of production. In a certain year, in so many working hours, so many pairs of boots were turned out. In the following year, twice as many in the same time. But how may we compare and add together the productivity of labor in the fields - let us say - of pig-breeding and orange-culture? Is this not as silly as the comparison between music, bills of exchange, and sugar-beets, of which Marx spoke so scornfully? Such objections may be answered in two ways; in the first place, all the useful products appropriated by society may be measured comparatively, as useful energies; we already express rye, wheat sugar-beets, and potatoes, in calories; if we have not yet advanced so far as to be able to express these other things in actual practice, we must not attach too much importance to this inability; we must recognize that such a process will ultimately be possible; in the second place, we are already able to compare with each other, by indirect and complicated methods, quantities of quite varied objects. This is not the place for indicating the method pursued, but we shall adduce a simple case. If, for example, in a certain year, in a certain number of hours of labor, there were produced 1,000 pairs of boots plus 2,000 packages of cigarettes plus 20 machines, and in another year, in the same labor period: 1,000 pairs of boots plus 1,999 packages of cigarettes plus 21 machines plus 100 woolen sweaters, we may maintain without error that the productivity of labor has increased on the whole. Of course, we can also imagine the objection that not only products of consumption are produced, but also instruments of production. This would, of course complicate the calculation considerably, but suitable methods may be devised for including this circumstance.

Thus, the relation between nature and society is expressed in the relation between the quantity of useful energy turned out. and the expenditure of social labor, i.e., the productivity of social labor. The expenditure of labor consists of two components: the labor that is crystallized and included in the instruments of production, and the "living" labor, *i.e.,* the direct expenditure of working energy. If the productivity of labor as a quantity be regarded from the point of view of the component material factors of this quantity, we find we are dealing with three quantities: first, the quantity of products obtained; second, the quantity of instruments of production; third, the quantity of the productive forces, i.e., living workers. All these quantities are mutually dependent. For, if we know what workers are involved, we shall also know what they will produce in a given length of time; these two quantities determine the third quantity, the product turned out. Taken together, these two quantities constitute what we call the *material productive forces of society*. If, in the case of a certain society, we know what instruments of production it controls, how many such instruments, what kinds of workers and how many, we shall also know what will be the productivity of social labor, and what will be the degree to which this society has conquered nature, etc. In other 'words, the instruments of production and the working forces give us a precise material measure for the stage attained in the social evolution.

We may also glance a little deeper; we may go so far as to say that the instruments of production determine even the nature of the worker. For example, when the linotype machine is added to the system of social labor, workers will be found to run the machine. The elements acting in the labor process are therefore not merely an aggregation of persons and things, but a system in which all things and all persons stand, as it were, at their posts, having become adapted to each other. The existence of certain means of production implies also the existence of workers to manipulate them. Furthermore, the means of production themselves may be distinguished into two great groups: raw materials and instruments of labor. Even the instrument of labor (tool) performs an active part; with it, the worker works the raw material. The existence in a certain society of certain tools necessarily implies the existence of the raw material for which these tools are intended (of course, in the normal course of reproduction). We may therefore definitely state that the system of social instruments of labor, i.e., the technology of a certain society, is a precise material indicator of the relation between the society and nature. The material productive forces of society and the productivity of social labor will find their expression in this technical system. "Relics of bygone instruments of labor possess the same importance for the investigation of extinct economical forms of society (societies of various types, *N. B.*) as do fossil bones for the determination of extinct species of animals. It is not the articles made, but how they are made and by what instruments, that enables us to distinguish different economic epochs."

The question may also be approached from another angle. The "adaptation" of animals to nature consists in an alteration of the various organs of these animals: their feet, jaws, fins, etc., which constitutes a passive, *biological* adaptation. But human society adapts itself not biologically, but technically, actively, to nature. "An instrument of labor is a thing, or a complex of things, which the laborer interposes between himself and the subject of his labor, and which serves as the conductor of his activity. He makes use of the mechanical, physical, and chemical properties of some substances in order to make other substances subservient to his aims . . .thus nature becomes one of the organs of his activity, one that he annexes to his own bodily organs, adding stature to himself in spite of the Bible."[2] Human society in its technology constitutes an artificial system of organs which also are its direct, immediate and active adaptation to nature (it may be stated parenthetically that this renders superfluous a direct bodily adaptation of man to nature; even as compared with the gorilla, man is a weak creature; in his struggle with nature he does not "interpose" his jaws, but a system of machines). When viewed from this point of view, the question leads us to the same conclusion: the technical system of society serves as a precise material indicator of the relation between society and nature.

In another passage in *Capital,* Marx says: "Darwin has interested us in the history of Nature's Technology, *i.e.,* in the formation of the organs of plants and animals, which organs serve as *instruments of* production for sustaining life. Does not the history of the productive organs of man, of organs that are the material basis of all social organization deserve equal attention? " Technology discloses man's mode of dealing with Nature, the process of production by which he sustains his life, and thereby also lays bare the mode of formation of his social relations, and of the mental conceptions that flow from them" (*Capital,* vol. i, Chicago, 1915, p.406, footnote). "The use and fabrication of instruments of labor, although existing in the germ in certain species of animals, is specifically characteristic of the human labor-process, and Franklin therefore defines man as a tool-making animal" (*ibid.,* vol. i, p. 200). It is interesting to observe that the earliest tools were actually constructed "according to the image" of the organs of the human body. "Utilizing the objects found 'at hand' in the immediate environment, the first tools put in their appearance as a prolongation, expansion, or reduction of bodily organs" (Ernst Kapp: *Grundlinien einer Philosophie der Technik,*Braunschweig, 1877, p.42). "Blunt tools are anticipated in the human fist, while edged tools are anticipated in the finger-nails and the incisor teeth. The hammer, with its pene, gives rise to the various forms of axe and hatchet; the index finger, held rigid, with its sharp nail, is imitated in the borer; a single row of teeth is duplicated in file and saw, while the gripping hand and the closing jaw are expressed in the head of a pair of tongs and in the jaws of the vise. Hammer, axe, knife, chisel, borer, saw, tongs-all are primitive tools" (*ibid., pp.* 434q.). "The finger, crooked, becomes a hook; the hollow of the hand, a bowl; sword, spear, rudder, shovel, rake, plow, trident, represent the various directions and postures of arm, hand and fingers" (*ibid., p.* 45)~ The example of primitive tools also shows how simple instruments were developed into more intricate ones: "The staff evolves into a number of different forms; it becomes a club for purposes of vigorous aggression; a pointed stick for turning over the ground; a spear for palings and for throwing at game" (Friedrich von Gottl-Ottlilienfeld:*Wirtschaft and Technik* in *Grundriss der Nationalokonomie*, vol. ii, p. 228).

The close connection between technology and the so called "cultural wealth" is obvious. We need only to compare present-day China and Japan. In China-by virtue of a number of circumstances - the productivity of social labor, and the social technology, developed very slowly, and China may therefore be considered, for the moment, a stagnant civilization. The new capitalist technology will here exert a revolutionizing influence. In Japan, on the other hand, great advances in technical evolution have been made in recent decades, and Japan's culture has correspondingly developed rapidly; a glance at the state of Japanese science will show this.

In the early Middle Ages, culturally at a lower level than so called antiquity, "technology made a great retrogression as compared with antiquity, and many methods and mechanical inventions of the ancient world were forgotten " The sole exception was the technique of warfare and the metallurgy of iron connected with that technique" (W. K. Agafonov: *Modern Technology,* in Russian, vol. iii, p.16 . Obviously, no cultural accumulation was possible on this technical foundation: society's living sap was too poor to make a "full life" possible. The swift growth of Europe coincides with the capitalist machine technology; the century 1750-1850 witnessed a revolution in technology; steam-engine, steam transportation, coal, machine methods in obtaining iron etc. There followed the application of electricity, turbine engines, Diesel motors, the automobile, aviation. The technical basis of society, and its productive forces, rose to unprecedented heights. Under these circumstances, of course, human society was capable of developing a very intricate and versatile "mental life". If we examine the ancient civilizations, with their comparatively intricate mental life, the backwardness of even *their* technology as compared with the capitalist technology of modern Europe and America is very striking. More or less complicated machines were used chiefly for construction work, water supply systems, and mining. Even the greatest establishments came into being not by reason of their perfect instruments, but owing to their use of an immense number of living labor forces. "Herodotus reports that 100,000 men carried stones for three months for the pyramid of Cheops (2800 B.C.), and ten years had to be spent in the preliminary work of making a road leading from the quarries down to the Nile" (Agafonov:*ibid.*, p.5). The comparative poverty of ancient technology is apparent from the definition of a "machine", given by the ancient Roman engineer Vitruvius "A machine is an articulated connection of wood, affording great advantages in lifting weights" (*ibid.*, p.3). These wooden "machines" were used chiefly for "raising weights", but they had to be supplied with much human or animal labor.

141

d. The Equilibrium Between Nature and Society; Its Disturbances and Readjustments

Considered as a whole, we find that the process of reproduction is a process of constant disturbance and reestablishment of equilibrium between society and nature.

Marx distinguishes between *simple* reproduction and reproduction *on an extending scale.*

Let us first consider the case of simple reproduction. We have seen that in the process of production, the means of production are used up (the raw material is worked over, various auxiliary substances are required, such as lubricating oil, rags, etc.; the machines themselves, and the buildings in which the work is done, as well as all kinds of instruments and their parts, wear out); on the other hand, labor power is also exhausted (when people work, they also deteriorate, their labor power is used up, and a certain expenditure must be incurred in order to reestablish this labor power). In order that the process of production may continue, it is necessary to reproduce in it and by means of it the substances that it consumes. For example, in textile production, cotton is consumed as a raw material, while the weaving machinery deteriorates. In order that production may continue, cotton must continue to be raised somewhere, and looms to be manufactured. At one point the cotton disappears by reason of its transformation into fabrics, at another point, fabrics disappear (workers, etc., use them) and cotton reappears. At one point, looms are being slowly wiped out, while at another they are being produced. In other words, the necessary elements of production required in one place must be produced somewhere else; there must be a constant replacement of everything needed in production; if This replacement proceeds smoothly and at the same rate as the disappearance, we have a case of simple reproduction, which corresponds to a situation in which the productive social labor remains uniform, with the productive forces unchanging, and society moving neither forward nor backward. It is clear that this is a case of stable equilibrium between society and nature. It involves constant disturbances of equilibrium (disappearance of products in consumption and deterioration) and a constant reestablishment of equilibrium (the products reappear); but this reestablishment is always on the old basis: just as much is produced as has been consumed; and again just as much is consumed as has been produced, etc., etc. The process of reproduction is here a dance to the same old tune.

But where the productive forces are increasing, the case is different. Here, as we have seen, a portion of the social labor is liberated and devoted to an extension of social production (new production branches; extension of old branches). This involves not only a replacement of the formerly existing elements of production, but also the insertion of new elements into the new cycle of production. Production here does not continue on the same path, moving in the same cycle all the time, but increases in scope. This is *production on an extending scale,* in which case equilibrium is always established on a new basis; simultaneously with a certain consumption proceeds a larger production; consumption consequently also increases, while production increases still further. Equilibrium results in each case in a wider basis; we are now dealing with *unstable equilibrium with positive indication.*

The third case, finally, is that of a decline in the productive forces. In this case, the process of reproduction falls asleep: smaller and smaller quantities are reproduced. A certain quantity is consumed, but reproduction involves a smaller quantity still; less is consumed; and still less is reproduced, etc. Here again, reproduction does not repeat the same old cycle in each case; its sphere grows narrower and narrower; society's condition of life becomes poorer and poorer. The equilibrium between society and nature is reestablished on a level that goes lower and lower each time.

Society meanwhile is adapting itself to this continually narrowing standard of living, which can only be done by the partial disintegration of society. We are here dealing with *unstable equilibrium with negative indication*. The reproduction in this case may be termed *negatively* extended reproduction, or extended *insufficiency of production.*

Having discussed the subject from all angles, we have found the same result always, each case depending on the character of the equilibrium between society and nature. Since the productive forces serve as a precise expression of this equilibrium, these forces enable us to judge its character. Our remarks would apply just as well if we were speaking of the *technology* of society.

e. The Productive Forces as the Point of Departure in Sociological Analysis

From all that has been said above, the following scientific law results inevitably: any investigation of society, of the conditions of its growth, its forms, its content, etc., must begin with an analysis of the productive forces, or of the technical bases, of society. Let us first take up a few of the objections that are made - or might be made - against this view.

In the first place, let us consider some objections advanced by scholars who in general accept the materialist point of view. One of these, Heinrich Cunow, says [8] that technology "is related to a very great extent with the conditions of nature. The presence of certain raw materials *(das Vorkommen bestimmter Rohmaterialien)* determines, for example, whether it is possible for certain forms of technology to develop at all, as well as the direction which they will take. For instance, where certain species of stone, or woods, or ores, or fibers, or shell-fish, are not present, the natives of these regions will of course never be able to develop of themselves these natural substances, or make tools and weapons from them." At the beginning of this chapter we have already adduced data as to the influence of the natural conditions. Why should we not begin with these conditions in nature? Why should the starting point of our methodology not be nature itself? There is no doubt that its influence on technology is as great as Cunow says, and, in addition, nature of course existed before society. Are we not therefore sinning against true materialism when we base it on an analysis of the material technical apparatus of human society?

However close a examination of the question will show how erroneous are Cunow's conclusions. To be sure, where there are no deposits of coal, no coal can be dug from the ground. But, we might also add, you can't dig it out with your fingers either; and it will be somewhat hard to make use of it if you don't know its useful qualities. "Raw materials", in fact, do not "exist" in nature as Cunow says. "Raw materials" according to Marx are products of labor, and they have as little existence in the bowels of nature as has a painting by Raphael or Herr Cunow's waistcoat (Cunow is here confusing "raw materials" with all sorts of "objects of labor).[2] Cunow completely forgets that a certain stage of technology must have been reached before wood, or, fibers, etc., may play the part of raw materials. Coal becomes a raw material only when technology has developed so far as to delve in the bowels of the earth and drag their contents into the light of day. The influence of nature, in the sense of providing materials, etc., is itself a product of the development of technology; before technology had conquered coal, coal had no "influence" at all. Before technology with its feelers had reached the iron-ore, this iron-ore was permitted to sleep its eternal slumber; its influence on man was zero.

Human society works in nature and on nature, as the subject of its labor. But the elements existing as such in nature are here more or less constant and therefore *cannot explain changes*. It is the social technology which changes, which adapts itself to that which exists in nature (there is no possibility of adapting oneself to empty space; it .is the cannon, and not the hole, that is manufactured). Technology is a varying quantity, and precisely its variations produce the changes in the relations between society and nature; technology therefore must constitute a point of departure in an analysis of social changes.[10]

L. Mechnikov expresses this idea very stupidly: "Far be it from me to give support to the theory' of geographical fatalism, which is often opposed as a propagating principle of the all-determining influence of the environment in history. In my opinion . . . the changes must be sought not in the environment itself, but in the mutual relations arising between the environment and the natural capacities of its inhabitants for cooperation and *team work* of a social order (my italics, N. B.). It follows that the historical value of one geographical environment or another-even assuming that it remain physically unchanged under all circumstances - can and must vary with the degree of capacity of its inhabitants for voluntary*team work"* (Mechnikov, *ibid.*, pp.27, 28). All of which does not prevent Mechnikov himself from overestimating "geography". (*Cf.* Plekhanov's criticism in the collection *Criticism of Our Critics*.) The passive character of the influence of nature is now recognized by almost all geographers, although bourgeois scholars of this type of course know nothing of historical materialism. Thus, John McFarlane *(Economic Geography,* London) writes concerning the "natural conditions of economic activity" (chap. i): "These physical factors " do *not determine the economic life absolutely,* but they do have an influence upon it, which is unquestionably more noticeable in the earlier stage of human history, but which is just as real in the advanced civilizations, after man has learned to adapt himself to his environment and to draw, more and more, an increased benefit from it." The role played by coal, and the dependence of our industry upon it, are well known. As the technique of winning and working peat changes, the significance of coal may decrease, and this would involve an immense dislocation of the industrial centers. The progress of electrification assigned a more important role to aluminium, formerly of subsidiary importance. Water as a form of power was once of great importance (the millwheel, then declining, and now again rising; turbines, "white coal"). Space relations in nature remain the same; but distances are decreased for men by the use of transportation devices; the development of aviation is changing the picture still more.

This influence of transportation (a very variable quantity, depending on technology) is of decisive importance even in the geographic location of industry. Extremely interesting observations on this point are to be found in Alfred Weber's "Theory of the Location of Industry", in his *Industrielle Standortslehre* in *Grundriss*, pp.58, 59, *et seq.*, Section vi; also in Weber's *Uber den Standort der Industries,* part *i: Reine Theorie des Standortes,* 1909.

A poetic expression of the growing power of man over nature, his *active* power, is given by Goethe in his poem Prometheus"

> Cover thy spacious heavens, Zeus,
> With clouds of mist,
> And, like the boy who lops
> The thistles' heads,
> Disport with oaks and mountain-peaks;
> Yet thou must leave
> My earth still standing;
> My cottage, too, which was not raised by thee;
> Leave me my hearth,
> Whose kindly glow
> By thee is envied.

(Translated by Edgar Alfred Bowring, *The Poems of Goethe,* New York, 1881, pp.191, 192.)

It is therefore obvious that the differences in the natural conditions will explain the different evolution of the different nations, but not the course followed by the evolution of one and the same society. The natural differences, when these nations combine into a society, later become a basis for the social division of labor. "It is not the absolute fruitfulness of the soil, but its differentiation, the manifoldness of its natural products, which constitutes the basis of the social division of labor, and which spurs man on, to the multiplication of his own needs, abilities, instruments and modes of labor, owing to changes in the natural circumstances in which he dwells" (Marx, *Capital*, vol. i).

Another group of objections to the conception of social development that we have advanced above is based on the decisive and fundamental importance of the growth of population. For the tendency to multiplication is ineradicably present in human nature, where it has existed since before the beginnings of history. This tendency is of animal, biological nature; it is older than human society. Does not this process stand at the beginning of the entire evolution? Does not the increasing fruitfulness and density of the population determine the course of social evolution?

Actually, this would be reasoning backward along a law of nature, for it is on the stage of development of the productive forces, or, what amounts to the same thing, on the stage of technical development, that the very possibility of a numerical growth of population depends. A more or less continuous increase in population is nothing more nor less than an extension and growth of the social system, which is possible only when the relation between society and nature has been altered in a favorable direction. It is not possible for a greater number of persons to live unless the bases of life are widened. On the other hand, an impoverishment of these bases of life will inevitably express itself in a smaller population. The question of how this happens is another matter whether it is by a lowering of the birth rate, or by its artificial regulation, or by a process of dying out, by an increase in the mortality from diseases, by a premature exhaustion of the organisms and a decrease in the average length of life; the fact remains that this fundamental relation between the bases of the life of society and the quantity of its population will express itself in one way or another.

Besides, it is entirely erroneous to represent the growth of population as a purely biological ("natural") process of multiplication. This process depends on any number of social conditions: on the division into classes, the position of these classes, and consequently, on the forms of the social economy. Now, the forms of society, its structure, as we shall show below, depend on the level reached in the evolution of its productive forces. It is quite clear that the relation between the growth of technology and the movement of population, *i.e.,* alterations in its number, are not at all simple. Only naive persons could imagine that the process of multiplication proceeds as primitively and simply among human beings as among animals. For example, for an increase of population, in society, it is always necessary that the productive forces should be increased, otherwise, as we have already shown, the excess population will have nothing to eat. And, on the other hand, an increase in material well-being does not always and in all classes produce a more rapid multiplication: while the proletarian family may be artificially limiting the number of its children because of the hard conditions of life, a society lady may be renouncing motherhood in order not to spoil her figure, while a French peasant wishes to have no more than two children because he does not want his farms to be divided up. The movement of population is therefore a result of a number of social conditions, and is dependent on the form of society and on the situation of the various classes and groups within society.

We may therefore make the following statement with regard to population; an increase in the population indisputably presupposes an increase in the productive forces of society; in the second place, each epoch, each form of society, the varying situations of the various classes, result in special laws for the movement of population. "An abstract law of population exists for plants and animals only, and only in so far as man has not interfered with them"; " "every special historic mode of production has its own special laws of population, historically valid within its limits alone".[11] But the historic mode of production, *i.e.,* the form of society, is determined by the development of the productive forces, *i.e.,* the development of technology. We thus see that

149

the absence of natural law in the movement of population is a decisive factor, while the growth of the productive forces, and the uniformity of this growth (or decline), of themselves determine the movement of population.

The bourgeoisie has repeatedly attempted to replace the social laws by means of "laws" showing the necessity of the divinely ordained poverty of the masses, and that this condition is independent of the social order. It is to this effort that we must trace the overestimating of "geography", etc., in the doctrine of environment, natural phenomena being dragged in by the ears in order to explain historical events. Thus, Ernst Miller "proved" the dependence of historical evolution on terrestrial magnetism; Jevons "explained" industrial crises by means of sun-spots, etc. Here belongs also the famous attempt of the English clergyman economist, Robert Malthus, to explain the discomforts of the working class on the basis of man's sinful desire for multiplication. Malthus' "abstract law of population" is formulated in the thesis that population grows more rapidly than the means of subsistence; the latter increase in arithmetical progression while the population increases in geometrical progression. Among modern scientists, the conceptions of bourgeois scholars are undergoing radical changes, and Malthus' theory is now in disfavor; this is due to the fact that (first in France, then in other countries also) the increase in population is so slow that the bourgeoisie fears a lack of able-bodied soldiers (cannon-fodder), and therefore attempts to encourage the working class to produce more children.

The Physiocrats were already aware of the dependence of population increases on the stage reached by the productive forces. Le Mercier de la Rivière (*L'ordre naturel et essentiel des sociétés politiques*, 1767, pp.5, 6) says: "If men should nourish themselves with products furnished by the earth itself . . . without any preliminary labor, an immense extent of area would be required for the subsistence of even a small number of persons; but we know from experience that by reason of our natural constitution (*l'ordre physique de notre constitution*) we tend to multiply considerably. This natural property would be a contradiction, a discord in nature . . . if *the natural order of reproduction of the means of subsistence did not permit them to multiply to the same extent as we do:"* (My italics, N. B.) Further on, we read: "I am not at all afraid of the arguments that will be brought to bear against me, based on certain American tribes, in order to prove that the natural order of births makes cultivation unnecessary. I know there are some tribes that have practically no cultivation (*ne cultivent point ou presque point*) of the soil; yet, though soil and climate are equally favorable to them, they destroy their children, kill their old, and make use of medicaments to prevent the natural course of birth." Ernst Grosse *(Formen der Familie and Formen der Wirtschaft*, 1896, p.36) says among other things: "The Bushmen and the Australians are accustomed, for a good cause, to wear `hunger-belts'. The Patagonians suffer need practically always. And in the tales of the Eskimos, famine plays " a great role ". A population limited to such imperfect production can of course never become very numerous ". Therefore, primitive hunters usually see to it themselves that their numbers shall not exceed what can be fed with the available foodstuffs. Infanticide with this purpose is very common in Australia. A large child mortality takes care of the rest" - "We even hear, of tribes in the Polynesian Islands, that they have regulations permitting only a minimum of children to each family, a fine being imposed for violations." (P. Mombert: *Bevölkerungslelare* in *Grundriss der Sozialökonomie,* part ii, Tiibingen, 1914, p.62.) . Mombert mentions the following facts after describing the economic advance in the Carolingian Era (transition to the three-field system, etc.): "As a consequence of this great expansion in the production of foodstuffs, we meet with an exceptionally large increase of population in Germany" (p.64.). In the Nineteenth Century, Europe presents an immense advance in the field of agricultural production, "accompanied by a great increase in the European population, far exceeding any such increase in the past" (p.64). There ensues a period in which the increase in population, due to the above cause, moves faster than the increase in the means of subsistence. The result *is:*emigration to America. The same law may be observed in Russia (cf. the studies of M. N. Pokrovsky).

We must finally point out a number of other objections to the theory of historical materialism, namely, those theories that are known as "racial theories". These theories may be described as follows: society consists of men; these men do not appear always the same in history, but different; they have different skulls, different brains, different skin and hair, different physical structure, and consequently, different abilities. It is clear that at the banquet of history there will be many called but few chosen. Some races have shown themselves to be "historical", for the names of these races re-echo over the world, and the professors of all the universities concern themselves with them; other races, the "lower races", are by nature capable of nothing; they cannot produce anything of note; at bottom, they constitute a historical nonentity; these races are not worthy of the name "historical races". They may serve at best as a fertilizer for history, as the peoples of colonies, as "savages" of various kinds, tilling the soil for European bourgeois civilization. It is this difference of race that is the true reason for the differing evolution of society. Race must be the point of departure in the discussion of evolution. Such, in broad outline, is the *race theory*. On the subject of this theory, G. V. Plekhanov made the following perfectly correct observation: "In considering the question of the cause of a certain historical phenomenon, sensible and serious people often content themselves with solutions which solve nothing at all, being merely a repetition of the question in other forms of expression. Suppose you put one of the above mentioned questions to a `scholar'; ask him why certain races develop with such remarkable slowness, while others advance rapidly on the path of civilization. Your `scholar' will not hesitate to reply that this phenomenon is to be explained by racial qualities. Can you see any sense in such an answer? Certain races develop slowly because it is a racial quality with them to develop slowly; others become civilized very rapidly, because their principal racial characteristic is the ability to become civilized very rapidly."[12]

In the first place, the race theory is in contradiction with the facts. The "lowest" race, that which is said to be incapable, by nature, of any development, is the black race, the Negroes. Yet it has been shown that the ancient representatives of this black race, the so called Kushites, created a very high civilization in India (before the days of the Hindoos) and Egypt; the yellow race, which now also enjoys but slight favor, also created a high civilization in China, far superior in its day to the then existing civilizations of white men; the white men were then children as compared with the yellow men. We now know how much the ancient Greeks borrowed from the Assyro-Babylonians and the Egyptians. These few facts are sufficient to show that the "racial" explanation is no explanation at all. It may be replied: perhaps you were right, but will you go so far as to say that the average Negro stands at the same level, in his abilities, as the average European? There is no sense in answering such a question with benevolent subterfuges, as certain liberal professors sometimes do, to the effect that all men are of course equal, that according to Kant, the human personality is in itself a final consideration, or that Christ taught that there are no Hellenes, or Jews, etc.[13] To aspire to equality between races is one thing; to admit the similarity of their qualities is another. We aspire to that which does not exist; otherwise we are attempting to force doors that are already open. We are now not concerned with the question: what must be our aim? We are considering the question of whether there is a difference between the level, cultural and otherwise, of white men and black men, on the whole. There is such a difference; the "white" men are at present on a higher level, but this only goes to show that at present these so called races have changed places.

This is a complete refutation of the theory of race. At, bottom, this theory always reduces itself to the peculiarities of races, to their immemorial "character". If such were the case, this "character" would have expressed itself in the same way in all the periods of history. The obvious inference is that the "nature" of the races is constantly changing with the conditions of their existence. But these conditions are determined by nothing more nor less than the relation between society and nature, *i.e*, the condition of the productive forces. In other words, the theory of race does not in the slightest manner explain the conditions of social evolution. Here also it is evident that the analysis must begin with the movement of the productive forces.

There is great disagreement among scholars concerning race and race subdivisions. Topinard (quoted by Mechnikov, *ibid.*, p. 54) correctly remarks that the designation "race" is being used for quite subsidiary purposes, far instance, we hear of an Indo-Germanic, Latin, Teutonic, Slavic, English, race, although all these designations mark accidental aggregates of the most varied anthropological elements. In Asia, the races were mixed so often and so thoroughly that the race which is characteristic of original Asiatic conditions is perhaps to be sought beyond the Pacific Ocean or at the Arctic Circle. In Africa, the same process was frequently repeated. In America, where a similar condition may be observed in historical times, we find no primitive races, but only the results of endless mixtures and cross-breedings. Eduard Meyer very convincingly observes: "As for the question of race, it is of course possible that the human race appeared at its origin in a number of varieties, or was subdivided into such at an early epoch; I am incompetent to judge of this. But it is absolutely certain that all the human races are constantly mingling " that a sharp line may not be drawn between them - the tribes of the Nile Valley are a typical example - and that so called pure racial types may be found only in places where certain tribes have been kept in a condition of artificial isolation owing to external circumstances, as, for example, on the islands of Borneo and Australia. But there is no justification for the assumption that we are dealing with primitive natural conditions of the human race even here; it seems far more probable that this homogeneity, on the contrary, is the result of isolation" (*ibid.*, pp.74., 75). Professor R. Michels *(Wirtschaft und Rasse,* in *Grundriss der Sozialökoromie,* part ii, p.98 *et seq.)*, gives a number of interesting examples, excellently showing the mutability of so called race traits, in the field of labor. For example: the power of resistance of Chinese workers is very high, enabling them to bear heavy burdens; thence the widespread use of Chinese coolies. But it is quite clear that the "burdens" imposed upon the coolies are a result, in part, of a semi-colonial enslavement. Negroes are considered poor workers, but a French proverb says: "I have worked like a negro" (*j'ai travaillé comme un nègre*). Negroes rarely became employers, perhaps because they were boycotted by the whites, etc. The examples in the domain of national differences are even more interesting: "When the first railroads were built in Germany, a German uttered the warning that railroads were of no value in view of the German national character, which - thank God! - was expressed in the splendid principle of *festina lente*("make haste slowly"); railroads could be of use perhaps to a different race, a different mode of life, a different mode of thought. Kant rebuked the Italians for their practical-mindedness., for their highly developed banking system; yet today we know that other regions take precedence of Italy in this respect," etc. Michels draws the absolutely correct conclusion "that the degree of economic utility of any people is about equivalent to the degree of technical and moral-intellectual `civilization' attained by it at the given moment" (p.101).

The adherents of the race theory succeeded in making their most absurd statements during the World War, which they attempted to explain as a race conflict, although the absolute ridiculousness of this notion was manifest to any person in his sound mind; for the Serbs, allied with the Japanese, were fighting the Bulgarians; the English, allied with the Russians, were fighting the Germans. Gumplowicz is considered the principal advocate of the race theory in sociology.

BIBLIOGRAPHY

The books named after the previous chapters; also: L. Mechnikov *Civilization and the Great Historical Rivers* (in Russian). P. Maslov: *Entwicklungstheorie der Volkswirtschaft.* P. Maslov: *Die Agrarfrage,* vol. i. P. Maslov: *Kapitalismus.* N. Bukharin: *Die Oekonomik der Transformationsperiode,* chap. vi. Cunow: *Die Stellung der Technik in der Marxschen Wirtschaftsauffassung* (*Die Neue Zeit,* vol. 39, part ii, no.15). Rosa Luxemburg: *Die Akkumulation des Kapitals* (on the process of reproduction). Karl Kautsky: *Entwicklung und Vermehrung in Natur und Gesellschaft.* Karl Kautsky: *Are the Jews a Race?*

NOTES

[1]Karl Marx: *Capital*, Chicago, 1915, vol. i., pp.198, 199.

[2]*Ibid.*, p.199.

[3]Karl Marx's letters to Kugelmann, in *Die Neue Zeit,* 1901-1902, part ii, No. 7, p.222.

[4]*Capital,* Chicago, 1915, vol. i, pp.197, 198.

[5]*Ibid.*, p.198.

[6]Karl Marx: *Capital*, vol i, p.201.

[7]Karl Marx: *Capital*, vol. i, pp.199-200.

[8]Die Neue Zeit, Vol. 39, part ii, pp.350 *et seq.*

[9]"If, on the other hand, the subject of labor has, so to say, been filtered through previous labor, we call it raw material. All raw material is the subject of labor, but not every subject of labor is raw material." (*Capital*, Vol. i, p. 199.)

[10]Cunow's mistakes do not prevent him from raising a number of very appropriate objections to Gorter, P. Barth, and others, who confuse the method of production with technology. We shall discuss this subject later.

[11]*Capital*, vol. i, p.693.

[12]*A Criticism of Our Critics* (in Russian), St. Petersburg, 1906, p.283

[13]*Cf.* for example, Khvostov, *Theory of the Historical Process*, p.247: "It is extremely probable that . . , the truth is on the side of the advocates of race equality."]

6: THE EQUILIBRIUM BETWEEN THE ELEMENTS OF SOCIETY

a. Connection between the Various Social Phenomena; Formulation of the Question

In our discussion of the equilibrium between society and nature, we found that this equilibrium is being constantly disturbed and constantly reestablished, that there it is subject to contradictions which are constantly overcome and then set up anew, and then again overcome, and that this constitutes the fundamental course of social evolution or social decline. W e must therefore give some attention to this "internal life" of society.

In discussions as to the relative standard of social evolution, we often hear such judgments as: "the degree of social evolution is determined by the quantity of soap used"; others measure the stage of this advance by the extent of the ability to read and write; still others, by the number of newspapers; a fourth group, by the state of technical progress; a fifth group, by the stage of development of the sciences, etc. A German professor (Schulze-Gaevernitz; see his book *Volkswirtschaftliche Studien aus Russland*) has advanced the proposition that the stage of civilization is best indicated by the manner of constructing toilet conveniences. We find that beginning with the latter and rising to the most sublime products of the human mind, everything has been used as a standard by which to measure the stage of social development.

Where is the truth? Whose yardstick is the true yardstick? Why have there been so many different answers to this single question?

A consideration of all the above answers will show that each of them is more or less correct. Does not the use of soap increase with the growth of "culture and civilization"? It does; so does the number of newspapers, or the social technology, or science. At any given time, the social phenomena of the period are always related with each other; just what this relation is, is another question, which we shall discuss very soon. But that there is such a relation no one can doubt; that is why all of the above answers are right. Just as the age of a man may be approximately determined on the basis of the structure and hardness of his bones, or on the appearance of his face (his color, wrinkles, growth of hair, etc.), or his mode of thought, or his mode of linguistic expression, so we may also judge the stage of growth of society on the basis of a number of indications, for all these indications are connected with other indications, and with still others, etc. If we stand face to face with beautiful products of art, or complicated systems of science, we rightly declare that these things could not be produced except in a highly developed society. We should make the same remark in the presence of a rich and complicated technology, and our remark would be just as correct. The fact that the most varied social phenomena are connected, are mutually conditioned, is almost self-evident. A series of simple questions will convince the reader immediately. Was futurist poetry possible, for example, a century ago? No, it was not. Could Eskimos living on the ice have invented wireless telegraphy? Is it possible for present-day science to predict man's fate from the stars? Could Marxism have originated in the Middle Ages? It is obvious that all these things are impossible. Futurism could not have appeared one hundred years ago, because life was then calmer and quieter; futurism grew up in pavemented cities, with their noise and racket, their nervous exhaustion, in the militaristic turmoil of a dissolving bourgeois civilization. This poetry of the brazen blare could no more have grown up one hundred years ago than ivy could grow on a recently tarred roof. Eskimos living on the ice could not have invented the wireless telegraph, for they cannot even handle an ordinary telegraph instrument. Present-day science does not occupy itself with such idiosyncrasies as reading the stars, because science at its present level despises these things. Marxism could not have begun in the Middle Ages, because the proletariat was not yet in existence, and therefore there was no soil in which the Marxist theory could grow. Now we have a highly developed technology, a proletariat, a great number of newspapers, advertising on a tremendous scale, trusts, futurism, aeroplanes, the electron theory, Mr. Rockefeller's dividends, strikes of coal-miners; the Communist Party, the League of Nations, the Third International, electrification projects, armies consisting of millions, Lloyd George, Lenin, etc.; and all these things are manifestations o£ the same period, the same epoch, just as we may also regard as manifestations of another epoch (the Middle Ages) all of the following: the power of the Popes at Rome, a comparatively low level of technology, compulsory labor of peasant serfs, science in the hands of priests (scholastic philosophy), the search for the philosopher's stone (which would turn base metals into gold, etc.), the inquisition, poor roads, illiteracy even among kings, village-commons, witches, trade guilds, dog Latin (spoken and written by scholars), robber knights, etc. Lenin, Lloyd George, Krupp, these have no place in the Middle Ages. And, on the other hand, we do not expect to find on the Red Square in Moscow, a medieval tournament with knights doing each other to death for the favor of a lady's smile. "Other times, other songbirds; other songbirds, other songs." There is no doubt of the general connection between social phenomena, of the "adaptation" of certain social phenomena to others, in other words, of the existence of a certain equilibrium within society between its elements, its component parts, between the various forms of social phenomena.

Auguste Comte already stated that the various phases of social life are always adapted to each other at any period (the so called *consensus*). Müller-Lyer (*Phasen der Kultur,* München, p.344) states this even more clearly: "Any sociological function, any cultural phenomenon, for instance, art, science, manners, economy, state organization, freedom of the individual, philosophy; the social position of woman, etc., down to the use of soap, and the like, may be taken as the measure of the cultural level. And, if all the cultural phenomena should develop parallel to each other and at the same rate, it would not matter which of these criteria should be applied." One of the latest writers of the hard-pressed German bourgeoisie, Oswald Spengler (*Der Untergang des Abendlandes,* München, 1920, vol. i, p.8), writes: "How many people know that there is a profound relation in form between the differential calculus and the dynastic state principle of the epoch of Louis XIV, between the ancient state form of the polis (in Greece) and Euclidean Geometry, between the perspective drawing of western painting and the conquest of space by railroads, telephones, and long-range guns, between contrapuntal instrumentation in music and the economic credit system?" Spengler's formulation may be disputed, but there is no doubt of the correctness of his thought: that the most varied social phenomena are interrelated.

b. Things, Persons, Ideas

We defined society above as an aggregation of persons. In the broader sense, however, society also includes things. Present-day society, for instance, with its vast stone cities, its giant structures, its railroads, harbors, machines, houses, etc.; all these things are material technical "organs" of society. Any specific machine will at once Lose its significance as a machine outside of human society; it becomes merely a portion of external nature, a combination of pieces of steel, wood, etc. When a great liner sinks to the bottom, this living monster with its powerful engines that cause the whole marvelous structure of steel to vibrate, with its thousands of appliances of every possible kind, from dishrags to wireless station, now lies at the bottom of the sea and the whole mechanism loses its social significance. Barnacles will attach themselves to its body, its wood constructions will rot in the water, crabs and other animals will live in the cabins, but the steamer ceases to be a steamer; having lost its *social* existence, it is excluded from society, has ceased to be a portion of society, to perform its social service, and is now merely an object - no longer a *social* object - like any other part of external nature which does not come in direct contact with human society. Technical devices are not merely pieces of external nature: they are extensions of society's organs; we may therefore take a broader view of society than we have thus far done; we may make it include also things, i.e., society's technical apparatus, its system of working devices. Strictly speaking, not all things are included among the means of production; some may even have a very remote relation with this production, aside from the fact that they themselves constitute products of material production: for example, books, maps, diagrams, museums, picture galleries, libraries, astronomical observatories, meteorological stations (we always speak of their "physical equipment"), laboratories, measuring instruments, telescopes and microscopes of every kind, test-tubes, retorts, etc. All these things are not directly connected with the process of material production and consequently are not a part of social technology, may not be considered among the material productive forces; nevertheless, everyone knows their function; they are not merely sections of external nature; they also have their "social existence"; they also must be included under our concept of society in its broader application.

We have seen in chapter iv that society constitutes a system of *persons* considered together; now we see that *things* must also be so considered. But, in the narrower sense of the word, we understand by "society" not merely the aggregate of persons involved, but the connected system. We first regarded these persons as material bodies at work. Society therefore, as we have explained, is above all a working organization, a *human* working apparatus. But we know very well that human beings are not merely physical bodies, they think, feel, wish, pursue goals and are constantly changing in their thoughts and desires. The relations between persons are not only material working relations, but also psychical relations, "mental" relations; society produces not only material objects: it also produces the so called "cultural values": art, science, etc.; in other words, it produces *ideas* in addition to things. These ideas, once they have been produced, may be developed into large *systems of ideas.*

The trinity of elements in society therefore includes: things, persons, ideas. We must by no means assume that these are independent elements: it is, of course, clear that if there were no people there would be no ideas, that ideas exist only in people and do not swim about in space like oil on the surface of water. But this does not prevent us from distinguishing these three elements; it is likewise clear that there must be a certain equilibrium between the three elements. Roughly speaking: society could not exist, unless the system of things, the system of persons, and the system of ideas were adapted each to the other. We shall have to go into this more in detail; we shall then understand the relation between phenomena that is so manifest on the surface, and concerning which we spoke in the preceding paragraph.

c. Social Technology and the Economic Structure of Society

We have already pointed out that in a consideration of social phenomena it is necessary to begin with the social, material productive forces, with the social technology, the system of tools of labor. We may now supplement these remarks. In speaking of the social technology, we of course meant not a certain tool, or the aggregate of different tools, but the whole *system* of these tools in society. We must imagine that in a given society, in various places, but in a *certain order*, there are distributed looms and motors, instruments and apparatus, simple and complicated tools. In some places they are crowded close together (for instance, in the great industrial centers), in other places, *other* tools are *scattered*. But at any given moment, if people are connected by a labor relation, if we have a society, all these instruments of production-tools and machines, large and small, simple and complicated, manual or power-driven-are united into a single system. (Of course, a certain *type* of tool is always predominant: at the present time this is the type of machines and mechanisms, while formerly it was that of hand tools; the significance of apparatus and self-acting machinery is increasing more and more.) In other words, we may consider the social technology as a whole, in which each of the parts at a given moment is socially necessary (inevitable). Why may it be so considered? Wherein lies the unity of all the parts of the technical system of society?

In order to grasp this matter fully, let us suppose that on a certain day - let us say, in modern Germany, all the machines serving the purposes of coal mining should miraculously ascend to heaven. The result would be a cessation of practically the entire industrial life. It would be impossible to obtain fuel for factories and shops; all the machines and instruments in these factories would stop working, *i.e.,* would be eliminated from the process of production. The technology of one branch would thus influence practically all the other branches. As a matter of fact, the various branches of production constitute a whole, not only in our thoughts, but objectively, in reality; they make up a single social technology. The social technology, we reiterate, is not therefore a mere aggregate of the various instruments of labor, but is their connecting system. On any individual part of this system depends all the rest of the system. At any given moment, also, the various parts of this technology are related in a certain proportion, a certain quantitative relation. If, in a certain factory, we must have a certain number of spindles and a certain number of workers to provide material for a certain number of looms, the more or less normal progress of social production throughout society will also involve the presence of a certain definite relation between the number of blast furnaces and the number of machines and mechanical tools in metallurgy, as well as in the textile industry, the chemical industry, or any other industry. To he sure, this relation may not be precisely *fixed*, as in a single factory; but between the "technological systems" of the various branches of production there does exist a certain necessary relation, which may in unorganized society be the result of a blind natural process, while in organized society it is the result of a conscious process; but it exists in all society. It is inconceivable, for instance, that a factory should have ten times as many spindles as it needs; it is likewise inconceivable that ten times as much coal should be mined as is needed, and that the machines and appliances used in mining coal should be ten times as numerous as is required in order to supply the other branches of production. Thus, as there is a definite relation and a definite proportion between the various branches of production; there is also in social technology a certain definite relation between its parts as well as a definite prevailing proportion. This circumstance changes the mere aggregate of tools, machines, instruments, etc., into a system of social technology.

This being the case, it is also clear that each given system of social technology also determines the system of labor relations between persons.

Is it conceivable, for instance, that the technological system of society, the structure of its tools, should be along certain lines, while the structure of human relations should be along entirely different lines? More concretely: is it possible that the technological system of society should be based on machines, while the productive relation, the actual labor relation, should be based on petty industry working with hand tools? Of course, this is an impossibility; wherever a society exists, there must be a certain equilibrium between its technology and its economy, *i.e.,* between the totality of its instruments of labor and its working organization, between its material productive devices and its material human labor system.

Let us explain by means of an example, namely, by means of a comparison between so called "ancient society" and present-day capitalist society; let us begin with technology. Albert Neuburger,[1] who is inclined more to exaggerate than belittle the accomplishments of ancient technology, says: "Aristotle in his *Problems of Mechanics* enumerates for us the auxiliary mechanical devices made use of in ancient times. They include only the following: the draw-well (lever with counter-weight), the equal-armed balance, the unequal-armed, or Roman balance (steelyard), the tongs, the wedge, the axe, the windlass, the cylindrical roller, the wagon-wheel, the shaft, the pulley, the sling, the rudder, the potter's wheel, as well as revolving wheels of copper or iron with different directions of revolution, which very probably are equivalent to our toothed wheels (gear-wheels)."

These are the most rudimentary technical appliances, otherwise known as "simple machines" (lever, inclined plane, tongs, rollers). It is obvious that not much advance was possible with such devices, which were used chiefly in the working of metals. It is clear that only the metallic skeleton of the productive forces constitutes the first permanent basis for their development. Yet, of the metals worked, gold was the most important; the greater quantity of metal was used for the manufacture of objects intended for non-productive consumption. The sole exception is blacksmith work, by means of which rather primitive tools were produced with the aid of hammer, anvil, tongs, file, vise, and other comparatively simple instruments (producing principally axes, hammers, hoes, horseshoes, nails, chains, pitchforks, shovels, spoons, etc.); the casting of metals stood chiefly in the service of turning out statues and other non-productive objects. It is therefore not surprising to learn that Vitruvius defines a "machine" as a "device made of wood".

"For whole centuries technology stood still," says Salvioli,[2] of course not meaning an absolute stagnation, but an extremely slow development of ancient technology.

These technical devices naturally also determined the *type of worker,* the degree of his skill, and also the working relations, the productive conditions.

There could only be one type of worker under such a technology: a hand worker, a petty artisan. Blacksmiths, carpenters, masons, weavers, goldsmiths, miners, wagon-builders, saddlers, harness-makers, lathe-workers, silversmiths, potters, dyers, tanners, glassmakers, locksmiths, etc., etc., such are the types of productive workers.[3] Thus, the social technology conditioned the character of the living working machinery, i.e., the type of worker, his labor "skill". But this technology also conditioned the relation between the persons at work. As a matter of fact, because we see here enumerated a number of types of workers, it is plain that we are dealing with a division of production into a number of branches, each one of which produces only a single type of worker. This is called the *division of labor.*

The cause of this division of labor was the existence of corresponding labor tools. But this division of labor was of a peculiar kind: "The division of labor could not here lead to the results which it has had in modern societies, for in ancient times this division was not a function of the machine process. It was not an outgrowth of a system of great factories (*de grandes usines*), but of petty and medium-sized industry."[4] "Large-scale production was foreign to the ancient world, which never advanced beyond the stage of petty artisanry."[5] Here is a different form of productive labor conditions, also based, as we have seen, on the system of technology. Even when we learn of great structures being raised, we must remember that they were often accomplished by means of petty labor. Thus, in the case of the construction of one of the great aqueducts at Rome, the government signed a contract with three thousand master masons; these worked together with their slaves. And in cases where production was on a comparatively large scale, it could, under the prevailing system of technology, exist only by making use of forces lying outside the economic system: for instance, slave labor, whole armies of slaves being imported after the conclusion of victorious wars, who were sold and distributed to the great estates and the slave-operated factories (*ergastula*). Under a different system of technology, slave labor would have been impossible: the slaves spoil delicate machinery, and slave labor does not pay. Thus, even such a phenomenon as the labor of imported slaves can be explained, under the given historical conditions, by the tools with which social labor works. Or, to take another example: we know that, in spite of the rather high development of commercial-capitalist conditions in ancient times, the economy of that period was on .the whole a natural economy (payments in commodities, in *kind*, rather than in money). People were not in close economic relations; the exchange of commodities was much less developed than in our day; great quantities of products were turned out in the great estates (*latifundia*) and in jail-like shops, for their own consumption. This is also a definite stage of labor, a form of productive relation, and again the explanation is evident: it can be explained on the basis of the low development of the productive forces, the weakness of technology. Under such a technical system, it was difficult to attain a great excess production. In a word, it is evident that the relations between people in the labor process are determined by the stage of advance in the evolution of technology; the ancient economy was, as it were, *adapted to* the ancient technology.

Let us compare this condition with that under capitalist society. Taking up, in the first place, the matter of technology, it is sufficient to cast a glance over a list of some of the branches of production. Let us consider only two of the groups of capitalist industry: the construction of machinery, instruments and apparatus, as one branch, and the electro-technical industry, as another branch. Here is the picture that presents itself:

I. Manufacture of machines, instruments and apparatus
a. power machines
locomotives

stationary engines

other power machines

b. manipulating machinery in general use

machines for working metals, wood, stone, and other materials

pumps

lifting cranes and carrying machines

other machines

c. manipulating machinery in various special branches

spinning machinery

agricultural machinery

special machinery for the obtaining of raw materials

special machinery for the manufacture of arms and ammunition

special machinery for turning out delicate products

manufacture of various kinds of machines

d. repair-shop machinery

e. boilers, appliances and inventory

steam boilers

boilers, appliances, and inventory for special branches (excluding working machinery)

f. machine instruments and machine parts

machine tools

machine part

g. mill construction

h. ship-building and the construction of marine machinery

i. the construction of airships and aeroplanes, and their parts

j. gas tanks

k. production of vehicles

bicycles, and their parts

motor-cars

railroad cars

wagon-building and carriage-building

production of other means of transportation, not including water and air transportation

l. manufacture of clocks and watches, and their parts

m. production of musical instruments

production of pianos

production of other musical instruments

n. optical and other delicate mechanical devices, also the preparation of zoological and microscopical specimens

the preparation of optical and delicate mechanical instruments, including cameras and other photographic apparatus

the production of surgical instruments and apparatus

the production of zoological and microscopical apparatus

o. the production of globes and lamps (except such as are connected with the

electrical industry)

II Electrical Industry

- a. manufacture of dynamos and electro-motors
- b. manufacture of storage batteries and other batteries.
- c. manufacture of cables and insulated wire
- d. manufacture of electrical measuring instruments, counters and clocks
- e. manufacture of electrical apparatus and installation inventory
- f. manufacture of lamps and searchlights
- g. manufacture of electrical medical machinery
- h. manufacture of weak current apparatus
- i. manufacture of electrical insulating devices
- j. manufacture of electrical products of great establishments
- k. repair stations for electrical products of all kinds.[6]

It is sufficient to compare this list with the "machines" spoken of by Aristotle or Vitruvius, to understand the tremendous difference between the technology of ancient society and that of modern capitalist society. Just as the ancient technology determined the ancient form of economy, so capitalist technology determines the present-day capitalist economy. If we could enumerate the entire population, let us say, of ancient Rome and of present-day Berlin or London, and divide these populations into trades, by their actual occupations, the profound gulf that separates us from ancient times would become apparent. We now have (as a result of our machine technology) types of workers that never existed in ancient times. Instead of the petty artisans (for instance, the *fabri ferrarii*),[2] we now- find, in our society, electricians, machinists, machine constructors, boiler-makers, engine-lathe workers, frazers, optical instrument makers, compositors, lithographers, railroad workers, locomotive engineers, firemen, steam-hammer attendants, harvesting machinery workers, mowing machinery workers, sheaf-binding machinery workers, tractor repairers, electrical engineers, chemists, specialists on steam-boilers, linotypers, etc., etc. These types of workers did not exist even in name, for no corresponding branch of production, and consequently no appropriate tools of labor, existed in this field in ancient times. But even if we take up those species of workers whose names are still the same and who existed in earlier days, we shall find that there is again a great difference. For instance, what is there in common between the present-day weaver who works in a great textile factory and the artisan or slave weaver in ancient Greece or Rome? The latter would feel as much out of place in a modern factory as would Julius Caesar in a New York subway train. We have *different* labor forces, of *different* labor skill. Our labor forces are the product of a different technology, and they have become adapted to that technology.

The existence of a great number of industrial branches which were not present in earlier times results chiefly in the fact that the division of labor today is entirely different. But the division of labor constitutes one of the fundamental conditions of production. The modern division of labor is determined by the modern instruments of labor, by the character, description, and combination of machines and tools, *i.e.,* by the technical apparatus of capitalist society. The typical form of a modern industrial establishment is that of the large factory. We no longer have the small production unit, the artisan industry, nor even the domestic industry of the *latifundium* owner; we have instead a gigantic organization embracing thousands of persons, distributed to their various posts in a definite order, and performing their allotted tasks. If, as an example of a capitalist enterprise, we take Mr. Ford's automobile factory in Detroit; its emphatically modern character is the first trait to strike the eye: a precise division of labor, much machinery, operating automatically under the supervision of the workers, the strict adherence to a correct succession of operations, etc. Parts of the product are carried along by slowly moving belts or platforms, and the various types of workers at their machines execute their specific tasks on the partly finished articles as they go by. The entire labor process has been calculated down to the second. Each displacement of the worker, each motion of hand or foot, each inclination of the body, all have been foreseen. The "staff" supervises the general course of the work; everything goes by the clock, or rather, the chronometer. Such is the division of labor and its "scientific efficiency" according to the Taylor system. Such a factory, if we consider its human structure, i.e., the relations between the individuals composing it, also constitutes a productive relation, in which the distribution of persons and their relation with each other are determined by the system of machinery, the combinations of machines, the technology, the organization of the factory inventory.

"The present development of technology must be considered as the dominating factor in the organization of labor ". The machine does not stand alone in the factory; all the machines are arranged in groups; they are related to each other or connected in their operations. The transfer of a job from one machine to another . . in the eyes of the technical supervisor, is a calculable quantity. The labor plan, the distribution of location in labor, transportation, are likewise precisely regulated, made automatic, standardized . . . and gradually changed into a precisely calculated mechanism of operative administration. . . In the general system of this *movement of things,* the *movement of man turned out* (also his *influence* on others) . . often to be a determining oasis . . . there arose a system of scientific movement" (A. Gastev: *Our*

Tasks - Labor Organization, in the *Annual of the Labor Institute, No.* t, Moscow, 1921, pp.12, 13, in Russian). An idea of the many branches of work in the great metal factories will be given by the branches found in Russian factories: mechanical, electrical, blacksmith, boiler, molding, casting steel, iron foundry, iron rolling, heating metals, Martin blast furnaces, Siemens ovens, crucibles, carriages, chemical treatment of wood, construction work, auxiliary operations. The following categories of workers were found in the Putilov Works in 1914-1916: locksmiths, lathe-workers, milling machine workers, planers, chiselers, borers, welders, stampers, ussemblers, blacksmiths, hammerers, pressers, pointers, stokers, furnace foremen, rollers, machinists, cutters, potters, molders, smelting furnace workers, paperers, joiners, carpenters, painters, tinsmiths, plumbers, cable workers, unskilled workers, men and women (*cf. Metal Workers' Gazette,* St. Petersburg, 1917, p.13, in Russian). Many of the names of these occupations show that they are bound to a specific instrument, tool, or machine. *In a certain combination of these working onstrumerits, in their distribution in the plant, a certain distribution. of men is also involved, the latter being determined by the former.*

Precisely as the production relations in ancient Greece or Rome were an outgrowth of the system of technology characteristic of petty and medium production, so the conditions of large-scale production in modern times are a result of the modern technology. Here again, there is a relative equilibrium between the social technology and the social economy.

We have above observed that the poor technology of ancient times resulted in a poor exchange process, and that the economy remained for the most part economy *in kind*: the relation between the economies was very loose; such were the definite production relations of antiquity. But modern capitalist technology permits the sending forth of huge quantities of products. The division of labor also has its influence in causing the entire production to be made for the market. For the manufacturer does not himself wear the millions of pairs of suspenders turned out by his factory. Therefore, the production conditions of the commodities economy are also a consequence of the technology of our day.

We have approached the question from four different angles: first, the nature of the labor forces; second, the distribution of labor between them; third, the extent of production, i.e., of the organization of individuals in the various economies; fourth, the relations between these various economies; and in every case we have seen from the example of the two different societies chosen (the ancient and the modern) that the *combinations of the instruments of labor (the social technology) are the deciding factor in the combinations and relations of men,* i.e. *in social economy.* But there is another phase of the production relations, namely, the question of the social classes, which is to be discussed later in detail; let us consider this question now from the standpoint of the production relations.

In considering the relations of men in the production process, we observe everywhere (except in the so called primitive communism) that the groupings of men are not accomplished in such manner as to cause the various groups to lie in a horizontal line, but rather in a vertical line. For example, in the conditions of medieval serfdom, we find at the top the owners of the estates, under them the administrators, mayors, supervisors, and at the bottom the peasants. In capitalist production relations we find that men are not only distributed among molders, machinists, railroad workers, tobacco workers, etc., all of whom - in spite of the great differences between their tasks - are working along the same lines-occupying the same relative station in production; but we find that here too a number of persons stand above the others in the labor process: above the workers are the "salaried employees" (the medium-grade technical staff: master mechanics, engineers, specialists, agricultural experts, etc.); above these "salaried men" stand the higher officials (superintendents, directors); above them are the so called owners of enterprises, capitalists, the commanders-in-chief and controllers of the destinies of the production process. Let us also consider the *latifundium* of a rich Roman landlord. Here again we find a regular gradation of persons; on the lowest rung of the ladder are the slaves ("the speaking instruments", *instrumenta vocalia*, as the Romans termed them, as distinguished from the "semi-speaking instruments", *instrumenta semi-vocalia*, namely, bleating cattle, and the "mute instruments", *instrumenta muta*, inanimate objects); above the slaves stand the slave drivers, overseers, etc.; then come the superintendents; finally we have the owner of the *latifundium* himself, with his honored family (his wife usually had charge of certain domestic operations). A blind man can see that we are dealing with differently constituted relations between persons at work. All the persons enumerated participate in one way or another in the labor process and therefore have certain definite relations to each other. In classifying them, we may divide them according to their trades and callings; but we may also divide them according to their classes. If our division is on the basis of occupations or callings, we shall have blacksmiths, locksmiths, lathe-workers, etc. In the higher class, chemists, mechanics, boiler-engineers, textile experts, locomotive specialists, etc. It is obvious that the locksmiths, lathe-workers, machine-workers, stevedores, are in one class, while the engineer, the specialist, etc., are in another class; the capitalist, who has control of all, is again in another class. These persons cannot all be thrown into the same pot. In spite of the division between the work performed by the locksmith, the turner and the compositor, they all stand in the same relation to each other in the general labor process. Quite different is the relation between locksmith and engineer, or between locksmith and capitalist. Furthermore, the locksmith, turner, linotyper, individually and as a body, are in the same relation to all the engineers and in the same remoter relation to all superintendents, "captains of industry", capitalists. The greatest differences here are in the productive function, in the productive significance, in the character of the relations between men; the capitalist in his factory distributes and arranges his workers as he might things or tools; but the workers do not "distribute" the capitalists (under the capitalist system of society); they "are distributed" by these capitalists. This is a relation of "master and servant", as Marx says, with "capital in command". It is their different function in the production process that constitutes the basis for the division of men into different social classes.

An important point to be noted here is the nature of the relation between the process of production and that of distribution, since we have seen that the latter is, so to speak, the reverse side of the social process of production. Concerning this subject of the process of distribution, Marx says the following: "In the most shallow conception of distribution, the latter appears as a distribution of products and to that extent as further removed from and quasi-independent of production. But before distribution means distribution of products, it is, first a distribution of the means of production, and, second, what is practically another wording of the same fact, it is a distribution of the members of society among the various kinds of production (the subjection of individuals to certain conditions of production). The distribution of products is manifestly a result of this distribution, which is bound up with the process of production and determines the very organization of the latter. To treat of production apart from the distribution which is comprised in it, is plainly an idle abstraction. Conversely, we know the character of the distribution of products the moment we are given the nature of that other distribution which forms originally a factor of production" (*A Contribution to the Critique of Political Economy,*Chicago, 1913, p.286).

These sentences of Marx deserve more of our attention.

We find, first of all, that the process of the production of products determines the process of the distribution of products. If, for example, production is carried on in independent establishments (by various capitalist enterprises, or by individual artisans), each establishment no, longer producing all of its requirements, but turning out some special product (watches, grain, iron locks, hammers, tongs, etc., as the case may be), it is obvious that the distribution of the product will take the form of exchange. Persons producing locks cannot clothe themselves in such locks or consume them for dinner, nor can persons producing grain lock their barns with grain; they must have locks and keys for this purpose. The manner of production which is followed also determines the manner of distributing the product; this distribution may not be considered as independent of production. On the contrary, it is determined *by* production and, together with it, constitutes a section of *material social reproduction.*

But production itself involves two further "distributions": first, the distribution of persons, their arrangement in the production process, depending on their function, as already discussed; second, the distribution of production tools among these persons. These "distributions" are a part of production or, in the words of Marx, are "involved" in production. We have seen, for example, in one of the systems of society discussed, namely, capitalist society, that its "distribution of persons" also includes a division into classes, based on the difference of function in the productive process. But this varying "distribution of persons", depending on their varying assignment in production is also connected with a distribution of the means of labor: The capitalist, the owner of the *latifundium,* and the estate owner control these means of labor (factory and machinery, the estate and the compulsory shops, the soil and structures), while the worker has no instruments of production aside from his own labor power; the slave does not even own his own body, nor does the peasant serf. It is therefore obvious that the varying function of classes in production is based on the distribution of instruments of production among them. In his review of Marx's book, A *Contribution to the Critique of Political Economy,* Engels says: a "Economy deals not with things but with relations between persons and in the last analysis between classes; but these relations always are bound up with *things* and appear as *things*."[8] For example, the current class relations in capitalist society, namely, the relations between capitalists and workers, are bound up with a *thing:* the instruments of production in the hands of the capitalists, controlled by the latter, not owned by the workers. These instruments of production serve the capitalists as tools for the obtaining of profits, as means of exploiting the working class. They are not mere things, they are things in a special social significance, in that they here serve not only as means of production, but also as a means of exploiting wage laborers. In other words, this *thing* expresses the relation between classes, or, in the words of Engels, these class relations are bound up with the *thing.* In the last analysis, this *thing,* in our example, *is capital.*

The special form of production relations, therefore, existing in the relations between classes, is determined by the varying function of these groups of persons in the production process, and the distribution of the means of production among them. This fully conditions the distribution of the products.

The capitalist obtains profit because he owns instruments of production: because he is a capitalist.

The class relations in production, *i.e.,* the relations bound up with the varying distribution of the means of production, are particularly important in society. It is they which determine in the first place the outline of society, its system or, in the words of Marx, its economic structure.

Now, the production relations are extremely numerous, and varied. If we recall, furthermore, that we are considering the distribution of products as a portion of reproduction, it also becomes clear that the relations between persons in the process of distribution are also included in the production relations. In a complicated system of society there are innumerable such relations, such as, between merchants, bankers, clerks, brokers, tradesmen of all kinds, workers, consumers, salesmen, traveling salesmen, messengers, manufacturers, ship-owners, sailors, engineers, unskilled workers, etc., etc., which all constitute production relations. All are interwoven in the most varied combinations, the most peculiar patterns, the most unusual confusions. But the fundamental scheme of all these patterns is important; namely, the relations between the great groups known as social classes. The system of society will depend on the classes included in society, their mutual position, their functions in the production process, the distribution of instruments of labor. We have a capitalist society if the capitalist is on top; we have a slave system if the estate owner is on top, and in control of everything; we have a dictatorship of the proletariat if the workers are on top. To be sure, even the absence of all classes would not mean the disappearance of society, but merely the disappearance of class society. There were no classes, for example, in the primitive communist society, nor will there be any in the communist society of the future.

We observed above that the production relations change with the social technology; a glance at the actual historical development of any society will be sufficient to show that this principle also holds good in such production relations as are simultaneously class relations. Great shifts of classes have taken place, for instance, before the eyes of the present generation. Not many decades ago, there was still a considerable class of independent artisans, which subsequently declined because of the growth of the machine technology, and, consequently of large-scale production, of the factory system. Simultaneously, the proletariat increased, as did also the industrial upper bourgeoisie, while the small artisan disappeared. The class alignment necessarily changed, for with the changes in technology there are also associated changes in the distribution of labor in society; certain functions in production disappear or fall into the background; new functions arise, etc., simultaneously, class groups are altered; in a society having a low stage of the productive forces, industry will not be highly developed, while the social economy will still be rural and agricultural in character. It will not surprise us to find the rural classes predominating in such a society, with the class of country squires standing at the head. On the other hand, in a society with highly developed productive forces, we shall find a mighty industry, cities, factories, villages, etc., with the urban classes attaining great influence. The landed proprietor yields place to the industrial bourgeoisie or other sections of the bourgeoisie; the proletariat becomes a great power.

A constantly progressing realignment of classes may totally change the form of society. This will particularly be the case if the class at the bottom comes out on top, a process which is to be described in the following chapters. For the present we shall merely state that class relations also - the most important part of production relations - change with the changes in the productive forces. "These social relations between the producers, and the conditions under which they exchange their activities and share in the total act of production, will naturally vary according to the character of the means of production. With the discovery of a new instrument of warfare, the firearm, the whole internal organization of the army was necessarily altered, the relations within which individuals compose an army and can work as an army were transformed, and the relation of different armies to one another was likewise changed. We thus see that the social *relations within which individuals produce, the* social *relations of production, are altered, transformed, with the change and development of the material means of production, of the forces of production*" (Karl Marx: *Wage-Labor and Capital*, New York, Labor News Company, 1917, pp.35, 36). In other words: "The organization of any specific society is determined by the condition of its productive forces. With an alteration of this condition, the social organization also will necessarily change sooner or later. Social organization is therefore in unstable equilibrium [2] at all points where the social forces of production are growing"[10] (or falling, *N.B.*).

The totality of the production relations, therefore, is the economic structure of society, or its mode of *production*. This is the human labor apparatus of society, its "*real basis*".

A consideration of the production relations will show that they depend on the manner in which the persons involved are distributed in space. The *relation is* expressed in the fact that each personas already shown, has his place as a screw in the mechanism of a watch. It is precisely this definite situation in space, in the "theater of labor" that makes of this arrangement, this distribution, a social relation of labor. No doubt, every object is situated in space, moves in space, but here men are joined, particularly, by the *definiteness* of their working positions, as it were. This is a material relation like that of the parts in the mechanism of a watch. We must not overlook the fact that the critics of historical materialism are constantly confusing terms because the word "material" has a number of meanings. Thus, the historical process, for instance, is traced back to material "needs" or "interests", whereupon the refutation of historical materialism is proclaimed, since it has been rightly shown that "interest" is' not a material thing in the philosophical sense of the word, but obviously psychical. We admit that interest is not matter; but it is too bad that even certain "advocates" of *historical* materialism (who usually associate Marx with some bourgeois philosopher, since they are opposed to *philosophical* materialism) are guilty of such a confusion in terms. Max Adler, for instance, who weds Marx to Kant, regards society as a totality of psychical interactions; for him everything is psychical. Here is a specimen of this nature: "A *relation is,* however, by no means `matter' in the sense of philosophical materialism, which puts matter on the same level with psychic substances. It is always difficult to find a relation between the `economic structure', `the material element' of historical materialism, and the `matter' of the former theory, no matter how this theory be understood . . . and what is true of the cause is also true of the effect. Instruments of production are rather products of the `human mind:" (Max Zetterbaum: *Zur materialistischen Geschichtsauffassung* in *Die Neue Zeit,* Vol. 21, part ii, p.403.) Zetterbaum is confused by the fact that machines are not made by soulless men. But as men themselves are not begotten by corpses, he considers everything in society to be a product of spirit without body - a very virtuous spirit therefore. It follows that the machine is psychical, and society has no "matter". But is obvious that sinful flesh is somewhere involved, for even a sinless spirit could not beget men and machines. Furthermore, a fleshless spirit would not even desire to occupy himself with such affairs. What remains of the "relation"? We must again point out to Herr Zetterbaum that the solar system is a material system; that we call it a system because its parts (sun, earth, other planets) are in definite *relations* to each other, occupy a certain position in space at any given moment. Just as the totality of planets, in certain relations with each other, constitutes the solar system, so the totality of persons in production relations constitutes the economic structure of society, its material basis, its personal apparatus. Kautsky, who sometimes confuses technology and economy most sinfully, also makes some very vulnerable statements. All such claims may be answered by the following passage from the arch-bourgeois, Werner Sombast. This professor, who is quite free from materialism, tells us: "Figuratively speaking, the economic life may be considered as an organism consisting of a body and a soul. The external forms of the operations of the economic life are its body; the forms of economic and factory operation, the most varied organizations within which and with the aid of which the economic process continues." (Werner Sombart: *Der Bourgeois,* München and Leipzig, 1913, pp.1 & 2.) Of course, the entire economic structure of society must be included under the head of economic form and economic organization, being therefore, "figuratively speaking", the body of this society.

d. The Outlines of the Superstructure

Among the remaining phases of social life which we must now consider are such phenomena as the social and political system of society (the state, the organization of classes, parties, etc.); manners, customs and morals (the social norms of human conduct); science and philosophy; religion, art, and finally, language, the means of communication between men. These phenomena, excepting the social and political system, are frequently referred to as our "mental" or "spiritual culture".

The word *culture* comes from a Latin verb meaning "to cultivate". Culture therefore means everything that is the work of human hands, in the wider sense, *i.e.,* everything produced by social man in one form or another. "Mental culture" is also a product of the social life, is included in the general life-process of society. It cannot be understood unless it be interpreted as a portion of this general life-process. Yet, certain bourgeois scholars would isolate this "mental culture" absolutely from the life-process of society, *i.e.,* they would deify it, make it an entity independent of the body, a disembodied spirit. Thus, Alfred Weber *(Der soziologische Kulturbegriff,* in *Verhandlungen des zweiten deutschen Soziologentages,*Tübmgen, 1913), who considers the expansion of social life, its intricacy and wealth, as a process of external civilization, writes: "But we feel today that culture is superior to all these things; that culture means something different to us ". Only when " life, rising above its necessities and utilities, has assumed a higher level than these things, only *then have we a culture*" (pp.10, 11; Weber's italics). In other words, culture is a portion of life, but is not determined by the necessities and utilities of life, *i.e.,* it transcends the bounds of society, is not conditioned by this society. It is obvious that such a point of view would lead to a renunciation of science and an acceptance of faith. Note that Weber's chief proof is the fact that "we feel".

A useful transition to a consideration of this "mental culture" is a study, in broad outline, of the *social and political structure of* society, which is directly determined, as we shall see, by its economic structure.

The most obvious expression of the social and political structure of society is the state power, which will be understood if we understand the necessary condition for the existence of a society of classes. For in such a society the various classes must have different interests. Some possess all; others, practically nothing; some are in command, and appropriate to themselves the products of the work of others; others obey, carry out the commands of strangers, and yield up what they have produced with their own hands. The position of the classes in production and distribution, i.e., the condition of their existence is their function in society, "their social being", results also in the growth of a specific consciousness. As everything in the universe is the result of the conditions that bring it about, the various situations of the classes must result in a difference in their interests, aspirations, struggles, even in their death struggles. It is interesting to observe the nature of the equilibrium existing in the *structure* of a society of classes. The fact that such a society, in which, in the words of an English statesman, there are in reality two "nations" (classes), can exist at all, without danger of disintegrating at any moment, is of itself very striking.

Yet there is no doubt of the existence of class societies. In some way or other, a unifying bond has been attained in such societies, a sort of hoop holding together the staves of the barrel; this hoop is the state, an organization of all society, with its threads, retaining them all in the system of its tentacles. If we should ask how the state originates, we should not be satisfied with any answer attributing a supernatural origin to the state, nor with any declaration that the state stands beyond all classes; for the simple reason that classless persons do not exist in a class society. There would therefore be no material with which to construct an organization standing outside of all classes or above all classes, no matter how often this may be asserted by bourgeois scholars.

The organization of the state is altogether an organization of the "ruling class".

It now becomes of interest to determine which is the ruling class, for we shall then understand which class is represented by the state power, which subjugates all the other classes by means of its strength, its force, its mental system, its widely ramified apparatus. The question is not difficult to answer. In capitalist society, we find the capitalist class dominant in production; it would be absurd to expect to find the proletariat permanently dominant in the state, for one of the fundamental conditions of equilibrium would now be lacking; either the proletariat would also seize control of production, or the bourgeoisie would seize the state power. The existence of a society with a specific economic structure also involves the adaptation of its state organization; in other words, the economic structure of society also determines its state and political structure. The state, furthermore, is a huge organization embracing an entire nation and ruling many millions of men. This organization needs a whole army of employees, officials, soldiers, officers, legislators, jurists, ministers, judges, generals, etc., etc., and embraces great layers of human beings, one superimposed on the other. This structure is a precise reflection of the conditions in production. In capitalist. society, for example, the bourgeoisie is in control of production, and therefore also of the state. Following upon the manufacturer comes the factory superintendent himself, often a capitalist; the same is true of the ministers of a capitalist state, its politicians in high places. From these circles are recruited the generals for the army; the intermediate positions in production are filled by the technical specialist, the engineer, the technical mental worker; these mental workers occupy the posts of intermediate officials in the state apparatus; they often furnish the army officers. The lower employees, as well as the soldiers, are furnished by the working class. Of course, there are many fluctuations, but the structure of the state authority corresponds closely, on the whole, to the structure of society.

If we should assume, for a moment, that by a miracle the lower employees had raised themselves above the higher employees, our assumption would involve a loss of equilibrium in the whole of society, i.e., a revolution. But such a revolution also cannot take place unless corresponding alterations have already been accomplished in production. Here also it is apparent that the structure of the state apparatus itself reflects the economic structure, i.e., the same classes occupy relatively the same positions.

Let us give a few examples from various times and places. In ancient Egypt, the administration of production was practically identical with that of the state, the great landlords heading both. An important fraction of production was that turned out by the landlord state. The role of the social groups in production coincided with their caste, with whether they were higher, middle, or lower officials of the state, or slaves (Otto Neurath: *Antike Wirtschaftsgeschichte,* Leipzig, 1909, p.8). "The families of the 'great' are of course landholding families, but they are also, above all, a *bureaucratic* nobility." (Max Weber: *Agrarverhältnisse im Altertum,* in *Handbuch der Staatswissenschaften,* vol. i.) Sometimes the combination of state authority and leadership in production was emphatically formulated. In the Fifteenth Century, the banking house of the Medici ruled the Italian trade-capitalist Republic of Florence: "The Bank of the Medici and the Florentine State Treasury were identical. The bankruptcy of this commercial firm occurred at the same moment as the collapse of the Florentine Republic" (M. Pokrovsky: *Economic Materialism,* Moscow, 1906, p.27, in Russian). In the second half of the Eighteenth Century, the landlords were dominant in Russian production, ruling over the peasant serfs. These landlords therefore also controlled the state, being specially organized as a privileged nobility. When the peasants rose under Pugachov, the landlord-empress Catherine II served as an incarnation of the existing state power, when she aided - as "landholder of Kazan" - in forming a cavalry regiment

186

for putting down this "rabble", wherewith she aroused a veritable storm of imperial fidelity among the Kazan landlords. Her frequent association with French free-thinking philosophers did not prevent Catherine from introducing serfdom into Ukraine, a contrast which has been well stated by A. Tolstoi:

"The great population
In your lands
Longs for Freedom
From your hands.
Then spake she full of noble zeal:
Messieurs, vows me comblez,
Whereupon she extended serfdom
To cover Ukraine also."

In the United States, financial capital, a clique of bankers and trust magnates, is dominant in production; they also control the state power to such an extent that congressional decisions are not made before they have been most thoroughly discussed behind the scenes by combined capital.

But the social and political structure of society is not limited to the state authority. The ruling class, as well as the oppressed classes, present the most varied organizations and forms of common action. Each class usually has its vanguard, consisting of its most "class-conscious" members, and constituting the political parties competing for domination in society. Usually, the ruling class, the oppressed classes, and the "middle classes", each have their specific party. Since there are various groups existing within each class, it is obvious that a class may have a number of parties, though the most permanent and fundamental of its interests can be expressed only in one party. Besides the regularly organized bodies, there may be a number of other bodies: the present-day American capitalists, for example, have not only organizations to combat the workers, but also special organizations for election manipulations (Tammany Hall, for example) and organizations for recruiting strike-breakers, organizations of industrial spies (the Pinkerton and other detective agencies), the secret groups of the most influential capitalist firms and the most powerful politicians, following strictly conspirative methods; the official state organs always carry out the will of these bodies. In Russia, there was an auxiliary organization of the state of the landed proprietors, namely, the semi-criminal band of the "Black Hundred" which had affiliations with the reigning Romanov dynasty. This role was played in Italy, in 1921, by the Fascisti, and in Germany by the Orgesch.[11] The oppressed classes also have a number of economic organizations in addition to their parties (for instance, the trade unions), not to mention fighting organizations and clubs, in which we may include such bodies as the "bands" of Stenka Razin or Pugachov.[12] In short, all organizations waging the class war, from the *jeunesse dorée* of the German student fraternities up to the state power itself, on the one hand-from the party to the club, on the other hand; all these are a portion of the social and political structure of society. Their basis is as clear as day; their existence is a reflection and an expression of *classes;* here also economy conditions *politics.*

In our consideration of this "political superstructure", we cannot afford to lose sight of the fact that - as the above examples alone would show - this political superstructure is not merely a personal apparatus. It consists, for all society, of a combination of things, persons, and ideas. For instance, in the state apparatus, we have a specific apparatus of things, a specific hierarchy, a certain specific system of ideas (procedure, laws, ordinances, etc.), etc. In the case of the army, which is a portion of the state, we have a special "technology" (cannons, rifles, machine-guns, commissary supplies), its specific arrangement of men, "distributed" in a certain way, and its own "ideas", which have been insinuated into the minds of all the members of the army by means of a complicated military drill and a special educational apparatus (spirit of subordination, discipline, etc.). Viewed from this angle, the picture of the army will suggest the following inferences. The technology of the army is determined by the general technology of productive labor in the given society; cannons cannot be manufactured before the casting of steel has been learnt, *i.e.,* before the necessary means of production have been obtained. The distribution of persons, the structure of the army, depends on the military science and also the class alignment of society. On the existence of weapons, and on the nature of these weapons, depends the division of the army into artillery, infantry, engineers, cavalry, sappers, etc.; on this will depend what types of soldiers, superiors, persons with special functions (for example, telephone operators) are present in the army. On the other hand, the class alignment of society will determine from what social layer the staff of officers is recruited; by the representatives of what class the actions of the army are controlled, etc.; finally, the specific mental attitudes with which the army is imbued are conditioned, on the one hand, by the army structure (memorizing regulations, *cadavre* obedience, etc.), and on the other hand by the class structure of society. In the Tsar's army the slogan was "Obey the Tsar", "For God, Emperor and Fatherland"; in the Red Army the slogan is "Preserve discipline in order to protect the workers against the imperialists." These examples are sufficient to show that the social and political superstructure is a complicated thing, consisting of different elements, which are interrelated. On the whole, this structure is determined by the class outline of society, a structure which in turn depends on the productive forces, *i.e.,* on the social technology. Certain of these elements are directly dependent on technology ("the art of war"); others depend on the class character of society (its. economy), as well as on the technology of the superstructure itself ("army management"). All the elements of the superstructure are therefore directly or indirectly based on the stage that has been reached by the social productive forces.

A special place among human organizations is held by the organization of the family, i.e., the living together of men, women, and children. This clan organization, which was constantly changing, was based on certain economic conditions. "The family, also, is not only a social, but preeminently an economic formation, based on the division of labor between man and woman, on 'sexual differentiation' " Primitive marriage is nothing else than the expression of this economic union." (Müller-Lyer, ibid., p.150; *cf.* Marx: *Capital*, vol. i, Chicago, 1915, p.386: "Within a single family " there arises a primitive distribution of labor based on differences of sex and age . . . .") The family thus arises as a firm unit by reason of the alterations in the economic order of the clan, which was a primitive state of communism (the original form of relation between the sexes was promiscuity, i.e., unregulated sexual relations between men and women). M. N. Pokrovsky characterizes the primitive Slavic family as follows: "The members of this family, workers in the same economy, soldiers of the same detachment, and finally, worshipers of the same god, participants in the same rite" (*History of Russia*, Moscow, 1920, pp.17, 18, in Russian). But the economic basis of such a family is further clarified by the following fact. "It would be erroneous," "to assign a dominant importance to these says M. N. Pokrovsky, blood ties: they are customary, but not inevitable. Such collective establishments were conducted in the North (of Russia) by persons who were strangers to each other, on the basis of contracts; they founded such communities, not for all time, but for a definite period, for instance, for ten years " Here also, the economic connection antedates the ties of blood, the 'relation' in our sense of the term" (ibid., p.16). The changed forms of family relations, in accordance with the economic conditions, may be traced even in modern times: we need only to compare the peasant family, the workers' family, and the modern bourgeois family. The peasant family is a firm unit, for it is based directly on production. "There must be a woman in the house," for who else would milk the cows, feed the pigs, cook the food, tidy the rooms, wash, take care of the children, etc.? The economic significance of the family is so great that marriages are dictated by specific economic calculation: "there is no woman in the house". Economically considered, the members of the family are "workers" and "eaters". Built up on this comparatively rigid basis, the peasant family is itself characterized by patriarchal rigidity, when untouched by the "corrupting" influence of the city. The workers' family is different. The worker has no economy of his own. His "household" is a consumption economy only; it consumes its wages. Simultaneously, the city, with its saloons, restaurants, laundries, etc., makes the household largely superfluous. Finally, large-scale industry disintegrates the family, forcing the proletarian woman to work in a factory. More mobile, less stable forms of family relations arise from these circumstances. In the upper middle class, private property requires the preservation of the family. But the increasing parasitism of the bourgeoisie, and the growth of entire strata who live by cutting coupons, transform the wife into a thing, into a bedizened but very stupid plaything, a boudoir appurtenance. The various forms of marriage (monogamy, polygamy, polyandry, etc.) are likewise dependent on the conditions of economic evolution. Furthermore, it must not be forgotten that sexual intercourse has practically never been limited to the family. The forms of prostitution, and their distribution, are again connected with the economy of society; we need only to point out the rôle of prostitution in the capitalist system. It seems reasonable to assume that communist society, which will definitely abolish private property and the enslavement of women, will witness the disappearance both of prostitution and the family.

The other phases of the "superstructure" are a result of man's living in society, or in individual sections of society, in a condition either of outright conflict or of incomplete harmony. The expression of this condition is the social necessity of social norms, including customs, morals, law, and a great number of other standards ("rules of decent behavior", "etiquette", ceremonial, etc.; also the constitutions of the various societies, organizations, brotherhoods, etc.), all of which are produced by the accumulation of contradictions in a mature and complicated

191

society. The most striking of these contradictions *is* the class contradiction, which therefore "demands" a mighty regulator for the purpose of suppressing this contradiction at certain times; the state power with its legal decisions, its standards of law, constitutes such a regulator. There are also subsidiary contradictions between the classes, within the classes, also within trades, groups, organizations, and in all human categories in general. Regardless of his class position, each individual comes in contact with all kinds of people, is subject to various influences which interact at many points; he finds himself placed in swiftly changing circumstances, which may disappear and later again assert themselves. Contradictions are here found at every step, and yet society and certain groups within it continue their relatively permanent existence. The capitalists, owners of enterprises, traders, merchants, compete in the market; yet they rarely resort to armed conflict with each other within the same state, and their class does not collapse because of the competitive struggle between its members. While buyers and sellers have distinctly opposed interests, they do not belabor each other physically. There are unemployed persons among the workers, whom the capitalists attempt to win over during a strike; but not every such person can be utilized; the class bond among the workers is too strong. This condition is a result of a great variety of standards existing by the side of the legal standards. These supplementary norms impress themselves on the minds of men, apparently from some inner source, and appear sacred to them, being voluntarily adhered o. Of such nature, for example, are the rules of morality, which are represented in a commercial society as eternal and immutably sacred laws, radiating their own light and binding on all decent eople; similar is the case with customs, "duties to the great departed", "rules of decency", "courtesy", etc.

In spite of the alleged "supernatural" character of these laws, their earthly roots may easily be traced, regardless of the pious awe of all their submissive adherents. A closer observation forces us to recognize two fundamental conditions: first, that these laws are subject to change; second, that they are connected with class, group, occupation, etc. It is also obvious that "in the last analysis" they are likewise conditioned by the level attained by the productive forces. In general, these rules indicate the line of conduct conducive to a preservation of the society, class, or group in question, and requiring a subordination of the individual to the interests of the group. These norms are therefore *conditions of equilibrium* for holding together the internal contradictions of human social systems, whence it results that they must more or less coincide with the economic structure of society. It is impossible, for instance, in any society, for the system of its *dominant* manners and customs to be in permanent contradiction with its fundamental economic structure. Such an opposition would mean the complete absence of the fundamental condition for social equilibrium. It is on the basis of the economic conditions that law, customs and morals are evolved in any society; they change and disappear with the economic system. Thus, in capitalist society, the capitalist controls things (instruments of production), a condition which is reflected in the laws of the capitalist state, in the so called right to private property, which is protected by the entire apparatus of the state power. The production conditions of capitalist society are juridically termed *property relations*; these relations are supported by many laws. A condition under which the laws of capitalist society would not protect the property relations of this society, but destroy them, is inconceivable. Similarly, the "moral consciousness" of capitalist society reflects and expresses its material being. Thus, in the field of private property, morality teaches that theft is to be condemned; honesty and the inviolability of the property of others are inculcated. And quite naturally, for without this moral law which has imbedded itself in the minds of men, capitalist society would at once disintegrate.

Apparent contradictions to the above can be easily disposed of. While communists do not believe in the sacredness of private property, they do not approve of stealing. It may be urged that this indicates the presence of something that is sacred for all men, that cannot be explained by earthly causes. The facts of the case are quite different: it is true that communists by no means recognize the inviolability of private property; the nationalization of factories is an expropriation of the bourgeoisie; the working class appropriates "the property of others", transgresses the right of private property, undertakes a "despotic intervention in the right of property" (Karl Marx: *The Communist Manifesto*). But communists condemn stealing, for the reason that individual thefts by each worker from the capitalists, for his own advantage, would not result in a common struggle, but would make the worker a petty bourgeois. Horse-thieves and swindlers will not fight in the class struggle, even though they may be offspring of the proletariat. If many members of the proletariat should become thieves, the class would break down and be condemned to impotence; therefore, communists condemn stealing, not in order to protect private property, but in order to maintain the integrity of their class, to protect it from "demoralization" and "disintegration", without which protection the proletariat can never be transformed into the next following stage. We are therefore dealing with a *class standard* in the conduct of the proletariat. It is obvious that the rules we have considered are determined by the economic conditions of society.

The proletarian standards, of course, are in contradiction with the economic conditions of capitalist society. But we have been speaking of *dominant standards*; as soon as the proletarian standards become dominant, capitalism will be a thing of the past (see next chapter).

A number of examples will be given to explain the above statements. In the sexual field, at a certain stage of development, when the clan was still based on bland relationship and members of other clans were considered enemies, marriages between close relations were not objectionable; particularly sacred was a marriage with one's mother or daughter (in the ancient Iranian religion).

When the productive forces were at a low level, and the social economy could not afford any superfluous ballast, manners and morals required the *slaying of old men*, as is reported by the ancient historians Herodotus, Strabo, etc. This was the cause for the voluntary self-poisonings (reported by Strabo) of old men. On the other hand, where these old men had a function in production or administration, morality required that they be honored (*cf.* Eduard Meyer: *Elemente der Anthropologie*, pp.31-33, *et seq.*). The close-knit nature of the clan, its solidarity when combating enemies, assumed the form of blood revenge, in which women also participated. Thus, we read in the Nibelungenlied:

"Chriemhilda did revenge her wrongs,
    in way that will affright;
She slaughtered, without fear or shame,
    the king, and loyal knight!
They both were singly manacled,
    in fast and dreary place;
So that those knights ne'er saw again each other,
    face to face,
Save when she took her brother's head to Hagen,
    with own hand,
Chriemhilda vengeful wrath was such,
    as baffles ail command."

(*Das Nibelungenlied, or Lay of the Last Nibelungers,* English transl. by Jonathan Birch, Berlin, 1848.)

Eduard Meyer correctly says: "In content, the laws of morality, of customs, and of justice, depend on the social order and the communal views of the community, prevailing at the time " They may therefore be diametrically opposed in content, if they represent different societies and different periods" (*ibid.*, p.44). In ancient China, a peculiarly constructed feudal state authority with a great stratum of officials of various degree, was of great importance. The rule of this feudal-bureaucratic stratum was ideologically based on the teaching of Confucius, a system of rules of conduct. One of the most important points in this moral teaching was the doctrine of respect and submission to those in authority (*Hiao*); "Calumniesmust be borne, even though they drive us into death, if the honor of the master require it; one can (and should) always make good *all* the master's errors by *faithful* service; such was*Hiao*" (Max Weber: *Gesammelte Aufsätze zur Religionsphilosophie,* Tübingen, 1920, vol. i, p.419). Violation of *Hiao* was the only sin. One who did not understand this, who therefore had no grasp of "propriety" (a fundamental conception in the Confucian doctrine) was a barbarian. "Respect (*Hiao*) toward one's feudal lord was enumerated together with that toward parents, teachers, superiors in the official hierarchy, and officeholders in general" (*ibid.,* p.446). Discipline, like respect, is a worthy virtue. "Insubordination is worse than baseness" (p.447). The case may be generally stated: "Better be a dog in peace, than a man living in anarchy," as Cheng Ki Tong says (p.457). "Like any code for officials, the Confucian code of course also condemned any participation by officials in business, directly or indirectly, as ethically objectionable and not in accord with their rank" (p.447). Friends must be chosen only from one's own rank, for they can fulfil all the ceremonies; the population consists of "stupid men" (*yun min*), as contrasted with the man of princely station. Characteristically enough, this entire system of standards supporting the feudal noble regime was called the "great plan", *hung fan,* (p. 454). It is obvious that this teaching is closely related with the system of society. The numerous "Chinese ceremonies" were in reality based on the dominant currents of thought, and served as a complicated silken tissue enmeshing the social structure and guarding the existing order.

Or, let us consider the medieval knights of Northern France, in the Twelfth and Thirteenth Centuries, who sang of their fair ladies and fought tournaments "for them"; their "ideal" views of "honor and love" bore all the earmarks of a *caste* honor (*cf.* H. Helmolt, *Weltgeschichte,* Leipzig and Vienna, vol. v). The chief role played by knighthood in society was that of war and strategy. The "standards" therefore had to serve the purpose of training a military type of man, segregated in a special class. "A knight, who " had shown himself to be a coward, was cast out, publicly outlawed by the herald, cursed by the Church; his escutcheon and arms were destroyed by the hangman, his shield tied to the tail of a horse and smashed by the animal in his swift course "" "For *training in the profession of* arms, there were *tournaments,* in addition to military campaigns and feuds" (p.496).

"As the capitalist relations grow, the dominant customs, morals, etc., change. Generous wastefulness is replaced by a desire for accumulation and the corresponding virtues." "A decent man is not honored by his lordly manner, but by his keeping order in his establishment" (W. Sombart, *Der Bourgeois*, p.140). "One must refrain from revelry, must appear only in decent company; must not be addicted to drinking, gambling, women; one must be a good `citizen' even in one's external conduct, for reasons of business interest. For, such a moral conduct of life *raises one's credit"* (*ibid.,* pp.162, 163). Of course, this pious Protestant morality was succeeded by a different morality when the situation of the bourgeoisie changed, the business of the firm no longer depending on the conduct of its owner.

It is an even easier matter to show how law changes with the economic structure, for here the class character of law is manifest everywhere. But even such intangible standards as those of *fashion* depend - as may be easily proved - on social conditions. For a bourgeois it is "indecent" not to dress in accordance with his standing; for this class trait of clothing indicates "persons of quality". Even revolutionists are subject to the caprices of fashion; a party fashion in the revolution of 1905 was the wearing of black blouses by the Social-Democrats (a sign of the proletariat), while the Social-Revolutionists preferred red ones (revolutionary peasantry); you could hardly find a dozen intellectuals in any big city, who had participated in the revolution and yet ignored these passively accepted party fashions.

In addition to a class morality, we also have subdivisions of this morality, for example, professional ethics, the vocational morals of physicians, lawyers, etc. There is also a thief morality ("there is honor among thieves"), which is rather strictly complied with. All the standards above mentioned constitute firm bonds emphasizing the unity of a society, a class, a vocational group, etc.

Science and Philosophy are also a category of social phenomena. We shall see that the latter is based on all the accomplishments of the former. Any fairly advanced science is a very complicated thing,, not limited to systems of ideas alone. The sciences have their technique, their physical apparatus, instruments, appliances, charts, books, laboratories, museums, etc.; any laboratory or any scientific expedition, to the North Pole or to Central Africa, will serve as an illustration; they also have their personal apparatus, sometimes highly organized (for example, scientific congresses, conferences, academies and other organizations, with their periodical and other publications); and finally, there is the system of ideas, of thoughts in orderly arrangement, constituting the science in the proper sense of the word.

The following principle is of fundamental importance: every science is born from practice, from the conditions and needs of the struggle for life on the part of social man with nature, and of the various social groups, with the elemental forces of society or with other social groups. "The savage has had the most varied experiences; he can distinguish venomous and edible plants, pursue the traces of game and protect himself from beasts of prey and venomous serpents. He can make use of fire and water, select stones and wood for his weapons, smelt and work metals. He can count and calculate with his fingers, make measurements with his hands and feet like a child, he sees the firmament, observes its motions and the changed positions of sun and planets. All or most of his observations are made casually or for the purpose of a useful application. These primitive observations are the germ of the various sciences. The latter can only exist when freedom from material cares has resulted in a sufficient quantity of comfort and leisure, and when the intellect has been sufficiently strengthened by frequent use, to make *observations per se . .* , a matter of interest."[13] Science therefore can begin only when the growth *of* the productive forces has left free time for scientific observation. Also, the original material of science is material taken from the field of production. It should therefore not surprise us that the immediate maintenance of life by production, i.e., the interests *of* production, gave the first impulse to the growth of science. Prac*tice* created theory and impelled it onward.

Astronomy arose from the need of finding one's bearings by the stars in desert plains, from the significance of the seasons in agriculture, the need of a precise division of time (astronomical control of clocks, for instance), etc. Physics was intimately connected with the technique of material production and warfare. Chemistry arose on the basis of an expanding industrial production, particularly mining; the beginnings of chemistry are already found in Egypt and China, in the manufacture of glass, dyeing, enameling, the production of paints, metallurgy, etc.; the word *chemistry is* derived from *chemi,* "black", thus suggesting its Egyptian origin. Alchemy is found among the ancient Egyptians, the outgrowth of the desire to find the law of transmutation of metals into gold; in the Fifteenth Century, chemistry was much aided by medicine. Mineralogy arises from the use of metals in production, and their study for purposes of production. Botany originally consisted of a knowledge of healing plants, later of useful plants, still later, of plants in general. Zoology developed from the necessity of understanding the useful and harmful qualities of animals. Anatomy, physiology, pathology, started from practical medicine (the first "specialists" in this field were Egyptian, East Indian, Greek and Roman physicians, such as the Greek Hippocrates, the Roman Claudius Galenus, etc.). Geography and ethnography were developed by trade and colonial warfare. The ablest commercial peoples of antiquity (for instance, the Phwnicians, Carthaginians, etc.), were also the best geographers. Geography was neglected in the Middle Ages, a great renewal of interest in the subject coming in modern times, beginning with the Fifteenth Century, in the era of the colonial wars waged by the trade-capitalist nations, and the half-commercial, half-predatory, half-scientific voyages connected with these wars. The voyages and discoveries were performed chiefly by the predatory commercial nations: Portugal, Spain, England, Holland. Ethnology was also encouraged by colonial policy, the practical question being the learning of a method of utilizing savages for labor for the advantage of the "civilized" bourgeoisie. Mathematics, the science that is apparently most remote from practice, was nevertheless of practical origin; its original tools were those first used in material production: the fingers, hands, feet (counting on one's fingers), the quinary, decimal, vicenary systems; the original designations for the angles, etc., after the bend in the knee; units of length: the ell, foot, etc. (cf. Cantor: *Vorlesungen über die Geschichte der Mathematik*, Leipzig, 1907, vol. i). The material basis of mathematics was the needs of production: surveying ("geometry" means "earth-measurement"), the erection of buildings, measuring the content of vessels, shipbuilding; still earlier, the number of cattle; in the commercial period, commercial arithmetic, inventory, balance-sheet, etc. The Egyptian and Greek geometers, the Roman *agrimensores,* the Alexandrian engineers (for instance, Hero of Alexandria, who invented a sort of steam-engine) were simultaneously the first mathematicians (Rudolf Eisler: *Geschichte der Wissenschaften,* Leipzig, 1906). The case of the social sciences (as already discussed in our Introduction) is in no way different. History arose from the need of knowing the "destinies of nations", for purposes of practical politics. Legal science began with the collection and codification of the most important laws, again for practical purposes. Political economy arose with capitalism, originally as a science of merchants, serving the needs of their class policy. The philological sciences arose in the form of "grammars" of the various languages, as a result of commercial relations and the requirements of intercourse. Statistics began with merchants' "tables", each dealing with a specific country (likewise, the first beginnings of political economy; one of the earliest economists, William Petty, calls one of his works: *"Political Arithmetic")*, etc., etc. New sciences are arising from production before our very eyes, for instance, the technical experiences acquired in the application of the Taylor system give rise to so called *psycho-technxcs,* the psychophysiology of labor, the theory of the organization of production, etc.

With the gradual extension, division, and specialization of the sciences, their direct or indirect dependence on the stage of the productive forces nevertheless continues in evidence. As the natural human organs, in the direct process of material production in society, are "extended," and by this extension, "contrary to the Bible", are enabled to embrace and manipulate a much greater material, so the "extended" consciousness of human society is *science,* increasing its mental compass and enabling it to grasp and consequently better to control, a greater mass of phenomena.

It is interesting to note that many bourgeois scholars, when speaking concretely of science, involuntarily assume this materialist standpoint. But they dare not pursue it to the end. Thus a well-known Russian scholar, Professor Chuprov (junior) speaks of the "significance of science" as follows: "While life remains uncomplicated, men in their daily affairs content themselves with the 'experiences of life', an accidental method of accumulating incoherent bits of knowledge and habit, passed on from father to son as a tradition. But as the sphere of interest widens, these formless bits of knowledge cease to fulfil requirements; there arises a need for systematic work; consciously and planfully devoted to an understanding of the surrounding universe, *i.e.,* science. As soon as men have learned that *scientia et ptentia humana in idem coincident* (science and human knowledge are identical), and that *quod in contemplatione instar causae est, id in operatione instar regulae est* (that which appears as cause in observation, is the rule in the effect), they grasp the thought that *ignoratio causae destituit effectum.* (failure to recognise the cause destroys the result), and learn to appreciate science as the basis of practical labor"(*Outlines of the Theory of Statistics,* St. Petersburg, 1909, pp.21, 22, in Russian).

The connection between the state of science and the productive forces of society is of manifold nature. This connection must be studied from a number of angles, for it is not as simple as may first appear. We shall therefore have to turn our attention, in our consideration of science, to its technique, its special organization of work, its content, its method (or alleged method), for all these components interact mutually and produce the level of the given science at a given time. Each of these elements will lead back directly or indirectly to the social technology.

In the first place, the very existence of society is possible only after the productive forces have attained a certain level in their development. If the labor surplus is absent or limited and not increased, the growth of science is impossible.

"This desire for science could not be displayed before man had satisfied his other appetites . . . . Certain very old observations are handed down to us from China, India, Egypt, but it is interesting to note that they were but imperfectly developed in those countries" (A. Bordeaux: *Histoire des sciences physiques, chimiques et géologiques au XIX siècle,* Paris and Liege, 1920, p.11).

The content of science is determined in the last analysis by the technical and economic phase of society; these are the "practical roots", which explain why an identical scientific discovery, invention, or study, may be achieved simultaneously in different places, perhaps quite "independently". The "ideas" are said to be in the air, meaning that they grow out of the existing stage of life. That has been produced by the level of the productive forces.

In his *Histoire,* A. Bordeaux mentions the following discoveries resulting, as he puts it, from the presence of ideas "in the air", and from the conditions of life *(par l'existence des idées dans l'air et par les circonstances de la vie): the* discovery of the relation between heat and mechanical work, induction, the induction coil, the Gramme ring, the infinitesimal calculus (mentioned not only by Leibnitz and Newton, but also by their predecessors Fermat, Cavalieri, etc., as far back as Archimedes). Bordeaux concludes: "As for science, . . . it shows " how difficult it is to determine which *person* really made a certain discovery" (*ibid.,* p.8). Let us note that the practical object of a science by no means presupposes that *each*scientific principle *directly* influences practice. Assuming the theorem A to be important for practice, and that this theorem cannot be proved except with the use of the theorems, B, C, D, and that the three latter theorems are of no *direct* practical value (being, as we say, of "purely theoretical interest"), these theorems nevertheless are indirectly of practical significance as links in a single scientific chain. There are no useless or worthless scientific systems, just as there are no useless mechanical tools.

While the problems have been put chiefly by technology and economy, their solution in many sciences depends on alterations in the *scientific technique,* whose instruments are of extraordinary importance in widening the horizon. The microscope, for example, was invented in the first half of the Seventeenth Century and of course, had an immense influence on the evolution of science by favoring the development of botany, zoology, anatomy, in creating a new branch of science, bacteriology, etc. Equally obvious is the role of technique in astronomy (equipment of observatories, varieties of telescopes, devices for photographing stars, etc.). , In its turn, scientific technique depends on the material production in general (is a product of material labor). In scientific work, we usually find a corresponding *organization of this work*, also influencing the state of scientific knowledge. The division of scientific labor (specialization in science), the organization of great scientific units (e.g., laboratories), the establishment of scientific bodies and scientific intercourse are extremely important. All these phases, again, are ultimately determined by the economic and technical conditions; thus, modern chemical laboratories grow with the industrial plants to which they are attached; scientific intercourse becomes more frequent with the greater frequency of economic connections, etc. But technical and economic conditions also "condition" science in another respect. With the rapid expansion of technology, economic conditions and the entire standard of life are constantly changing, resulting not only in a swift growth of science, but in its acceptance of the concept of change as a guiding factor (use of the *dynamic* method, see chapter iii). Conversely, where technology is conservative and of slow growth, the economic life will also advance but slowly, and the human psychology infers that all things are permanent. Society then marks time and is governed by the principle of permanence. The *class characteristics* in the various branches of science also present themselves, reflecting either the *mode of thought* characteristic of the specific class, or the *interests of* the class. Mode of thought, interests, etc., are, in their turn, determined by the economic structure of society.

Let us give a few of these relations. In ancient times, technology - as we know - developed slowly, with a resulting slow advance in technical knowledge. "This neglect of technology has several causes: in the first place, antiquity was "entirely aristocratic in its attitude. Even prominent artists, such as Phidias, are classed as artisans; they are incapable of bursting through the stone wall " separating the aristocratic circle " from the artisans and peasants. . . A second cause of the slight progress of technical discovery in antiquity is in its slave-holding system " We therefore find a lack of any impulse to develop the machine as a substitute for manual labor " Science " was dead and the interest in technical problems, except for a few curiosities, such as water-clocks and water-organs, had died out" (Hermann Diels: *Wissenschaft und Technik bei den Hellenen,* in *Antike Technik,* Leipzig and Berlin,

1920, pp.31-33). Thence the character of the existing science: "The natural sciences probably arose as a by-product of artisan work. But since such work, as well as any manual work, was despised in ancient society, and as the slaves who observed nature were sharply distinguished from the masters who speculated and worked as amateurs at their leisure, often knowing nature only by hearsay, it is easy to explain much of the naive, vague and mystical nature of ancient natural science" (Ernst Mach: *Erkenntnis und Irrtum,* Leipzig, 1905, p.95, Mach's italics). In the Middle Ages we have a feeble and primitive technology, with feudal relations in economic life, an entire system of superiors has been elaborated, culminating in the landlord and monarch. It should not surprise us to learn that the dominant thought was not very mobile, resisting all that was new (heresy was punished with burning and quartering), not occupying itself with the investigation of nature, but delving in theological problems. The important problems of discussion were: the bodily size of Adam, whether he had brown or red hair, how many angels could stand on the point of a needle, etc. This immobile, conservative theological (formal, "scholastic") character of the science of the time, entirely opposed to experimental investigation, may be explained by the conditions of the social life, by the technical and economic relations, which ultimately rested on the stage of social evolution. The case became quite different, when capitalist relations began to grow. We now are no longer dealing with a rigid technology, but with one that is rapidly changing, with new branches of production constantly growing up; we now need mechanics, engineers, chemists, and not theologians or knights; warfare also requires scientific knowledge, as well as mathematics. It is natural that this shift in the technical and economic relations also necessarily resulted in a transformation of science: Scholasticism, Latin, Theology, etc., gave way to an experimental investigation of nature, to the natural sciences, to the Realist School. We have here given an example of the general transformation in the content of science. We might, with close study, also trace this transformation in the methods of investigation, the tools of scientific thought, and in many other phases of science.

An example of the influence of the class psychology, and consequently also of the class structure of society, is afforded by the organic theory in sociology, already mentioned by us. Professor R. J. Wipper says the following on this subject: "The comparison of society with an organism, the expression, the `organic connection of the individual with society', as contrasted with the connection in a mechanical society, all these comparisons, formulas, and antitheses were launched by the reactionary publicists of the Nineteenth Century. In setting up this organ as opposed to a mechanism, these publicists were attempting to distinguish their demands sharply from the didactic and revolutionary principles of the previous century (the Era of Enlightenment). `The state is a mechanism', was the old terminology: equal rights for all men, whose totality constitutes the sovereign people; `the state is an organism', was the new slogan: arrangement of men in a traditional social hierarchy, subjection of the individual to a `natural' group, .e., his subordination to the old social authority. Translated into concrete language, the 'organic' relations mean: serfdom, the guild system, subordination of workers to employers, defense of the honor and privileges of the nobility, etc." (Wipper: *A Few Observations on the Theory of Historical Knowledge,* in the collection *Two Intelligentsias,* Moscow, 1912, pp.47, 48, in Russian.)

We give below a few additional data on the history of mathematics, since it is commonly assumed that mathematics, being a purely contemplative science, has nothing in common with practical life. We take them from the very important work of M. Cantor (*Vorlesungen über die Geschichte der Mathematik,* Leipzig, 1907, vol. i). Mathematical knowledge arose among the Babylonians, developing on the basis of surveying, measuring the cubic contents of vessels, commercial arithmetic, and the need of a precise division of time (the calendar) into years, days, hours, etc. The original mathematical instruments were the fingers. Later, calculating machines: a rope with little rods (Sumerian: *tim)* in geometry; later, an instrument recalling the astrolabe. Mathematical study was closely connected with religion, the numerals at first indicating the gods, their celestial precedence, etc. Mathematics attained a high state of development among the Egyptians; the ancient mathematical *"Calculation Book of Ahmes"* (its precise title is: "Rules for obtaining a knowledge of all obscure things " of all secrets which are contained in objects") contains such headings as: "Rule for Calculating a Round Granary", "Rule for Calculating Fields", "Rule for Making an Adornment", etc. (*ibid.,* pp.58, 59). Arithmetical and occasionally algebraic operations are illustrated by means of problems clearly indicating the conditions of practice. This practice involves: distribution of grain, distribution of rye, calculation of receipts, etc. " (p.79 *et seq.*). The concluding statement of this mathematical primer clearly shows its connection with agriculture; we read: "Catch vermin, mice, gather fresh weeds, numerous spiders, beg (the god) Ra for warmth, wind, high water" (p.85). The fingers were obviously the first calculating instruments, later a sort of board (with knotted twine, as in the case of the Peruvians). The basis of geometry was surveying; besides problems in the measurement of fields, Ahmes also has problems for calculating the volume of granaries and the amount of grain they may hold (p. 98). The Greek historian Diodorus writes of the-Egyptians: "The priests teach their sons two kinds of writing, the so called sacred writing and a common writing. They diligently study geometry and arithmetic. For the river (the Nile) changes the country considerably each year, thus producing much litigation concerning boundaries between neighbors; such divisions cannot be adjusted without direct measurements made by a geometer. Arithmetic serves them in their *household affairs"* (p.303, my italics, N. B.). The astronomical, geometrical and algebraic rules were first connected with religious rites; they were sacred mysteries in which only a select few were initiated. The so called "harpedonapts" (rope-weavers, or literally, rope-knotters) possessed the trade secret of setting the rope, of placing it at the proper angle with the meridian, etc. (In fact, in general, the angles and sides of pyramids, the arrangement of their parts, had a certain sacred astronomical-scientific meaning, which was probably imparted to the "sons of the priests".)

Among the Romans, geometry advanced with the needs of landed property, which was so holy that even the gods possessed it. Mathematics attained its highest development ("exceptional period," according to Cantor). This exceptional condition of development was due to the presence of two practical problems: the construction of the calendar (the so called Julian Calendar; Julius Caesar himself wrote a book on the stars, *De astris*), and the great survey of the Roman Empire. The latter problem was solved under Augustus, the great Greek engineer and mathematician, Hero of Alexandria, being invited to conduct the work; for the first time a complete map of the entire empire was compiled. We later find, in Columella, a consideration of mathematics in its relations with agriculture; in Sextius Julius Frontinus, a treatment of mathematics as applied to the calculation of aqueduct tubes (the important mathematical symbol p, to represent the ratio between circumference and diameter of the circle). In the so called *Codex Arcerianus* (a legal-scientific reference work for administrative officials of the Roman Empire, in the Sixth and Seventh Centuries, A.D.), we find a number of articles on field-surveying for purposes of taxation (Cantor, *ibid.*, p.454).

The development of arithmetic was due chiefly to the demands of trade. Interest calculations, according to Horace an accomplishment of daily use, calculations of inheritance bequests, in accordance with the complicated Roman legislation, merchants' calculations - they were the motives underlying the evolution of arithmetic.

Among the ancient East Indians, we find astronomy,

algebra and the beginnings of trigonometry. The conditions in this country resemble those found among other ancient peoples. The mathematical chapters of a learned collected work (the *Aryabhattd)* give evidence, in the designations and content of the problems, of the living basis of Indian mathematics. A mathematical method, for instance, is suggested in the following verse: "Multiplications become divisions, divisions become multiplications; what was *profit* becomes loss, what was loss becomes *profit*" (p.17). In another passage we find the problem: "A sixteen-year-old female slave cost thirty-two *nishkas;* how much will a twenty-year-old slave-girl cost?" (p.618). Interest calculations follow (at the rate of 50 per cent. per month!); also problems for calculating all kinds of commercial transactions (p. 619), etc. The unknown quantities designated by x, y, x, in present-day algebra, were called by the Indians "coin" *(rupaka),* the positive quantities were "assets" *(dhana* or *sva)*; the negative quantities, "liabilities" *(rina*or *kshaya)* (p.621). Architecture and its mathematical rules were here also enveloped in mystery, having a specific astronomic and divine significance. The measurement of fields, the construction of palaces and temples, the calculation of contents, were the moving impulse in Indian geometry. Among the ancient Chinese, the evolution of mathematics proceeded along the same general lines, with the class character of science, its monopoly, more sharply expressed (there were three sets of numerals, one for state officials, one for science, one for civilian merchants. In a collection of laws *(Tcheou ly)*, we find the following mathematical offices: the hereditary dignity of court astronomer *(fong siang ski)* and court astrologer *(pao tshang shi)*; followed by the head-geometer *(liong jin)*, to whom was entrusted the laying out of the walls and palaces of cities, below him a special official for the measuring apparatus*(tu fang shi)*, who performed measurements with an instrument called *to küei,* namely, a shadow indicator, making the necessary calculations, etc. (p.676).

It is easy to conclude from the above: 1. that the content of science is given by the content of technology and economy; 2. that its development was determined among other things by the tools of scientific knowledge; 3. that the various social conditions now encouraged, now retarded progress; 4. that the method of scientific thought was determined by the economic structure of society (the religious, divinely mysterious character of ancient mathematics, in which even a *number* sometimes designated a divinity, is a reflection of the feudal-slaveholding order of society with its inaccessible ruler, its priestly officials, etc.); 5. that the class structure of society impressed its class stamp on mathematics (in part merely on the mode of thought, in part on the form of material interest, excluding ordinary mortals from the sacred mysteries). In modern times we find the same causal relations, but they are more complicated and, of course, different in form; the technology and the economic conditions have changed entirely.

Religion and Philosophy. Religion and philosophy are the next forms of the superstructure to which we shall devote our attention.

The thoughts and observations accumulated by human society give rise to the need of grouping and classifying them; science has resulted from this need. But science began, at a very early stage, to be subdivided into various branches, and within these special sciences there proceeded an "adaptation of thoughts to thoughts", *ie.*, a systematization. But, in addition, a need was felt for some thing that would hold together all these "knowledges" and "errors", that would realize an equilibrium between them. Religion and general science had to provide this uniting principle; it is that which had to furnish the answers to the most abstract and general questions: as to the cause of all existence; the nature of the universe; whether the universe is as it seems, or otherwise; the nature of mind and matter; the possibility of a knowledge of the universe; the nature of truth; the ultimate causes of all phenomena; the nature of truth; ultimate causes of all phenomena; the existence of limits to human knowledge, the defining of these limits; and a host of similar questions. Of course, our answer to these questions will influence our conception of any specific phenomenon. If, for instance, all depends on the will of God, who guides the world according to his divine plan, all our knowledge must be arranged in teleological or theological order, and at certain epochs science actually assumed this form. All phenomena then required us to seek the so called "hand of God", the divine purpose. But if the gods are not involved, if a causal relation is the only element of importance, our attitude toward the phenomena of the universe becomes quite different. If philosophy and religion, therefore, are the spectacles through which all facts are viewed at a certain stage in evolution, a study of the conditions *underlying* the construction of these "spectacles" is very important.

As for religion, we already know that its "essence" is a "faith" in supernatural powers, in miraculous spirits; this "faith" may be in one or more such forces, may be crude, or more intangible and ethereal. This notion of "spirit", "soul", etc., was a reflection of the particular economic structure of society at the time when the "eldest of the clan" - and later, the patriarch - arose (in the patriarchate; the case is essentially the same in the matriarchate), in other words, when the division of labor led to the segregation of administrative work. The eldest of the clan, the guardian of its accumulated experience in production, administers, commands, outlines the plan of labor, represents the active "creative" principle, while the rest obey, execute commands, submit to the plan handed out by their superior, act in accordance with another's will. This mode of production became a pattern for the interpretation of all phases of existence, particularly man himself. Man was divided into "body" and "spirit". The "spirit" guides the "body", and is as much superior to the body as the organizer and administrator is superior to the simple executant. In one passage, Aristotle compares the soul with the master and the body with the slave. All the rest of the world began to be considered in accordance with the same scheme of things:

211

behind each thing, man saw the "spirit" of this thing; all nature became animated with a "spirit", a scientific conception which is known as "animism", from the Latin *anima* (*"soul"*), or animus (*"spirit"*). This conception, once established, necessarily led to the origin of religion, beginning with the worship of ancestors, of the elders of the clan, of supervisors and organizers in general. Their "spirits" or "souls" were naturally considered to be the most intelligent, most experienced, most powerful spirits, capable of giving aid, and on whom all things depended. Here we already have a religion, showing in its origin that it also is a reflection of production relations (particularly those of master and servant) and the *political order of society* conditioned by them. The whole world was explained in accordance with the pattern used to explain life in society; in all its later history, religion shows alterations proceeding parallel with the alterations in the production relations and the social-political relations; in a society consisting of loosely connected clans, each with its own elders and princes, religion assumes the form of polytheism; should a centralized monarchy arise, it will be found paralleled in heaven, where a single God will mount the throne, as cruel as the ruler of the earth; the religion of a slaveholding commercial republic (for instance, the Athens of the Fifth Century B.C.) will show the Gods organized as a republic, even though the goddess of the victorious city, Pallas Athena, may be given unusual prominence. And, parallel with the hierarchy of officials found in any "respectable" state, we also find a corresponding organization of saints, angels, gods, etc., in heaven, arranged in accordance with their dignity, rank, and order.[14] Furthermore, a division of labor is instituted among the gods, as among mundane superiors; one is made a specialist for military affairs (Mars in the Roman mythology, St. George or the Archangel Michael, the Archistrategus, in the Greek Catholic Church); another for commercial matters (Mercury); a third, for agriculture, etc. The parallel even extends to amusing details; for instance, among the Russian saints there are "specialists" (like the *spetses* in Soviet Russia) for horsebreeding (Frol and Lavr). Any relation of domination and subjection is paralleled by a religion reflecting this relation. As actual life presents cases of war, enslavement, and insurrection, so religion teaches that these also occur in the celestial spheres; devils, demons, princes of darkness, are merely a heavenly parallel to the hostile leaders seeking to destroy the state on earth; in heaven they attempt to undermine the Emperor, the Almighty, and subvert the entire celestial order.

This theory of the origin of religion, which we accept absolutely, belongs, to A Bogdanov, and was first formulated in the Russian handbook: *Contributions to Social Psychology.*Later special investigations have entirely confirmed this conjecture, which is touched upon by H. Cunow in his book: *Ursprung der Religion and des Gottesglaubens,* Berlin, 1920. Cunow objects to the conception which would have religion emanate from the various observations of external nature, and rightly declares: "We may indeed, since each conceptual image is determined by the conception at its basis (its sub-stratum), maintain in a certain sense that both the natural environment and the social life determine the religious ideology; but, aside from the fact that the view of nature is in turn largely dependent on the degree to which man has succeeded in technically utilizing the forces of nature in the production of his material life (Herr Cunow should have remembered this when he took up a discussion of the productive forces, *N. B.*), the natural conceptual image furnished only the *external adornments,* one might almost say, only the *local color for the religious system of thought*" (p.20, my italics, *N. B.*). But Herr Cunow does not pursue this thought to its logical conclusion and falls a victim to the most incredible childishness. Thus, he states (p.24): "All natural and semi-civilized races are naturally (!) dualists." This recalls Adam Smith's designation of "exchange" as an "entirely natural" property of man, or the explanation of the origin of science in man's innate "tendency to causality". According to Cunow, the fact that man has both soul and body is "fortified" by dream-visions and the trance (fainting) condition (something apparently, leaves the body, later returning to it). But only that which is can be "fortified". Perhaps *death* is a phenomenon calling forth the notion of a "soul" separate from the "body". But Cunow himself gives us examples (pp.22, 23) of savages who do not understand the necessity of natural death, in fact, many tribes (John Fraser reports this of the Australians in New South Wales) ascribe death itself to "the mysterious malignance of an evil spirit" (p.23). In other words, this explains nothing at all. (We may mention in passing that M. N. Pokrovsky derives religion from the fear of death, from those departed, etc. But suppose even the conception that all men are mortal is lacking? It is obvious that Pokrovsky considers "natural" or primitive what is really a historical category, historical in its origin.) In Cunow's mind, religion evolves as follows: Beginnings of a spirit worship, then totem worship (totems are the birds, animals, plants, that were once the coats of arms of the tribes) and ancestor worship. But in almost all of the examples mentioned by Cunow, his "most primitive" spirits are the spirits of ancestors. In his chapter on "the beginnings of spirit worship", Cunow writes: "Only the spirits of close relations or, at any rate, of members of the same horde are regarded as well disposed. And not always even these; the spirits of the dead of strange hordes and tribes are all considered as hostile" (pp.39, 40). The name "Father" is given to the spirit of either parent (p.40), to that of grandfather and great-grandfather (p.41), to any spirit at all (p.41), etc. Cunow gets nowhere by this method. On p.6 he accepts the formula that religious impressions are called forth by the "impressions . . . of *social life*"(my italics, *N. B.*). But on p.17 he has already ceased to speak of the social nature of the spirit, now speaking of "its own nature, its own origin, growth and decay, *particularly death*"(Cunow's italics). But Cunow will surely not dare term birth and death as specifically social phenomena! In reality, what is true of external nature is also true of the biological nature of man: the impressions of all these phenomena, (death, sleep, trance, as well as thunderstorms, earthquakes, will-of-the-wisps, the sun, etc.) furnish a partial material out of which the total is built up from the point of view of dualism; a dualism by no means innate, but arising from the fundamental conditions of *social life.*

We are giving so much attention to Cunow because his book - on the whole quite valuable, is almost the only Marxian work on the history of religion. Eduard Meyer (*ibid.*, p.87) considers the fundamental cause for the origin of religion to lie in the direct presence of a "causality instinct" and an (also "directly given"!) dualism; man experiences within himself two parallel sets of phenomena in causal relation with each other.: on the one hand, phenomena of consciousness (feeling, conceiving, volition), on the other hand, bodily movements, arbitrary actions, resulting from the above. *"The dualism of body and soul is therefore a primitive experience, and not the product of reflection, of however primitive a nature".* This marvelous theory "on the one hand" flies in the face of the facts and "on the other hand" explains nothing: it contents itself with a description of that which requires explanation. Professor Achelis comes closer to a correct understanding of the matter (*Soziologie,* in *Sammlung Göschen,* Leipzig, 1899, pp.85 *et seq.*); he considers religious conceptions to be "merely a mirror of social-political conceptions and institutions" (p.91). Even death was able to arouse the attention of the savage, only in *society* (p.97; Achelis is closer to the truth here than Cunow). All the differentiations in political power and standing, shown by the various concrete forms of organization, are here found faithfully reflected; the chieftains and kings among men are paralleled by the great gods among the lesser spirits, the imposing figure of a more or less generally recognized ruler predominates - quite on the earthly pattern - in the motley crowd of different gods" (p.96). But Achelis' excellent (because it is Marxian) chapter on religion does not prevent him from shamefully distorting Marx, from never mentioning him by name, and from taking off his hat to religion! Here we are obviously dealing with a contradiction between the evolution of science and the interests of the bourgeoisie.

We shall now furnish examples for the correctness of the Marxian standpoint. For the ancient Babylonians (two or three thousand years before Christ), "heaven is a prototype of earth, everything earthly is created in accordance with the heavenly pattern, an indissoluble bond exists between the two" (Professor B. A. Turayev: *History of the Ancient Orient*, vol. i, p.124, in Russian). The gods are the protectors (spirits) of individuals ("God", "My God", are equivalent to our "patron saints"), of streets, cities, regions, etc. "The divinity is indissolubly connected with the destinies of its city . . its magnitude grew with the expansion of the city territory, if the inhabitants annexed other cities, the divinities of the subject peoples were subjected to the home divinity; on the contrary, the removal of a divine image from the city and the destruction of its temple were equivalent to the political destruction of the city" (p.124.). By the side of the great gods (Anu, Enlil, Ea, Sin, Shamash, etc.), there are also a number of smaller spirits, of celestial (*ihihi*) and terrestrial spirits (*anunaki*).Parallel with the formation of the Babylonian monarchy proceeds that of the celestial monarchy: "The rise of Babylon carried in its wake certain changes in its Pantheon. The god of Babylon had to take the place of honor. Such a god was Marduk, whose name was of Sumerian origin. He was the god of the sun in springtime. The dynasty of Hammurabi (a Babylonian king whose code of laws has been found in excavations on the site of ancient Babylon, N. B.) elevated him into a supreme god" (p.127). The following "evolution" took place in the case of the other great gods: "Enlil, king of heaven and earth, handed Marduk " the domination over the four lands of the world and his name as ruler of these lands." As for Ea, Marduk was proclaimed his first-born son, to whom his father had graciously ceded his rights and his power, his role in the creation of the world (p.127). When the Babylonian monarchy, had struck firm root, there "gradually arose" the conception of unified power, manifesting itself in countless visible forms, and accordingly bearing countless different names. The priests began to maintain that the other great gods were merely manifestations of Marduk. "Ninib is Marduk of Strength, Nergal is Marduk of Battle, Enlil is Marduk of Might and Dominion" (p.129). Here is a fragment of a hymn of prayer to the god Sin, excellently characterizing the monarchic construction of the celestial power: "Lord, ruler of the gods, sole great lord in heaven and on earth . . Thou who hast created the earth, founded the temples and given them names, Father, begetter of gods and men " mighty leader, whose mysterious depth has been sounded by no god " Father, Creator of all beings; Ruler, thou who desirest the destinies of heaven and earth, whose bidding is inexorable, who providest warmth and cold, who rulest living things, what god is like unto thee? Who is great in Heaven? Thou alone; and on earth who is great? When thy word resounds in the heavens, the ihihi fall into the dust, when it resounds on earth the anunaki kiss the dust . . . Ruler ! In thy rule on heaven and earth, none is like unto thee among the gods, thy brethren", etc. (quoted from B. Turayev, *ibid.*, p.144). Sin is here depicted almost as a celestial emperor, before whom all appropriate ceremonies are carried out (bending the knee, kissing the ground, etc.). It is self-evident that the official religion always has expressed chiefly the idea of the *ruling* class, as we may note even in little things. For instance, in the feudal period, when warlike virtues were esteemed highest, and the ruling class, representing particularly the warlike great landlords, only those feel at home in the hereafter who have fallen in battle, while those "for whose gifts in the hereafter no one can have much concern", namely, the poor, fare but poorly.

Max Weber furnishes us with a mass of valuable material concerning the religion of the ancient East Indians, in his interesting investigations on the economic morality of the world religions (*ibid.*, vol. ii, *Hinduismus and Buddhismus*). Here the economic and vocational stratification of society into classes directly assumes the form of castes, later confirmed by religion.

According to the old legal code of Manu, the four chief castes are - the Brahmans (priests, scholars, noble literati), Kshatryas (noble knights, warriors), Vaiçias (farmers, later also usurers and merchants), and Sudras (slaves, artisans, etc.). A caste is thus "always essentially a purely social, eventually a vocational subdivision of the social community" (p.34). The Brahmans and Kshatryas control everything and everybody. The Vaiçias are considered only as a "pure" caste, worthy of handing food or water to the Brahmans. The Sudras are divided into "pure" and "impure"; a noble will accept no water from the latter; no barber may cut the nails of their feet, etc. Below the impure Sudras there are also other "impure" castes; some may not enter any temples; others are so "impure" that even to touch them is defiling; in some cases approaching within sixty feet of such a person is an "impurity" for a noble or other "pure" person. Food is rendered "impure" by the mere glance of the "impure", etc. (p.46); even the excrement of a Brahman may have religious significance (p.62). Thousands of rulers and religious ceremonies support the existing order. Kings and rulers are descended from the Kshatryas; the aristocratic nature of the state extends also to the economic life (price-fixing, taxes in kind, national storehouses), with a monstrous bureaucratic mechanism (p.69). Max Weber considers the following as the two fundamental religious ideas growing out of this soil (pp.117-121): the idea of transmigration (*samsara*) and the doctrine of reward and punishment (*karma*). All acts of men are recorded; each has his account, his good and evil actions being balanced: after death, he will be reincarnated in the form to which the balance-sheet of his actions, at the moment of his death, entitles him. He may come to life again as a king, as a Brahman; he may be transformed into a worm in the entrails of a dog. The basis of the most important virtues is the observance of the caste order. The slaves, the impure, must know their place. He who is unfailing, who never forgets his "impurity", may perhaps in the life after death become a noble; but on earth the caste system is not to be tampered with.

"Accidents of birth" do not exist; the individual is born into the caste which is his by reason of his conduct in an earlier life (p.120). This doctrine expresses most distinctly the social order and the interests of the ruling classes, but we find this reflection even earlier. For instance, the gods of the Vedas (ancient sacred hymns) "are functional and heroic gods of a type externally similar to those in Homer, and the heroes of the Vedic period are warlike kings dwelling in mountain fastnesses and fighting in chariots, having retinues ... and with ... a predominantly cattle-breeding peasantry" (p.29). The characteristic gods are "Indra, god of thunderstorms and therefore (like Yahveh) a warlike and heroic god of impetuous character . . and Varuna, the wise, all-seeing functional god of the eternal order, particularly the legal order" . . . (p.29). It should be remembered that the heavens were originally destined only for the Brahmans and Kshatryas- (*cf.* p.119). Alongside of the official religion of the ruling classes, there was also a religion of the people, often including, among other things, sexual manipulations. The Vedas designate one of these cults as an "evil custom of the *subjected ones*". We are, therefore, dealing with class religions. For instance, here is the description of the religious split in Southern India (reminding one somewhat of the schism in the Russian Church): a portion of the *lower castes* and the *royal artisans,* coming from other parts, there opposed reglementation by the Brahmans, and thus arose the still existing schism of the Valan-gai and the Iden-gai, the castes "to the right" and "to the left" (p.324). Among the ancient Greeks, the feudal order, and later the slave order, were reflected in heaven, Zeus being the chief of all the gods, Demeter the goddess of agriculture, Hermes, the god of trade and intercourse, Hellos the god of the liberal professions (arts).

The class struggle proceeded along these lines. In Athens, in the Fifth Century (period of highest culture and incipient decay), religion was one of the chief weapons of the ruling class of the commercial "democracy". "In the opinion of Sophocles (one of the "orthodox" poets of the time, N. B.), the entire world will perish if faith ceases, for all the moral and state regulations, according to Sophocles, depend on the will of the gods" (Eduard Meyer: *Geschichte des Altertums,* vol. iv, p.140). The opposition element of the nobility and the declassed strata make use of a criticism of religion in order to criticize the existing order. The merchant democracy imposes the death penalty for expressions of doubt as to the existence of the gods.

The ancient Slavs present the same picture. Ancestor worship, worship of tribal gods, of house-gods, of vocational gods, are found here also. The most important national god was that of the traders and noble warriors, simultaneously also god of thunder: Perim. Paradise was reserved for departed princes and their retinue; there was no place for ordinary mortals (M. N. Nikolsky: *Primitive Religious Faith and the Origin of Christianity,* in Pokrovsky's *History of Russia* vol. i, in Russian; Nikolsky himself finds the origin of religion in the fear of the departed, etc.). Let us now consider the modern forms of the Christian religion. The Russian "Orthodox" Church was a precise reflection of Byzantine-Muscovite absolutism. God is the emperor; the Mother of God the empress; St. Nicholas the Wonder-Worker and the other popular saints are his ministers of state. Under them is an entire nation of officials (angels, archangels, cherubim, seraphim, etc.). Due division of labor exists between these heavenly courtiers. Saint Michael is Commander-in-Chief; the Mother of God is first lady of the court; Saint Nicholas is principally the god of fruitfulness of the soil; Saint Pantelemon is a sort of medicine-man; the victorious Saint George is the divine warrior; etc. The more distinguished saints have finer honors: better halos, fairer raiment, sacrifices. etc. The class struggle repeatedly assumed religious forms in Russia (schisms; the sects of the Stundists, the Flagellants, Molokans, etc.). We cannot pursue this subject here, but merely point out that the Russian designations for divinity distinctly indicate the true origin of these precise notions of godhood: "Lord" (*Gospod*) is practically the same as *gospodin* ("master"); "God" (*Bog*) has the same root as *bogaty* ("rich"). Ruler, heavenly father, judge, father, etc., such are the names of the feudal-noble monarch who looks upon the people as his slaves. Absolutism had good reason to be content with the "Orthodox" Church.

Religion, as a super-structure, consists not only of a system *of ideas* that have been fitted into a pattern, but like science it also has a corresponding *personal* organization (ecclesiastical organization) and a system of special methods and rules in the worship *of* God (the "services": "liturgy", high mass, low mass, with many ceremonials, conjurations, magic formulas and a great number of unintelligible magic incantations), the god's cult.

This phase of the religious superstructure is also indissolubly bound up with the course of social life. "The Church has at every epoch reproduced and repeated contemporary society within itself, in its economic and cultural traits. In the period of the feudal magnates, the church was a feudal magnate, while democratic elements and the forms of financial economy were expressed by the Church in the period of the rise of the cities", etc.[15] The original form of the professional clergyman was the sorcerer, mountebank, clairvoyant, prophet, soothsayer, etc., whom Eduard Meyer considers as the earliest social classes known to us. In general, the highest class of priests were a portion of the ruling class, reflecting its division of labor, some of the rulers becoming military leaders, others priests, others legislators, etc. It does not surprise us to find the Church "reproducing and repeating contemporary society".

The dominant church also constitutes an economic organization whose economic conditions are a portion of the general economic conditions of society as a whole. "Thus, we learn from the legal code of laws of Hammurabi, king of Babylonia, that the Temple of the god Shamash executed many transactions and usually collected 20 per cent. interest, the rate rising.to 33⁻ per cent. and even to 40 per cent. in the case of loans on grain.[16] In the Middle Ages, the Roman Catholic Church was a veritable feudal kingdom with a tremendous economic system, imposts and taxes (the so called "tithes") and administrative mechanism. Similarly, the monasteries and *lavras* (groups of monasteries) in Russia accumulated immense wealth; characteristically enough, the magnificent edifice of the Moscow Stock Exchange belonged to the Troitsa-Sergius Lavra. The Church, in addition to serving as a pacifier of the masses, restraining them from violations of the established order of things, itself was and still is a portion of the exploiting machinery, constructed according to the same general plan as the larger exploiting society.

Society, except in its initial stage, was always *class* society; its production relations were those of domination and submission; its political system was a reflection and an expression of this condition. Its religion justified this condition and secured its acceptance by the masses, sometimes by very skilful means (as in the case of the Hindoo doctrine of reincarnation and compensation, discussed .above). But this conciliation did not always last; the oppressed classes, unable to free themselves entirely from the religious mode of thought, would set up their own religion in opposition to the orthodox religion; so called "heresies" arose in opposition to the orthodox Church doctrine; we now have an official Church and also special religious groups of "dissenters", sometimes organized illegally and conspiratively, with priests and prophets of their own, who are also their political leaders.

A short time ago, such a view of religion and the church would have been considered as downright blasphemy, but even bourgeois investigators who have made a special study of the subject now accept this view. One of the best modern students of religion, Max Weber, arrives at the following conclusion with regard to Asiatic religions: "On the whole we observe everywhere the same group of cults, schools, sects, orders of all kinds, which is also characteristic of occidental antiquity. Of course, the competing tendencies were not looked upon with equal favor by the temporary majority in the ruling classes, or by the political powers. There were orthodox and heterodox persons, the former including a number of more or less legitimate schools, orders, and sects. Particularly important for us is the observation that they were distinguished from each other socially. In the first place, . . . according to the strata of society in which they existed; in the second place, however, ... according to the species of salvation ministered to the various strata of their adherents. We find the former case, where, for instance, an upper social class that rigidly condemns the entire religion of redemption is opposed by popular soteriologists [17] among the masses, as was typical of China. But we also find the various social strata following different forms of soteriology." [18] As an example of the class struggle waged under a religious flag, we may take the so called (Protestant) Reformation, the first onslaught of certain classes on feudal rule and its expression in Western Europe, the Roman Catholic Church. The ruling princes all sided with the Pope; the petty provincial nobility and the bourgeoisie with the moderates, headed by Luther; the artisans, semi-proletarians and a portion of the peasants joined the extreme sects (Anabaptists, etc., sometimes not without an element of communism). The religious struggle, slogans, groups of adherents, of the various tendencies were a precise reflection of the struggle, the aspirations, and the alignments in the socialpolitical field.

The religious superstructure is thus determined by the material conditions of human existence; its nucleus is the reflection of the social-political order of society. Other ideas group themselves about this nucleus, but their simple axis remains the social structure as transferred to the invisible world, and furthermore, as viewed from a specific class standpoint. "Soul" is here also a function of social "matter".

The following objection might be raised in the case of capitalist society: while religion continues to exist in that society-throughout Europe in the form of monotheism - the capitalist social order has different forms of bourgeois domination in politics (monarchy, republic)., and while production relations are based on domination and submission, they are not monarchic in character; the capitalist is a monarch in his own factory, but in society the class of capitalists usually does not operate through a single person. The Marxian theory affords, however, the only possible explanation of the religious forms of our day; the apparent contradiction above mentioned is easily disposed of.

In feudal society, the monarchs and princes and officials under them had control of the semi-natural economy (economy in kind) but under capitalism we have a powerful, new, impersonal regulator, of elemental nature: the market, with its incalculable caprices, exalting some and destroying the lives of others, playing with men as a blind, irrational inscrutable force. "What is our life? A trifle; let the luckless dog bemoan his lot," says the poet; divinity now distributes the lots. The Greeks and Romans already had their Parcae, their Moira, their Ananke ("necessity"), a compulsory force superior even to the gods; this conception was associated with the growth of exchange relations and the consequent commercial wars which endangered the very existence of Greece. The gods (the individual God also) have not always been disembodied spirits; they were fond of eating and drinking, they cohabited with women, assuming the form of a dove for the purpose, in the case of the "Holy Ghost". (In Greece, where homosexual practices were 'frequent, Zeus adopted the shape of an eagle in his intercourse with the boy Ganymede.) But the economic evolution which brought about an economy based on exchange and undermined the feudal political system, not only plucked from the god his eagle's and dove's feathers, but deprived him of his beard, his mustaches, and the other attributes of his previous incarnations. The pious bourgeois now believes in God as an unknown, unknowable, divine power on which all things depend, but with no external relation with man: the divinity is a spirit, not a crude aboriginal form. The condition may be stated as follows: economy is characterized, on the one hand by a relation of domination and submission, and on the other hand by unorganized exchanged relations; the preservation of religion at all is due to the former circumstance, while the latter explains the meagre and fleshless character of God today.

But we must not forget that we are here considering only the fun*damental* ideas of religion. The subsidiary notions must always be explained from the peculiar conditions of development.

In concluding our consideration of religion, we must not fail to point out that the proletariat - holding our view of religion - is faced with the necessity of *actively combating it.*Hermann Gorter, in his book *Der historische Materialismus,* not only departs from philosophical materialism, but takes a purely petty bourgeois and opportunistic view of the attitude which would regard religion as every man's private affair. His view of this attitude is that it is equivalent to our paying no attention to religion, which will disappear of itself. But nothing "disappears of itself" in society; as early as in the days of Marx, we find the latter, in a brilliant essay (*Critique of the Goths Program*),[19] poking fun at the Gorter view of "religion a private matter". Marx considers this slogan to mean merely that the workers must demand of the bourgeois state that it shall not poke its police nose into things that do not concern it; but it by no means signifies that the workers are to be "tolerant" of all the remnants of the wretched past, of all the powers of reaction. We may not regard Gorter's point of view on this subject as at all revolutionary or communist; it is a genuinely Social-Democratic point of view.

We now turn our attention to *Philosophy,* which is a meditation on the most abstract questions, a generalization of all knowledge, a science of sciences. When the sciences had not yet developed or been differentiated from each other, philosophy and religion (from which it had not yet parted company) also embraced purely scientific questions, including that fragmentary knowledge of nature and man that was available at the time. But even after the various sciences began to exist independently, philosophy still retained a field of its own, namely, the common element of all the sciences and particularly the subject of man's knowledge and of its relation to the world, etc. Philosophy must coordinate science in spite of the tatter's manifold subdivision; must furnish a common framework for all the things that are known, serving as a foundation to the total view of life (*Weltauffassung*). At the beginning of this book, we discussed the question of causality and teleology, which is not specifically a question of physics, or political economy, or philology, or statistics, but a universal concern of all the sciences: a philosophical question; similar is the question of the relation between "mind" and "matter", in other words, "thought" and "being". The individual sciences do not give special attention to this question, but it concerns them all, as do also tech questions as: do our senses correctly reflect the outer world? does this world exist as such? what is truth? are there limits, or not, to our knowledge? etc. As each science classifies and systematizes the ideas connected with its domain, so philosophy continues to assemble and systematize our total knowledge from a single point of view, thus creating an orderly structure of the whole. Philosophy might therefore be said to occupy the highest place in the human spirit and it is more difficult to trace its earthly and material origin than in the case of other subjects. Yet here again we may ascertain the same basic law of nature: the final dependence of philosophy on the technical evolution of society, the level attained by the productive forces. Inevitably, we here encounter a complicated form of such dependence, for philosophy does not issue forth directly from technology, being separated from the latter by a number of links. A few examples will make this clear. We have stated that philosophy systematizes knowledge, the general results of the individual sciences; it therefore is directly conditioned by the stage at which these sciences stand; if for any cause the social sciences develop, philosophy will shade off in that direction; but if, at the given time, the natural sciences engage the general attention, the fundamental note of philosophy will be quite different. These results are produced by the social psychology, the general mental attitude, prevailing in the given time and place, which is in turn an expression of the alignment of classes, the conditions of their existence; these "conditions of existence in general" are governed by the situation of the classes in the social economy, and the latter is the result of the given level of the productive forces. We thus find a number of links interposed between the productive forces (technology) and philosophy.

If a certain philosophic doctrine is gloomy in its nature (a pessimistic philosophy), or asserts the impossibility of all knowledge, or the vanity of all things, their frail and transitory nature, we must look for an explanation to the current psychology from which such a philosophy is born. Detailed investigation will show that such gloomy thoughts do not arise independently, but that they must express a defeat of some section or class of society, or of all classes of society; there seems to be no escape, the love of life has been lost; a gloomy philosophy is the product of this mood. Or, suppose a certain society is involved in a passionate struggle between the classes and their parties; this condition will be reflected in the philosophy of the period, for man does not lead a double life: it is the same man or the same class that is engaged in the political struggle and cogitating on the "final cause" of things. Such social struggles will place their stamp on the psychology and be reflected in the "sublimest" constructions. Or, if we assume a society whose tempo has become excessively slow: life creeping along monotonously day by day; today another yesterday, tomorrow another today, etc.; tradition, routine, time-honored precedent, control all things; no changes in technology, in social life, in science; men die, other men are born, with thoughts precisely like those of their predecessors, etc. Such a rigidity of a whole society will necessarily cause its philosophy to be based in general on the notion of immutability, of permanence. The causal chain may be traced back as follows: a philosophy of inertia; a science of inertia; a social psychology of inertia; a technology of inertia. Examples might be multiplied, but we consider that the ultimate dependence of philosophy on the social economy and technology has been proved.

The entire history of philosophic thought will support the above.

In ancient Greece, usually considered the classic home of philosophy, the earliest philosophical systems arose in the Ionic commercial cities. These cities lay on the great maritime routes between Asia Minor and Europe; the meshes of economic relations with Egypt also centered here. More than anywhere else in the world as then known (Sixth and Fifth Centuries, B.C.), trade, artisan work, and slave industry - particularly trade - were developed here. Together with economic intercourse with other countries, there was an exchange of ideas, influence of Babylon, Egypt; "cultural life" flourished. We have the beginnings of the natural sciences, astronomy, geometry, arithmetic, medicine. On this basis, the first philosophical systems also grew up: so called natural philosophy, i.e., a philosophy connected with the natural sciences, its task being to find the natural basis of all being. The Ionic school (Thales, Anaximander, Anaximenes, and their disciples) sought the unity of matter now in water, now in air, now in infinity, etc. In addition to their observations on the "essence of things", we find many scientific observations among these philosophers; Anaximander, for example, devised a geographical map that remained in use for some time. In the Ionic school, philosophical thought was not yet separated from scientific observations connected with practice. We then find a growth of wealth, its accumulation, an increase of slave labor, of parasitism in the higher classes of society; simultaneously, an increased contempt for labor, for the life of the worker, for production, for a direct engaging in trade (not through employees); all this retarded the development of scientific technical thought, transforming philosophy into a thoroughly unworldly "speculation". But it does not follow that philosophy therefore "developed out of itself"; it continued to be shaped and conditioned by the social life. For instance, let us consider the philosophy of one of the greatest Greek philosophers, Heraclitus of Ephesus; he was born in a rich commercial city which had passed through many tribulations (wars, civil wars, etc.). "In the Era of Tyrants, Ephesus was as much torn by internal dissension as any other Ionic city" (Edward Meyer, *ibid.*, p.216). The commercial aristocracy had struck deep roots here and was politically dominant over the agrarian aristocracy. Heraclitus was of an old noble family, which had retained feudal-royal traditions, "and he was, if not a partisan of the aristocrats, yet a fanatical opponent of the democracy, of rule by the blind mob" (p.217). Being a counter-revolutionary, he shunned politics himself, and he even expounded his philosophy in a particularly obscure, semi-conspirative language. "One is worth tens of thousands for me, if he is the best one," he wrote. "What manner of sense and reason have they (the present rulers, *N. B.*)? They run after minstrels and permit the mob to teach them, since they know not that most men are evil and few good. Rather than all other things, the best choose a single thing, namely, eternal fame among mortals; but the mob feed themselves like cattle" (p.218). It is to this principle of the persecuted aristocracy of birth that we must trace the philosophy of Heraclitus, born among turbulent transformations and dissensions. Society, torn by many conflicts, nevertheless exists as a whole, with all its contrasts and confusions. Such is the universe also. The essence of each thing consists in the fact that it is a whole and not a whole, concordant and discordant, constructive and destructive, one consisting of all and all of one . . . . It is precisely in these contrasts that we have the unity, the "essence of things" (p.220). It is folly to speak of peace when there is no peace; one cannot have peace when the enemy prevails. Therefore: "War is Father and King (!) of all things, he has made some men gods, others men, some slaves, others free men." "Homer, who wished to see struggle (*eris*) eliminated from among gods and men, was not aware that he was thus renouncing all new birth" (p.220). It is absurd to speak of peace when all is in commotion and change. As a matter of fact, there is nothing rigid and immutable. "We cannot step into the same river, for ever different water flows along." We hear it said everywhere that. the present order is good, but truth is relative. "The ocean is the purest and the impurest water, potable and beneficent for fishes, non-potable and ruinous for men" (p.220). It matters not that merchants and democratic upstarts now rule the city; we must not regard only the surface of things, but must penetrate below the surface: "The sense is deceived; even the eye, a better witness than the ear" (p.219). Changes are constantly maturing in life; what exists must perish. "Fire lives through the death of Earth, Air through the death of Fire; Water lives through the death of Air, Earth through the death of Water." Not only are the classes constantly succeeding one another, but social things also are constantly changing place. *"Everything is exchanged against fire, and fire against everything, as commodities against gold and gold against commodities"* (p.221). The essence of society is this substance of gold, which can purchase everything; the omnipresent and impenetrable power of gold. Therefore, Fire, the incarnation of this force, is the essence of things, the life-giving force, from which all else emanates. "The life spirit also, the soul, is Fire and warmth." Market, competition, war, are elemental in nature; they are a compulsory and omnipotent fate. Therefore God also is not a human being with curly hair, but a fleshless, inevitable universal law; "the predestined compulsion of fate (eimarmeun auaukh), imposing its eternal regulations, its 'measures' on all things, which they may not exceed without falling forfeit to the Erynnyes, the hand maidens of justice." But divinity, reason, Logos, fate, ruling the world, will ultimately reestablish justice, which has been crushed to earth; the day of judgment will come when "Fire will fall upon all things and seize and judge them." "Dike (Justice) will take hold of the architects and witnesses of falsehood" (p.222).

We can thus see the factors of the social life of his times peering through the philosophy of Heraclitus, woven in a peculiar pattern: the nature of the economy developing under the banner of gold, the class struggle, the aristocracy as an opposition party, the hope for a better future, words of encouragement, faith in victory, a support for this faith in the fact that all things are changing, the assumption of an impersonal destiny and a mysterious Reason ruling the world - these reflections of the laws of a commercial world, with competition and warfare, rejecting productive labor; the aristocrats by birth, hating the mob; the traditions of the nobility and the feudal warrior caste, etc., etc, These are the social roots of Heraclitus' philosophical constructions. Quite characteristically, while Heraclitus, a member of the opposition and representing the aristocracy, and therefore not interested in preserving the existing order of things, was defending the principle of change, of contradictions, of struggle, of dynamics, the philosophers of the other - the ruling-school - were with equal vigor defending the principle of immutability and permanence. The greatest of these philosophers was Parmenides. Anaxagoras, a close associate of the leader of the Athenian commercial democracy in the Fifth Century, Pericles, and the official state philosopher of Athens, so to speak, made a very ingenious attempt to shift the center of gravity of this passionate philosophical dispute. "The Hellenes," he taught, "have no right to speak of rising and passing away, for existing things clearly show that what is present now is produced by mixture and elimination" (Eduard Meyer, *ibid.*, p.235). In other words, Aiiaxagoras represents the point of view of gradual evolution; which is precisely what we should expect from the social position of his class. Anaxagoras, by the way, among his other ideas, also did much to advance the atomic theory.

We cannot dwell in detail here on Greek philosophy. It was manifestly incapable of finding a solution by making it up of whole cloth and elaborating intangible impressions of social life, which was meanwhile becoming more and more confused. The extremely complicated struggle and the very restless condition of the leading cities produced numerous currents, disputes, and criticisms; the social ties, standards, and traditional morals were falling into decay. Men "were becoming confused". Parallel with this tendency, the whole of philosophy accomplished a sudden shift in the direction of a so called practical philosophy, *i.e.,* considerations concerning the nature of man, morality, etc. Instead of investigating the essence of the universe, attention began now to be given to the essence of man, of standards of conduct, of duty, of "good" and "evil"; on the one hand we have the sophists, subjecting everything to their criticism, on the other hand Socrates. We have already mentioned, at the beginning of this book, the greatest philosopher of slaveholding antiquity, a man of outspoken "Black Hundred" tendencies, Plato, with his perfected system of philosophical idealism, incorporating, at one and the same time, pure reason and the Good as well as the big stick for the slaves. We may take another example, from the period of the decay of the Roman Empire, simultaneously a period of decay of the entire ancient Mediterranean civilization. The cities grew with tremendous rapidity; commodities were accumulated by plundering colonies and exploiting slaves; the ruling class was absolutely parasitic, as were also the great numbers of free *lumpenproletariat,* corrupted by state alms; the slaves were oppressed as never before; such, in broad outline, is the internal situation. Seneca, a philosopher of the Stoic school, a rich man, imparts the philosophy of life to his friend Lucilius: "What is there that can tempt you away from death? You have tasted all the enjoyments that might make you hesitate; none of them are strange to you; you have had your fill of all. You know the taste of wine and of honey; is it not a matter of indifference to you whether one hundred or one thousand bottles of them pass down your throat? Also, you have tasted oysters and crabs. Thanks to your splendid living, nothing remains untasted for you in the years that are to come. And can you not separate yourself from these things? What is it you may still have to regret? Friends? Home? Do you really value them so highly that you would sacrifice yourself for them to the extent of postponing your supper-hour? Oh, had it been in your power, you would have extinguished the sun itself, for you have accomplished nothing worthy of the light. Confess it: you are hesitating to die, not because you will be sorry to leave the Curia, the Forum, or the beauties of nature. You are merely sorry to leave the flesh-market, and yet you have already tasted all its supplies." (*Seneca: Letter to Lucilius,* here quoted from N. Vassilyev: *The Question of the Decay of the Western Roman Empire, Transactions of the University of Kazan,* vol. 31, in Russian). This is a philosophy of absolute individualism, of persons recognizing no social ties; a pessimism, an advocacy of death, a fruitless criticism of all social institutions, a worship of abstract reason which despises all things; such is the philosophy of the time. Is it not a faithful reflection of the psychology of an over-sated, decaying, parasitic class, which has lost all taste for life? This psychology is an outcome of the social-economic conditions prevailing at the time.

In the Middle Ages, the dominant system in Europe was that of feudalism, with a huge hierarchy of subjection; the Church also was constructed along these lines. Standards of law, manners, religion, all these forms of the superstructure were expressive of this system and served to consolidate it. It is obvious how significant a role must here be played by religion. For the foundation of religion is a relation of domination and subjection; consequently, particularly on the firm foundations of feudalism, a system of religious, spiritual serfdom necessarily and inevitably flourished. Therefore, philosophy also is distinctly religious in tone; it served as the maidservant of divinity (*ancilla theologiae*).

The typical orthodox philosopher of the Middle Ages, Thomas Aquinas (1225-1274; his principal work is the *Summa Theologiae,* "Theological Encyclopedia") clearly reflects the feudal conditions in his philosophy. The world is divided into two portions: the everyday visible world and the "forms inhabiting it". The highest and "purest" form is God. In addition to God, there are certain particular, specific "forms" (*formae separatae*), arranged according to certain degrees of dignity or rank: angels, the souls of men, etc. This entire philosophical system is based on the idea of constancy, of tradition, of authority. "Step by step, as the bourgeoisie developed, there also developed an immense advance of science; astronomy, mechanics, physics, anatomy, physiology, again received attention. The bourgeoisie needed, in order to develop its industrial production, a science that would investigate the properties of natural bodies and the mode of operation of natural forces. Hitherto, however, science had been only the humble handmaiden of the church. . . Now science rebelled against the church; the bourgeoisie needed science and joined in the rebellion" (Friedrich Engels: *Über historischen Materialismus, Die Neue Zeit*, 1893, vol. ii, part i, p.42). These needs for further growth were even reflected in cases where an agrarian aristocracy was at the helm. Thus, in England, the first harbinger of the great upheaval in the entire conception of the universe, and consequently in philosophy also, was Lord Francis Bacon (1561-1626). Bacon held that nature should be studied in order to be controlled. For this, we need above all "the. art of invention" (*ars inveniendi*); the old scholastic nonsense, and even Aristotle, must be thrown into the scrap-heap. Now, "the old is done for; reason is victorious" (*vetustas cessit, ratio vicit*). Marx considered Bacon as the founder of English materialism. "For him, natural science was true science and the physics of the senses was the most distinguished part of natural science . . . . In his teaching, the sciences cannot deceive us; they are the source of all knowledge. Science means experimental science; it consists of the application of a rational method to that which is perceived by the senses. Induction, analysis, comparison, observation, experiment, are the principal conditions for a rational method. Among the properties inherent in matter, motion is the first and foremost" But Marx also discovers many "theological inconsistencies" in Bacon. (Karl Marx and Friedrich Engels: *Die heilige Familie*, 1845, pp.201 *et seq.*, also quoted by Engels in *Über historischen Materialismus,* cited above.) In view of the period and the point of view of Bacon's class, we could not expect any other condition.

French materialism in the Eighteenth Century declared war most emphatically on the feudal conception of the universe, in the field of philosophy, just as the bourgeoisie was declaring war on feudal society in the field of politics and economy. This materialism supported and energetically expounded the doctrine of the English philosopher Locke, according to which man has no "innate ideas", all the psychical elements in man being merely a "modification" of feeling; this phase of the doctrine is termed *sensualism*. Feeling is declared a property of matter. Simultaneously, Locke believed in the omnipotence of human reason and of "rationalism", the whole being permeated with an individualism that is also found expressed in the field of "practical philosophy" (the "rights" of the individual, the "freedom" of the individual, etc.). This philosophy, extremely revolutionary in its time, is an outgrowth of the revolutionary position of the bourgeoisie of the period, which was destroying the feudal world, its traditions, its Church, its religion, and its theological and conservative philosophy. The revolutionary attitude of the bourgeoisie may easily be explained by the social economy of the Eighteenth Century and by the conditions of the productive forces, which had encountered, in the feudal system, a great obstacle in their development, and which, operating through the bourgeoisie, the petty bourgeoisie, the artisans, and the semi-proletarians, were obliged to break down these barriers.

In order to make the dependence of philosophy on the course of social life even clearer, we shall consider as our final example the philosophy of the bourgeoisie in the period of its decay, after the imperialist world war of i9t4-1918. The great crisis of the war, the crisis in economy, the social crisis which is bringing about a collapse of capitalism before our eyes, shattering its entire cultural structure to its very foundations, is producing among the ruling classes a psychology of despair, of profound skepticism, of pessimism, a lack of confidence in one's own forces, in the power of the intellect in general; this results in a return to mysticism, a seeking for the mysterious, an inclination toward occult rites and ancient religions, by the side of a reawakening of the modern form of parlor magic, spiritualism. In many of its traits, this philosophy recalls that of the ruling classes in the declining period of the Roman Empire. We shall close with a few specimens of this philosophy, characteristic of the collapse of capitalism.

Paul Ernst (*Der Zusammenbruch des deutschen Idealismus,* Leipzig, 1918) is our first example. Ernst offers a criticism of the capitalist organization which led to war; this blind organization oppressed the individuality of man. "Whence can a change come? There is but one way: humanity must bethink itself of itself; it must become aware of the fact that the most distinguished task imposed upon it by God (!) is that of setting goals for itself and its actions" (p.400). Ideal wisdom, says Ernst, is found in China! "We must attain clarity on the point that the foundations for the sufferings of men do not lie in institutions, but in the attitudes creating institutions " Why has capitalism never succeeded in gaining a foothold in China? For the simple reason that the Chinese loves and honors agricultural work, and always succeeds in obtaining the little parcel of land (!) that he needs, and can produce on it what is required for his simple tastes ". We want nor reforms or revolutions, but an introspective return to true morality" (pp.406, 407). The ultimate source of all the goals are men of a higher order. "The highest of our metaphysical thought we owe to men who lived naked in the for forests in India and nourished themselves on grains of rice, begged by their disciples" (p.418). Therefore, we are to infer, according to Ernst, that the highest forms and methods of knowledge are those devised by men who have sucked the divine wisdom from their own thumbs; the highest forms of life are those of the Chinese peasant and his virtuous spouse. The solution offered by present-day philosophical thinking is: a flight from civilization, which has run into a blind alley.

Hermann Keyserling says in his *Reisetagebuch eines*

Philosophen: "All truth (is) in the last analysis symbolical; the sun more correctly expresses the character of the divine . . .than does the best formulation of a conception. Therefore, all the worshipers of God are right in the eyes of God" (the author is not joking; he is serious! N. B.). "The divine reveals itself to man everywhere in the frame of his intimate prejudices." According to Keyserling, the Hindu fakirs are the ideal in faith and knowledge; for there is no cruder superstition than the belief in the insurmountable character of natural determinism. . . Man is spirit in his profoundest essence, and the more he recognizes this, the more firmly he believes it, the more of his fetters will fall away from him. It is therefore possible that, as in the Hindu myth, perfect knowledge may even overcome death (pp.282, 283). "And he who is perfectly instructed, he who is of spiritual practices, utilizes faith according to his desire as an instrument. So far had gone the greatest among the Indians. . .They knew that all religious formations were of human origin. But they sacrificed now to this god, now to that, devout in their hearts, knowing well that this practice is useful to the soul" (p.284), etc., etc.

Oswald Spengler says in *Der Untergang des Abendlandes* (München, 1920): "Systematic philosophy is today infinitely remote from us; ethical philosophy has reached its termination. There is still a third possibility, corresponding to Hellenic skepticism, within the Western mentality" (p.63). This is a skeptical *history* of philosophy. Spengler considers the entire history of humanity and puts the idea of fate in the place of the idea of causality. It devolves upon each society, according to Spengler, to accomplish a cycle, running from youth to age and terminating in death; the European cultural cycle has exhausted its creative powers and is on the downward path. Our task is to predict this downward motion and adapt ourselves to the inevitable.

The bourgeois philosophers, like the over-satisfied Roman higher bureaucrats, and the effeminate noble "sages" make journeys to foreign countries, in quest of men going about naked, in order to learn the great secret. Spengler predicts the fate of the Roman Empire for Europe, but he is reckoning without his host; while his glances have been turned to India and China, he has been blind to the proletariat at home. While in "ancient times" the lower classes were only capably of bringing about the "philosophy" of Christianity, we now have Marxian communism which cannot but gain strength in the ruins of the "Abendland" (occident). This communism has its *own* philosophy, a philosophy of action and battle, of scientific knowledge and revolutionary practice.

We thus are again led to conclude that philosophy also is not a thing that is independent of social life, but that it is a quantity that changes in accordance with the changes in the various phases of society, i.e., in the last analysis, with the changes in economy and technology.

We shall now take up another order of social phenomena - art. Art is as much a product of the social life as is science or any other outgrowth of material production; the expression "objects of art" will make this apparent. But art is an outgrowth of the social life in the further sense that it is a form of mental activity. Like science, it can develop only at a certain level of productive labor, in default of which it will wither and perish. But the subject of art is sufficiently complicated to justify an investigation of the manner in which it is determined by the course of social life; the first question requiring an answer is: what is art; what is its fundamental social function?

Science classifies, arranges, clarifies, eliminates the contradictions in the thoughts of men; it constructs a complete raiment of scientific ideas and theories out of fragmentary knowledge. But social man not only thinks, he also feels; he suffers, enjoys, regrets, rejoices, . mourns, despairs, etc.; his thoughts may be of infinite complexity and delicacy; his psychic experiences may be tuned according to this note or that. Art systematizes these feelings and expresses them in artistic form, in words, or in tones, in gestures (for example, the dance), or by other means, which sometimes are quite material, as in architecture. We may formulate this condition in other words: we may say, for example, that art is a means of "socializing the feelings"; or, as Leo Tolstoi correctly says in his book, art is a means of emotionally "infecting" men. The hearers of a musical work expressive of a certain mood will be "infected", permeated, with this mood; the feeling of the individual composer becomes the feeling of many persons, has been transferred to them, has "influenced" them; a psychic state has here been "socialized". The same holds good in any other art; painting, architecture, poetry, sculpture, etc.

The nature of art is now clear: it is a systematization of feelings in forms; the direct function of art in socializing, transferring, disseminating these feelings, in society, is now also clear.

What conditions the development of art? What are the farms of its dependence on the course of social evolution? In order to answer these questions, we must analyze an art - we have selected *Music* for this purpose - into its component parts. Our investigation will show the following elements: 1. the element of *objective material things*, the musical technology: musical instruments and groups of musical instruments (orchestra, quartette, etc.; the combinations of instruments may be likened to combinations of machines and tools in factories); also, physical symbols and tokens: systems of notation, musical scores, *etc.*; 2. the *human* organization; these include many forms of human association in musical work (distribution of persons in the orchestra, the chorus, in the process of musical creation; also, musical clubs and societies of all kinds); 3. the *formal* elements of music, including rhythm, harmony (corresponding to *symmetry* in the graphic and plastic arts), etc.; 4. the *methods* of uniting the various forms, principles of construction, what corresponds to style in some arts; in a broader sense, the type of artistic *form*; 5. the *content* of the art work, or, if we are dealing with an entire movement or tendency, the content of all the works; we are chiefly concerned here not with the *method* of performance, but with its substance, let us say with the choice of "subject" of presentation; 6. as a "superstructure of the superstructure", we may also include, in music, *the theory of musical technique* (theory of counterpoint, etc.).

Let us now consider the various causal relations between the evolution of music and social evolution in general, which is ultimately based on the economic and technical evolution of society.

First. We shall not again emphasize the fact that art may not flourish before a certain level has been attained in the productive forces of society.

Second. Only in a certain social "atmosphere" may art (and specifically, music) be singled out for development from among the innumerable forms of the superstructure. For example, in discussing the question of technology and art among the Greeks in the Fifth and Fourth Centuries B.C., we found that there was no growth of technical or natural sciences at all, but that philosophical speculation was widespread. There is no doubt that the "superstructure" in general rises at a fast pace if social technology is moving at a fast pace; but there is also no doubt that the superstructure does not move forward (or backward) *uniformly*; nor does *material* production advance uniformly; for instance, the manufacture of sausages may not keep abreast of the evolution of the productive forces to the same extent as the construction of locomotives or the production of castor oil. Certain forms of production usually develop much faster than others; in fact some such forms may be entirely absent, for certain reasons. The "superstructure" shows the same conditions: in Athens, in the Fifth Century B.C., technology fared badly, while speculative philosophy flourished. In America, in the Twentieth Century, technology is supreme and philosophy is neglected. Church hymns (a branch of the general field of music) were once universal, but it would be difficult to find many persons today - except a few :moldy old men and pious old women - who are fond of the conventional hymns. The mental "shoots" of society are the highest outgrowth of the superstructure, and we naturally expect that shoot to burgeon that happens to receive the most generous supply of sap. In ancient Athens it was an "ignoble" thing, worthy only of stupid artisans, to concern oneself with an investigation of nature by means of experiment; the disfavor in which the natural sciences were held is easy to understand; it was a result of the class alignment, of the social economy, which in its turn was conditioned by the social technology. Similarly, in the case of music, hymns might be quite important at an epoch when music still the "handmaiden" - as was also philosophy - of religion. But such hymns are as appropriate to a highly developed capitalist society as General Ludendorff's trousers to Father Sergius. The function of music in society is therefore dependent on the state of the latter, on society's mood, means, views, feelings, etc. The explanation of the latter is found in the class alignment and the class psychology, which are ultimately based on the social economy and the conditions of its growth.

Third. The "technique" of music depends in the first place on the technique of production. Savages cannot build pianos; this prevents them from playing the instrument or composing pieces for it. It is sufficient to compare the primitive musical instruments (aside from the natural instrument, the human voice), those developed from horn and pipe, from the needs of the chase,[20] with the complicated construction of the modern piano, to grasp fully the function of these instruments. "Music is not possible as an independent art until appropriate tools have taken shape and developed: the instruments and their development." [21] "Music can express the gamut of emotions only within the scale of the available instruments."[22] The production of such things as the telescope and the piano are a portion of the social material production; it is obvious that musical "technique" (now meaning the instruments) depends on the technique of this material production.

Fourth. The organization of persons is also directly

connected with the bases of the social evolution. For instance, the distribution of the members of an orchestra is determined precisely as in the factory, by the instruments and groups of instruments; in, other words, the arrangement and organization of these members is here conditioned by musical technique (in our restricted sense of the word) and, through it, based on the stage in social evolution, on the technique of material production as such. Similarly, the organization of persons in another musical field, let us say, a musical society, is the result of a number of conditions of social life, principally, a love of music (resulting from the social psychology, as above discussed), the opportunities afforded the various classes to indulge this predilection (for instance, the amount of unoccupied time available to the various classes, *i.e.*, the class alignment and the degree of productivity of social labor), which elements govern the number of members, the extent and nature of their activity, the character of the membership, etc. Or, in the case of the creative process, we also find a number of forms for the human relations involved, the oldest of which is the impersonal stage (individual names are not handed down), the so called "folk songs". Here the art work is produced in an elemental manner by thousands of nameless artists. Quite different is the case when the individual artist works "on order", by the command of a prince, king or wealthy man. The case is again different when the artist works as an artisan for an unknown market, on whose caprices he depends. An artistic production may also result when the latter assumes the form of a social service, etc. These forms of human relations are obviously based directly on the economic structure. In the slaveholding system, the musicians were slaves; not so long ago, we still had serf musicians in Russia, performing and composing not to satisfy a market requirement, but at the command of a feudal magnate. Of course, these elements are expressed in the art work.

Fifth. The *formal elements* (rhythm, harmony, etc.) are also connected with the social life. Many of these elements are already present in prehistoric times, even in the animal kingdom. Karl Bucher says [23] concerning rhythm among horses: "Rhythm springs from the organic nature of man. Every normal use of his animal body he seems to control, as a regulating element of economic utilization of energy. The trotting horse and the laden camel move as rhythmically as the rowing fisherman and the hammering blacksmith. Rhythm awakens a feeling of well-being; it therefore not only renders work easier, but is a source of esthetic pleasure and the element of art to which all persons respond, regardless of their mental nature." Quite true; but rhythm has also developed - as Bucher points out in his work - under the influence of social relations and particularly under the direct influence of material labor (the "workers' songs", like the Russian *Dubinushka*, arose on the same basis; rhythm here is an instrument of labor organization). In other words, while the formal (such as rhythm) may have arisen in prehistoric times, became man, they do not evolve from within them but under the influence of social evolution.

A further circumstance is worth mentioning. At a certain stage of development, only the simplest rhythms are available to man ("as monotonous as the singing of cannibals"); he has *no ear* for the complicated rhythm perceived by a man at a *different* stage of development. A. V. Lunacharsky, in one of his essays on art, says: "From all of the above (*i.e.,* the determining role of economy, *N. B.*) it by no means follows that . . . the forms of creative work may not have their own immanent psycho-physiological laws; they have such laws and are *entirely* conditioned by them (my italics, *N. B.*) in their specific *form,* while the content is given by the social environment." We learn later on what is meant by this: "The immanent psychological law of evolution in art is the law of complication. Impressions of similar energy and intricacy begin, after a number of repetitions, to exert less and less force on the mind, and to be capable of suggesting a lower intricacy. We experience a sense of monotony, of boredom ('it gets on my nerves'); it follows that every school of art will

243

naturally seek to make more complicated and to enhance the effect of its works" (A. V. Lunacharsky: *Further Remarks on the Theatre and Socialism*, in the collection *Verslziny*, p.196 *et seq.*, in Russian). We thus find the "psycho-physiology" contrasted with the "economy"; the "content" is left to economy, the "form" to psycho-physiology. This point of view seems to us to be at least insufficient, if not wrong. As a matter of fact, if we consider the evolution of those elements that we regard as formal, we shall find that this evolution has by no means proceeded at a uniform rate. The music of the savage, the number of harmonious tones produced by him, was very poor; yet, the social evolution itself was not characterized by great speed; manifestly the musical supply lasted for a long time, did not produce "boredom" for a long time. "Antiquity did not know our modern harmony and made use of unison arrangements; it took a long time for it to become accustomed to the octave. . . We have reason to believe that it is only recently that the fourth has been recognized as a harmonic interval" (L. Obolensky: *The Scientific Bases of the Beautiful and of Art*, p.97, in Russian). Therefore, the formal elements become more complicated as a consequence of the *more complicated structure of life* for *an increasing intricacy of life alters the psycho-physiological "nature" of man.* The "crude" hearing of the savage is as much a function of social evolution as is the "fine" hearing of the inhabitants of the great capitalist cities with their extremely delicate nervous organization. The "immanent laws" therefore, are merely another phase of the social evolution. And since the social evolution is conditioned by the evolution of the productive forces, they constitute "in the last analysis" a function of these productive forces. For, man alters his nature *in accordance with his influence on the external universe.*

Sixth. The type, the *style*, is also conditioned by the course of social life. It embodies the current psychology and ideology; it expresses those feelings and thoughts, those moods and beliefs, those impressions, those current forms of thought, that "are in the air". Style is not only external form, but also "embodied content with its corresponding objective symbols"; the history of the styles is an expression of the "history of the systems of life".[24] "The style of form is a reflex of the social vitality." [25] The religious music of the ancient Hindoo hymns (the *Vedas*) have not the same "style" or construction as - let us say - a French music-hall song or the battle-song of the revolution, the Marseillaise. These productions are the outgrowth of different environments, different social soils, and their form is consequently different; the religious hymn, the battle-song, the vaudeville song, cannot be composed or constructed in the same way; even their form expresses different feelings, thoughts, and views. This difference is a result of the difference in the situation of the societies or classes involved, and this difference is conditioned by the economic development and consequently, by the state of the productive forces. Furthermore, the style depends also in high degree on the material conditions of the specific work of art (for instance, instrumental music is conditioned by the nature of the instrument) as well as by the method of artistic creation (we have already discussed the organization of persons in music), etc. All these phases likewise depend on the fundamental causal relation in social evolution.

Seventh. The content ("subject"), almost impossible to isolate from the form, is obviously determined by the social environment, as may be readily seen from the history of the arts. It is obvious that artistic form will be given to what is engaging the attention of men in one way or another at the given moment. The creative spirit is not stimulated by subjects that do not hold its attention, but those things that constitute the central interest of society or of its various classes are given treatment, thus reflecting this general interest in the form of "mental labor". "There is indeed a certain moral temperature governing the general condition of manners and minds (*des esprits*)."[26] "The artistic family (Taine here means a specific 'school' or tendency in art. *N.B.*) is situated within a larger community; namely, the surrounding world, whose taste conforms with that of the *school*. For the state of

245

morals and of mental life is the same for the public as for the artists; the latter are not isolated men." [22] These statements by Taine are entirely correct, but Taine seems incapable of thinking them out to their ultimate conclusions, which would lead him into the acceptance of impious materialistic inferences. We have again and again discussed, in another shape, this question of the "moral of the *"milieu"*, of which Taine speaks; both "mental life" in general, feelings and moods, do not develop out of themselves; we know that this social consciousness is the social being, *i.e.,* the conditions of existence of society and its various parts (classes, groups). These conditions also give birth to the various "tastes". As a result, the content of art is also determined, in the last analysis, by the fundamental natural law character of social evolution; its content is a function of the social economy, and therefore of the productive forces.

Eighth. Musical theory is obviously directly connected with all the foregoing, and therefore "subject" to the movement of the productive forces of society.

We have outlined the fundamental chains of causality that exist in music; they do not at all exhaust the subject; in the first place, probably not all of these relations have been enumerated above, and, in the second place, there is in addition a mutual interaction of all these elements, resulting in a much more complicated and confused pattern, the general outlines of which, however, follow the scheme above indicated. Nor does it follow that the other arts will show precisely the same pattern as we have traced in the case of music. Each art has certain special earmarks: for instance, the material objects involved in singing are reduced to a minimum (there are notes, but the "musical instrument" remains the human voice alone); in architecture the role of the material, the tools, the purpose of the buildings (temple, residence, palace, museum, etc.), is of immense importance; the student must not neglect such distinctions, but we shall always find that the following holds, good: *directly or indirectly, art is ultimately determined in various' ways by the economic structure and the stage of the social technology.*

At the early stages in its evolution, when human society had barely begun to turn out surplus products, art was in direct contact with; practical material life. The earliest forms of art are the dance and; music, and so much of poetry as was involved in the combination..; The original aim of these arts was to produce a mood of unity, as a preparation for a certain act (a sort of practice or repetition of the: act itself). Among certain "savage" tribes, the "council-dances", the "terrifying war-dances", etc., accompanied by the clapping of hands,` later also by primitive musical instruments, are examples of such dances. Rhythm developed together with work, as a principle *of* organization, as is excellently shown by Karl Bücher. The "challenging" dance of the New Zealanders may be taken as an example; it is accompanied by terrible grimaces and the utterance of threats (in order to frighten the opponent); also, the dances and songs representing the chase, fishing, etc. A particularly important part is played by the so called *work-song,* constructed on the rhythm of the work performed, the text being developed from the sound involuntarily ejaculated in the course of this work. The songs of the shepherds, or of the Bedouins as they direct the steps of the camels on their travels through the desert, etc. - these are *directly* connected with the daily labor of the environment. As society grows, and new ideologies arise, as "civilization", etc., increases, art of course absorbs all these elements and ceases to be *directly* connected with the material life of production. For instance, as religion develops, music, the dance, etc., become a part of the cult. In Egypt, the ruling classes made a sort of mystery of music; the priests were scholars and musicians; religious music concerned them chiefly; the enslaved masses had their own music "at home, in the fields" (Kothe, *ibid.,* p.11). We find the same condition among the East Indians, whose musicians formed a privileged caste (special families of musicians and singers): among the Assyro-Babylonians, whose conditions required them to wage war more frequently than other nations. Their music is principally military and military-religious in character (as suggested by, the instruments: cymbals, kettle-drums, etc.). The earliest musical works of the Greeks, of which we know, were the work-songs of shepherds, and war songs ("songs of victory"); only later, songs of social and family type (laments on the dead, wedding-songs, etc.): Among the Romans, there were chiefly shepherd and peasant songs (their instrument was the reed, *fistula*) and war-songs (the loud brass instruments were first introduced by the Romans. the trumpet, *tuba;* curved horn, *lituus;* a sort of trombone, *buccina,*etc.). Similarly, the other forms of art also have their roots in practice. Primitive painting, ornament, has its origin in poetry; for example: the; ornaments in many cases still suggest the earlier combination of pot and woven basket. Furthermore, the beginnings of painting simultaneously serve as the beginnings of writing. The first step in the development of script were drawings set down to aid the memory. The Bushmen, as well as the East Indians, attempt to record certain visible objects on stone. The hieroglyphic inscriptions of the Egyptians, the Mexican symbols, are above all depictions of objects. Tattooing is closely connected with this practice. "The practice of tattooing of words and syllables developed from more primitive forms. The earliest stage was that of pictorial representations on the human body (tattooings), with the purpose not only of securing religious effects (warding off spirits, etc.), but also of making known the tribe, the rank, age, etc., of those marked in this manner" (R. Eisler: *AIlgemeine Kulturgeschichte,* 3d ed., Leipzig, 1905, p.42). Markings for the purpose of producing terror, and adornments, must also be considered here. Since such adornments had the purpose of causing admiration and producing an impression, they were used chiefly in warfare (cf. Lippert: *Allgermeine Kulturgeschichte);* they include, for instance, the "war-masks" of Germanic tribes, which were used in war, according to Tacitus (here is the germ of sculpture). Architecture is chiefly "technical" in character, as will be readily understood; originally it amounted merely to the construction of (materially) useful edifices. "The Greek temple and Gothic spire are both merely the permanent representations of useful wooden constructions" (John Ruskin: *Lectures on Art,* New York: Maynard, Merrill & Co., 1893, p.42). "The lovely forms of these were first developed in civil and domestic building, and only after their invention, employed ecclesiastically on the grandest scale" (*ibid.,* p.141). Of course, the*direct* influence of production relations made itself particularly noticeable here; in Egypt, the firm construction of the houses with their receding walls, was due to the overflowing of the Nile, as such walls were capable of offering more resistance to the rush of waters. Columns were used as props before the arch and vault were known.

In order to show the dependence of form, and therefore of style, on the social environment, we shall offer a few examples in this field, taking our material chiefly from the interesting investigations of Wilhelm Hausenstein. In the primitive reproductive arts, we may discern two periods: a purely naturalistic period (representing things as they were) on the one hand, and a conventionalized ornamentation and symbolic drawings, with little resemblance to reality, on the other. In the former case, we have drawings of bisons, horses, mammoths, reindeer, scenes of the chase, etc., found on the walls of caves, or drawn on the bones of horses, the teeth of mammoths, or reindeer antlers, etc. In the second period, we have chiefly conventionalized idols and human and animal figures. Max Verworn explains this circumstance as follows: "The palaeolithic hunter of the earlier period did not yet possess, as far as we know, the notion of the soul. " He looked for nothing behind things (*i.e.,* was not yet an animist, *N.B.*). He had no metaphysics; he concerned himself only with what he perceived, fully resembling the Bushman in this respect." On the other hand, "all tribes among whom the conception of the soul and other religious conceptions have gained a control over life, as among negroes, American Indians, South Sea Islanders, we find extremely ideoplastic (" *i.e.,* symbolic not ʻnaturalisticʼ, or in Verwornʼs words, 'physioplastie', *N. B.*) art." (Max Verworn: *Zur Psychologie der primitiven Kunst, Naturwissenschaftliche Wochenschrift,* New Series, vol. vi, Jena, 1907; also quoted by Hausenstein, *ibid.,* p.38). Hausenstein observes that Verworn does not pursue the thought to its conclusion; Hausenstein finds the nucleus of the matter in the fact that the hunter is more an individualist, the peasant more of a collectivist. But the fact of the matter is that "ideoplastic art", like religion, grows with the growth of particular conditions of production, namely, the relation of domination and subjection In the feudal era, this relation attains huge dimensions in production and ; the gulf between the slave and the despot may indicate the extent of this relation. This condition determines the specific style of all feudal eras, has brilliantly analyzed by Hausenstein. The power and domination of the divine despots, of mighty feudal kings, of Pharaohs, their unattainable sublimity, valor, audacity, etc., as opposed to common mortals - this is the essential point expressed in the feudal styles of the Egyptians, Assyro-Babylonians, of the earliest Greeks, Chinese, Japanese, Mexicans, Peruvians, East Indians, as well as in the Romanesque and early Gothic art of Western Europe (Hausenstein: *Versuch einer Soziologie der bildenden Kunst,* in *Archiv für Sozialwissenschaft und Sozialpolitik,* May, 1913, pp.778, 779). Literary examples from the epochs mentioned will support this statement. From the legal code of the Babylonian king Hammurabi, whom we have mentioned before, we take the words: "I am Hammurabi, the incomparable king. With the mighty weapon given me by Zamama and Innanna, with the wisdom given me by Ea, with the reason bestowed upon me by Marduk, I have destroyed the enemies to the North (above) and to the South (below), have terminated dissension, have bestowed prosperity upon the laid . . . .The great gods called me . . . . I am the beneficent shepherd . . . . I am Hammurabi, the King of Truth, upon whom Shamash bestowed the quality of justice. My words are good, my deeds incomparable, sublime. . .They are a pattern for the wise, to attain fame" (quoted from Turayev, *ibid.,* pp.114,

115). The following eulogy of a king is found on an Egyptian tomb: "Praise the king in your bodies, bear him in your hearts. He is the god of universal wisdom living in hearts . . . . He is the radiant sun illuminating both the earths more than the disk of the sun; he makes more things green than the great Nile; he fills both the earths with power, he is breath-giving life . . . .The king is sustenance. Multiplication is his lips, he is the begetter of what is, he is Hnum, original Father of man . . . .Battle for his name," etc. (*ibid.*, p.325). Meanwhile, "in good society", the lower stations were despised. An Egyptian father, giving paternal advice to his son, wants the latter to become a court scribe, and speaks of the lower trades as follows: "I have never seen a smith serve as an envoy, or a jeweler as an ambassador; but I have seen a smith working at his forge; his fingers were like the hide of a crocodile; he spread an odor worse than rotten fish-roe. . . The peasant wears an eternal garment (*i.e.,* never changes it, N. B.). His health may be compared with that of a man lying under a lion . . . . The weaver in his workshop is weaker than woman; his feet lie against his stomach; he has nowhere to breathe. If he does not complete his daily task, he is beaten like lotus on a swamp," etc. (*ibid.,* p.231). The Egyptian king Yakhmos says of himself: "The Asians approach full of fear and are judged by him; his sword enters into Nubia, the fear of him into the land Fenekha; the fear of his splendor is like that of the God Min," (*ibid.*, p.272). Fritz. Burger thus characterizes the ancient Egyptian, *i.e.,* feudal, art *(Weltanschaasungsprobleme und Lebenssysteme iii der Kunst der Vergangenheit*, pp.43, 44): "Egyptian art is an embodiment of the notion of immortality, not as mere symbol, however, but as a reality (the `eternal' pyramids, of unusual permanence, statues, etc., *N. B.*). . . A powerful suggestion of force emanates from them; they make us bend the knee; they have the awe-inspiring quality of a higher existence incorporated within them they bear witness to the disciplined strength of life in its dreadful tension, to a super-personal eternal power, whose pride keeps us at a distance, to the soulless severity of a being that is indifferent to all mere matters of detail; they reflect the brilliancy of their master's light, as remote as the stars." Therefore: "Every feudal civilisation carries on a worship of quantity" (Hausenstein: *Die Kunst und die Gesellschaft*, p.46). The huge pyramids, the gigantic monuments of the Pharaohs or the Assyrian-Babylonian kings, are a form of greatness and might; art is monumental and frontal; the "interior decoration" of the present-day bourgeoisie would not have sufficed for feudal conditions; the bearing of the figures of rulers is prescribed exactly: upright stature, not human, but half divine, as opposed to the slaves and ordinary mortals (the ancient Greeks designated the bearing of a slave, etc., by the word *proskynesis, i.e.,* "dog-like creeping"). One of the best specialists on Egypt, Ehrmann, maintains that the human body is represented in a number of different forms in Egyptian painting, according to the social rank: it is natural for ordinary mortals, conventionalized for superiors; virile power is represented by a wide chest, not foreshortened as perspective would require; among the Egyptians, the chest is always given its full width, even if the figure stands in profile. The same spirit also prevailed in archaic, feudal, early Greek art (the heroic "energetic power of early Attic art", "the severe energy of the Dorians", the so called "Doric style"; (*cf.* B. Haendcke: *Entwicklungsgeschichte der Stilarten,* Bielefeld-Leipzig, 1913, p.10). Approximately the same condition is found among the East Indians, Peruvians, Mexicans, Chinese and Japanese. "When the Mexican Aztec succumbed to the Conquistadors under Hernando Cortez, the style of this kingdom was almost identical both socially and aesthetically with the style of the feudal despotism," (Hausenstein, *ibid.*, p.77). In literature we find in addition to the eulogies of kings, in inscriptions and elsewhere, also heroic warlike epics, and the heroic-knightly drama; among the Greeks, the Iliad and the Odyssey; among the Japanese, the knightly drama, glorifying the fidelity of the Samurai, who were the feudal masters; among the Incas, likewise the heroic drama, etc. A divine sublimity, a crude strength, both inaccessible to ordinary mortals, are expressed also in medieval European art, particularly in the architecture of the cathedrals, built in the course of many years by great numbers of unknown persons; later, in the bourgeois epoch, these gloomy and solemn structures began to be designated as "citadels of the spirit".

The transition from the feudal style to the bourgeois styles begins everywhere with the growth of trade, of commercial capital, or trade. capitalist relations, in the Athens of the Fifth Century, in the Italian commercial city republics of the Renaissance, later in the commercial cities of all Europe. The process was finally completed with the definite collapse of feudalism, *i.e.,* with the victory of the French revolution (1789-1793). In the place of the masses, held down by the feudal system, by the scale of hierarchic relations, we have the bour*geois individual* with his commercial calculations, his thoughts of profit, "a man and a citizen". In music the situation is as follows to the Sixteenth Century, the *community*principle prevailed (i.e., in the sense of feudal restrictions, serfdom, but after all a form of organization, *N. B.*); the individual was relegated entirely to the background. He was absorbed in the family, the community, the Church, the guild or brotherhood, the state. Accordingly, choral music was the prevalent form of the times. But now the individual also wished to make himself felt (*i.e.,* the energetic, vigorous bourgeois individual, then still "young" eager for knowledge, capable of practical calculations, *N. B.*),and therefore we find individual singing and . . . the musical drama growing up by the side of the chorus" (Kothe, *ibid.,* p.159*).* The new musical style (*stile rappresentativo, i.e.,* the style of theatrical performances, of opera, of drama), practically constituted a transition to recitative, *i.e.,* half singing, half conversation; melody, rhythm, etc.; all were subordinated to a faithful representation of the words of the text. ("It is extremely interesting to note the concomitants of the circumstance that this new musical style arose simultaneously in three quarters," writes Kothe, *ibid.,* p.161, "so that it is difficult to determine the real `inventor'." The reader should recall, in this connection, Bordeaux' remark concerning the similar condition in science, already mentioned in our discussion of that "superstructure"). The trained merchant replaced the royal-feudal religious banner with a desire for the earthly, for the individual human. Leonardo da Vinci, one of the greatest artists of all times and peoples, and one of the most significant of all humans, magnificently expressed the new tendency of thought in many fields: as a philosopher, inventor, natural scientist, mathematician, an incomparable artist, and even as a poet. "Leonardo renounces all mysticism. He reduces the fact of human life to the law of circulation, well known and well drawn by him. With cold cynicism, he analyzes the structural laws of the world of human forms, and with an intellectual brutality that is above all sentimentality, he graphically depicts the sexual act... He approaches the problem of light by the path of knowledge; the influence of light and atmosphere on form becomes the problem of experimental optics. The rhythm of graphic composition is for him a geometrical secret; the wonderful panel with Saint Anna, the Madonna, the Jesus child, and the Lamb, is doubtless the outcome of very exhaustive mathematical combinations, of painful thought concerning the theory of curves" (Hausenstein, *ibid.*, pp.100-102). Realism, rationalism, individualism, these are the "-isms" of the Renaissance. In poetry, the path of transition from the Medieval-Gothic style to the new style is successively marked by Dante, Petrarch, Boccaccio, etc. The "content" of this art is a criticism of feudal churchdom, a rejection of the feudal style in favor of an elegant style of the world; realistic, but also personal, individual. The connection with the social life is here clearly evident.

Unfortunately we cannot dwell on all the art forms, for instance, on the Baroque, on which, by the way, we have an excellent Marxian work by Hausenstein, *Vom Geist des Barock*(München, 1920). We shall proceed at once to the modern period. Just before the French Revolution, the so called Rococo style prevailed, the social basis of which was the rule of the feudal aristocracy and the financial oligarchy (haute finance), parvenus who bought ducal and princely titles and adopted aristocratic manners. Positions of tax-farmers were sold, manipulations and dubious financial operations were carried on on the Stock exchange; commercial and colonial policy, domination by the nobility, which needed money and sold its titles, rich burghers who bought these titles (also purchasing the young scions of the nobility "as husbands for their daughters), etc., such was the environment "up above". This environment determined the manners peculiar to this gallant "period". Life was dominated by love, not as a powerful passion, but in the form of philandering, which had become the trade of elegant idlers. The ideal type was that of the specialists in deflowering virgins (the *deverginateur*); the frivolous doctrine of the "proper moment" for this operation constituted practically the spiritual axis of the age. Rococo art, with its delicate and absolutely erotic curves, is a perfect reflection of these traits in the social psychology (*cf.* Hausenstein: *Rokoko; Französische und deutsche Illustratoren des XVIII Jahrhunderts,* München, 1928). With the growth of the bourgeoisie, with their battle and victory, a new style was brought forth, the best representative of which is, in French painting, David. This style was the embodiment of the bourgeois virtues of the revolutionary bourgeoisie: the ancient "simplicity" of its forms expressed its "content", concerning which Diderot wrote that art must have the purpose of glorifying great and fine deeds, of honoring unhappy and defamed virtue, of branding flagrant vice and of inspiring tyrants with fear. Diderot also advised dramatists "to get close to real life"; he himself blazed the trail in literature for the so called "bourgeois drama" (*Cf.* Fr. Muekle: *Das Kulturproblem der französischen Revolution,* vol. i, Jena, 1921, pp.177 *et. seq.*); which was called *le genre honnête* (Beaumarchais' *Le Mariage de Figaro* may be taken as a specimen). The social roots of this *genre honnête* are perfectly manifest. If, after having viewed a painting by Watteau, of the Rococo School, we return to our room and open J. J. Rousseau's *Nouvelle Héloise,* we shall find we have entered a different sphere (George Brandes: *Main Currents of the Nineteenth Century Literature,* New York, vol. i, p.17). This changed *artistic* sphere corresponds closely with the changed *social* sphere; the burgher has become the hero in the place of the enervated parlor butterflies of the aristocracy, and he begins to create his *genre honnête.*

For purposes of contrast, it would be very interesting to consider the art of the dying bourgeoisie. This art has been expressed with `particular sharpness in Germany, where, by reason of the military collapse and the Peace of Versailles, on the one hand, and the constant menace of a proletarian uprising on the other hand, the general basic note in the life of the bourgeoisie has become particularly gloomy; where the capitalist mechanism is deteriorating most rapidly, and where, therefore, the process of "unclassing", of transforming bourgeois intellectuals into human "riff-raff", is rapidly proceeding, into individuals thrown from their course by the pressure of great events. This condition of hopelessness is expressed in a strengthening of individualism and mysticism. There is a convulsive grasping for a "new style", for new forms of generalization, without any possibility of finding them; each day brings some new "-ism", which does not hold the ground for long. Impressionism is followed by Neo-Impressionism, then by Expressionism, etc. A vast number of tendencies and experiments, an accumulation of paper theories, but no reasonably solid synthesis. This may be observed in painting as well as in music, poetry, sculpture, in short, all along the line. Bourgeois reactionaries, timidly recording the gradual disintegration of their culture, of their:: class, formulate this process in some such way as this; a faith in the mysterious is developing; a belief in witchcraft and miracle-workers, in spiritualism and theosophy. "The head of a group of so called occult devotees writes book after book and delivers lecture after lecture " Diligent spiritualists, Christian Scientists, or theosophists, have a lot to say, but are neither moved by the alleged revelations,`nor moving by their communication" (Max Dessoir: *Die neue Mystik und die neue Kunst,* in *Die Kunst der Gegenwart,* Leipzig, 1920, p. 130). "Our latest artists also maintain that what they create is the expression of the*contents of visions* (my italics, *N. B.*), and that each art work consists of 'ecstatic gestures' of the soul" (p.132). We are asked to consider this as an expression of magic idealism; "in poetry, sacrificing the sentence to the word, or even Dadaism (the derivation of this name from 'da-da', the earliest sound produced by infants, is illustrative of the childish attitude characteristic of this tendency, N. B.) ; in painting and sculpture, a crude childish trifling " Christian Scientists, astrologers and their ilk, distort the admitted fact that wisdom is not exhausted by the logic of syllogisms, into a laudation of prenatal negro metaphysics" (*ibid.,* pp.133, 134). Little closed groups, cliques, leagues, are promulgated, within which the. artists surrender themselves to a mysterious contemplation of the hereafter and the joys of this wondrous creation. Together with this tendency, we find an inclination toward "emotional communism", an indication of the profound fall of the bourgeoisie as a class. Mysticism is therefore triumphant. Jules Romains (*Manuel de deification,* quoted by Dessoir,*ibid.,* p.137), requires "a state of mystical rapture as a condition for the conquest of the world by art", and Dessoir, having become sufficiently tired of this image, expresses the single hope that this unhealthy mysticism may in some way be healed by a return to the path of faith in the God of earlier days! (p.138). An expressionist theorist, Theodor Daubler (*Der neue Standpunkt,* Leipzig, 1919, p.180), excellently expresses this essentially and profoundly individualist point of view of the disintegrated social atoms: "The: center of the world is in every ego, even in the ego-justified work." Of course, this point of view leads to mysticism. "We hear everywhere pronounced the cry: 'Away from nature!' It is obvious what this means, as far as expressionist poetry and graphic art are concerned: a departure from what is supplied us by the senses, a transcending of the limits of sensuous experience, a tendency to elevate oneself to that which lies behind phenomena" (*ibid.*, p.142). In music we are led to super-music, to anti-music, without harmony, with. out rhythm, without melody, etc. (Arnold Schering: *Die expressionistishe Bewegung in der Musik,* in the work already quoted, *Einführung in die Kunst der Gegenwart,* pp.142 *et seq.*). A general social evaluation of all this business from the point of view of capitalist culture is given by Max Martersteig (*Das iiingste Deutschland* in *Literatur and Kunst, ibid.*, p.25): "The states of rapture produced by the suffering of monstrous things must yield place to reason. No variety of war psychosis or disarmament psychosis may any longer, serve as an excuse for fragmentary and anarchic work." The author invokes a spirit of "highest responsibility", but his invocations will be of no avail, for it is impossible to find a new sublime synthesis in the decaying temple of capitalism; debris and ruins, an incoherent mystical babbling and the "ecstasies" of theosophical sects, will now be inevitable. Such always has been the case in civilizations destined to early extinction.

We shall also say a few words on fashions, which have already been touched upon. In certain respects, fashions are related to art (in "*style*": *e.g.*, the garments and costumes of the Rococo period corresponded perfectly with the Rococo art). In other traits, fashion is connected with standards of conduct, with the rules of decency, customs, etc. Fashions therefore also develop in accordance with the social psychology, the succession of its forms, the rate of change, depending in turn on the character of this social development. Here, for instance, we find the roots of the inordinately swift changes of fashions at the end of the capitalist period. "Our inner rhythmics (corresponding to the headlong course of life, *N. B.*) require shorter and shorter periods for each new impression" (Georg Simmel: *Die Mode,* Leipzig, 1918, p.35). Wherein lies the social significance of ions? What is their role in the current of social life? Here is Simmel's brilliant answer: "They are . . . a product of the division along class lines, the case being similar to that of a number of other social formations, particularly with honor, having the double function of holding a group together and at the same time keeping it separate in other groups . . . . Thus, fashions on the one hand express one's connection with those of equal rank, the unity of the circle defined by these fashions, and simultaneously the exclusiveness of this group as opposed to those further down in the scale" (*ibid.*, pp.28, 29).

Language and *thought,* the most abstract ideological categories *of* the superstructure, are also functions of social evolution It has sometimes been fashionable among Marxists or pseudo-Marxists to declare that the origin of these phenomena has no relation with historical materialism. Kautsky, for example, went so far as to claim that the powers of human thought are almost unchanging. Such is not the case, however; these ideological forms, so extraordinarily important in the life of society, constitute no exception to the other ideological forms of the superstructure in their own origin and evolution.

A preliminary question must first be disposed of: namely, the doubt that at once appears in a discussion of language and thought. It is customary to admit that language is a social relation, a tool in the intercourse between men, an instrument of cohesion; and that Marx is right when he states that it would be absurd to speak of an evolution of language if men did not speak to each other. But the case with thought seems different, for each individual thinks, has his own brain, and only a mystic could attempt to seek the roots of this individual human thought in society. This objection is based on an incomplete understanding of the close relation between thought and language. Thought always operates with the aid of words, even when the latter are not spoken; thought is speech minus sound. The process of thinking is a process of combining concepts, which are always dealt with in the form of word symbols. A person who has made excellent progress in a foreign language may begin to think in that language. In fact, it is easy to find illustrations, in the reader's own experience, of the fact that the process of thought, of rumination, is accomplished with the aid of words. This being the case, and if we admit that speech is associated with society in its origin as well as in its growth, it results logically that the same must be true of thought. And the facts show that the evolution of thought has coincided with that of language. One of the most distinguished philologists, Ludwig Noiré, says: "The social activity directed *toward* a common goal, the most ancient *labor* of the elders of the clan, is the source from which language and reasoning originated."[28] Human speech is as much an outgrowth of the sounds ejaculated during labor as are music and song. Philology has shown that the original basis of the vocabulary is the so called action roots, the earliest words being such as designated chiefly an action (verbs). In the later growth of language, objects also received their designations (nouns), insofar as these objects were prominent in the labor experience of man; such names were given chiefly to the tools used, and were developed from the verbal terms for the actions involved. Parallel with this evolution proceeded the consolidation of more definite *concepts* out of the mass of material which - figuratively speaking - filled man's head, echoed in his ears, appeared before his eyes, etc. But the *concept is* the *beginning of thought.*

The further evolution of thought and language proceeds along the lines followed by the other forms of the ideological superstructure; namely, they follow the evolution of the productive forces. In the course of this evolution, the external world ceases to be a world *per se,* becomes man's world; ceases to be mere matter, becomes material for human action; instruments of material labor, coarse at first, later more and more delicate, as well as instruments of scientific knowledge, together with the countless "feelers", such as machines, telescopes, acute reasoning, aid society in its annexation of more and more of this external world to society's sphere of labor and knowledge. A vast number of new concepts, and consequently of new words, is the result; language his enriched and is made to include the totality of subjects that constitute the concern of human thought and speech, *i.e.,* of human communication.

The "fullness of life" results in the "richness" of language. As some shepherd tribes ("pure cattle breeders") have no subject of conversation but their cattle, owing to the fact that the low level of their productive forces restricts their entire life to the sphere of production, and their language therefore remains directly connected with the process of production. If, as a result of enhanced productive forces, a huge and complicated ideological superstructure has been erected, language will of course embrace this superstructure also, *i.e.,* the connection of language with the process of production is more and more indirect; the dependence of language on the technique of production is now an indirect dependence; the causal chain now runs *through* the dependence of the various superstructural forms on the process of production, and even the latter dependence may no longer be a direct one. The increased :number of words borrowed from foreign languages is a good example of the manner in which language grows. Such borrowings result from an economy of universal dimensions and the development of a number of practically identical things in many countries, or of events having universal significance *(telephone, aeroplane, radio, Bolshevism, Comintern, Soviet,* etc.). It would lead us too far afield to point out in detail that the character, the *style* of a language also changes with the conditions of the social life; but it is worth while to mention that the division of society into classes, groups, and occupations also impresses its mark on a language; the city-dweller has not the same language as the villager; the "literary language" is different from "common" speech. This difference may become so great as to prevent men from understanding each other; in many countries there are popular "dialects" that can hardly be understood by the cultured and wealthy classes; this is a striking example of the class cleavage in language. And the various occupations have their special languages; learned philosophers, accustomed to dwell in a world of subtle distinctions, write - and sometimes even speak - a language that only their fellows can understand. The desire to indulge in such forms of expression is partly due to the same cause that produces fashions in dress; namely, to distinguish these persons from "everyday mortals". Thus, a Russian noble landowner would show his "class" by bringing back with him from Paris, clothes of foreign design, an expensive mistress, and an accentuated pronunciation of the letter *r*. Wundt shows that the peculiar intonation of the Puritans also had this social character; they not only took the names of patriarchs and prophets, but even imitated in their speech the chanting tones in which the Bible is still read aloud in the Jewish synagogues. Wundt rightly observes that the philologist cannot afford to consider language as a phenomenon that is isolated from human society; on the contrary, our conjectures as to the evolution of linguistic forms must accord with our view of the origin and evolution of man in general, the growth of the forms of social life, the origin of customs and law.

Thought has not always followed the same lines. Certain respectable scholars find that science originates in man's mysterious and universal inclination toward causal explanations, but they do not consider the question of the cause of this extremely laudable tendency. But we may now consider the mutability of the types of thought to have been definitely established. Thus, Lévy-Brühl devotes a whole book [29] We are quoting chiefly from Professor A. Pogodin's Russian work, *Border-Regions between the Animal and Human*, in *New Ideas in Sociology*, Collection No.4 to the mode of thought of savages, which he considers entirely different from the present "logical" thought, terming it pre-logical. In savage thought, details and specific things are often not distinguished from the general or even the whole; one thing is confused with another. The entire world is not a system of things, but a system of mobile *forces*, man being one of these; individual man is not a personality: personality is absolutely socialized, being absorbed in society and not distinct from the latter. The "fundamental law" of savage thought is not the concept of causal succession, but what Lévy-Brühl terms the law of "participation" (*loi de la participation*), if it is possible to exert an influence on any object under conditions which-from our point of view-preclude such a possibility. "The law of participation permits him to shift from the individual to the group and from the group to the individual without the slightest difficulty. Between a bison and bisons in general, between a bear and bears in general, between a reindeer and reindeers in general, this psychology accepts a mystical participation.[30]

This psychology has no place for the species as an aggregate, or for the individual existence of its members, in our sense of these words." Lévy-Brühl himself finds a connection between this type of thought and a certain type of social existence, in which personality had not yet been differentiated from society, i.e., he connects this stage of thought with primitive communism.

Causality, as found among savages, is not *our* causality, but an animistic causality, the result of the inclination of the savage to seek a spiritual, divine, or daemonic principle operative in all situations. All things that come to pass have been "ordained" by someone: *cause* seems identical with a *command* emanating from a superior spirit. The law of causal succession becomes the whim of the Supreme Being, the spiritual ruler (or rulers) of the universe. Therefore, while the tendency to seek causes seems to be present in man, savage man seeks causes of a specific kind, causes emanating from a certain higher power. Of course, this type of thought is also related with a certain social order. It is typical *for a society that already shows the presence of a hierarchy in production and social polity.*

The further course of development presents the same process; it has already been touched upon in our discussion of philosophy. The above examples suffice to show that *thought and the forms of thought are a varying quantity, and that this variability is based on the variability in the evolution of society, its organization of labor, and its technical backbone.*

An excellent recapitulation of this subject is the magnificent formulation made by Karl Marx in his *A Contribution to a*

Critique of Political Economy:

"In the social production of their lives, men enter into specific, necessary relations, independent of their wills, production relations, which correspond to a certain specific stage in the evolution of their material productive forces. The totality of these production relations constitutes the economic structure of society, the real basis, over which there rises a legal and political superstructure, and to which there correspond specific social forms of consciousness. The mode of production of material life conditions the social, political, and mental life-process in general. It is not the consciousness of men that determines their being, but, on the contrary, their social being determines their consciousness" (*Zur Kritik der politischen Okonomie*, Stuttgart 1915, p.IV.).

The huge "superstructure" that rises over the economic basis of society is of rather intricate internal "structure". It includes material things (tools, instruments, etc.), the most various human organizations, furthermore, strictly coordinated systems of ideas and forms; furthermore, vague, non-coordinated thoughts and feelings; finally, an ideology "of the second degree", sciences of sciences, sciences of arts, etc. We are therefore obliged, in 8t precise analysis, to resort to a certain definition of terms.

We shall interpret the word "superstructure" as meaning any type of social phenomenon erected on the economic basis: this will include, for instance, social psychology, the social-political order, with all its material parts (for example, cannons), the organization of persons (official hierarchy), as well as such phe. nomena as language and thought. The conception of the superstructure is therefore the widest possible conception.

The term "social ideology" will mean for us the system of thoughts, feelings, or rules of conduct (norms), and will therefore include such phenomena as the content of science (not a telescope, or the personal staff of a chemical laboratory) and art, the totality of norms, customs, morals, etc,

Social psychology will mean for us the non-systematized or

but little systematized feelings, thoughts and moods found in the given society, class, group, profession, etc.

e. Social Psychology and Social Ideology

In our treatment of science and art, law and morality, etc., we were dealing with certain unified *systems* of forms, thoughts, rules of conduct, etc. Science is a unified, coordinated system of thoughts, embracing any subject of knowledge in its harmony. Art is a system of feelings, sensations, forms. Morality is a more or less rigid coordination of rules of conduct giving inner satisfaction to the individual. Many other ideologies may be similarly defined. But social life also includes a great mass of incoherent, non-coordinated material, by no means presenting an appearance of harmony, for instance, "ordinary, everyday thought" on any subject, as distinguished from "scientific thought". The former is based on fragments of knowledge, on disorderly, scattered thoughts; it is a mass of contradictions, or incompletely digested notions, freakish conceptions. Only when this material has been subjected to the sharp test of criticism, and stripped of its contradictions, do we begin to approach science. But, alas, we live in "every-day" life! Among the countless mutual interactions between men, out of which social life is built up, there are many such non-coordinated elements: shreds of ideas (yet expressing a certain knowledge), feelings and wishes, tastes, modes of thought, undigested, "semi-conscious", "vague conceptions of God" and "evil", "just" and "unjust", "beautiful" and "ugly", habits and views of daily life; impressions and conceptions as to the course of social life; feelings of pleasure or pain, dissatisfaction and anger, love of conflict or boundless despair, many vague expectations and ideals; a sharp critical attitude toward the existing order of things, or a delighted acceptance of this "best of all worlds"; a sense of failure and disappointment, cares as to the future, a bold burning one's bridges behind one, illusions, hopes of the future, etc., *etc., ad infinitum.* These phenomena, when *of social* dimensions, are the *social* psychology. The difference between the social (or "collective") psychology and ideology is merely in their degree of systematization. The social psychology has often been apparent in bourgeois society in the mysterious envelope of the so called "popular spirit" or Zeitgeist, frequently conceived as a peculiar single social soul, in the literal sense of the word. But, of course, a *folk-soul,* in this sense, does not exist, any more than there can exist a society which is an organism with a single center of consciousness. Society then becomes a huge monster lying in the midst of nature

In the absence of such an organism, we can hardly speak of a mysterious folk-soul or a "popular spirit", in this mystical sense. Yet we do speak of the *social* psychology, to distinguish it from the individual psychology. This apparent contradiction may be answered as follows: the mutual interaction between men produces a certain psychology in the *individual.* The "social" element exists not between men but in the brains of men; the contents of these brains are a product of the various conflicting influences, the various intersecting interactions. No mental life exists except that which is found in the individual "socialized" human being, who is subject to all such interactions; society is an aggregate of socialized humans and not a huge beast of whom the individual humans are the various organs.

G. Simmel excellently describes this: "When a crowd of people destroy a house, pronounce a judgment, utter a cry, we here have a summation of the actions of the individual persons, constituting a single event recognized as a realization of a *single* conception. A frequent confusion takes place here: the *single* physical *result of many,* subjective mental processes is interpreted as the result of a single *mental process, namely, a process in the collective soul"* (G. Simmel: S*oziologie; Untersuchungen über die Formen der Vergesellschaftung,*Leipzig, 1908, pp.559 560). Or - to use another example - when some new and greater thing than their individual aspirations or actions arises from the mutual interaction of men, "when examined closely " we find that such cases also involve the conduct of *individuals,* who are influenced by the fact that each is surrounded by other individuals; this results in nervous, intellectual, suggestive, moral transformations of man's mental constitution as compared with its operation with regard to different situations, in which such influences are absent. If these influences, mutually interacting, produce an internal modification in all the members of the group, in a like direction, their total action *will* no doubt have a different aspect from that of each individual, if each had been placed in a different, isolated situation" *(ibid.,* p.560).

Yet such words as *Zeitgeist, popular mood,* etc., are not without meaning: they indicate the existence of two conditions that may be noted everywhere: they indicate the real existence, first, of a certain predominant current of thoughts, feelings, moods, a prevailing psychology, at any given time, giving color to the entire social life; second, the alteration of this prevailing psychology according to the "character of the epoch", i.e., according to the conditions of social evolution.

The prevailing social psychology involves two principal elements: first, *general psychological traits,* perhaps found in all classes of society, for the situations of the various classes may have certain common elements in spite of class differences; second, the psychology of the ruling class, which enjoys such prominence in society as to set the pace for the entire social life and subject the other classes to its influence. The former case is illustrated in the feudal eras, in which the feudal lord and the peasant present certain common psychological traits: love of traditional practices, routine, submission to authority, fear of God, generally backward ideas, suspicion of innovation, etc. This results from the fact that both classes live in a stagnant and almost inert society; the more mobile psychology is later developed in the cities. Another cause of this condition is the unlimited authority enjoyed by the feudal lord on his estate and by the peasant in his family. The family then was an organized labor unit; in fact, the labor bond remains an important element in the peasant family to this day. The authority of the feudal lord is therefore found paralleled in the patriarchal order of labor relations in the family, as expressed in the complete submission to the "head of the family": "the old man knows!" At a certain stage of social evolution, the *Zeitgeist* was a conservatism of feudal nobility and peasant serf. In addition, of course, the prevailing social psychology also presents factors characteristic of the feudal lords alone, which were disseminated only by virtue of the dominant position of the feudal nobility.

Much oftener, however, we encounter cases in which the social 'psychology, i.e., the prevailing social psychology, is that of the ruling class. In the second chapter of the *Communist Manifesto*, Marx says: "The prevailing ideas of a period have always been simply the ideas of the ruling class." The same might be said of the social psychology prevalent at a given time. Our discussion of ideologies has already shown a number of examples of feelings, thoughts, moods, predominant in society. Let us examine a specific case: the psychology of the Renaissance, with its highly developed pursuit of pleasure, its parading of Latin and Greek words, its ingenious erudition, its love of distinguishing one's own ego from the "mob"; its elegant contempt for medieval superstition, etc.; this psychology obviously has nothing in common with that of the Italian *peasantry* of the same epoch; but was a product of the commercial cities, and of the *financial* cities, of the *financial-commercial aristocracy* in those cities. At precisely this period, *the* city began to control the provinces; the cities were ruled by bankers, who married into the families of the prominent nobility. The psychology of this class was the ruling psychology; it is expressed in many monuments - literary and other monuments - of the epoch. The development of the productive forces among *the* ruling class causes mighty levers to be fashioned for molding *the* psychology of the other classes. "The three or four metropolitan sheets will, in our future, determine the opinion of the provincial papers and therefore the *popular will*", is the frank statement of Oswald Spengler,[31] the philosopher of the German bourgeoisie of the present day.

Yet, it is obvious that no *permanent,* uniform, integral "social psychology" may exist in a class society; at most there are certain common traits, whose importance should not be exaggerated.

The same applies to so called "national characteristics", "race psychology", etc. It goes without saying that Marxists do not "in principle" deny the possibility of certain common traits in all the classes of one and the same nation. In one passage, for instance, Marx even allows for a certain influence of race, in the following words: "The same economic basis - the same in its principal conditions - may present infinite variations and gradations in their manifestation, owing to countless different empirical circumstances, natural conditions, racial relations, historical influences working from without, etc., which cannot be understood without analyzing these empirically given circumstances" (Marx: *Capital,* vol, iii). In other words, if any two societies are passing through the same stage of civilization (feudalism, let us say), they will nevertheless present certain (perhaps unimportant special traits. These special traits are the result of certain deviations: in the conditions of evolution, as well as of the special conditions of evolution in the *past,* It would be absurd to *deny* such peculiarities, as it is impossible to deny certain peculiarities in the "national character," "temperament," etc. To be sure, the presence of a class *psychology* may by no means be taken as a proof of certain special "national" traits (Marx, for instance, spoke of the philosophy of Bentham as a "specifically English" phenomenon; Engels described the socialism *of* the economist Rodbertus as a "Prussian junker socialism," etc.). We may therefore also agree with Dr. E. Hurwicz - now Cunow's companion-in-arms in the noble task of destroying the Bolsheviks - when he writes: "Vocational psychology does not exclude the possibility of national psychology", and "the psychology of caste does not differ in this respect from the local psychology:

neither precludes the possibility of a national psychology" (E. Hurwicz: *Die Seelen der Völker,* Gotha 1920, pp.14, 15). But the facts are these: Marxists *explain* these national traits on the basis of the actual course of social evolution; they do not merely point at them; in the second place, they *do* not overestimate these peculiarities, or remain oblivious of the forest because of its many trees, while the worshipers of "national psycholy," etc., lose sight of the forest altogether; in the third place, they do not set down the absurd things cooked up by learned and unlearned babblers and philistines on the subject of the "national soul". Everyone knows, for example, that any Russian philistine considers philistinism to be a permanent and immutable quality of the Germans; yet the German workers are now proving that such is not the case. We all know also how much humbug has been written about the "Slavic spirit". When Hurwicz exclaims with rapture that Bolshevism is merely a topsy-turvy Tsarism, that the government methods in both cases are the same, etc., he reveals to us not the properties of the *"Russian* spirit", allegedly responsible for this similarity, but the qualities of the spirit of an international *petty bourgeois,* now serving *as a* prop to the Social-Democratic parties.

The class psychology is based on the aggregate of the conditions of life in the classes concerned, and these conditions are determined by the position of the classes in the economic and social political environment. But the intricacy of any social psychology must not be overlooked. For example, similarities of *form* may be found in quite different class psychologies; thus, two classes engaged in a life and death struggle with each other of course represent an entirely different content of feelings, aspirations, impressions, illusions, etc., while the form of their psychology may quite similar: passionate zeal, furious and fanatical aggression, even their specific forms of heroic psychology.

The fact that the class psychology is determined by the totality of the conditions of the class life, based on the general economic situation, should not lead us to ascribe the class psychology to selfish interest, which is a very frequent error. No doubt class interest is the main sinew of the class struggle, but class psychology includes many other elements. We have already observed that the philosophers of the ruling class in the period of the decline of the Roman Empire preached self-extermination with some success, because their preaching was an outgrowth of the psychology of this class, a psychology of repletion, satiety, of disgust with life. The causes for this psychology may be definitely traced; we have already found its roots in the parasitic rôle of the ruling class, which did nothing and merely lived in order to consume, to try out, to surfeit itself with all things, as was natural in view of its economic situation, its function (or lack of function) in the general economy. The psychology of satiety and necromania was a class psychology. Yet we may not say that Seneca, when he preached suicide, was expressing the interest of his class.[32] The hunger strikes in the Tsarist prisons, for example, were acts in the class struggle, a protest in order to fan the flame of conflict, a symbol of solidarity, a device to maintain the ranks of the fighters, and this struggle was dictated by class interests. At times, despair seizes the masses or certain groups, after a great defeat in the class struggle, which is of course connected with class interest, but the connection is somewhat peculiar: the conflict went on under the impulse of the hidden springs of interest, but now the fighting army has been defeated; the result is: disintegration, despair, a longing for miracles, a desire to escape mankind; thoughts turn heavenward.[33] After the defeat of the great insurrections in Russia in the Seventeenth Century, which had taken the form of religious dissent, "protest assumed many varied forms under the influence of defeat and despair": retirement to the wilderness, self-incineration. "Hundreds, even thousands, seek their death in the flames .... ecstatic dreamers clothe themselves in pure funereal raiment and lie down in the coffins that have already been prepared, to wait for the crack of doom." [34] This psychology also finds expression in the two contemporary poems quoted by Melgunov

Dear Mother Desert,
Release me from earth's sufferings,
Receive me in your arms,
Dear Mother Desert,
Kind Mother, keep me.

and:

Coffin of pine-wood,
There will I lie,
Waiting for the last trump.

It is obvious that the phenomenon of class psychology is of very complicated nature, not capable of direct interpretation as *interest* only, but *always to be explained by the concrete environment in which the specific class has been placed.*

In the psychological structure of society, *i.e.*, among the various forms of the social psychology, we must not omit to mention the psychologies of groups, occupations, etc. There may be several groups within one class; thus, the bourgeoisie includes a bourgeoisie of high finance, a trading bourgeoisie and an industrial bourgeoisie; the working class includes the aristocracy of skilled labor, together with slightly skilled labor and wholly unskilled labor. Each of these groups has special interests and special characteristics; thus, the highly skilled worker likes his work and is even proud of being superior, as a worker, to the others; on the other hand, he is ambitious, and assumes certain bourgeois inclinations, together with his high collar. Each occupation bears its mark; when we berate the bureaucrats, we mean a certain professional psychology of negative virtue: routine, red-tape delays, precedence of form over substance, etc. Vocational types of psychology arise, their mental traits a direct result of the character of their activity, whence follows also a corresponding tinge in their ideology. Friedrich Engels says: "Among the practical politicians and the theorists in jurisprudence, and among the jurists in particular, this fact is first completely lost sight of. Since in each single instance the economic facts must take the form of juristic motives so as to be sanctioned in the form of law, and since, therefore, a backward view must be taken over the whole existing system of law, it follows therefrom (in the opinion of these persons, N. B.) that the juristic form appears to be the whole and the economic content nothing at all."[35] His trade psychology will quickly betray a man; a minute's conversation will tell you whether you are dealing with a clerk, a butcher, a reporter, etc. It is a characteristic fact that all these traits are international; you find them everywhere. By the side of the class psychology, which is the plainest, most pregnant and most significant form of the social psychology, we find a group psychology, a vocational psychology, etc.; being determines consciousness. In this sense we may say that each grouping of men-even in an amateur chess club or chorus-imparts a certain-sometimes almost imperceptible -stamp on its members. *But since the existence of a certain grouping of persons is nevertheless always associated with the economic structure of society, being ultimately dependent on the latter, it follows that all the varieties of the social psychology are quantities to be explained by the social mode of production, the economic structure of society.*

What is the relation between the social psychology and the social ideology? The social psychology is a sort of supply-chamber for ideology; or, it may be compared with a salt solution out of which the ideology is crystallized. At the beginning of this section, we stated that the ideology is distinguished by the great *coordination* of its elements, *i.e.,* the various feelings, thoughts, sensations, forms, of which it is composed. The ideology systematizes that which has hitherto been not systematized, *i.e.,* the social psychology. The *ideologies are a coagulated social psychology.* For example, early in the history of the workers' movement, there was a certain crude discontent among the working class, a sense of the "injustice" of the capitalist order, a vague desire to replace this system by some other system; we could not call this an ideology. Later, however, this vague tendency was definitely formulated. Things were coordinated, a set of demands (a program, platform) arose, a specific "ideal" began to appear, idealism, etc.; here we have an *ideology*. Or, we may find that the discomforts of a situation, and the aspiration to cast it off, find expression in a work of art; here also we have an ideology. It is sometimes difficult to draw the line sharply; the actual process is a slow solidification, consolidation, crystallization of the social ideology out of the social psychology. A change in the social psychology will of course result in a corresponding change in the social ideology, as we have pointed out above. The social psychology is constantly changing, simultaneously with the alterations in the economic conditions from which they grow, for the latter bring about a constant regrouping of these social forces, a growth of new relations, based on the successively altered levels of the productive forces as has been already point out.

Having given a number of examples in our discussion of ideology, we need not dwell upon the alterations in social psychology as connected with the alterations in ideology; we shall merely point out that the latest books are now devoting considerable attention to the question of the so called "spirit of capitalism", ix., the psychology of the entrepreneurs. For instance, the works of Werner Sombart *(Der Bourgeois,* etc.), Max Weber, and more recently Professor Dr. Hermann Levy *(Soziologische Studien über das englische Volk,* Jena 1920). Marx wrote, in the First Volume of *Capital:* "Protestanism, by changing almost all the traditional holidays into workdays, plays an important part in the genesis of capital" (Chicago, 1915, p.303, footnote) Marx repeatedly points out that the bigoted, frugal, parsimonious, and at the same time energetic and persistent mentality of Protestanism, abhorring the pomp and luxury of Rome, is identical with the mentality of the rising bourgeoisie. People poked fun at this statement; but now prominent bourgeois scholars are developing this very theory of Marx, of course without giving credit to its originator. Sombart proves that the most varied traits (avarice for gold, untiring lust for adventure, inventive spirit, combined with calculation, reason, sobriety) gave rise to the so called capitalist spirit" by reason of their united presence. It goes without saying that this spirit could not have developed out of itself, but was shaped by an alteration in the social relations; parallel with the growth of the capitalist "body" proceeded a growth of the capitalist "spirit". All the fundamental traits of the economic psychology are reversed: in the pre-capitalist era, the basic economic notion of the nobility was that of a "decent" life, "according to station". "Money exists in order to be spent," wrote Thomas Aquinas; things were managed poorly, irrationally, without proper bookkeeping; tradition and routine predominated; the tempo of life was slow (almost every other day a holiday) initiative and energy were lacking. On the other hand, the capitalist psychology, which replaced the feudal-chivalrous psychology, is based on initiative, energy, briskness, rejection of routine, rational calculation and reflection, love of accumulating riches, etc. The complete upheaval in men's minds proceeded simultaneously with the complete upheaval in the production relations.

f. The Ideological Processes considered as differentiated labour

The question of ideologies and of the superstructure in general must also be considered from another standpoint. We have already seen that the various forms of the superstructure are a composite quantity, by the nature of their construction, and include things as well as persons; the ideologies themselves are a sort of mental product. This being the case, we necessarily consider the forms of the superstructure in their evolution (and consequently also the ideological process) as a special *form of social labor (but not of material production;* the two must not be confused) In the beginnings of "human history", i.e., at the time when surplus labor did not exist, we find practically no ideology. Only later as surplus labor arises, "a class which is relieved of directly productive labor is formed by the side of the great rnajority which does nothing but toil; this new class takes care of the common concerns of society: supervision of labor, affairs of state, justice, sciences, arts, etc. Therefore, we find at the basis of the division into classes: the law of the division of labor" (Friedrich Engels: *Die Entwicklung der Sozialismus von der Utopie zur Wissenschaft,* Berlin, 1920, p.49) In one passage, Marx designates priests, lawyers, the ruling classes, etc., as the "ideological classes". In other words, the ideological processes may be considered as a specific form of labor within the general labor system. This labor is not material production, nor does it constitute a portion of this material production, but results from the latter, as our study of ideologies has shown, and sets up an independent domain of social activity. The increasing division of labor is an expression of the increasing pro ductive forces of society, wherefore the growth of the pro ductive forces conditions also a division of labor in the field of production, accompanied by an isolation of the ideological labor having its own division of labor. "The division of labor is not a characteristic of the economic world; its growing influence may be observed in the most varied fields of society, in the increasing specialization of political, administrative, legal functions. The same thing may be observed in art and science." [36] We may now view the whole of society as a huge working mechanism, with many subdivisions of the divided social labor. This great labor aggregate may be divided into two great categories, first, material labor, "production" as such; second, the various forms of labor in the superstructure, the work of supervision, etc., as well as *ideological* labor as such, The organization of this labor goes hand in hand with the organization of material labor, and is along the same general lines; it includes a class hierarchy, those holding the means of production being at the top, and those without such means at the bottom. In the process of material production (1) those in charge have a special role in this process, which is (2) determined by the fact that the means of production are in their hands, and (3) they also have control of distribution by virtue of this circumstance; such also is the case in almost all the branches of "superstructural" labor. The army has already served as an illustration; the same might be noted in science and art. A great technical laboratory, under capitalist society, has an internal organization similar to that in the factory. The theatre, under capitalism, has its owner, its manager, its actors, its "supes"; its technical employees, its clerks, workers, just as in a factory. We consequently find here, (*i.e.,* in a class society) various functions *socially connected* with *these persons;* the higher function involves, so to say, a possession of the "means of mental production", constituting a class monopoly; in the distribution of the products of *material* production (men live, of course, by consuming material commodities), the possessors of these "instruments of mental production" obtain a greater share of the social product than their subordinates.

We know how firmly the ruling classes have clung to the monopoly of knowledge. In antiquity, the priests who held this monopoly barred the "temples of science", to which they admitted but a few chosen ones; knowledge itself was enveloped in the shroud of a divinely awful mystery, accessible to only a few of the wise and just. The store set by this monopoly by the ruling classes is apparent, for example, from the following words of the well-known German idealist philosopher, F. Paulsen: "Anyone whose social conditions force him to remain a manual worker by trade and status, would not find it a gain to have received the schooling of a scholar; such training would not enhance, but darken his life" (Friedrich Paulsen: *Das moderne Bildungswesen,* in *Kultur der Gegenwart,* part i, section i, p.24; we may observe in passing that this gigantic work, the *Kultur der Gegenwart* - a product of the finest brains among the German professors - is dedicated to Emperor William II!). Apparently the honored philosopher and idealist regards a man as bound down to the compulsory labor of capitalism, even in his mother's womb, and deprives him of education even before he has seen the light of the sun.

The monopoly character of education was the principal reason for the opposition of the Russian intellectuals to the revolution of the proletariat; conversely, one of the principal achievements of the proletarian revolution was the abolition of this monopoly.

: An inspection of material production will show that it is divided into a number of branches; in the first place, into manufacturing and agriculture, both of which are further subdivided into a great number of sections, from mining operations and grain-growing to the manufacture of pins and the raising of lettuce. Here, as in the "superstructure", there are large subdivisions (such as those previously considered, i.e., administration, the setting of standards, of science, of art, of religion, of philosophy, etc.); furthermore, each of these subdivisions is further ramified (for instance, science now consists of many branches; so does art). In material production, as we have seen, a certain rough proportion must exist - if society is to go on - between the various branches of production. Even in a blind, capitalist social order, with no social plan of production at all, but rather with anarchy in production, i.e., a disproportion between the various branches of production, even here we find a constant adjustment within this anarchy; violent disturbances of this proportion meet with their reaction, of course, not without much pain, and not for long periods, but there is a certain temporary equilibrium, for otherwise capitalist society would go to pieces as the result of a single industrial crisis. While it is possible for a society to exist in spite of the fact that there is no harmony between its material production and the other forms of its labor, the non-material forms, such a society will not grow but decline. For instance, where too much labor is allotted to the maintenance of theaters, the government mechanism, or the church, or art, the productive forces themselves will decline. It is obvious that this would be the case, for instance, in a community in which there was one worker and seven men supervising and calculating his product, with two others encouraging him by singing, and another man governing the whole process. Since all must eat, it is obvious that such a labor system would not endure for long. But it is also quite obvious that - in spite of all the effort the workers might put in - a working community would fare very badly unless its various members formed a coordinated system, in which their product was duly tabulated, and in which certain individuals took care of relations with the outside world. Therefore, if society as a whole is to endure, there must exist within it a certain condition of equilibrium (though it be unstable) between the material work as a whole and the superstructural work as a whole. Let us assume for a moment that all the scholars (mathematicians, engineers, chemists, physicists, etc.) in the United States of America should disappear overnight; the huge production of that country could not go on, based as it is, on scientific calculation, but would decline. Let us assume, on the other hand, that 99 per cent. of the present workers should suddenly be miraculously transformed into learned mathematicians, not participating in production. The resulting bankruptcy would be complete; society would perish. Not only is a certain proportion (even though its limits be indefinite) necessary in any society between the total material labor and the total superstructural labor, but the distribution of labor within the superstructure, i.e., among the various forms of the "mental" supervising and other activity, is also of importance. As there is a certain equilibrium between the various forms of material labor (these various forms tend to equilibrium, as Marx puts it), so there must be a certain modicum of such equilibrium between the branches of ideological work, in fact, of the "superstructural" work in general. The coordination of these ideological "branches of production" is ultimately determined by the economic structure of society. Why, for instance, was so vast a quantity of national labor in ancient Egypt devoted to the construction of the huge pyramids, great Pharaonic statues, and other monuments of feudal art? For the simple reason that Egyptian society could not have maintained itself without constantly impressing upon the slaves and peasants the sublimity and the divine power of their rulers. In the absence of newspapers and telegraph agencies, art served as the ideological bond; it was therefore a *sine qua non* for this society and took an enormous share of the country's labor budget. Similarly, "ethics", the establishment of moral standards, assumed a very important place in Greece at the end of the Fifth Century B.C, because the question of the relations between men and of the regulation of these relations, had become particularly acute, even for the ruling classes, who were impelled by the great gulfs that had opened up, to seek to conciliate divergent tendencies. Art is but feebly developed in the United States of America of our day, while the same country is a pioneer in the study and application of the science of organized production as a whole (the Taylor system, vocational psychology, psychophysiology of labor, etc.), because American capitalism does not need to resort to art in order to mould the minds of the people; this task is excellently performed by a capitalist newspaper press that has been perfected to the point of virtuosity; the question of a national production, a "scientific management", is of immense importance in the life of such a system.

A certain proportion between the parts is therefore necessary in the field of "superstructural" (and consequently of any ideological) labor, so long as society is in a state of equilibrium, this proportion between the various branches of mental work, and their distribution, being determined by the economic structure of society and the requirements of its technology.

An interesting application of these observations may be made to the *school,* which is one of the fields of ideological labor. Indeed, schools (universities, high schools, elementary schools) are the sphere of common social labor in which instruction is given, in which the labor forces are endowed with a certain skill, a specific "training", simple human labor power being thus transformed into *specific* labor power. One person studies medicine, another *law,* military science, engineering, etc. The same condition of affairs is found throughout the field of instruction, *i.e.,* all those special processes in which specific abilities are imparted to men, which are required for the performance of more or less specialized functions; essentially there is no difference between the trade school that turns out locksmiths, and the educational institution that turns out the geniuses of the pulpit, or the Tsarist cadet school, producing its crack officers. It follows that: the school system, its division into various branches (commercial schools, trade schools, cadet schools, schools of engineering, universities, *etc.) are an expression of society's need for various kinds of skilled - material and mental-labor.*

A few examples will clarify our thought.

In the Middle Ages, the school stood in the sign of the priesthood. Feudal society could not exist without a tremendous development of religion. Therefore: "The monastic and cathedral schools and the overwhelming number of chancellor universities, the life in the bursae, and the instruction in the artistic faculty - all these had a monastic priestly tinge, everything having been devised and arranged according to the ecclesiastical theological spirit" (Theobald Ziegler: *Geschichte der Pädagogik,* in *Handbuch der Erziehungs- und Unterrichtslehre für höhere Schüler, vol.* i, Miinchen 1895, P. 33). "Except the few medical and legal professional schools, the universities as well as the lower schools were concerned above all with the *training of clerics"* (ibid.). In addition, there were schools for training knights; in these, "education" no longer served to develop priestly "labor power", but brightly "labor power". The boys were instructed chiefly in seven virtues *(probitates); these* were "the seven *probitates* of the knight, six of them being purely physical arts *(equitare, natare, sagittare, cestibus certare, aucupari, scacis ludere:* riding, swimming, archery, fencing, hunting, chess-playing) and the remaining one, *versificare,* poetry and music" (*ibid.*). Obviously, this must have produced a different type of man, necessary for feudal society.

But now we have the growth of cities, the commercial bourgeoisie, etc.; the result of this condition is well described by Professor Ziegler, whom we have already quoted: "But (p.34) new educational needs arise in another field. In the blossoming cities, the *merchant* and the *artisan* (my italics. N.B.) required a different practical education than was given to the scholar or judge; the erection of schools by the city was resorted to, for the purpose of providing these circles with the necessary important instruction."

With the development of industrial capitalism and the increasing demand for skilled labor, the so called trade school is born in the field of material labor. "In order to support the national industry, governments and private persons began to establish trade and artisan schools, destined to provide such vocational instruction to the pupils as they had formerly obtained in the master's shop" (N. Krupskaya: *Popular Education and Democracy*, Moscow, 1921, p.94., in Russian). This school undergoes certain changes with the growth of *large-scale* industry, and the increasing demand for masters, supervisors, foremen, etc. (*ibid.*, p.96). Simultaneously, the intermediate schools and higher trade schools, giving more prominence to natural science and mathematics, now flourish on a very large scale, also commercial universities, agricultural schools, etc

The above cited German idealist philosopher, F. Paulsen, expounds the significance of capitalist education with frank brutality. These passages in his work are so instructive and give so precise a picture, that we must present them unabridged (Paulsen's frankness may be explained by the fact that he is contributing to a thick and heavy volume which will not fall into the hands of the workers; he therefore writes for the capitalist bandits only, and can afford to tell tales out of school)

"The actual outline of the educational system is determined everywhere, in the main, by the outline of society and its stratification. . . The form of the public educational system will always reflect the condition of the society producing it. Society shows everywhere a double stratification: a grouping according to the form of the social performance of labor, and a grouping by property relations. The first grouping furnishes the division into vocational stations; the difference in property gives rise to the division into social classes. Both have an influence on the educational system; the main outlines of the social performance of labor, the vocational social station, determine on the whole the varieties of instructional type; *the class membership or the property standing of their families to a great extent determines the distribution of young men to the various courses*. . . It (society) needs and has motor, executive, and mentally operating and guiding functions and organs. The first group includes all those whose labor achievement is essentially that of bodily strength and manual dexterity; here we should place the industrial workers and artisans of all kinds, rural workers and small peasants, and, lastly, those employed in trade and transportation as the lowest executive instruments. The second, group includes those whose vocational task essentially is that of controlling the social labor process and giving instructions and guidance to manual laborers; here belong the factory owners and technical specialists, managers of great farms, merchants and bankers, higher employees in trade and transportation, also subaltern officials in the service of nation and community. The third group, finally, includes those professions customarily classed as "learned"; their practice requires an independent grasping and extending of scientific knowledge: here belong research workers and inventors, also the incumbents of the higher places in the civil and military service, in church and school, physicians, engineers in high position, etc." (Paulsen, in *Kultur der Gegenwart,* part i, section i, pp.64, 65). The grading of the schools corresponds to these three groups. Paulsen's statements are an excellent indication of the school mechanism: on the one hand, it provide the necessary number of labor forces for each material and mental task; on the other hand, the higher ideological functions always remain fixed to a certain class, the educational monopoly, and with it the capitalist order of society, being thus maintained. But Paulsen is wrong in placing himself and his ilk *over* the manufacturers and bankers whose boots the learned gentlemen lick on all necessary and unnecessary, occasions.

Thus the school illustrates the practical roots of all ideologies. If any mathematician should be indignant at our suggesting that his "pure science" has any earthly import, we shall merely ask him to inform us why mathematics is studied by the merchants' sons in the commercial high schools, the would-be agronomists in the agricultural schools, the would-be engineers in the engineering schools, etc. He may reply that only the riff-raff of the profession would consent to give them instruction; we should then ask him why 'pure mathematicians - who really seem quite ignorant of practical life - should deliver lectures before persons preparing for the professions of engineering or agriculture. Our mathematician may go so far as to say that there are some scholars that give no instruction, deliver no lectures. But surely - as we should then assert - these men write books which are read by professors who give instruction to future engineers who make use of what knowledge they acquire in order to calculate problems in the construction of bridges, steam-boilers, electrical power stations, etc.

Furthermore, the case of the school indicates the relative need of the specific society for various types of skilled labor, including the "highest".

The various sciences are therefore as much interconnected by the bond of labor as are the various branches of material labor. Likewise, the other branches of ideological labor are connected with the sciences, *all being based ultimately and constantly on material labor.*

g. The Significance of the Superstructure

We may now take up a more detailed study of the significance of all the varieties of the superstructure, including the ideologies, which may best be done in a critical examination of the objections commonly raised by the opponents of the theory of historical materialism.

First, there are the objections to the practical roots of ideology, to the claim that the forms of the "superstructure", including those of ideology, have any significance as services. We are told that scholars or artists very often are not concerned at all with the practical role played by their thoughts or constructions. On the contrary, the scholar, in his search for "pure truth", is merely expressing his love of this goddess; his marriage to her is a love-match, based on no practical considerations of any kind. Similarly, we are told that the true artist loves art for art's sake. Art is his highest goal; art alone gives life meaning for him. As a. jurist may declare that he would wish to see the world destroyed; rather than that justice be not done (*fiat justitia, pereat mundus!*), so the true musician would give everything else in the world for a single glorious symphony. The true artist lives for his art, the, scholar for science, the jurist for the state (Hegel, for instance, considers the Prussian junker capitalist state to be the highest manifestation of the world-spirit in human history, and therefore worthy of receiving self-sacrifice), etc.

Now, is it true that scholars and artists have this attitude, or are they pulling the wool over the eyes of the public? While the latter may sometimes occur, we have not the right to approach the subject from this angle. Thousands of examples prove that a true scholar, or artist, or theoretical jurist, loves his vocation as he loves himself, without regard to its practical phases. But it would be wrong to have the matter end there, *for the subject of the psychology of the ideologists is* not to be confused with their *objective role;* man's view of his labor is not identical with the role, the significance, of his labor for *society.* Let us examine

285

the growth of an ideology. Mathematics, for instance - arose on the basis of practical needs - became specialized and divided off into a number of branches. The specialist is not aware of the practical needs satisfied by his science. He is interested in his "own work"; the more he loves it, the more productive will it be. Other persons, working in other fields, will apply his theory. Before the days of specialization, the practical significance of science was apparent to everyone; now it has been lost. Knowledge formerly served practice, even in men's minds; it still serves practice, but the minds of the closeted specialists represent knowledge as entirely divorced from practice. The causes are not far to seek; man's thinking is influenced by his being. To a man working in one ideological field only, this field must appear as the navel of the earth, about which all else revolves. This man lives in the atmosphere of his specialty, for - as Engels has excellently put it - ideology is simply the "occupying oneself with thoughts as with independent entities developing independently, subject only to their own laws."[37] Before the days of specialization, a man might have thought: "I guess I'll take up some geometry, in order to measure the fields down by the shore next year." But the mathematical specialist would probably say: "I have got to solve this problem; it is my life-work." Somewhat different in expression, but identical in sense, is Ernst Mach's formulation of the case: "For the artisan, and more still for the scientist, the quickest, simplest mental acquisition - with the slightest mental outlay - of a certain field of natural phenomena is *itself* an economic object, in which, *although it was originally a means to an end, there is now no longer a thought of physical need,* once the corresponding mental impulses have developed and demand exercise." [38] Thus, the system of the superstructure, from the social-political to the philosophical phase inclusive, is connected with the Cmnomic basis and the technical system of the specific society, being a necessary link in the chain of social phenomena.

In this connection, Engels says in a letter addressed to Franz Mehring, dated July 14, 1893: "Ideology is a process accomplished, to be sure, by so called thought, but with a false consciousness. This mess does not know the actual motive forces behind it, otherwise it would not be an ideological process. Being a process of thought, it derives its content as well as its form from pure thought, either on its own part or on that of its predecessors. It works with mere mental material, which it assumes and accepts as the product of thought, and for which it does not seek any more remote process, that may be independent of thought, and all this is self-evident to this process, for it regards all action, since it works through thought, as also in the last instance based on thought " This illusion of an independent history; of national constitutions, legal systems, ideological conceptions, in each special field of knowledge, is the element that leads most persons astray mentally" (Mehring: *Geschichte der deutsehen Sozialdemokratie,* Note to Book i, Stuttgart 1919, p.386).

Another frequent objection to our theory results from pretending that it declares economy to be the only true element in life, all other elements being childish folly, illusions, vague mists. This conception represents historical materialism as stating the existence of various factors in history: economy, politics, art, etc., some of which are very important, others unimportant, with the economic "factor" as the only real "factor", all the others being a sort of fifth wheel of the wagon. This representation of the Marxian conception is then diligently bombarded with refutations; it is pointed out that many other things are important besides economy; but it would be erroneous to interpret our view of ideology in this way; the superstructure is not "child's play". We have shown that a destruction of the capitalist state would make capitalist production impossible, that a destruction of modern science would involve also that of large-scale production and technology; that an elimination of the means of human intercourse, language and literature, would cause society to disintegrate. The theory of historical materialism does not deny the importance of the superstructure in general and of the ideologies, in particular, but explains them. As we have shown in our chapter on Determinism and Indeterminism this is quite a different attitude.

It would be equally incorrect to consider the various "factors" from the point of view of their unequal value; to admit the importance of economy, but to belittle that of politics or science. Many misunderstandings result from such an interpretation. Why attempt to set up a scale of the relative importance, of these "factors" when we recall that capitalist economy could not exist without capitalist politics? It would be difficult to decide whether - in a rifle - the barrel or the trigger was the more important; or - in the human body - the left hand or the right foot; or - in a watch - the spring or the cog-wheel. Some things are more important than others; economy is more important than dancing; but in many cases it is absurd to make such a statement A system may contain sections that are of equal importance for the existence of the whole. The trigger is as important in a rifle as the barrel; a single screw in a piece of mechanism may be as important as any other part, for without it the mechanism might cease to be a mechanism. Similarly, in a consideration of the "superstructural" labor, as a portion of the total social labor, it would be equally absurd to ask either of the following questions: Which is more important for modern industry, metallurgy or mining? Which is more important, direct material labor, or labor in economic administration? At certain stages in evolution, the two may be inseparable. "This theory (the theory of these factors, N. B.) played the same role in the evolution of social science. The progress of natural science has shown us the unity of these forces, the modern doctrine of energy. Likewise, the progress of social science has necessarily led to a displacement of the theory of factors - this product of social analysis - by a *synthetic conception of social life.*" [39] We therefore reject the theory of factors. But there remains a basis for the distinction between material production and the superstructure, and for a study of their mutual relations.

The true difference is in the different character of their functions. The administration of production does not play the same part as does production itself. The former eliminates, friction, systematizes and coordinates the various elements of work, or to put it differently - institutes a certain adjustment of work. We have also seen, for instance, that morality, customs, and other standards, coordinate men's actions and keep them within certain bounds, thus preventing society from disintegrating. Science likewise (let us suppose we are speaking of the natural sciences) ultimately serves as a guide for the process of production, increases its effectiveness and regulates its operation. We have defined the similar function of philosophy, which coordinates and regulates (or seeks to do so) the contradictions between the various sciences, due to their division of labor.

Philosophy arises from the sciences, as the administration of production arises from production; neither is "primary"; both are "secondary", neither "original", both "derivative"; yet, philosophy controls the sciences, to a certain degree, for it imparts to them their "common point of view", their "method", etc.

Another example that has already been treated is that of language; the latter grows out of production, develops under the influence of the social evolution, *i.e.,* its evolution is determined by the natural law of social evolution. The function of language is to coordinate man's actions, for mutual understanding is the simplest form of adaptation, coordination, in relations, actions, even - to a certain extent - in feelings, etc. The fundamental import of the distinction between material production and ideological labor - or any other "superstructural" labor - should now be clear: Their mutual relation is in the fact that ideological labor is a derived quantity, also constituting a regulating principle. With regard to the whole of social life, the distinction lies in their *difference of functions.*

We have now practically answered also the question as to the reverse relation, "the influence of the superstructure on the economic basis and on the productive forces of society". The superstructure, growing out of the economic conditions and the productive forces determining these conditions, in its turn, exerts an influence on the latter, favoring or retarding their growth. But, in either case, there is no doubt of this reverse process. In other words: *a constant process of mutual cause and affect is in operation between the various categories of social phenomena.* Cause and effect change place.

But if we recognize this mutual influence, what becomes of the bases of Marxian theory? For most bourgeois scholars admit a mutual interaction. May we still say that the productive forces and the production conditions are the basis of our analysis? Are not our own hands destroying what they have built up? These doubts are quickly disposed of. However numerous these mutual, influences, the basic fact remains: *at any given moment the inner structure of society is determined by the mutual relation between this society and external nature,* i.e., *by the condition of the* material *productive forces of society; the change in form, however, is determined by the movement of the productive forces.* We go; further than merely to admit the existence of a set of mutual relations, for we understand that all the countless processes at work within society, all their intersecting, colliding, accumulating forces and elements are operating within a common frame, provided by the mutual relation between society and nature. Perhaps our opponents will attempt to controvert this principle, already known to Goethe in its general outlines, and expressed by him in his poem, "The Metamorphosis of Animals", a poem not so well known as his "Metamorphosis of Plants".

Alle Glieder bilden sich aus nach ew'gen Gesetzen,
Und die seltenste Form bewahrt im Geheimen das Urbild.
Also bestimmt die Gestalt die Lebensweise des Tieres.
Und die Weise zu leben, sie wirkt auf alle Gestalten
Mächtig zurück. So zeiget sich fest die geordnete Bildung
Welche zum Wechsel sich neigt durch düsserlich wirkende Wesen.

[The following inadequate English translation of these lines is submitted, existing collections of Goethe's poems in English having neglected this poem:

All the limbs take shape according to laws immortal,
Even unusual forms always remaining close to original type
... Thus the animal's mode of life determines its figure
As well as its habits; it has a mighty reverse influence
On all types. Thus the orderly formation is firmly shown,
Tending to fluctuate as influenced by beings working from without.

TRANSLATOR.]

This thesis is irrefutable; it follows that our analysis must begin with the productive forces, that the countless mutual dependences between the various parts of society do not eliminate the basic, ultimate dependence of all social phenomena on the evolution of the productive forces; that the diversity of the causes operating in society does not contradict the existence of a *single unified causal relation in social evolution.*

We cannot take up here the individual objections of the various bourgeois scholars; their number is legion. Essentially, they are all chewing the same old insipid cud. Let us take one of the latest "critical" essays as an example; Professor V. M. Khvostov expounds Marx's theory as follows, "It consists on the whole (!) in assigning, among the historical factors (!), the chief place to the economic factor (!) . . . all other phenomena being shaped under the one-sided (1) influence of the economic conditions" (Khvostov: *Theory of the Historical Process,*in Russian, p.315). After our recent remarks in large type, we need hardly to inform the reader whether Khvostov's conception of Marxian theory is a correct one. But, to do him justice, Mr. Khvostov constitutes no exception; on the contrary, the greater the erudition displayed in the refutation of Marx, the greater the 'ignorance displayed in expounding his doctrine.

We shall take one more specimen of "refutation" (from the

same professor): "I believe(!) that man is characterized by the most varied aspirations. In the first place, he is concerned with preserving his physical existence, for which he undertakes certain actions. In the second place, he makes an effort to evaluate the universe in himself, and this is a peculiar human tendency, independent of any material calculations. In the third place, man also possesses such desires as, for example, the love of domination, the love of freedom; men also have religious, esthetic, needs, a need for the sympathy of their surroundings, etc," *(ibid.,* pp. 317-320). Having served us this chowder of human needs, Khvostov draws the conclusion that a "monistic explanation . . . is impossible". But Khvostov's example, quoted above, will serve to indicate the full absurdity of his view (quite current among "scholars" all over the world), as well as the necessity for a monistic explanation. In fact, is it not a parody of scientific thought; to consider the tendency to religion, to domination, etc., as eternal categories? Khvostov never even thinks of asking for an *explanation* of them. Religion exists; how shall we explain it? Well, by means of man's need of religion. Domination exists; why? Simply because: man has a desire for domination. Is this not similar to "explaining" sleep as due to a force that "puts to sleep"? Can anything be explained in this way? By the use of this method, everything in the world can be "explained" without turning an eyelid: the state is explained by the desire for the state; art, by the desire for art; the circus by the desire for the circus; Khvostov's explanations, by the need felt for Khvostov's' explanations; walking, by the desire for walking; and so on, *ad infinitum.* Such a "theory" of the historical process is not worth a penny. "The love of liberty is an inherent tendency in man." Nothing could be farther from the truth! Was the "love of liberty" an inherent tendency in Nicholas II, during his reign, or in his class? Of course not. In spite of Khvostov, this noble impulse is not, therefore, present in all men. When we have understood this, we are faced with the next question: "Why do certain men have this tendency; while others do not?" And then -

oh, horror! - we must go back to the conditions of their existence, etc. The same applies to all the rest of Khvostov's "different needs". The scholars of the bourgeoisie, in kicking against the traces of a monistic interpretation, are in reality fighting against any form of explanation at all.

h. The Formative Principles of Social Life

We are now prepared to discuss the general question of the possibility of distinguishing a definite "characteristic" of each specific "era". Shall we perhaps find that the connection existing between all the social phenomena will express itself in the existence of some element common to all? We have seen that they are all determined "in the last analysis" by the productive forces and the production relations. How may this connection be recapitulated in a few words? How shall this problem be approached? Let us consider art, one of the "finest", "most complicated" phenomena of mental life. In each epoch, as we have seen, art has its own "style", expressing itself in specific forms, indicative of the specific content (let us recall the example of the Egyptian art), which - in turn - is indicative of a specific ideology; the ideology is the outgrowth of a specific psychology; the psychology of a specific economy; the economy of a specific stage of the productive forces.

Now, if we observe a certain definiteness of forms in all the fields of social life, may we assert that all these fields have their style? We may; it is as reasonable to speak of the "style" of science", as of the style of "art". We may speak of a "style of life", i.e., of typical, specific forms of life. [40] We may in a certain sense speak of the style of the social economy, meaning precisely what Marx terms the "production relations", the "mode of production", the "economic structure of society". As the style of a certain building is determined by the specific combination of its elements, so the "style" of social economy expresses itself in the peculiarities of the production relations, the specific manner in which the elements of the social whole are connected with each other. "The peculiar shape and manner in which this union is realized distinguishes the various epochs of the social structure."[41] But in addition to the "mode of production", there is also a "mode of conception", as Marx puts it. Such is the "style" of the ideology of the given period in general, i.e., that special combination of ideas, thoughts, feelings, forms, characteristic of the specific epoch, "the uniformity of scientific thinking, of conceptions of the world and of life", to use the words of Professor Marbe.[42]

Is it possible thus to distinguish the "mode of production" and the "mode of conception"? Is it possible to distinguish between the economic "style" of a specific society and the ideological "style"? From what has been said concerning the superstructures in general and the ideologies in particular, it is certain that we have the right to do this.

We may show this by means of an example: feudal society; the *economic* style of feudal society is expressed in the principles of a fixed hierarchy, the idea of rank. Marx characterizes the feudal epoch as follows: "Here, instead of the independent man, we find everyone dependent, serfs and lords, vassals and suzerains, laymen and clergy. Personal dependence here characterizes the social relations of production just as much as it does the other spheres of life organized on the basis of that production":[43] This character of the economy and the other spheres of life is precisely the "style" of the epoch, the hierarchical arrangement by rank, in economy; the hierarchical dependence in the other spheres of life; the hierarchical "style" of the entire ideology. Indeed, the entire philosophy of man was then religious, and religion is a philosophy that explains everything in a hierarchical manner; *according to rank*. Science is permeated with this idea of rank; so is art; and we find this condition expressed in the "style", In the Middle Ages, rank *is* the "style" of all of life. And the uniformity of this style proves the dependence of the "mode of *conception*" on the "mode of production", of the system of ideas on the system of persons, the latter in turn being conditioned by the system of objects, i.e., by the social material productive forces. Such a basic stratum of style as is here afforded by hierarchy or rank, may be termed the "formative principle *of* social life", based, as we have seen, on the production relations.

This unity in the style of life is so obvious that even many bourgeois scholars come very close to accepting this view. Karl Lamprecht, for example, sets up the doctrine of the "dominant of personality," i.e., the prevailing type of psychology, changing with the conditions of the epoch, in which the old dominant is destroyed and a new one arises, a new "style of life" being created (K. Lamprecht: *Moderne Geschichts. wissenschaft,* Berlin 1920, pp. 77 et seq.). In the solution of the question of formative principles, we also have a fairly simple solution of the question raised by Hammacher. The latter mobilizes the following chief objection to the theory of historical materialism: "It remains a constant problem why only the economic relations could obtain admission into the historical soul" (Emil Hammacher: *Das philosophisch-okonomische System des Marxismus,* Leipzig, 1909, p.178). This enigma is easily solved. Men are influenced not only by economic stimuli, but by everything that lies within the sphere of their experience; the general *formative* principles are determined, however, by the production relations, which are therefore "reflected" also in the ideological fields. This may be best observed in the case of religion. No doubt sunlight, thunder, death, sleep, all found "admission to the historical soul." But the conception of godhood, of a "sublime power", of "rank" in creation, did not arise until rank had already been established in social life, Into this frame, all "appropriate" phenomena were jammed in, including sleep and death. Approaching the subject from another angle: in bloody despotisms, the god of war was frequently the chief of all the gods. Being the god of war, he naturally also became god of thunder and lightning, which were the most awful "belligerent" forces of nature. Thunderstorms made an impression on the "historical soul", but this material was shaped by the frame of the social relations. We might ask why the social relations give shape to this material; where is the inner relation? The reason is very simple: the social environment has the foundations of its life in the production relations " "We know that the uniformity of psychical phenomena may be traced back to the uniformity in the conditions of these phenomena" (Marbe, ibid., p.52). Many facts taken from this field are "to a certain extent cultural products; Huber (in *Zeitschrift für Psychologie*, vol. 59, 1911, pp.241, *et seq.)* has shown that in experiments in psychological association, the quality of the reaction words depends, among other things, on the vocation and the habits of life of the persons experimented on" (Marbe, *ibid.*). In other words, different answers will be given to the same question (for instance, a request for a certain word), depending on the "habits of life" of the persons experimented on. It is, therefore, not surprising to find the social psychology and ideology to be dependent on the mode of production of material life, and simultaneously on the productive forces.

i. Types of Economic Structure; Types of Various Societies

Any investigation of society will encounter certain historical *types* of society. In other words, there is no such thing as society "in general"; we are always dealing with society in a specific historical raiment; each society wears the uniform of its time. For we know that any specific society is an aggregate of human beings in constant interrelation with each other, these interrelations being based on the labor relations of men, on the system of *production relations*, if these mutual labor relations be visualized at any given moment. But this system of production relations is the aggregate of human beings arranged in a specific manner, namely, of beings connected not only by a labor bond, but by a specific type of such bond. It is therefore evident that society exists only on a specific labor basis, and as this specific basis, the specific mode of production, gives rise to a specific mode of conception (view of life), it follows that it will condition the type of society as a whole, and not only in its material productive or economic portion. The technology conditions the mode of production; the mode of production conditions the view of life; this chain uniting the material, human, and mental system creates a certain type of society. As we distinguish genera, species, and families in the animal world so we distinguish *social types* in sociology. This has been repeatedly emphasized, but we must again point out as our basic thought, that this difference between the social "types" may be traced not only in the economic field, but also in any other series of social phenomena. The type of a society may be inferred from its ideology as well as from its economy. Feudal art permits one to draw conclusions as to feudal conditions of production; feudal conditions of production enable one to make inferences as to feudal art, or religion, or feudal thinking in general, etc., etc. The deciphering of certain literary monuments excavated by the archaeologists enables us to form a picture of the life and manners of races that have disappeared. A reading of Hammurabi's Codex makes the economic life of Babylon live in our minds. The Iliad and the Odyssey permit us to form a conception of early Greek history, etc.

The historical forms of society, the specific nature of these forms, are applicable not only to the economic basis, but also to the aggregate of social phenomena, for the economic structure also determines the political structure and the ideological structure. One being given, the other is also given. To be sure, this does not mean that a type of society must be so sharply distinguished from another as to leave no common traits between them. "Epochs in the history of society are no more separated from each other by hard and fast lines of demarcation, than are geological periods." [44] On the contrary, in actual reality we find that each new social type, each new social structure may present very great and decisive remnants of the old economic formations.

For example, we find in modern capitalist society a great number of remnants of earlier economic forms. Thus the entire great class of the peasantry, with its economic life, may be considered on the whole as a remnant of the feudal ages; the petty artisans likewise, etc. "Pure" capitalism implies a bourgeoisie and a proletariat, but not a peasantry, not an artisan class, etc. If such "purity" cannot be found in the *economic* structure, it is obvious that there will be a certain "mingling of ideas" in the *ideological* field also. Capitalist society may therefore present us with many remnants of feudal ideology, for instance, among the landed nobility and the peasantry, rural classes that are based on earlier agricultural relations, and which still retain certain traditional traits. The interweaving of economic forms will be accompanied by an interweaving of ideological forms, with the result that there never is an absolutely uniform "mode of production", and of course - still less - a uniform "mode of conception" (for, the latter varies even among the various classes that may at the given moment be a part of the same economic structure). It does not follow, however, that we cannot and should not distinguish between the various types of production relations. For, in any actually existing society, a certain type of production relations is *dominant,* and there is also therefore a certain prevalent "view of life". Werner Sombart is right when he says: "I distinguish a certain epoch in the economic life by the *predominance* of a specific spirit in a specific period.[45] Marx, speaking of capitalism, likewise terms it "the form of society in which capitalist production is predominant".[46] As we may distinguish between ape and man in the animal kingdom, in spite of their many common traits, so we may distinguish also between the various forms of society in spite of their common traits; in spite of the fact that the "higher" forms frequently present quite useless remnants of older forms (so called "rudiments"), which are incomprehensible at first sight.

In chapter iii, we have already spoken of the necessity of distinguishing, in any treatment of society, the social form which is rooted in the peculiarities of the economic structure.

This conception has been vigorously and repeatedly opposed by official bourgeois science, which is hostile to the notion of a radical transformation of social relations. Bourgeois scholars themselves now admit that the crux of the matter is in the above fact. Thus, Dr. Bernhard Odenbreit writes: "Marx, as is only natural in the case of a `revolutionary', has a particularly sharp eye for the historical, transitory nature of all social institutions. This general social understanding is joined with a consciously critical reflection on the narrower field of political economy" (Plenge: *Staatswissenschaftliche Beiträge, No. 1; B.* Odenbreit: *Die vergleichende Wirtschaftstheorie bei Karl Marx,* Essen-on-Ruhr 1919, p.15). Precisely so! The "sharp eye" for that which is changing will be found only in the revolutionary. This is, of course, one of the principal reasons for the superiority of the social sciences of the revolutionary proletariat over the social sciences of the counter-revolutionary bourgeoisie.

In so called primitive communism, the oldest form of society known to us, the type of production relations in which the economic "personality" is not yet isolated from the "horde", We also find the corresponding forms of consciousness: absence of religion, of ideas of rank, even of the notion of personality, of the individual *per se.* Similarly, a consideration of so called feudal society shows that its "essential traits consist on the one hand in the splitting up of the land into a number of independent estates, principalities, and privileged holdings, and on the other hand in the organization of these holdings by means of contractual vassal relations."[47] The style of economy is here hierarchic; likewise, the style of politics, of the ideology. As we have already seen, the notion of *rank* is everywhere prevalent. The basis is the large landed estate (*nulle terre sans seigneur,* "no land without its master"), inert and uneventful. The economic bonds are bonds between feudal landowners and serfs; these relations are stable immobile, and - from the point of view of the members of feudal society - immutable; everything is "fixed" in its place in the hierarchic order. Let the shoemaker stick to his last! The same;

condition was reflected in the political superstructure that was expressive of these production conditions.

"The hierarchic tendency of feudal life was elevated by the learned jurists of the Thirteenth Century into a theory and a system " [48] The preachers have a clear vision of the horizontal distribution of society as a whole, even though it be divided into masters and servants. The latter are admonished to follow the words of the apostle commanding slaves to obey their masters, since God has installed kings and dukes on earth, and other men in order that the latter might obey the former. God so disposed things as to enable the weak to depend on the strong." [49] The entire conception of life is religious, *i.e.*, permeated with the notion of rank, or, to use another term, it is authoritarian. Its rigidity, its fidelity to tradition, are a natural result. Science consists chiefly in interpreting tradition and the Sacred Scriptures; art is "divine", magnifying in its form and content the "higher" celestial and terrestrial powers; the dominant morality and the dominant manners and morals are those inculcated by feudal fidelity, noble arrogance, pious awe of the commandments of ancestors, respect for "gentle bearing" and "gentle lineage". *Quod licet Jovi, non licet bovi.* In other words, we are here dealing with a specific *social "species"*, a specific form of society, *beginning with its material basis, and rising to the "highest" forms of social consciousness.*

Let us now consider capitalist society, whose economic basis is an entirely different type of relations. "The contrast between the power, based on the personal relations of dominion and servitude, that is conferred by landed property, and the impersonal power that is given by money, is well expressed by the two French proverbs, *Nulle terre sans seigneur,* and *L'argent n'a pas de maître.*"[50] In this sentence, Marx has revealed one of the fundamental relations in capitalist society, namely, the connection between the various enterprises *through the market,* whence results also the impersonal power of this market and the impersonal, "abstract" power of money. But there is another phase also: the impersonal, social power of money turned to capital nevertheless finds its master, in so far as a simple commodities production is transformed into a capitalistic production.

"Just as every qualitative difference between commodities is extinguished in money, so money, on its side, like the radical leveler that it is, does away with all distinctions. But money itself is a commodity, an external object, capable of becoming the private property of any individual. Thus social power becomes the private power of private persons."[51] From this follows another trait in the economy of capitalist society, namely, its hierarchic character. This trait has also been brilliantly outlined by Marx, particularly in his chapter on cooperation [52]: "The control of the capitalist is " in form " despotic. As cooperation extends its scale, this despotism takes forms peculiar to itself. Just as at first the capitalist is relieved from actual labor so soon as his capital has reached that minimum amount with which capitalist production, as such, begins, so now he hands over the work of direct and constant supervision of individual workmen, and groups all workmen into a special kind of wage laborer. An industrial army of workmen, under the command of a capitalist, requires, like a real army, officers (managers), and sergeants (foremen, overlookers), who, while the work is being done, command in the name of the capitalist. The work of supervision becomes their established and exclusive function."

The capitalist mode of production is therefore twofold in character: on the one hand, it is the summation of the individual private economies, "enterprises", united by the anarchic bond of the market, through exchange, the blind elemental force of the market controlling each individual economy; on the other hand, it is a hierarchic system, with "capital in command". Naturally, this mode of production has also produced its corresponding view of life. Its "style" must reflect its twofold nature. And indeed, "the view of life" of capitalist society is characterized on the one hand by what Marx terms the *fetishism of commodities,* and on the other hand by the principle of *rank,* which we have already observed in feudal society. The combination of these two "formative principles" results in the fundamental style of the "view of life" prevalent in the capitalist world.

We must now define the *fetishism of commodities*. In a society of commodities capitalism, the enterprise works "independently" for an unknown market. But each labor here constitutes a section of the social labor, all the sections being mutually dependent; but the social relation between men, actually at work for each other, is concealed to the eye. If we were dealing with a socialist economy in which all things proceed according to plan, it would be perfectly clear at first glance that men are working for each other, that each individual type of labor is merely a section of the general social labor, etc. The relations between men would then be clear, the mists dispelled. But the case in the capitalist world is quite different. Here the labor relation *between men* is invisible, being concealed by the manipulations of the market, where commodities are shifted, sold and bought. The market is not rationally controlled by men, but, through its prices, controls men. Men observe the *movements* of *commodities* without understanding that they are working for each other, all men being related by the common labor bond. The latter appears to them as a specific miraculous power of commodities, as a "value" of these commodities. Relations between men present themselves as relations between commodities. That is what we mean by the *fetishism of commodities*, the ascribing to commodities of qualities truly inherent in human labor. This fetishism, which causes "a definite social relation between men . . . to assume in their eyes the fantastic form of a relation between things",[53] constitutes the peculiar earmark of the capitalist "view of life". We have already observed that bourgeois scholars, artists, philosophers, etc., are irritated by discussions concerning the social roots of science, art, or philosophy. They are out and out fetishists, for they disregard the social connections, being unable to conceive of their inspired, divine labor as merely a portion of the total *social labor*.

The fetishism of the capitalist world is very graphically indicated in the field of the so called moral standards, of "ethics," a favorite topic with the learned professors. We have already ascertained that the ethical norms are the rules of conduct for the preservation of the society, or of the class, or of the vocational group, etc. They have a necessary, social, service significance. Yet, in fetishistic society, this human and social significance of standards is not recognized. On the contrary, these standards, i.e., the technical rules of conduct, appear as a "duty", dwelling far above men, like any other external divine compulsion. This inevitable fetishism of ethics is excellently expressed by the bourgeois *philosophic genius,*Immanuel Kant, in his doctrine of the "categorical imperative".

The proletariat must approach the question from a different angle. The proletariat must not preach a capitalistic fetishism. For the proletariat, the standards of its conduct are technical rules in precisely the sense of the rules according to which a joiner constructs an arm chair. The latter, wishing to construct an armchair, will plane, saw, glue, etc., which acts are involved in the labor process itself. He will not interpret the rules of woodworking as something foreign to him, of supernatural origin, whose victim he is. The attitude of the proletariat in its social struggle is precisely the same. If it would attain communism, it must do this and that, as the joiner at work on his armchair. And everything required, from this point of view, must be done. "Ethics" will ultimately, in the case of the proletariat, be transformed into simple and easily understood technical rules of conduct, such as are required for communism, and thus it will really cease to be ethics *at all.* For the essence of ethics is in the fact that it involves norms enveloped in a fetishistic raiment. Fetishism is the essence of ethics; where fetishism disappears, ethics also will disappear. For instance, no one would think of designating the constitution of a consumer's store or of a party as "ethical" or "moral", for anyone can see the human significance of these things. Ethics, on the other hand, presupposes a fetishistic mist, which turns the heads of many persons. The proletariat needs rules of conduct, and it needs to have them very clear, but it has no need of "ethics", i.e., a fetishistic sauce to flavor the meal. Of course, it is obvious that the proletariat will not at once succeed in liberating itself from the fetishism of the commodities society in which it lives; but that is another question.

The fetishism of the ideology of capitalism and commodities is merged with the principle of "rank", and these two fundamental formative principles constitute the nucleus of the capitalist mode of thought, the framework for the ideological material. Capitalist society is thus a special type of society, with special characteristic traits in all the "levels" of social life, up to the highest ideological superstructure. *The type of economic structure,* therefore, also determines the type of the social-political structure and of the ideological structure. Society has a basic "style" in all the dominant phenomena of its life.

j. The Contradictory Character of Evolution; External and Internal Equilibrium of Society

We have examined above the phenomena of social equilibrium; but we must not lose sight of the fact that we are dealing with a mobile equilibrium, *i.e.,* a situation in which equilibrium is being constantly disturbed, then reestablished on an altered basis, then again disturbed. We are dealing, in other words, with a process of contradictions, not of rest; we are not discussing a condition of absolute adjustment, but a struggle between opposites, a dialectic process of motion. In considering the structure of society, *ie.* the mutual relation between its parts, we may not conceive of this relation as a perfect harmony between these parts. Every structure involves internal contradictions; in every social class form, these contradictions are very sharp. Bourgeois sociologists, while recognizing the mutual relation of the various social phenomena, do not understand the internal oppositions of the social forms.

In this respect, the entire school founded by the originator of bourgeois sociology, Auguste Comte, is very interesting. Comte recognizes the relation between all the social phenomena (the so called "consensus") in which its "order" is expressed. But the contradictions within this "order", particularly such as lead to its inevitable destruction, do not receive his attention. On the other hand, for the advocates of dialectic materialism, this phase is one of the most essential, perhaps *the* most essential phase. For, as we have seen, the contradictions in any given system are precisely the "moving" element, leading to an alteration of forms, to a characteristic transformation of species in the process of social evolution or social decline.

In our consideration of the social structure, we have seen that its alterations are closely connected with the alterations in the relation between society and nature. The latter equilibrium we have designated as an *external* equilibrium, while the equilibrium between the various series of social phenomena has been called the *internal* equilibrium of society. If we now regard all of society from the point of view of a contradictory evolution, we are at once faced with a number of questions: in the first place, we shall find the existence of contradictions within each series of social phenomena (for example, in economy, the contradictions between the various labor functions; in the social-political structure, the contradictions between classes; in ideology, contradictions between the ideological systems of the classes, etc., not to mention many other contradictions); we shall find also, without difficulty, the contradictions between economy and politics (for instance, when legal standards have been outdistanced by the economic evolution, and a "reform" becomes mature); between economy and ideology; and between psychology and ideology (for instance, the need of something new is felt, but the new has not yet been expressed in ideological form); between science and philosophy, etc. These are contradictions *between the series of the various social phenomena.*

Both elements are a necessary part of the internal

equilibrium; but there is a contradiction between society and nature, *a* disturbance of equilibrium between society and its environment, which finds its expression in the movement of the productive forces. This is the field of external equilibrium. Of course, there is another extremely important case of contradiction, namely, that *between the movement of the productive forces and the social-economic structure of society* (and all the rest of the social structure).

In this case, the relation obtaining between society and nature comes in conflict with the relations developed within society. Obviously, this conflict, this contradiction, must play a very important role in the life of society, for it concerns the bases of the existing "order", the "pillars" on which the given order rests.

We have here sketched only the principal questions involved in the social contradictions, the investigation of which is to be the subject of the next chapter, which will deal with society in motion. Thus far, we have considered chiefly the *structure of society, of* the given social form. We shall now undertake a treatment of the transitions from one structure to another. Again we emphasize that the law of social equilibrium is a law of mobile equilibrium, that includes antagonisms, contradictions, incompatibilities, conflicts, struggles, and - this is particularly important - that it cannot dispense, under certain circumstances, with catastrophes and revolutions, which are absolutely inevitable. Our Marxian theory is the revolutionary theory.

BIBLIOGRAPHY

Karl Marx: *Capital,* particularly vol. i. Kautsky: Introduction (in German) to Salvioli's *Le Capitalisme dans le monde antique.* Lenin: *State and Revolution.* Friedrich Engels: *The Origin of the Family, Private Property, and the State.* Alexandrov: *State, Bureaucracy, Absolutism* (in Russian). Korsak: *The Society of Law and the Society of Labor,* in *Outlines of the Realistic World-Conception* (in Russian). Kautsky: *Ethics and the Materialistic Conception of History.* Kautsky: *Foundations of Christianity* (New York, International Publishers, 1925). Stepanov's essays on religion (in Russian). Pokrovsky: *Geschichte den russischen Kultur.* Friedrich Engels: *Über den historischen Materialismus.* Plekhanov's essays on art; the studies (in Russian) of A. V. Lunacharsky, P. S. Kohan, V. M. Fritsche. K. Bucher: *Arbeit und Rhythmus.* B. Odenbreit: Die *vergleichende Wirtschaftstheorie bei Karl Marx* (a good compilation. of quotations from Marx on the types of societies). A. Bogdanov: *Short Outline of Ideological Science* (in Russian). Cunow: *Ursprung den Religion.* Cunow: *Die Marxsche Geschichts-, Gesellschafts- and Staatstheorie* (vol. i and ii).

NOTES

[1]*Die Technik des Altertums,* Voigtlanders Verlag, Leipzig, 1919, p.206.

[2]*Der Kapitalismus im Altertum*, p.101.

[3]*Gustave Glotz: Le travail dans la Grèce ancienne*, Paris, Felix Alcan, 1920, pp.265-276; Paul Louis: *Le travail duns le monde romain*, Paris, 1912, pp.234-244.

[4]Glotz, *op. cit.*, p.275.

[5]Salvioli, *op. cit.*, p.131.

[6]Rudolf Meerwarth: *Einleitung in die Wirtschaftsstatistik,* Jena, Gustav Fischer, 1920, pp.43- 44.

[7]Artisans working with iron.

[8]*Die Neue Zeit*, vol. 39, part i, p.420.

[9]Readers who are displeased with the "theory of equilibrium" should note this terminology.

[10]G. Plekhanov: On *the Materialistic Interpretation of History, in A Criticism of Our Critics* (in Russian), p.324.

[11]An abbreviation *for Organisation* Escherich - TRANSLATOR.

[12] The names of leaders in Russian Cossack and peasant revolutions against the Muscovite Tsars in the Seventeenth and Eighteenth Centuries, respectively. The name of Stenka (diminutive of Stepan) Razin is particularly popular in Russian folk poetry as that of a national liberator or robber chief. - TRANSLATOR.

[13] Ernst Mach: *Erkenntnis und Irrtum* ("Knowledge and Error"), Leipzig, 1915, p.82.

[14] See Karl Kautsky: *Foundations of Christianity* (New York International Publishers, 1925), pp.179-181, for a detailed parallel in the later Roman society. - TRANSLATOR.

[15] Wipper: *Observations on the Theory of Historical Knowledge* (in Russian), p.46.

[16] Turayev, *op. cit.*, p.112.

[17] From Greek *Soter*, "Redeemer." Max Weber *is* speaking of the cases in which we find a complete religious and political system of ideas based on "world-redemption" or "world-salvation", the elimination of all social evils, the kingdom of God on earth. These aspirations of the oppressed classes assumed the form of "soteriology", *i.e.,* the doctrine of redemption and the "promised land". *N. B.*

[18] Max Weber, *op. cit., Die asiatische Sekte and Heilandsreligiasität*, p.364.

[19] This monograph is a criticism of the program adopted at the Congress of the German Social-Democracy at Goths in 1875. - TRANSLATOR.

[20] Kothe-Prohazka: *Abriss der allgemeinen Musikgeschichte*, Leipzig, 1919, p.4.

[21] Zu Märten: *Historisch-materialistisches über Wesen and Veränderung der Künste,* published by Jugend-Internahonale, Berlin, p.18.

[22] *Ibid.,* p.18.

[23] *Arbeit and Rhythmus,* Leipzig, 1919, p.454.

[24] Fritz Burger: *Weltanschauungsprobleme und Lebenssysteme in der Kunst der Vergangenheit,* p.23.

[25]Wilhelm Hausenstein, *Die Kunst and die Gesellschaft,* München, Verlag *Piper,* p.32.

[26]H. Taine: *Philosophie de l'art,* Paris, 1909, vol. i, p.55

[27]*Ibid.,* p.4.

[28]*Ursprung der Sprache,* Mainz, 1877, p.31. The italics are ours. *N.B.*

[29]*Les fonctions mentales dans les sociétés inférieures,* Paris, 1910.

[30]A. Pogodin correctly points out that "mystical" is hardly the proper word.

[31]*op. cit.,* p.49.

[32]This romantic love of death during the decay of Roman society will be found exhaustively treated in Kautsky: *Foundations of Christianity, d Study in Christian Origins,* New York, International Publishers, 1925, pp.114-128. TRANSLATOR.]

[33]Kautsky, *ibid.,* pp.128-141; 167-177; 383-387: TRANSLATOR.]

[34]S. Melgunov: *Russian Religious-Social Movements in the Seventeenth Century,* in the *Source-Book for Modern. History,* vol. i, p.619 (in Russian).]

[35]Friedrich Engels: *Feuerbach,* translated by Austin Lewis, Chicago, 1906, p.117.

[36]Emil Durkheim: *De la division du travail social,* Paris, 1893, p.2.

[37]*Ludwig Feuerbach* translated by Austin Lewis, Chicago, 1906, p.119.

[38]Ernst Mach: *Die Mechanik in ihrer Entwicklung,* Leipzig, 1921, 8th ed., p.6; *italics* are ours. - N. B.

[39]N. Beltov: On *the Materialistic Conception of History,* in *Criticism* of our Critics (in Russian), p.313.

[40]See what Simmel has to say on *Lebensstil* in his *Philosophie des Geldes,* p.480.

[41]Marx: *Capital,* vol. ii, pp.12, 13.

[42]Karl Marbe: *Die Gleichförmigkeit in der Welt, Untersuchungen sur Philosophie und positiven Wissenschaft,* München, 1916, p.86.

[43]*Capital,* vol. i, Chicago, 1915, pp.88, 89.

[44)]Marx: *Capital*, vol. i, p.405.

[45)]Sombart: *Der Bourgeois*, p.6.

[46)]Marx: *Theorien über den Mehrwert*, Stuttgart, 1910, vol. i, p.424.

[47)]N. P. Silvansky: *Feudalism in Ancient Russia*, St. Petersburg, 1907 (in Russian), p.45.

[48)]The author is speaking of feudalism in Western Europe. N. B.

[49)]L. P. Karsavin: *The Civilization of the Middle Ages*, Petrograd, 1918 (in Russian), p.99.

[50)]Marx, *Capital*, vol. i, Chicago, 1915, p.163, footnote.

[51)]*Capital*, vol. i, pp.148, 149.

[52)]*Capital, vol. i, p.364.*

[53)]*Capital, vol. i, p.83.*

7: DISTURBANCE AND READJUSTMENT OF SOCIAL EQUILIBRIUM

---

a.The Process of Social Changes and the Productive Forces

The process of social changes is closely connected with changes in the condition of the productive forces. This movement of the productive forces, and the movement and regrouping of all social elements, involved in it, is nothing more nor less than a process of constant disturbance of social equilibrium, followed by reestablishments of equilibrium. Indeed, a progressive movement of the productive forces implies above all that a contradiction has arisen between the social technique and the social economy: the system loses its equilibrium. The productive forces have increased to certain extent; a certain regrouping of persons must be undertaken, for otherwise there is no equilibrium, *i.e.*, the system cannot permanently endure in its present form. This contradiction'. eliminated by means of the following regrouping of men: economy "adapts itself" to the condition of the productive forces, to the social technology. But the regrouping of persons in the economic apparatus also implies a necessary regrouping of persons in the social-political structure of society (a different combination parties, a different alignment of the forces of the parties, etc.) Furthermore, the same condition necessarily demands a change in legal, moral, and all other standards. For the contradiction can be solved only in this way, or, what amounts to the same thing, the equilibrium between the system of persons and the system of standards cannot be reestablished in any other way. The same true also of the entire

311

psychology of society, as well as of its ideology. G. V. Plekhanov has brilliantly stated this: "The origin, change, and destruction of the association of ideas, under influence of the origin, change and destruction of certain combina nations of social forces, to a predominant extent explain the history of ideology." [1] The new "combination", *i.e.,* the new relation between persons, comes in conflict with the old combination (the old associations of ideas). This means a destruction of the internal equilibrium, which is reestablished on a new basis, a new "combination" of ideas originates, *i.e.,* where there is an adaptation on the part of the social psychology and the social ideology, which equilibrium is again disturbed, etc., etc.

We now encounter a problem that is of immense theoretical and practical significance.

We may conceive of the restoration of social equilibrium as proceeding in either of two ways: that of a gradual adaptation of the various elements in the social whole (evolution), and that of violent upheaval (revolution). We have seen from history that revolutions do sometimes occur; they are historical facts. It will be interesting to learn under what circumstances the adaptation of the various elements of society proceeds by evolution, and under what circumstances by revolution.

This will involve a discussion of a number of other questions concerning the dynamics of society. We know, for instance, that any given society is constantly undergoing change, experiencing internal regroupings, alterations of form and content, etc. We know that this process is connected with the evolution of the productive forces. But we sometimes witness changes within the limits of the identical social-economic structure; and, at other times, a transition from one "species" of society to another, the substitution of one "mode of production" for another "mode of production". When will the one result, and when the other?

A general description of the process of social evolution is given by Marx in his A *Contribution to the Critique of Political Economy*:

"At a certain stage of their development, the material forces of production in society come in conflict with the existing relations production, or - what is but a legal expression for the same thing - with the property relations within which they had been at work before. From forms of development of the forces of production these relations turn into their fetters. Then comes the period of social revolution. With the change of the economic foundation the entire immense superstructure is more or less rapidly transformed. In considering such transformations, the distinction should always be made between the material transformation of the economic conditions of production which can be determined with the precision of natural science, and the legal, political, religious, aesthetic or philosophic - in short, ideological forms in which men become conscious of this conflict and fight it out. Just as our opinion of an individual is not based on what he thinks of himself, so can we not judge of such a period of transformation by its own consciousness; on the contrary, this consciousness must rather be explained from the contradictions of material life, from the existing conflict between the social forces of production and the relations of production" (*A Contribution to the Critique of Political Economy,* New York, 1904, p.12).

Marx therefore conceives of revolution as intervening when the equilibrium between the productive forces of society and the foundations of its economic structure is disturbed; such is the content of the conflict solved by revolution; this; of course, means the transition from one form to another. But so long as the economic structure still permits the productive forces to evolve the social changes will not take the form of revolution; we shall here find evolution instead.

This question will be taken up in detail later, but we shall now emphasize the following point. *According to Marx, the cause of revolution is not at all to be sought in a collision between economy' and law, as many critics of Marxism maintain, but in a collision between the productive forces and economy,* which is quite a different matter, as will be shown in the sequel.

b.The Productive Forces and the Social-Economic Structure.

We have stated that the cause of revolution, of a violent transition from one type to another, must be sought in a conflict proceeding between the productive forces, and their growth, on the one hand, and the economic structure of society, *i.e.,* the production relations, on the other hand. The following objection might be raised: since the evolution of the production relations is conditioned by the movement of the productive forces, is not the constant alteration of the production relations in itself a result of the conflict between the productive forces and the antiquated production relations? If we take the example of the growth of productive forces in capitalistic society, we shall find that this growth has involved extensive regrouping of persons in the economic process. The old middle class melted away, the artisan class disappeared, the proletariat increased, great enterprises grew up. The human network of production was constantly changing. Further more, did not one form of capitalism lead into another; for instance, was not industrial capitalism followed by financial capitalism, entirely without revolution? Yet, all these changes were the expression of a constant disturbance of equilibrium (a conflict) between the productive forces and the production relations. While the productive forces were growing, they collided with the petty artisan conditions; this was a disturbance of equilibrium; the economy of the artisan was no longer compatible with the increasing technique. The lost equilibrium was again and again restored, already on a new basis, for the new economy was also increased, corresponding to the new technique. It therefore obviously follows that not *every conflict between the productive forces and the production relations results in revolution,* that the case is much more complicated than that. To determine which kinds of conflict produce a revolutionary crisis we must take up an analysis of the various kinds of production relations.

Production relations are, of course, all kinds of relations between persons, arising in the process of the social economic life, *i.e.*, in the production process, which also includes the distribution of means of production, as well as in the process of the distribution of products. Of course, these production relations are of many kinds: a broker in Paris, who buys shares of a New York trust, is thus assuming a certain production relation to the workers and owners, the superintendents and engineers, of the factories belonging to this trust. The banker who employs bookkeepers stands in a certain production relation with them. Likewise, the joiner has certain production relations with the lathe-workers in the same factory, or with the fish-wife from whom he buys a herring, or with the foreman above him. But the same joiner also has certain relations with the fisherman who catches the herring, with the weaver who is one of the many persons concerned in the manufacture of his trousers, etc., etc. In short, we have a truly endless quantity of different and varied production relations, distinct from each other according to the type of relation. Our task therefore will be to differentiate between the various species of these relations, and to determine *what is the species* of production relations in which a conflict would lead to revolution.

In order to have a sound actual basis for our answer, we must learn how revolutions have actually operated, i.e., in what manner they have solved the contradiction between the evolution of the productive forces and the economic basis of society. To be sure, this conflict has always been waged by men; the class struggle has been a hard one. What has been the outcome of the victorious revolution? First a *different political power.* Second a different place of classes in the process of production, a different *distribution of instruments of production,* which, as we know, are directly connected with the situation of the classes.

315

In other words, the struggle during a revolution is waged for the control of the most important instruments of production, which in a class society in the hands of a class which consolidates its rule over things, and through them, over persons, by the additional power of its state organization. This leads us to the decisive point in our search for those production relations that require a revolution for their destruction, in order that society may continue to develop its productive forces. In the Third Volume of *Capital*, Marx categorically states the problem of the form of society and points out the *fundamental*, specific element in the total phenomenon of the productive relations: "The *specific* economic form, in which unpaid surplus labor is pumped out of the direct producers, determines the relations of rulers and ruled, as it grows immediately out of production itself and reacts upon it as a determining element Upon this is founded the entire formation of the economic community which grows up out of the conditions of production itself, and this also determines its specific political shape. *It is always the direct relation of the owners of the conditions of production to the direct producers,* which reveals the innermost secret, the hidden foundation of *the entire social construction, and with it of the political form* of the relations between sovereignty and dependence, in short, of *the corresponding form of the state.*" [2] The matter therefore stands as follows: among all the varied production relations, one type of such relations stands foremost, namely the type that is expressive of the relations between the classes which hold the principal means of production in their hands, and the other classes which hold either subsidiary means or no such means at all. The class that is dominant in economy will also be dominant in politics and *will politically fortify* the specific type of production relations which will give security to the process of exploitation operating in favor of this class. "Politics," to use; the expression found in one of the resolutions of the Ninth Congress of the Russian Communist Party, "is the concentrated expression of economy."

The same thing may be stated in somewhat different words. We have observed that not all the production relations are here concerned, but only of the economic domination supported by a specific relation to things, to instruments of production. In the language of the jurists, we are concerned here with fundamental "property relations", with relations of *class property in the instruments of production.* These property relations are identical with the fundamental production relations; they are merely another way of saying the same thing, legally this time, instead of economically. And these relations are now associated also with the political domination of the specific class; they are maintained by this domination, fortified and extended at any price.

Within this frame, all possible variations of "evolutionary nature" may take place; but we may pass beyond the frame only with the aid of a revolutionary upheaval. For example: within the limits of capitalist property relations, artisan trades may perish, new forms of capitalist enterprises may originate, capitalist organizations of unheard-of varieties may spring into being; individual members of the bourgeois classes may become bankrupt; individual members of the working class may become petty or even large-scale industrialists; new social strata (for instance, the so called "new middle class", *i.e.,* "the technical mental workers") may grow up. But the working class cannot become the owner of the means of production, nor can it (or its representatives) secure command of production, or dispose of the most important instruments of production. In other words: however much the production relations may shift under the influence of the increasing productive forces, *their fundamental character remains the same.* If this fundamental character should come in conflict with the productive forces, it will break up. This is revolution, which affords a transition to another form of society. "To the extent that the labor process is a simple process between man and nature, its simple elements remain the same in all social forms of development. But every definite historical form of this process develops more and more its material foundations and social forms. Whenever a certain maturity is reached, one definite social form is discarded and displaced by a higher one. The time for the coming of such a crisis is announced by the depth and breadth of the contradictions and antagonisms which separate the conditions of distribution, and with them the definite historical form of the corresponding conditions of production, from the productive forces, the productivity, and development of their agencies. A conflict then arises between the material development of production, and its social form."[2]

Revolution therefore occurs when there is an outright conflict between the increased productive forces, which can no longer be housed within the envelope of the production relations, and which constitutes the fundamental web of these production relations, *i.e.* property relations, ownership in the instruments of production. This envelope is then burst asunder.

It is easy to see why this should be the case, why precisely *these* production relations should constitute the most immutable, the most conservative form: for they are the expression of the economic monopoly rule of a class, as affirmed and expressed in its political domination. And, of course, it is only natural that such an "envelope" as would express the fundamental interests of the class would be held together by this class to the bitter end, while alterations *within the envelope,* not disturbing the essential bases of the existing society, may and do proceed rather painlessly. It follows, among other things, that there are no "purely political" revolutions: every revolution is a social (class-displacing) revolution; and every social revolution is a political revolution. For the production relations cannot be overturned without also upsetting the political congelation of these relations; on the other hand, if the political power is broken, this also means the destruction of the domination of this class in economy, for "politics is the concentrated expression of economy". Some persons consider that the French Revolution differs from the Russian Revolution in the sense that the former was a political revolution and the latter a social revolution. For, in the Bolshevik Revolution, politics and political changes did not play a greater role than in the French Revolution, while the alterations in the production relations were incomparably greater.

This "objection" is merely a confirmation of the statements we have made above. Let us consider this question of the political phase. We all know that during the French Revolution the power passed from the hands of one set of owners into the hands of another set. The bourgeoisie destroyed the feudal commercial state and organized the state of the bourgeoisie. In Russia, on the other hand, the organization of all owners was swept away. The political upheaval went far deeper, corresponding to the deeper penetration of the displacement of the production relations (nationalization of industry, abolition of landed estates, beginnings of the socialist order of society, etc.).

Therefore: *the cause of revolutions is the conflict between the productive forces and the productive relations,* as *solidified in the political organization of the ruling class. These production relations are so emphatic a brake on the evolution of the productive forces that they simply must be broken up if society is to continue to develop. If they cannot be burst asunder, they will prevent and stifle the unfolding of the productive forces, and the entire society will become stagnant or retrogressive,* i.e., *it will enter upon a period of decay.*

From the above remarks, the reader will understand why society was able to transform itself, for instance, from the primitive communist condition, by way of evolution, into a patriarchal society, and then into a feudal society. Under primitive communism, there was no class rule over the means of production and no political power for the protection of such a rule. On the contrary, such rule, as well as the use of force, grew up by evolutionary process from the primitive communist production relations, owing to the growth of private property, etc. The productive forces expanded, accompanied by an increasing differentiation, an increasing experience on the part of the eldest of the clan, the development of private property, a segregation of the ruling class thus formed. Formerly, there had been no ruling class, no ruling power; therefore, there was nothing to be destroyed; therefore, the transition took place without a revolution.

H. Cunow, who in his two-volume work reduces Marx to an innocent liberal lamb, writes the following concerning revolution: "When Marx, accordingly, speaks in the above sentence of social conditions and social revolution (in his *Critique of Political Economy. N. B.*), he does not mean, as is suggested by others, a political fight for power, but the transformation of the social conditions of life following upon the blossoming forth of a new and altered mode of production". According to Marx's view, an alteration in the mode of production, particularly if the state government should seek to maintain by force the antiquated laws corresponding to an older stage in the economic relations, may lead to a political revolution or eruption of the masses of the people; but this need not necessarily be the case. The upheaval of the political and social conditions of life, as well as the ideologies, brought about by a change in the economic structure, may be achieved gradually *without uprisings and street battles* (for instance, by parliamentary methods)." (Heinrich Cunow: *Die Maxsche Geschichts-Gesellschafts- und Staatstheorie*, Berlin 1921, vol. ii, p.315). The above quotations from the honorable Social-Democratic professor are a horrible example of the mental confusion of a vulgar-liberal eclectic. In fact, in the sentence in which Marx speaks of revolution, he considered its cause to be, as we have seen, the conflict *between the productive forces and the production relations*. The revolutionary solution of this conflict is precisely the breakdown of the production relations and the state forms expressing them. But in Cunow's mind, the new mode of production arises ready-made, Lord knows whence and how, perhaps *later* (!) leading to a political revolution. This is so gorgeous, so "brilliant," that it is hard to keep up with it.

Cunow considers the case of socialism somewhat as follows: capitalism will be peacably succeeded by the socialist mode of production; the capitalists in the government will observe this miracle and marvel thereat; and then they will begin, by the use of force (or perhaps without the use of force) to battle against the alterations already accomplished in the mode of production (*i.e.*, they will begin - if we may put it thus - to demand their profits, which everyone has been forgetting). Then, not until then, an indignant nation, fighting behind barricades, will drive them out. This is a fine cartoon for a humorous weekly, but hardly material for a learned work. Cunow provides us with a great accumulation of erroneous views. In the first place, the essence of the conflict is not properly formulated (Cunow is here copying from Mr. P Struve, whose article in Braun's*Archiv* was brilliantly annihilated by G. V. Plekhanov years ago); in the second place, the actual phase of the revolutionary process are entirely distorted; in the third place, revolution itself disappears altogether from revolution. What is revolution which does not even involve a political upheaval? The preceding alteration in the mode of production here does not operate catastrophically, but quite cautiously; it is reflected in politics by parliamentary manipulations; that is all. Herr Cunow here relinquishes the Marxian theory as thoroughly and shamelessly as he has been relinquishing Marxian practice in the latter years. And this, at a time when even the stupidest bourgeois professors seem inclined to regard revolutions as phenomena which constantly arise, with a sort of inner necessity, from a given condition of society. (*Cf. Schriften der deutschen Gesellschaft für Politik an der Universität Halle-Wittenberg,* ed. by Prof. H. Waentig, No. 1: *Die grossen Revolutionen als Entwicklungserscheinungen im Leben der Völker.*)

A brief examination of the causes of revolutions will be illuminating The bourgeois revolutions (the English Revolution of the Seventeenth Century, the French Revolution at the end of the Eighteenth) have been excellently characterized - in a few lines -

321

by Marx: "The revolutions of 1648 and 1789 were not mere English or French revolutions, but revolutions on a European scale. They were not a victory of a specific class of society over the old political order; they were the announcement of the political order of the new European society (i.e., the new production relations. *N. B.*). In them the bourgeoisie was victorious; but the victory of the bourgeoisie then meant the victory of the new order of society of bourgeois property over feudal property, of nationality over provincialism, of competition over the guild, of division (of the soil. *N. B.*) over the right of primogeniture, of domination by the owner of the soil over domination of the owner by the soil, of industry over magnificent idling, of bourgeois justice over medieval privileges" (Marx: *Aus dem literarischen Nachlass*, vol. iii, Stuttgart 1920, pp.211, 212). In the period of bourgeois revolution, the chief obstacles to development were the following production relations: first, feudal ownership of land; second, the guild system in the rising industry; third, trade monopoly, perpetuating the whole by means of countless legal standards. The private ownership of property by the landholders led to countless imposts; most peasants were obliged to pay a "hunger rent," and the internal market for industry was extremely limited. In order that industry might develop, *the feudal ownership laws had just to be broken* "The rents" says Thorold Rogers (in *The Economic Interpretation of History*, London, 1891, Fisher Unwin, p.174), speaking of English rents in the Seventeenth Century, "began as competitive rents and are rapidly transformed into hunger-rents, by which I mean such rents as leave the tenant a bare subsistence, with the result that he is enabled neither to save nor to undertake improvements" (quoted by Eduard Bernstein, in *Sozialismus und Demokratie in der grossen englischen Revolution*, Stuttgart 1908, p.10).

In France, before the Revolution, "the people languished under the burden of taxes raised by the state, of duties paid to the landowner, of the tithes for the clergy, and compulsory service for all three. In every province, you could observe hosts of five thousand, ten thousand, of twenty thousand persons, men, women, children, wandering about on the roads. In 1777 an official estimate placed the number of beggars at 1,100,000; famine was chronic in the villages, recurring at frequent intervals and devastating entire provinces. Peasants deserted their villages in great numbers, etc." (P. Kropotkin: *The Great French Revolution,* London, 1921, p.16). Taxes and tributes were of infinite number and variety (*ibid.,* p.36 *et seq.,* also Luchitski: *The Condition of the Agricultural Classes in France on the Eve of the Revolution, and the Agrarian Reform of 1789-1793,* Kiev 1912, in Russian). All of these were different manifestations and expressions of feudal landownership. Property in land, which reduced the peasants to mendicants, simultaneously prevented the growth of industry, gave clear evidence of its retarding effect on the productive forces in Russia also. (Starvation rents, impoverishment of the peasantry, insignificant domestic markets, etc. - this combination was also the main cause of the Revolution of 1905. S. Maslov: *Die Agrarfrage in Russland,* Stuttgart 1907; also, Lenin's essays: *On the Agrarian Question in Russia,* in Russian.)

The Guild organization of industry retarded the growth of the productive forces at every step; for instance, in English history there was not only a seven-year apprenticeship, but also a rule permitting merchants and masters in many branches of production to employ only the sons of freemen, having a certain amount of land, as apprentices. A system of petty regulations prevailed. Naturally, in view of the general dispersion of production, there was no possibility of a planful economy. On the other hand, this type of production relations was a frightful hindrance to all personal initiative. Technical progress had no possibilities of growth. The machine was considered a menace. Trade monopoly was also a heavy burden, likewise the immense unproductive national expenditures. This system as a whole therefore constituted a burden which had to be eliminated under the slogan of "liberty" (particularly the economic liberty to buy, sell and exploit). Of course, before this system of production relations finally perished, new production relations, expressive of the growth of the productive forces, had undermined this growth, but *they could not expand fast enough, they could not maintain themselves as the dominant system of such relations.* This period was the period of the dying feudal society, its social expression was in "unsuccessful" uprisings, insurrections, etc.; such were, for instance, the peasant wars and rebellions. In England, we have Wat Tyler's Rebellion, chiefly a protest by the English peasantry against the feudal order in the social and economic sense" (D. Petrushevsky: *Wat Tyler's Rebellion*, Moscow 1914, in Russian, Introduction). Professor Petrushevsky neatly characterizes this period in the following generalization: the disintegration of English feudalism in its final form, achieved in the Thirteenth Century, proceeded side by side with the disintegration of the economic bases from which it grew. This disintegration resulted from the economic evolution of English society, its gradual transition from a closed system of economy in kind to a money economy, a political-economy organization" (*ibid.*, p.19).

Turning now to the proletarian revolution, *i.e.,* the transition from the capitalist form of society to socialism (ultimately evolving into communism), we shall again find that the principal cause for this transition is the conflict between the evolution of the productive forces and the capitalist production relations: "The monopoly of capital (*i.e.,* the privileged position of the capitalist class with regard to the means of production. *N. B.)* becomes a fetter upon the means of production which has sprung up and flourished along with, and under it. Centralization of the means of production and socialization of labor at last reach a point where they become incompatible with their capitalist integument. This integument bursts asunder. The knell of capitalist private property sounds. The expropriators are expropriated." (Karl Marx: *Capital* vol. i, p.837). Marx's remarks mean this: the growth of the productive forces is above all an immense increase and centralization of technical tools, machines, apparatus, instruments *of* production in general. This growth involves also a corresponding regrouping of men. *In part,* this occurs in the sense that the centralization of instruments of production leads to a centralization of the labor forces, or, as Marx puts it, to a socialization of labor. But this is not sufficient to bring about an internal equilibrium of society. The evolution of the productive forces requires *planful* relations, *i.e. consciously regulated* production relations. But herein lies the chief obstacle in the capitalist structure: legally speaking, in the private! property of capitalists, or in a collective capitalist property, held by national capitalist groups. If the productive forces are to develop,., the capitalist integument must be *broken through*, namely, the property relations of capitalism, those basic production relations that are legally expressed in capitalist property and politically perpetuated in the state organization of capital. This fundamental contradiction map express itself in various ways. Thus, the World War was an expression of this contradiction. The productive forces of world economy "demand" a world regulation; the "national-capitalist integument" is too tight; this leads to war; war leads to a disturbance of the social equilibrium, etc. The trustified form of capitalism, the artificial restriction of production in order to boost profits, the monopoly of inventions (legally expressed in the patent laws), the restriction of the domestic market (low wages, etc.), immense unproductive expenditures, the obstacles placed by private property in the way *of* technical progress (for example, the objections of the real estate owner to having cables laid on his land, thus preventing a general system of electrification), etc.- all these are various expressions and functions of a single quantity: the fundamental contradiction between the growth of the productive forces and the integument of capitalist production relations.

The revolutionary upheaval accompanying the transition from one form of class society to another is a clash between the production forces and the property relations in a given society is not a sudden growth, but becomes perceptible long before *the* revolution *evolves,* during a long period, terminating in a destruction of those production relations that act as a hindrance to the further evolution of the productive forces. This "boiling point" is reached when the new production relations have already matured, concealed in the entrails of the old production relations (Marx: *A Contribution to a Critique of Political Economy,* New York, 1904, p.12).

Let us take a present-day example of this "hatching" of new relations in the womb of the old production relations. The capitalist structure includes the totality *of* production relations in capitalist society, the fundamental feature of which is the totality of relations between workers and capitalists, relations that may be expressed-as we have seen-by means of things (capital). The capitalist structure of society is therefore determined chiefly by the combination of the relations between the individual capitalists, and those between the individual workers. The capitalist structure of society is by no means fully expressed in the relations within the capitalist class nor is its "essence" to be found in the relations between the workers. This essence consists in the combination of both forms of the production relations of capitalism, the bond connecting and binding two basic classes, each of which constitutes in itself an aggregate of production relations, as stated above. The following is the picture of the manner in which a new mode of production matures within a certain old mode of production.

Within the production relations of capitalism, i.e., within the class combination, a portion of these production relations constitutes the basis for the new "socialist" order of society. We have already seen what Marx considers as the basis of the socialist order; namely, first, the centralized means of production (productive forces), second (particularly in production relations), "socialized labor", i.e., principally the relations within the working class, the totality of the production relations within the proletariat (production bond between all workers). It is upon this production relation of cooperation, maturing in the womb of capitalist production relations in general, that the temple of the future will rest.

We must also obtain clarity on another point; we have seen that the cause of revolution is the conflict between the productive forces and the basic production relations (property relations). Now this fundamental contradiction is expressed in a contradiction production, particularly in a contradiction between the *one* phase of capitalist production relations and the *other* phase. It is clear that the social centralized labor which is embodied in the proletariat becomes more and more irreconcilable with the economic (and therefore with the political) domination of the capitalists. This "socialized labor" demands a planful economy, and will not tolerate anarchy between classes; it is an expression of the organized nature of society, which cannot be fully realized in capitalist society, particularly not in the social field. For, class society is a contradictory, *i.e.,* unorganized society. Manifestly, the capitalists' will not and cannot relinquish their class rule. It is consequently, necessary to eliminate the rule of the capitalists, in order to achieve' the possibility of organization all along the line. We therefore encounter a conflict between the production relations embodied is the proletariat and those embodied in the bourgeoisie.

We are now prepared to understand the following. make history, the conflict between the productive forces and the production relations will not find its expression in an attack made:, by dead machines, *things,* on men, which would be a monstrous and ridiculous assumption. Obviously, the evolution of the productive forces places *men* in a position of outright opposed situations, and the conflict between the productive forces and the production relations will find its expression in a conflict *between men,* between *classes.* For, the relations of cooperation between workers find expression in the living man, in the proletariat, with its interests, aspirations, its social energy and power. The restrictive, dominant basis of the production relation of capitalism also finds u its expression in living men, in the capitalist class. *The entire conflict assumes the form of a sharp struggle between classes; the revolutionary struggle between classes; the revolutionary struggle of the proletariat against the capitalist class.*

The opportunistic troubadours of the Social-Democracy, such as H. Cunow, love to emphasize the "unreadiness" of present conditions, for which they again seek support in Marx, who said that no form of production is succeeded by another form until it has created a field for the further growth of the productive forces. These hoary sages proceed, therefore, to finecomb the surface of the earth in their search for villages - let us say in Central Africa - which are still unprovided with savings banks, and which still contain naked savages. We should like to meet such efforts with a quotation from one of our own books: "The World War, the beginning of the revolutionary era etc, *is precisely an evidence of the objective 'maturity* here spoken of. For here we have a conflict of the greatest intensity, as a consequence of an antagonism that had developed to enormous proportions and was constantly being reproduced, having grown up in the womb of the capitalist system. Its destructive force is a fairly precise indicator of the level attained by capitalist evolution, a tragic expression of the complete incompatibility of the further growth of the productive forces with the envelope of the capitalist production relations. We are here dealing with the collapse so frequently predicted by the creator of scientific communism" (N. Bukharin : *Okonomik der Transformationsperiode*, Hamburg 1922, p.67).

c.The Revolution and its Phases

We have seen that the starting point of revolution is the conflict between the productive forces and the production relations, which places the class that serves as the bearer of the new mode of production in a peculiar position, "determining" its consciousness and its will in a specific direction. The necessary condition for revolution is therefore a revolutionizing of the consciousness of the new class, an ideological revolution in the class that is to serve as the grave-digger of the old society.

It is worth while to dwell on this point, above all, to recognize that this revolution has a material basis. Furthermore, it is necessary to make clear why we are dealing with a violent alteration in the consciousness of a new class, namely, with a *revolutionary* process.

Each order of society is based, as we have again and again stated, not only on an economic basis, for all the ideologies prevalent under a given order of things serve as rivets to hold together the existing order.

These ideologies are not playthings, but in many ways serve as girders to maintain the equilibrium of the entire social body. It is obvious that if the psychology and the ideology of the oppressed classes were absolutely hostile to the existing order, the latter could not maintain itself. Any form of society will convince us that its existence is rendered possible on the whole by the psychology and ideology of class harmony, which is particularly well illustrated by the example of capitalism at the beginning of the World War of 1914-1918. While the working class had evolved an ideology that was independent of that of the bourgeoisie, the working class nevertheless was strongly imbued with a faith in the permanence of the capitalist world order, with an attachment to the capitalist state; the mentality of class harmony had great power. No true uprising of one class against the other was possible before the consummation of the entire psychological and ideological revolution. Such a mental revolution takes place when the objective evolution places the oppressed class in an "intolerable situation": causing it to feel clearly that no improvement can be obtained under the existing order. A class attains this realization when the conflict between the growth of the productive forces and the production relations has produced a collapse of the social equilibrium, and made it impossible to restore it on the old basis. If we trace the course of the proletarian revolution, we shall find that the working class had already developed a psychology and an ideology that were more or less hostile to the existing order, during the capitalist evolution of humanity. Marxism expressed this ideology in the clearest and most profound manner. But precisely for the reason that capitalism still could and did continue to develop, even paying higher wages to labor by plundering and mercilessly exploiting the colonies, the capitalists had by no means become "intolerable" in the actual consciousness of the masses of workers. In fact, in the working classes of Europe and America, a sort of "common interest" with the capitalist national state was felt Simultaneously, the *Marxian* Marxism, originating in the Revolution of 1848, had been replaced in the labor parties by a specific "Second International Marxism", which distorted the Marxian theory both with regard to the social revolution, as well as with regard to the doctrine of impoverishment, of collapse, of proletarian dictatorship, etc. This condition resulted in the betrayal by the Social-Democratic parties in 1914, and in the patriotic tendencies in the working class. Only the war, an expression of the contradiction in capitalist development, and its consequences, began to make clear that "things could not go on thus". The psychology and ideology of class harmony were gradually replaced by the psychology and ideology of civil war, and, in the purely ideological field, "Second International Marxism" began to be replaced by true Marxism, i.e., by what may be properly designated *as scientific communism.*

Therefore: this mental revolution consists in a collapse of the old psychology and ideology (they are burst asunder by the new turbulent facts of life) and the creation of a new truly revolutionary psychology and ideology.

The Social-Democrats will never understand this; in fact, they would prefer to believe that no proletarian revolution may grow from the soil of misery and starvation, wherefore no revolution growing from this soil can be a "genuine" revolution. Marx's conception of this matter, as stated in an editorial in the New

York *Tribune* of February 2, 1854, affords an interesting contrast to this view: "Yet, we must not forget that a sixth power exists in Europe, maintaining at certain moments its domination over all five so called 'great powers', and causing them all to tremble. This power is revolution. After having long dwelt in quiet retirement, it is now again summoned to the field of battle by crises and starvation". There is needed only a signal, and the sixth and greatest European power will step forth in shining armor, sword in hand, like Minerva from the brow of the Olympian. The impending European war will give the signal" (quoted by Cunow, vol. i, p.322). Marx therefore did not engage in idiotic statements as to the impossibility of a proletarian revolution after the war, that revolution could not be built up on starvation, etc. Marx may have been mistaken as to the *tempo* of evolution, but he brilliantly predicted the main landmarks of the course of events: crises, starvation, war, etc.

The second phase of revolution is *political revolution, i.e.,* the seizing of power by the new class. The revolutionary psychology of the new class becomes action. The oppressed class, encountering the concentrated power of the dominant class, namely, its state apparatus, disorganizes, in the process of struggle, the opponent's state organization, in order to break down the resistance it offers. This state organization is to a certain extent destroyed and then rebuilt, partly from elements of the old system, partly from new elements. We must here point out that the seizure of power by the new class is not and cannot be merely a transfer of the same state organization from one hand to another. Even socialist circles have been subject to this naive error. Marx and Engels specifically speak of the destruction of an old power and the creation of a new power, and naturally so, for the state organization is the highest expression of the power of the ruling class, its congelation, its concentrated authority, its principal fighting mechanism, its principal weapon of self-defense against the oppressed class. How could the oppressed class break the resistance of its oppressors without laying hands on the principal weapon of oppression? How can an economy be *defeated without disorganizing its powers?* Either the powers of the commanding class are on the whole uninjured, in which case the revolution may be regarded as lost; or they revolution is victorious, which usually amounts to the disorganization, the destruction of the forces (chiefly, the state organization) of the commanding class. But as the material power of the state authority finds its most important expression in the armed forces, *i.e.,* in the *army,* it is evident that whatever destruction has taken place has chiefly affected the whole army. The English Revolution in the Seventeenth Century showed this by destroying the state power of the feudal kings, their army, etc., and creating the revolutionary army of the Puritans, as well as Cromwell's dictatorship. The French Revolution also showed it, by disintegrating the royal army and creating another army on a new basis. The Russian Revolution beginning in 1917 has illustrated the same point in its destruction of the state mechanism of the feudal landowners and the bourgeoisie, its disorganization and destruction *of* the imperialist army, and its creation of a new state of an entirely new type, and a new revolutionary army.

Both Marx and Engels were well aware of this theoretically; we shall not take pains to prove this statement, as the reader will find the necessary material in Lenin's *State and Revolution,* the orthodox Marxian treatment of which is now recognized even by bourgeois scholars (such as Struve and particularly P. I. Novgorodtsev: On *the Social Ideal* Berlin 1921, in Russian). When forced into a corner, the Social-Democratic theoreticians now find themselves obliged to attack Marx openly, and to oppose the revolutionary, "destructive" phase of his doctrine. This grateful function has devolved upon Heinrich Cunow, (*ibid, vol. i,* p.310: "Marx kontra Marx"), who repeats Sombart's stupid fiction to the effect that the scholar Marx had inflicted great damage upon Marx the revolutionary. Cunow distinguishes two "divergent forms" of the theory of the founder of scientific communism; first, according to Cunow, the state is regarded by

Marx, *sociologically,* as a thing arising from the conditions of economic evolution, an organization fulfilling social functions; second, Marx also conceives the state from a *purely political* point of view, as a class instrument of oppression, responsible for all evil. The first point of view is that of a scholar; the second, that of an "optimistic revolutionary" (!). It is in the latter view, according to Cunow, that we must seek an explanation for Marx's hatred of the state and his effort to overthrow the state machinery of the bourgeoisie.

It is easy to point out the error in Cunow's view. He is wrong in contrasting the "social functions" of the state machine with its class-oppressing character. "Politics is the concentrated expression of economy." Capitalist production is inconceivable without the capitalist state. The capitalist production, of course, fulfills very important functions. But the fact of the matter is that during a revolution, the "important social functions" discard one historical garment and put on another, which takes place by a shift in classes, by a *break-up* of the old relations. Cunow's sophistries are a repetition of Renner's sophistries. During the war, Renner supported the Fatherland of the Hapsburgs and of capitalist profit by the following reasoning: uninstructed persons imagine capital to be a thing; Marx has shown that it is a social relation; this relation necessarily possesses two phases: capitalists and workers; consequently - this is Renner's inference - when you speak of the capitalist; you necessarily imply the existence of the capitalist; consequently in defending the worker, you must also defend the capitalist, for neither can exist without the other; such are the "interests" of the whole. All such considerations of course assume in advance that the wage worker wishes to remain a wage worker forever. In actual fact, however, revolution is not concerned with the "right" to be a wage worker, but with the "right" to *cease* to be a wage worker.

The political phase of revolution therefore does not involve a mere *seizure* of the *intact old machinery* by a new class, but more or less (depending on which class follows upon the old society) a *destruction of this machinery,* followed by the erection of a new organization, *i.e.,* a new combination of things and persons, a new coordination of the corresponding ideas.

The third stage of revolution is the *economic revolution.* The new class, now in power, makes use of its power as a lever for economic upheaval, breaks up the production relations of the old type and begins to erect new relations which have been maturing in the womb of the old order, and *in contradiction* with that order. Marx defines this period of revolution as follows, in his discussion of the proletarian revolution: "The proletariat will use its political supremacy to wrest, by degrees, all capital from the bourgeoisie, to centralize all instruments of production in the hands of the State, i.e., of the proletariat organized as the ruling class; and to increase the total of productive forces as rapidly as possible. Of course, in the beginning, this cannot be effected except by means of despotic inroads on the rights of property, and on the conditions of bourgeois production; by means of measures, therefore, which appear economically insufficient and untenable, but which, in the course of the movement, outstrip themselves, necessitate further inroads upon the old social order, and are unavoidable as a means of entirely revolutionizing the mode of production." [4]

We are now obliged to consider an important and fundamental question: in the typical case, how does this transformation, this reorganization of production relations, actually proceed, and how should it proceed?

The old Social-Democratic view on this point was quite simple. The new class - in the proletarian revolution, the proletariat - removes the commanding "heads", whom it dismisses more or less gently, and then assumes control of the social apparatus of production, which has been developed to a splendid and uninjured maturity in the bowels of the capitalist Abraham. The proletariat installs its own "heads", and the thing is done. Production goes; on without interruption, the process of production suffers no set back, the entire society sails on harmoniously on its course toward a full-blown socialist order. But a closer inspection of the revolution in the production relations will show us that these production relations, as viewed from the point of view of the labor process, are nothing more nor less than the total human labor mechanism, a system of interconnected persons, who, as we know, are related by a specific type of bond. Furthermore - an extremely important point - the labor functions of the various groups of persons in class society are connected with each other, *bound up with their class function.* Therefore a shifting of the class relations more or less destroys the old labor apparatus, causing the construction of a new one, precisely as in the political phase of the revolution. It is certain that a *temporary* decrease in the productive forces will result; every change in society must be paid for by discomfort. It is also evident that the degree to which the old apparatus is destroyed, the depth of the wound, depends above all on the extent of the shift in the class relations. In bourgeois revolutions the power of command in production passes from one group of owners to another; the principle of property remains valid; the proletariat retains its former place. Consequently, the destruction and disintegration of old institutions is far smaller than in cases in which the lowest layer of the pyramid, the proletariat, takes its place at the top. In such a case, an immense upheaval is inevitable. The old order: bourgeoisie, upper class intellectuals, middle class intellectuals, proletariat, is *destroyed.* The proletariat stands in splendid isolation; everyone's hand is raised against it. There results an inevitable temporary disorganization of production, which continues until the proletariat succeeds in rearranging the order of persons, uniting them with a *new* bond, i.e., until a new structural equilibrium of society has become effective.

This principle was enunciated by the present writer in his *Ökonomik der Transformationsperiode* (particularly chapter iii) to which those interested are referred. A few supplementary remarks may not be out of place. First, may this view be considered orthodox? We believe Marx interpreted the matter thus; at least, it is suggestive that Marx here uses precisely the same expression as that used in his discussion of the destruction of the state. He says that the envelope (integument) of capitalist production relations is "burst asunder" (*Capital,* Vol. 1, p.837); In other passages he speaks of a dissolving a "rebuilding". Obviously, a ` bursting asunder" of production relations must interrupt the "regularity of the production process", though a different condition might be more pleasant. Very probably this is the thought that peers through-though in rudimentary form-where Mark speaks of the economic "untenability", of a "despotic inroad" by the proletariat, which nevertheless, so to say, is profitable in the long run. Second, we have heard a number of objections with regard to the New Economic Policy in Russia. The objectors point out that in the *Ökonomik der Transfornaationsperiode* we are too one-sided in our defense of the Russian Communist Party in its blind attack on everything; for the facts of life now show that the mechanism should not have been destroyed; now, it would appear, we have become as mild and gentle as the Scheidemanns. In other words, the destruction of the capitalist production apparatus is represented as a *fact* in the Russian reality, but not as a general law of revolutionary transition from one form of society (capitalist) to the other (socialist). This "objection" is apparently based on a very careless conception of the matter. The Russian workers could not readmit the capitalists, etc., before they had given them a resounding thrashing and gained a firm foothold themselves, *i.e.,* until the conditions of the new social equilibrium had been established in their main outlines, but our critics would prefer to start from the other end. Even in our official mechanism (for instance, in the army) we are now admitting great numbers of the old officers in Russia, and giving them commanding posts. Could we have afforded to do this at the beginning of the revolution? Dared we *refrain from* destroying the old Czarist army? The army would then not have been ruled by workers, but would have ruled the workers, which has of course been sufficiently proved by the experiences with Ministers

Scheidemann and Noske in Germany, Otto Bauer and Renner in Austria, and Vandervelde in Belgium. Third, nine-tenths of the New Economic Policy of Russia is due to the peasant character of the country, *i.e.,* to specific Russian conditions. Fourth, we are of course speaking of the typical course of events. Under special conditions, we may have a state of affairs that will not involve destruction. For example, after the proletariat has been victorious in the most important nations, the bourgeoisie may perhaps surrender with all its mechanism.

The above point of view by no means maintains that all of society disintegrates into individual persons. On the contrary, it maintains that the various hierarchical strata of persons are segregated from each other; the proletariat cuts loose from the other strata (technical mental workers, bourgeoisie, etc.), but within itself, as an aggregate of persons, it closes its ranks more tightly, at least for the most part. This forms the basis for the *new* production relations (we have already seen that "socialized labor", chiefly represented by the proletariat, is the very element that has "become mature" within the framework of the old economic order).

The fourth (last) phase of revolution is the *technical revolution.* A new social equilibrium having been attained, i.e., a new and durable envelope of production relations having been created, capable of serving as an evolutionary form of the productive forces, an accelerated evolution of these forces now sets on; the barriers are down, the wounds inflicted by the social crisis are healed, an unparalleled boom begins. New tools are introduced, a new technical foundation is created, a revolution in technique takes place.. Now a "normal", "organic" period in the evolution of the new social form sets in, creating its corresponding psychology and ideology.

We shall now recapitulate. The starting point for revolutionary development was a disturbance of the equilibrium between the productive forces and the production relations, as evidenced in a disturbance of the equilibrium between the various portions of the production relations. This disturbance of the equilibrium between classes is expressed chiefly in the destruction of the psychology of class harmony. Furthermore, there is a sudden disturbance of political equilibrium, which is restored on a new basis, then a sudden disturbance of the economic structural equilibrium, also restored on a new basis, followed by the erection of a new technical foundation. Society begins its life on a new basis; all the functions of its life assume a new historical raiment.

d.Cause and Effect in the Transition Period; Cause and Effect in Periods of Decline

Our discussion of the process of revolution, which is equivalent to a process of transition from one social form to another, led us to the conclusion that this process, after its initial clash between the productive forces and the production relations, passes through a number of phases, *beginning* with ideology, *ending* in technique, a sort of reverse order, as it were. In this connection, it will be useful to examine a concrete example afforded by the proletarian revolution. Heinrich Cunow, self-appointed critic of Marx, finds a contradiction between two passages in Marx (one taken from the *Poverty of Philosophy,* the other from the *Communist Manifesto*). In the first passage we read: "The working class, in the course of evolution, will put in the place of bourgeois society an association which will exclude classes and their opposite, and there will no longer be any political authority as such, because the political authority is the expression of class hostility within bourgeois society." The other passage (*Comvnunist Manifesto*) defines the course of events as follows: "If the proletariat in its struggle with the bourgeoisie is forced to unite itself as a class, to make itself to eliminate the old production relations by force, in destroying these production relations it also destroys the basic conditions for the existence of class contradictions; it thus abolishes classes altogether, as well as its own class rule."[5]

Cunow makes the following reply: "This (the passage in the *Communist Manifesto. N. B.*) is, sociologically speaking, almost the direct opposite of the above sentence from Marx's *Poverty of Philosophy*. In the latter work, we have, first, the abolition of class stratification, in the course of social evolution, which is followed by its political (!) conquest, since the basis of the old state authority is thus destroyed. But in the *Communist Manifesto*, we have, first, the conquest of the state power, followed by the application of this power to an overthrow of the capitalist production relations, upon the disappearance of which the class contradictions and finally classes as such are abolished in the sequel." [6] Cunow therefore maintains that in the *Poverty of Philosophy*, Marx shows himself to be a learned evolutionist, while the *Communist Manifesto* reveals him as a crazy revolutionist. Mr. Cunow is here consciously distorting the facts, for he knows that the *Poverty of Philosophy* calls for a "bloody battle" ("bloody battle or non-existence; thus - only thus - does history put the question"). In the first passage, Marx is speaking of the period *after* the conquest of power, of the dying out of the power of the proletariat; he is not discussing any "political conquest", but he considers the political authority from the outset as a vanishing quantity. The same is the case in the *Communist Manifesto*. There is no doubt, therefore, that Marx considered the conquest of political power (*i.e.,* the destruction of the old state machinery and the *characteristic* new machinery) as a condition for the transformation of the production relations, brought about by a forceful "expropriation of the expropriators". We are therefore dealing with things in the reverse order. The analysis is not proceeding from economy to politics, but from politics to economy. In fact, since production relations are being altered by the lever of political authority, it follows that economy is determined by policy. Cunow is absolutely wrong when he says that we are here dealing with a sociology that precisely contradicts Marx's sociology. The proper word for this procedure is *forgery.*

It is important not to lose sight of the point of departure of the entire process, which is the conflict between the evolution of the productive forces and the property relations. The entire social's transformation is based on this beginning, and does not cease its harsh course until a new structural equilibrium has ensued in society. In other words: a revolution begins when the property relations have become a hindrance to the evolution of the productive forces; revolution has done its work, as soon as *new* production relations have been established, to serve as forms favoring the evolution of the productive forces. Between this beginning and this ending lies the reverse order in *the influence of the super structures.*

In the previous chapters we have seen that the superstructure is not merely a "passive" portion of the social process: it is a specific force, against which it would be absurd to argue, as even Mr. Cunow will admit. But just at this point we have an extended analysis, in time, of a reversed process of influence, which analysis results from the catastrophic character of the entire process, from the disturbance of all the customary functions. In so called "normal times", any contradictions arising between the productive forces and economy, etc., are quickly obliterated, are quickly absorbed by the superstructure, which passes it on to the economy and the productive forces, the cycle then beginning all over again, etc., etc. In this case, however, the mutual adaptation of the various sections of the social mechanism proceed with dreadful slowness, with torments, with immense sacrifice; and the contradictions themselves are here contradictions of immense proportions. It is not surprising, therefore, that the process of a reversed influence of the superstructure (political ideology, conquest of power, application of this power in reshaping the production relations) is of long duration, filling an entire historical period. But precisely this is the *peculiarity of the transition period,* which Mr. Cunow absolutely fails to understand.

The following also must be understood. Every superstructural force, including also the concentrated authority of a class, its state authority, is a *power;* but this power is *not unlimited. No* force can transcend its own limits. The limits imposed upon the political power of a new class that has seized the power are inherent in the existing state of economic conditions and therefore of the productive forces. In other words: *the alteration in the economic conditions that may be attained with the aid of the political lever itself dependent on the previous state of the economic conditions.* This may be best seen from the Russian proletarian revolution. In November, 1917, the working class seized power, but it could not think of centralizing and socializing the petty bourgeois economy, particularly the peasant economy. In 1921 it transpired that the Russian economy was even stronger than had been supposed, and that the forces of the proletarian state machinery were merely sufficient to maintain a socialization of large-scale industry, and not even all of that. Let us now approach another phase of the question. Let us attempt to understand the nature of the interruption of the productive forces, introduced by the revolutionary process; also, the temporary *reduction* in the level of these productive forces.

Unorganized society, of which capitalist commodities society is the most striking expression, always develops by leaps and bounds. We are aware that capitalism involves wars and industrial crises. We all know that these wars and crises are an "essential phase" of the capitalist order of society. In other words, the continued existence of capitalism necessarily involves crises and capitalist wars; this is a "natural law" of capitalist evolution. What is the meaning of this law, from the point of view of the productive forces of society? First, what is it that happens during a crisis? We have a cessation of factory work, an increase of unemployment, a lower production; many enterprises, small ones particularly, disappear; in other words, there is a partial *destruction of the productive forces.* Parallel with this process, there is an enhancement of the *organized forms* of capitalism; a strengthening of the large-scale enterprises, the formation of trusts and other powerful monopoly organizations. After the crises, there is a new cycle of development, a new growth on a *new* basis, under *higher* organizational forms, affording greater opportunities for the evolution of the productive forces. The possibility of continued evolution is therefore bought at the price of a crisis and a waste of productive farces during the crisis. To a certain extent, the case in capitalist wars is the same. These wars are an expression of capitalist competition; they result in a temporary decrease in the productive forces. After wars, bourgeois states rounded out their boundaries; great powers became greater; small states were swallowed up; capital assumed world-wide proportions, obtained a greater field of exploitation, the outlines within which the productive forces could develop were extended, a temporary decline was followed by a swifter process of accumulation. It may therefore be said that the possibility of an *expanded reproduction* was purchased, in this case also, at the price of a temporary decline in the productive forces.

The same law may be observed from the wider point of view; from which we regard the evolution of society. The significance, of revolution is in its elimination of an *obstacle* to the development of the productive forces. Strange as it may seem, in destroying this hindrance, revolution temporarily destroys a portion of its productive forces. This is as inevitable as the crises under capitalism.

The destructive effects of revolution ("debit side of revolution") may be considered under the following heads:

1. *Physical destruction of the elements of production.* Destruction of things and persons, in any form, during the civil war process, may be included here. If barricades are constructed of railroad cars, and men are killed (civil war and class war involve such sacrifices), this is equivalent to a destruction of productive forces. The annihilation of machines, factories, railroads, cattle, etc.; the injury and ruin of instruments of production by sabotage, failure

to repair or replace -absent parts, etc., absence of workers due to war, departure of mental workers, etc.; these are phases of the physical destruction of the productive forces.

2. *Deterioration of the elements of production.* Here belongs: deterioration of machinery for lack of repair and replacement; physical exhaustion of workers, intellectuals, etc, resorting to inferior substitutes (poorer metal, replacement of male labor by female and child labor; petty bourgeois elements in the factories, etc.).

3. Interruption of liaison between the elements of production. This is the main cause of the specifically revolutionary disintegration; it includes the disorganization of the production relations spoken of in our large-type text. (Destruction of liaison between the proletariat, on the one hand, and the technical mental workers and bourgeoisie on the other hand; disintegration of capitalist organizations; decay of liaison between city and country, etc., etc.). This does not mean a physical destruction of productive forces (things and persons), but their *elimination from the process of production;* factories not working, men idle. Also, there is the waste due to the initial "inability" of the new class, its incapacity to build up its organizations, its "mistakes", etc.

4. Shifting the production forces for unproductive consumption, including the readjustment of a great portion of the productive forces for military purposes; manufacture of cannons, rifles military supplies, other war materials. *cf. Oekonomik der Transformationsperiode,* chap, vi).

This enumeration is based on the proletarian revolution; obviously, any revolution will present the same classification, but the total "expense" of revolution will in general be lower in bourgeois revolutions.

History fully supports these theoretical principles. The peasant wars in Germany were followed by immense disorganization; French Revolution, with its financial crises, its monstrous price inflation, famine, etc., shows the same course. The Civil War in

343

the United States put the country back at least ten years. Later, the social transformation having been accomplished, a boom period will ensue, advances proceeding much more rapidly than any advances in the pre-revolutionary period, since society has now found a more appropriate envelope for its productive forces.

Therefore: the transition from one form of society to another is accompanied by a temporary lowering of the productive forces, which cannot in any other way find an opportunity for further evolution.

The law of decline is distinguished from the law of the transition period by the fact that the transition in the former case does not lead to a higher economic form; in this case, the decline in the productive forces will continue until society receives some impulse from without, or until its equilibrium has been found on a lower basis, whereupon we have a "repetition", or a permanent state of stagnation, not a higher form of economic relations.

An analysis of the causes of a decline will in general show that they are due to the impossibility of breaking down the given property relations; they therefore remain fetters on evolution, and react on the productive forces, so that the latter continue "going down" all the time. This may be the case, for example, when the

opposing classes in a revolution are of about the same strength, making a victory impossible for either class; the society is doomed.

The conflict between the productive forces and the production relations has determined the will of the classes in a specific manner. But revolution has not advanced beyond its earliest phases. The classes give battle; neither is victorious; production falls asleep; society dies out. Or, we may have the case in which the victorious class is incapable of disposing of the tasks imposed upon it, or, the revolution may not mature to the "boiling point"; but the evolution of the productive forces has been proceeding in an environment in which it has determined a quite specific class alignment, namely, a completely parasitic ruling class, and a completely demoralized oppressed class. Here there will be no evolution; sooner or later a simple, one might say a "bloodless", disintegration and dissolution will take place. Or, we may have a case of mixed type. All these cases show that the evolution of the productive forces has led to an economy and to such forms of "superstructure" as have a reverse influence of such nature on the evolution of the productive forces as to oblige them to go down. Of course, when the productive forces go down, the level of the entire social life will also go down.

Greece and Rome may be taken as examples of social decay, later Spain and Portugal. The ruling classes, maintained by the slaves conquered in countless wars, became parasites, also a portion of the free burghers. Their technology permitted them to wage wars, thus conditioning a corresponding economy, which produced a specific state order; but the material condition of the classes also determined their: being, their social psychology (a mentality of parasitic degeneration;, among the rulers; of degeneration by stupefaction and oppression among the oppressed). Such a superstructure was too heavy for its basis, the productive forces, which ceased to grow, ultimately becoming a negative quantity. In place of this perfectly simple explanation, most scholars present an unspeakable confusion, of which an excellent, specimen is afforded by the latest book of P. Bitsilli: *The Fall of the Roman Empire.*Vassilyev, a professor at the University of Kazan,.who enumerates - in a work already quoted by us - all the theories explaining the fall of the ancient world, particularly emphasizes thetheory of biological degeneration. This degeneration, in the case of ,x: the rulers, according to Professor Vassilyev, is a necessary consequence and the natural end of any civilization (with certain reservations): for, brawn is replaced by brain, the nervous system develops its wants, a biological deterioration results. Mr. Vassilyev therefore believes that the materialist Marxian conception of history should be replaced by the materialist *Vassilyev* conception, which is much "profounder". Mr. Vassilyev points out that the progress of the social sciences has taken the following path: first, there was an analysis of ideology; then, of policy; then, of the social order; then, of economy (Marx). We are told that we must now penetrate still more profoundly, descending to the material nature of man, his physiological constitution, the changes in which constitute the "essence" of the historical process. There is no doubt that the material nature of man changes; but, if we proceed beyond the limits of social laws, we must advance from biology to physics and chemistry, and then we shall become fully aware of Mr. Vassilyev's error. The fact of the matter is that the law of cause and effect in social *science* must be a *social* law. If we wish to explain the social properties of man's material nature, we must determine what are the social causes whose influence has altered the physiology (and also the psychology) of man. We shall then find that this phase is determined above all by the conditions of material being, *i.e.,* by the situation of the given groups in production. Mr. Vassilyev is therefore not digging deeper, but walking backwards; his theory is actually the time-honored theory of the inevitable aging of the human race. Besides being useless because it is based on a mere analogy with physical organisms, it is not capable of explaining the simplest phenomena. Why, for instance, has the infinitely more complicated European civilization not passed away, whereas Rome degenerated? Why did Spain "fall" and not England? Commonplaces about degeneration will explain nothing, for the simple reason that this degeneration is a product of social conditions. Only an analysis of these conditions can result in a proper view of the subject.

An analysis of the causality of the transition period and the periods of decay will also throw light on the question of what determines the evolution of the productive forces, and what is the influence under which they are changing. Obviously, they are changing *under the reversed influence of the basis, and of all the superstructural forms.* Marx himself recognizes this. Thus, he informs us in *Capital* (Chicago, 1909, Vol. iii, p.98): "Such a development of the productive power is traceable in the last instance to the social nature of the labor engaged in production; to the division of labor in society; to the development of intellectual labor, especially of the natural sciences." Strictly speaking, the matter does not end here : Marx emphasizes only the most important factors influencing the productive forces in industry. "But," our opponents may object, "why do you begin at just this point?" Our answer is: "For the simple reason that, no matter what interactions may be taking place within society, the internal social relations at any given moment will-insofar as we are considering society in its condition of equilibrium-correspond with the relation existing between society and nature."

e.The Evolution of the Productive Forces and the Materialization of Social Phenomena (Accumulation of Civilization)

A consideration of the process of production and reproduction, where the productive forces are *growing, will* present us with a general law; namely, as the productive forces grow, more and more labor is applied in the production of instruments of production. With the aid of these constantly increasing instruments of production, which are a part of the social *technique,* a much smaller part of the work than formerly will produce a much greater quantity of useful products of all kinds. When manual labor was used, comparatively little time was devoted to the manufacture of instruments of production. Men worked in the sweat of their brows with their insignificant, wretched tools, and their work was not very productive. But in a highly evolved society a great portion of their labor is devoted to the production of immense labor tools - machines, mechanisms - in order to produce further immense instruments of production, such as huge factories, electrical power stations, mines, etc., which

347

consume a large part of the human forces available. But the use of these tremendous instruments of production vastly increases the productivity of living labor; the investment yields more than compound interest.

In capitalist society, this law is expressed in the relative increase of constant capital as compared with variable capital. That portion of capital that has been devoted to the construction of factory plants, machines, etc., grows more rapidly than the portion put into wages. In other words, in the evolution of the productive forces in capitalist society, the *constant* capital grows more rapidly than the *variable* capital. We may state this in another manner, as the productive forces of society grow, they are being constantly realigned, with the result that an increasingly greater share of these forces goes into the branches producing instruments of production.

The growth of the productive forces, the accumulation of man's power over nature, is expressed in the higher and higher "specific" weight assigned to *things,* to dead labor, to the social technique.

It is reasonable to inquire whether similar phenomena are presented by other fields of social life, for we have seen that the superstructural labor is also labor, differentiated labor, which has been segregated from material labor. And we have seen that the outline of the superstructure includes both material elements and personal elements, as well as ideological elements proper. Where is there here an accumulation, an aggregation of "mental" culture? Do we here encounter anything resembling the material process of production?

Let us anticipate: Yes, there is such a similarity, expressed in the fact that the social ideology is crystallized or congealed in things which are quite material. Let us remember that we are enabled to reproduce the ancient "mental cultures" out of the so called "monuments" of earlier epochs; the remnants of old libraries, the books, inscriptions, clay tablets, statues, paintings, temples, old musical instruments, and thousands of other things. In a way, we may regard these things as a congealed, materialized ideology of ages long gone by, enabling us to judge the psychology and ideology; of their contemporaries with precision, as the remnants of working tools enable us to judge of the stage reached in the evolution of the productive forces, and even of the economy of these epochs. Furthermore, in the superstructural work, in ideological labor, instruments of *consumption* frequently serve also as instruments for further production. A picture gallery contains instruments of enjoyment; for the public which goes to view them, it consists of consumption products. But they are also instruments of production, not in the same sense - of course - as brushes and canvas, for the coming generations learn art, a new "tendency" in painting, from them. A new school of does not descend from heaven, but grows out of an earlier stage, even though it may renounce and denounce the old ideological system. Nothing is made of nothing. As, in the political field, the old state is destroyed during a revolution, while the new state will contain many old elements in a *new* arrangement, so, in the ideological field, even the greatest interruptions do not wipe out a certain succession and connection with the past: the new building is not constructed on the "bare ground". Paintings, for the painter, are an instrument of production, an accumulated artistic experience, a congealed ideology, from which any further movement in this field must take its start.

Perhaps the following objection might be made: "All this may be very fine, but what has the sublime doctrine of Christianity in common with the material symbols that have been traced on parchment or paper, or with the pigskin in which the Gospels are bound? What is the connection between the scientific ideology as such and the masses of paper that have been piled up in the libraries? Surely there is a difference between the ideologies, the most delicate product of the collective human mind, and such gross material things as books, considered as *things!*" But this argument may be due to a misunderstanding. To be sure, paper *per se,* or coloring matter, or pigskin, would in these cases have no meaning for us if they were without a social *being*. We have shown in chapter *vi* (*b. Things, Men, Ideas*) that a machine - considered outside of its social connection - is merely a piece of metal, wood, etc. But it has also a social being, in that men interpret it as a machine in the labor process. Similarly, the book, in addition to its physical being, as a piece of paper, also has a social being; it is considered as a book in the process of reading. Here, the book is a congealed ideology, an instrument of ideological production.

If we approach the question of the accumulation of mental culture from this angle, it will be easy to admit that this accumulation takes the form of an accumulation of things, of crystallized, material shapes. The "richer" a field of mental culture is, the more imposing, the broader the field of these "materialized social phenomena". Figuratively speaking (and not forgetting its character as an ideology), the material skeleton of mental culture is the "fundamental capital" of this culture, which increases with the "richness" of this culture, and is dependent "in the last analysis" on the stage reached in the material productive forces. The childish inscriptions, masks, rude images of idols, drawings on stones, art monuments, rolls of papyrus, other manuscripts, parchment books, temples and observatories, clay tablets, with their cuneiform writings; later, the galleries, museums, botanical and zoological gardens, huge libraries, independent scientific exhibitions, laboratories, sketches, printed books, etc., etc., are an accumulated crystallized experience of humanity. The new library stacks, with their new books, considered together with the olds stacks and books, are an interesting physical manifestation of collaboration of many generations in their uninterrupted succession.

We have become so accustomed to many phenomena in this field as to lose sight of the historical boundaries. Our present-day psychology and ideology, for instance, finds its crystallization in the daily newspaper. Yet, the newspaper itself is a modern phenomenon, beginning approximately in the

Seventeenth Century. No doubt important official news was already posted on walls ("published") in ancient Rome and among the Chinese (Eighth Century A.D.), but this was barely a beginning (*cf. K.* Bücher: *Das Zeitatngswesen* in *Kultur der Gegenwart*, Berlin and Leipzig, 1906, part i, section i.). Books, in our sense, are also not found before the invention of printing, when there were only rolls of papyrus and parchment codices, then the most perfect method of preserving the accumulated "wisdom of centuries", clay tablets:(Babylon) preserved in gigantic libraries. For example, Ashurbanipal's famous library (*cf.* Pietschmann: *Das Buch,* in *Kultur der Gegenwart).* Libraries (called by Leibnitz "treasuries of all the riches of the human spirit") may therefore be found in very ancient times, and it is to the remnants of such libraries that we owe most of our information on many secrets of times long past (a short study on libraries is found in *Die Bibliotheken,* by Fritz Milkau, in *Kultur der Gegenwart).* Important examples are: the above mentioned library of Ashurbanipal (Seventh Century B.C.), also the libraries of the most ancient ecclesiastical schools (Third Century B.C.). Hermann Diels (*Die Organisation der Wissenschaft,* in *Kultur der Gegenwart,* p.639) rightly observes: "Among all institutions of learning, libraries have ever been the most important and most essential means of preserving, disseminating and transmitting learning and of supplementing the evanescent *viva vox* of living teachers." Art objects, of course, play the same rôle, as preserved in collections, galleries, museums, cathedrals, etc.

The accumulation of mental culture is therefore not only an accumulation of psychological and ideological elements in the minds of men, but also an accumulation of things.

f. The Process of Reproduction of Social Life as a Whole

We are now in a position to recapitulate this subject:
A constant "metabolism" is taking place between nature and

society, a process of social reproduction, a labor process operating in cycles, constantly replacing what is consumed, extending its basis as the productive forces develop, and enabling mankind to widen the boundaries of its existence.

But the process of production of material products is simultaneously a process of production of given economic relations. Marx says: Capitalist production, therefore under its aspect of a continuous connected process, of a process of reproduction, produces not only commodities, not only surplus-value, but it also produces and reproduces the capitalist relation; on the one hand the capitalist, on the other, the wage-laborer."[2] This formula of Marx is not only applicable to capitalist production, but universally applicable in general. If we consider the case of the ancient slaveholding economy, each production cycle in it will be accompanied by the slaveholders' receiving his share and the slave his; in the next cycle, the slaveholder will also discharge his role, while the slave will discharge his; if reproduction should expand, the sole alteration will be in the fact that the share and power of the slaveholder, the number of his slaves, the amount of surplus labor produced by them, will become greater. Thus, the process of material production is simultaneously a process of the reproduction of those production relations, of that historical envelope, in which they are operative. On the other hand, the process of material reproduction is a process of constant reproduction of the corresponding labor forces. "Man himself," writes Marx, "viewed as the impersonation of labor power, is a natural object, a thing, although a living conscious thing, and labor is the manifestation of this power residing in him."[8] But at various historical periods, in accordance with the social technique, the mode of production, etc., specific labor forces, i.e., labor forces with the required skill, are available. The process of reproduction is constantly reproducing this skill; it therefore reproduces not only the things, but also the "living things", i.e., workers possessing certain qualifications; it also reproduces relations among them with expanding reproduction, it makes the adjustments corresponding to the new level of the productive forces, in this case assigning the persons, who may not be the same (for new types of skill, new "living machines" are required), to posts in the labor field which may not be identical. But the fundamental texture of the production relations nevertheless remains intact (except in the case of revolutionary periods) and continues to be reproduced on a progressively larger and larger scale.

If the totality of the various types of skill of the labor forces be designated as a social physiology, it may be said that the process of reproduction is constantly reproducing the economy of society and therefore also its physiology.

All types of work have thus far required a specific physiological type, a result of specialization. We may therefore distinguish - even by his external appearance - a transport worker from a metal works clerk, butcher, stool-pigeon, etc., not to mention a musician or a member of the "liberal professions" in general. Therefore, not only is the psychology of men their social psychology, but their physiological structure is a product of social evolution. As he works upon nature, man alters his own nature. What we call "social physiology" may not be considered as opposed to economy, for it is a part of economy. The difference simply is this: in discussing economy, we analyze the connections and the type of these connections between men, their: material relation with each other, what we call social physiology is not a connection, but a property of these same elements.

Simultaneously with the process of reproduction, we have a similar motion of the entire vast machine of social life: the mutual relations between classes are reproduced, also the conditions of the state organization; also the relations within the various spheres of ideological labor. In this aggregate reproduction of the entire social life, the *social contradictions* are also constantly reproduced. The partial contradictions, a disturbance of equilibrium emanating from the impulses imparted by the evolution of the productive forces, are being constantly absorbed by a partial realignment of society within the frame of the given mode of production. But the *basic* contradictions, those arising from the very nature of the given economic structure, continue to be reproduced on a larger and larger foundation, until they attain the proportions that bring about a catastrophe. Then the entire old form of production relations will collapse, and a new form arises, if the social evolution continues. "The historical development of the antagonisms, immanent in a given form of production, is the only way in which that form of production can be dissolved and a new form established."[2] This moment is succeeded by a temporary interruption in the process of reproduction, a disturbance which is expressed by the destruction of a portion of the productive forces. The general transformation of the entire human labor apparatus, the reorganization of all the human relations, brings about a new equilibrium, whereupon society enters upon a new universal cycle in its evolution, by extending its technical basis and accumulating its experience (as congealed in objects), which serves as the point of departure in any new forward step.

BIBLIOGRAPHY

Plekhanov: Articles attacking Struve in the collection, *Criticism of Our Critics* (the best work on the analysis of the production relations from the point of view of revolution). Rosa Luxemburg: *Sozialreform und Revolution.* Karl Kautsky: *Die soziale Revolution.* Karl Kautsky: *Anti-Bernstein.* Heinrich Cunow: *Die Marxsche Geschichts-, Gesellschafts-und Staatstlaeorie, vol. i.* Werner Sombart: *Sozialismus and soziale Bewegung.* N. Lenin: *State and Revolution.* N. Lenin: *The Proletarian Revolution and the Renegade Kautsky.* N. Bukharin: *Oekonomik der Transformationsperiode.* Hermann Beck (editor): *Wege und Ziele der Sozialisierung.* J. Delevsky (Social-Revolutionary): *Social Antagonisms and the Class*

Struggle in History. Karl Marx: particularly, *A Contribution to the Critique of Political Economy;* also, Marx's historical writings.

NOTES

[1]N. Beltov (Plekhanov) : Concerning *the Materialistic Interpretation History,* in *Criticism of Our Critics,* p.333. The italics are mine. *N. B.*

[2]Karl Marx: *Capital,* vol. iii, Chicago, 1909, p.919. My italics. *N.B.*

[3]Karl Marx: *Capital,* vol. iii, Chicago, 1909, p.1030.

[4]*Communist Manifesto,* Chicago, 1912, pp.40, 41; also quoted by Cunow, *ibid.,* Vol. i, p.321

[5]Quoted by Cunow, *ibid.,* p.182.

[6]*Ibid.,* vol. 1, pp.321, 222.

[7]Capital, Chicago, 1915, vol. i, p.633

[8]*Ibid.,* vol. i, v. 225.

[9]*Capital,* vol. i, p.534, 535.

8: THE CLASSES AND THE CLASS

a. Class, Caste, Vocation

WE have already seen the important function of the classes in the evolution of human society. Even the social structure in a class society depends chiefly on what classes exist in this society what is their mutual relation, etc. And we have seen that every great alteration in the social life is connected with a class struggle in one way or another. It is not unimportant to note that transition from one form of society to another is realized through a furious class struggle. This is why Marx and Engels opened the *Communist Manifesto* with the words: "The history of society existing up to the present is the history of class struggles. " We have already defined the general nature of a *class.* We now prepared to go into further detail.

A social class - we have seen - is the aggregate of persons playing the same part in production, standing in the same relation toward other persons in the production process, these relations being also expressed in things (instruments of labor). It follows that in the process of distribution the common element of each class is its uniform source of income, for the conditions in the distribution of products are determined by the conditions in production. Textile workers and metal workers are not two separate classes; but a single class, since they bear the same relation to certain other *persons* (engineers, capitalists). Similarly, the proprietors of a mine, a brick-field, a corset-factory, are all of one class; for regardless of the physical differences between the things they manufacture, they occupy a common ("commanding") position with regard to the persons engaged in the process of production, which position is also expressed in things ("capital").

The production relations are therefore at the basis of the class alignment in society. Other divisions have been made, which must now be disposed of. A frequent conception is the division into the classes of "poor" and "rich". A man having twice as much money in his pocket as another is considered as belonging to a different class, the basis of the division being in this case the amount possessed of the standard of living. An English sociologist (D'Ett) has gone so far as to draw a table of classes: the first and lowest class (paupers) have a budget of eighteen shillings per week; the second class, twenty-five shillings; the third, forty-five shillings, etc.[1]

This conception is not only very simple, but also naive and erroneous. From this point of view, a well paid metal worker in capitalist society would not be counted with the proletariat, while a poor person or artisan would fall into the working class. The lumpenproletariat would have to be considered as the most revolutionary class, as the power capable of realizing the transition to a higher form of society. On the other hand, two bankers, one of whom has twice as much money as the other, would have to be assigned to two separate classes. Yet, everyday experience shows us that the various classes of workers are far more likely to fight side by side than are the workers and artisans, or workers and peasants, etc. The peasant is not much inclined to feel any solidarity with the worker. At the other end of the scale, two bankers feel themselves to be members of the same family, though one be ten times as rich as the other. Marx already pointed out that the size of one's purse constitutes a merely quantitative difference, which may, to be sure, throw two individuals of the same class into violent opposition to each other. In other wards, the difference in "wealth" may not be considered as sufficient basis for the definition of a class, even though it have an influence within the frame of one class.

Another widely accepted theory is that which makes

the process of distribution the basis of the class division of society, *i.e.*, the distribution of social *income*. Thus, in capitalist society, the division of income into three principal groups, profits, ground rent, wages, gives rise to a distinction between three classes: capitalists, landlords, proletarians (wage workers). The share falling to each of these classes may only grow - for a given quantity of social income - at the cost of the share falling to another class. The members of one class are therefore united not only by common and uniform interests, but also by the opposition of their interests to those of other classes.

Unless we debase this theory to a mere consideration of who is getting more and who less, we at once encounter the following question: why are the persons who are united in a class reproduced as a class? How comes it that - let us say - in capitalist society certain types of income exist? What is the cause for the stability of these "types of income"? The mere putting of these questions shows the true statement of affairs. This stability depends on the relation to the *means of production,* which, in turn, *express the relation between men in the process of production.* The function of men in production, and the ownership in the interests of production, *i.e.,* the "distribution of persons" and the "distribution of means of production" are fixed quantities within the limits of the:existing mode of production. If we are dealing with capitalism, we have therefore a category of men who command the production process, who simultaneously control all sorts of means of production, and there is also a category of men working at the command of the former, subordinating their labor power to them, and producing commodity values. This circumstance is responsible for the fact that a certain natural law process prevails in the distribution of the products of labor (*i.e.*, in the distribution of income). We have therefore come to the point of considering the most important phases in production - the "distribution of persons" and the "distribution of things" - as the basis of class relations.

Nor could it be otherwise, as we may learn if we approach

question in the most abstract terms. Every class is obviously a certain "real aggregate", *i.e.,* it sums up all the persons related in uninterrupted mutual reactions, all the "living persons" whose roots are in production, and whose thoughts may reach into the skies. Each class is a special, definite human system within the great system known as human society. Our approach to the class must be similar, therefore, to our approach to society; in other words, the analysis of classes must begin with production. We must of course not be surprised to find classes differing from each other along various lines: in production as well as in distribution, in politics, in psychology, in ideology. For all these things are interdependent; you cannot crown a proletarian tree with bourgeois twigs; this would be worse than placing a saddle on a cow. But this connection is determined, in the last analysis, by the position of the classes in the process of production. Therefore, we must define the classes according to a *production criterion.*

What is the difference between a social *class* and a social *caste*? A class, as we have seen, is a category of persons united by a common role in the production process, a totality in which each member has about the same relative position with regard to the other functions in the production process. A social caste, on the other hand, is a group of persons united by their common position in the juristic or legal order of society. Landlords are a class; the nobility are a caste; the great landlords are defined by a common production type, not so the nobility. The noble has certain legal rights and privileges, due to his "noble station". Yet, economically speaking, this noble may be impoverished; he may barely vegetate; he may be a slum-dweller; but his station remains that of a noble; such is the Baron in Gorki's *Lower Depths.* Similarly, under the Tsarist government, workers' passports often contained the words: "Peasant from such and such a province, such and such a district, such and such a parish", although this worker had never been a peasant, had been born in a city and worked for wages since childhood. Such is the difference between *class* and *caste.* A person whose class character is that of a worker may (from the standpoint of Tsarist laws) be classified as a peasant. But have we any right to dwell on laws without descending deeper, since we know that politics (including law) is "the concentrated expression *of* economy"?

Of course, we must go deeper; we have ourselves pointed out that it is methodologically very important to approach the social alignments chiefly from the production angle. We find the question of *caste* excellently presented by Professor Solntsev, who has written the authoritative work on classes: "Socially unequal groups in the various stations appear as such and do not arise on the basis of the relations of the social labor process, of economic relations, but chiefly on the basis of legal and state relations. The caste is a *legal-political* category, which may express itself in various forms . . . . As distinguished from *caste,* the class alignment arose on the basis of economic conditions" (p.22). Solntsev denies that *caste is* synonymous with class, or that it is merely a legal-political raiment for class, while he admits that in ancient times, for instance, "the division into estates necessarily reflected certain class differences" (p.25), that "the class struggle assumes the peculiar form of a struggle between stations (estates)" (p.26). This somewhat vague statement obliges us to seek a somewhat clearer formulation. In the French Revolution the *tiers état* was a mixture of various classes, then but slightly differentiated from each other: it included the bourgeoisie, the workers and the "intermediate classes" (artisans, petty traders, etc.). All were members of the *tiers état* for the reason of their legal insignificance as compared with the privileged feudal landlords. This *tiers état* was the juristic expression for the class bloc opposing the dominant landlords. It follows that class and caste may not be taken as synonymous, while the shell of the caste may include on the whole a class *kernel* (a single estate corresponding to a number of class which remain classes, in spite of the vagueness in Solntsev's mind). On the other hand, class and caste may fail to correspond in another way, as already shown: one might belong to a "lower class" but "higher caste" (an impoverished nobleman may become a janitor or stoker), or the reverse: one may belong to a lower caste and higher class (a peasant may become a wealthy merchant) Evidently the "class content under the economic envelope" is here non-existent.

A correct theoretical statement of the case may not be obtained by a consideration of individual instances, but only from the point of view of typical mutual reactions within the frame of a specific economic order. The following fundamental circumstance is worthy of attention: the "estates" are abolished by the bourgeois revolutions, by the evolution of bourgeois conditions. Capitalism was incompatible with the existence of "estates", for the following reason: in pre-capitalist forms of society, all relations are far more conservative; the tempo of life is slower; alterations are less significant than under capitalism. The dominant class is the landed aristocracy, almost a hereditary class. This striking *immobility* in conditions made possible a consolidation of class privileges - as well as class duties - by means of a series of legal standards; this immobility enabled classes to be enveloped in the garment of the'. "estate". On the whole, therefore, the "estates" followed the same line as the classes or groups of classes, in their opposition to a certain class. But this harmony was brusquely disturbed by the entrance of the far more mobile conditions of commodities capitalism; the insignificant man became important; the *nouveaux.. riches* arose, a very frequent phenomenon (some of the great landlords assumed capitalist forms, others becoming impoverished,: while still others maintained themselves on the previous level, etc.)., Thus the mobility of capitalist relations completely undermines the existence of the "estates". The transition period of the disintegration of feudal relations is also expressed in the growing disharmony between the economic content of the classes and the legal envelope of the "estates". There now ensued the conflict that led inevitably to the collapse of the entire system of "estates". Its "caste" form was incompatible with the growth of capitalist production relations, as the class envelope of the production process is now becoming incompatible with the further growth of the productive forces. Thus, Marx wrote in his *Poverty of Philosophy:* "The condition for the liberation of the working class is the abolition of all classes, as the significance of the liberation of the *tiers état* . . . was the abolition of all the *estates*". Engels, elucidating this passage, adds the following: "Estates here mean the estates of the feudal state in the historical sense, estates with definite, limited privileges. The revolution of the bourgeoisie abolished the estates and their privileges. The bourgeois society now recognizes only classes. To term the proletariat the *fourth estate* was therefore to contradict history.'

Therefore: in the period of the stable precapitalist systems, the estates were the legal expression of the classes; the increasing incompatibility of these quantities (the disturbance of equilibrium between the class content and the legal form of the estates) was called forth by the growth of capitalist relations and the disintegration of not only the higher but also the lower of the old feudal classes. Under the feudal system, the peasantry as a class coincided in general with the peasantry as an estate; but the country bourgeoisie and the city proletariat began to differentiate from the peasantry, retaining, however, the garment of their former "estate" (caste), which, being ill adapted to the new conditions, have had to be discarded.

We must now examine the third category mentioned at the beginning of this chapter. Manifestly, *vocation* is connected with the process of production. At first glance, the difference between a vocation and class is based on the fact that the line between vocations is not drawn as a line in the relations between men, but as a line in their relations with *things*, depending on what *things*, with what *things* one works, what *things* are produced. The difference between metal turner and joiner and mason is not based on a different relation to capitalists, but simply on the fact that one works metals, the other wood, the third stone.

Yet the essence of the matter is not in the *thing*, for vocation is simultaneously a social relation; in the process of production, which unites many workers of different types, owing to the standards of the production process, a definite relation naturally prevails. However different these relations may be, they are all subsidiary to the differences that prevail in the principal phase: *the differences between the work of those who command and those obey, the differences expressed in the property relations.*

The classification by vocation, as a relation between person as a relation based on the relation toward technical tools, methods, objects of labor, coincides neither with the division of labor into commanding and obeying elements, nor with the corresponding distribution of instruments of production, *i.e.,* with the proper relations in these instruments of production.

Professor Solntsev is therefore wrong in declaring that vocation "is a *natural technical* category (Solntsev's italics, N. B.), that it is peculiar to human communities even in the prehistoric period, as w< as in the following stages that it is not an historical category coy nected with the social order" (*ibid.*, p.21), in short, that it is a eternal category. Vocations become vocations for the reason that certain kind of labor is usually performed throughout the individual's life: let the shoemaker stick to his last! But this does not signify that things have always been thus and must always remain thus. The increasingly automatic nature of technology will liberate men from this necessity and will show to what extent this category also been historical rather than permanent.

We are now prepared to take up a description of the important *classes.*

1. *The basic classes of a given social form* (classes in the proper sense of the word) are two in number: on the one hand, the *class* which commands, monopolizing the instruments of production; *on'* the other hand, the executing class, with no means of production, which works for the former. The specific form of this relation of economic exploitation and servitude

determines the form of the, given class society. For example: if the relation between the commanding and executing class is reproduced by the purchase of labor power in the market, we have capitalism. If it is reproduced. by the purchase of persons, by plunder, or otherwise, but not by the purchase of labor power alone, and if the commanding class gains control of not only the labor power but also of body and soul of the exploited persons, we have a slaveholding system, etc

In connection with capitalism, three classes are usually counted, as confirmed by Marx in the well-known passage at the end of volume iii of *Capital,* where the manuscript suddenly breaks off at the beginning of an analysis of the classes in capitalist society. "The owners of mere labor power, the owners of capital, and the landlords, whose respective sources of income are wages, profit and ground-rent, in other words, wage laborers, capitalists and landlords, form the three great classes of modern society resting on the capitalist mode of production." *(Capital,* Chicago, 1909, vol. iii, p.1,031) But the circumstance that the land-owning group constitutes a *great* "class" does not imply that it is one of the essential classes. Thus, we find the following passage in Marx, which Professor Solntsev erroneously quotes in his own support: "Objectified and living labor are the two factors on the contrast between which capitalist production is based. Capitalist and wage laborer are the sole functionaries and factors in production, their relation and opposition being a result of the very essence of the capitalist mode of production . . . . Production, as observed by James Mill, might therefore continue uninterrupted, if the landlord should disappear and be replaced by the state. . . This reduction in the number of classes directly concerned in production, to capitalists and wage laborers, *eliminating the landlord,* who only subsequently enters into the relation, as a consequence not of property relations produced within the limits of the capitalist mode of production, but of property relations *handed down* to capitalism - a reduction inherent in the nature of the capitalist mode of production, distinguishing it from feudal and ancient production - makes it an adequate theoretical expression of the capitalist mode of production and manifests its *differentia specifica."* (Marx: *Theorien über den Mehrwert,* Stuttgart, 1915, vol. ii, part i, pp.292 *et seq.*). Marx again makes the same statement in his treatment of nationalization of the soil.

The basic classes may be subdivided into their various elements. In capitalist society, the commanding bourgeoisie was partly industrial, partly commercial, partly banking, ere. The working class includes skilled and unskilled workers.

2. *Intermediate classes:* these include such social-economic groups as constitute a necessity for the society in which they live, *without being* a remnant of the old order. They occupy a middle position between the commanding and exploiting classes. Such are, for instance, the technical mental workers in capitalist society.

3. *Transition classes:* these include such groups as have emerged from the preceding form of society, and as are now disintegrating in their present form, giving rise to various classes with opposite roles in production. Such are, for example, the artisans and peasants in capitalist society, who constitute a heritage from the feudal system, and from whom both the bourgeoisie and the proletariat are recruited.

Thus, the peasantry is constantly falling to pieces under capitalism; economically speaking, it is differentiated; the rich peasant grows out of the medium peasantry, becoming a trader and, one step further up, a true bourgeois. On the other hand, the proletariat is also growing out of the peasantry, by some such process as this: the peasant has no horse; he becomes a farm laborer or seasonal worker; he becomes a true proletarian.

4. *Mixed class types:* these include such groups as belong to of class in one respect and to another class in another respect, for example, the railroad worker who runs a farm of his own, for which he hires a laborer; he is a worker from the standpoint of the railroad company, but an "employer" from the standpoint of

the hired man.

5. Finally there are the so call declassé groups, *i.e.;* of persons outside the outlines of social labor: the *lumpenproletariat,* beggars, vagrants, etc.

In an analysis of the "abstract type" of society, *i.e.,* any form in its purest state, we are dealing almost exclusively with its basic classes; but when we take up the concrete reality, we of course find ourselves faced with the motley picture with all social-economic types and relations.

The general cause of the existence of classes is defined by Engels in his *Anti-Dühring* as follows "" that all previous historical contradictions between exploiting and exploited, ruling and oppressed classes are explained by the same comparatively undeveloped productivity of human labor. As long, as the truly working population is so completely occupied by its necessary labor as to leave it no time' for conducting the common affairs of society - division of labor, business of the state, legal matters, art, science, etc.- so long did we necessarily have a special class which, freed from actual labor, looked after these matters; in which connection, it never failed to place more and more work upon the shoulders of the working masses, for its own advantage" (Friedrich Engels: *Herrn Eugen Dührings Unwälzung der Wissenschaft,* Stuttgart, 1901, pp.190, 191). In another passage (p.190), practically the same remark is repeated, with the added statement that society is divided into two classes. A recapitulation of the whole matter is this: "The law of the division of labor is therefore *the basic factor in the division into classes.*"

Professor Solntsev criticizes G. Schmoller, who finds the cause of the formation of the classes to be chiefly the division of labor, and attacks Schmoller's reference to Engels with the following words: "Engels actually shows the close connection between the process of class formation and the process of the division of labor; but " Engels regards the division of labor as only the necessary natural-technical condition for the formation of social classes, not as their cause; the causal basis of the formation of classes was found by Engels, *not* in the division of labor, *but* in the relation between production and distribution, *i.e.,* in processes of purely economic nature" (*ibid.,* p.303, my italics, *N. B.*). As we have observed above, when considering the question of vocation, we may not oppose the division of labor to the production relations, for the division of labor is likewise one of the varieties of the production relations. Schmoller's error (in his books, *Die Tatsachen der Arbeitsteilung,* Jahrbücher, 1889; *Das Wesen der Arbeitsteilung und Klassenbildung,* Jahrbücher, 1890) is in overlooking the difference between the stratification of vocations and the stratification of classes, thus reconciling class oppositions in the spirit of the organic school. The theory of L. Gumplowicz and F. Oppenheimer, which traces the origin of classes from extra-economic force, overlooks the difference between the abstract theory of society and the concrete facts of history. In actual history, the role of the extra-economic use of force (conquest) was very great, and had an influence on the process of class formation. But in a purely theoretical investigation, this condition may not be considered. Assuming that we are analyzing society *only,* "abstract society", in its evolution, we should find classes developing here also, by reason of the so called "internal" causes of development mentioned by Engels. Therefore, the role of conquests, etc., is merely a (very important) *complicating* factor.

b. Class Interest

We have seen that classes are specific groups of persons, "real aggregates", distinguished by their role in production, which role 1s expressed in the *property relations.* But these two phases in the production process also are accompanied by a third phase- the process of the distribution of products in one way or another. Production is paralleled by distribution.

The forms of distribution correspond to the forms of production. The position of the classes in production determines their position in distribution. The antagonism between administrators and the administrated, between the class monopolizing the instruments of production and the class possessing no means of production, is expressed in an antagonism in income, in a contradiction between the shares held by each class in the product turned out. This different "being" of the classes also determines their "consciousness". The contradictions of the "being", of the conditions of existence, are directly reflected in the growth of *class interests.* The most primitive and general expression of class interest is the *effort of the classes to increase their share in the distribution of the total mass of products.*

In the system of class society, the process of production is at the same time a process of the economic exploitation of those who work physically.

They produce more than they receive, not only because a portion of the product turned out (of *values,* in capitalist society) goes for extending production ("accumulation", in capitalist society), but also because the working class is supporting the owners of the instruments of production, is working for them. The most general interest of the dominant minority may therefore be formulated as the effort *to maintain and extend the opportunities for economic exploitation;* while the interest of the exploited majority is *to liberate itself from this exploitation.* The first of these two efforts has an eye only to society as it exists at present; the second is challenge to the existence of this society.

But the economic structure of society - as we have seen - is fortified in its state organization and supported by countless superstructural forms. It is therefore not surprising to find the economic class interest clothed also in the garment of political, religious, scientific interests, etc. The class interests thus develop into an entire system, *embracing the most varied domains of social life.* These coordinated interests, maintained in place by the general interest of the class, condition the construction of the so called "social ideal", which is always the quintessence of the class interests.

A few additional points require our attention in a discussion of class interests

First: *permanent, general interests must be distinguished from temporary, momentary interests.* The "momentary" interests may even constitute an objective contradiction to the permanent interests. The English workers, for instance, were acting in accordance with their temporary interests when they accepted a class harmony with the English bourgeoisie, supporting them in the imperialist war; they acted in the interest of their wages, which were increased at the expense of the colonial workers. But because they thus destroyed the solidarity of *all* the workers, and made a compact with their employers, they were opposing the general and permanent interests of their class.

Second: the professional *interests of a group* must not be confused with the general *interests of the class.* Thus, the dominant bourgeoisie may, in capitalist society, win over the aristocracy of labor (skilled labor), whose special interests then do not coincide with those of the entire working class; they are group interests, not class interests. Another example: during any war, the commercial bourgeoisie violates the commercial laws with all its might, although the bourgeois state itself established these laws, and is waging war in the interest of the bourgeoisie as a *class.* In other words, the group interests of the commercial section of the bourgeoisie is in this case at variance with the interests of the bourgeoisie as a *class.*

Third: alterations in *principle and tendency* in the momentary interests of the class, proceeding simultaneously with the alterations in principle of its social situation, must not be left out of account. The example of the proletariat will serve to illustrate this point. In capitalist society, its most permanent and general interest is the destruction of the capitalist system. Its partial demands always have this general tendency: the

369

conquest of strategic positions, the undermining of bourgeois society, the improving of the proletariat's material position, enhance its social strength, preparing its forces for the attack on the entire capitalist order. Now, let us assume that the proletariat has discharged its historical. task. It has destroyed the old state machinery, built up a new machinery, produced a new social equilibrium; temporarily, the proletariat assumes the place of the commanding class. Obviously, the *direction* of its interests has radically changed: all its partial interests, taken from the point of view of the general interests, are now subordinate to the idea of *fortifying and developing* the new conditions, organizing them, offering resistance to every attempt at destruction. This dialectic transformation is an outgrowth of the dialectic evolution of the proletariat itself, onice it has become a state power.

The common element behind both these opposed directions of interest is the construction of a new form of society, whose bearer is the proletariat, a construction which presupposes the destruction of the old envelope, which had become an obstacle to the evolution of the productive forces.

A new class, to be capable not only of destroying the old system of social relations, but of building up a new one, must necessarily turn its interests in the direction of *production, i.e.,* it must not approach social questions from the standpoint of division and mere distribution, but from that of a destruction of old forms for the purpose of a *construction* of forms with more perfect *production,* with more powerful *productive forces.*

c. Class Psychology and Class Ideology

The difference in the material conditions of existence that lie at the basis of the class stratification of society impresses its mark on the entire consciousness of the classes, i.e., on the class psychology and ideology. We already know that the psychology of a class is not always identical with the material interests of that class (for instance, the psychology of despair, escape from the world, longing for death); but it always results from the life conditions of this class, being *constantly* determined by the latter. Let. us consider a few examples of the manner in which the class psychology and the class ideology are actually conditioned by the economic condition of the class.

Our first example will be taken from the Russian Revolution. It is a matter of common knowledge that Russian Marxists and Social-Revolutionaries disagreed as to which class would lead society to socialism. The Marxists maintained it would be the working class, the proletariat; the Social Revolutionaries, on the other hand, claimed that the peasantry would take the lead in this field. The facts of life have supported the Marxists; the peasantry supported the proletarians in their struggle against the landlords and capitalists, because the proletariat guards the peasants' ownership of the soil and makes possible the development of peasant economy; yet the peasants are but little susceptible to communism and adhere to the old forms of tilling the soil, and of agriculture in general. It will be interesting to determine the reasons for this phenomenon, the heroic struggle of the proletariat and its incomparably, greater receptivity for communist reconstruction and communist ideology. It is not sufficient to reply that the peasants are not quite so poor, for then we might ask why the *lumpenproletariat* (beggars, declassed persons) did not furnish the chief detachments of fighters.

It is important to learn what are the traits that must be preset in a class in order to enable it to accomplish a transformation of society, to shunt society from the capitalist track to the socialist track.

1. Such a class must be one that has been *economically exploited and politically oppressed* under capitalist society; otherwise, the class will have no reason for resisting the capitalist order; it will not rebel under any circumstances.

2. It follows - to put the matter crudely - that it must be a *poor class;* for otherwise it will have no opportunity to feel its poverty

as compared with the wealth of other classes.

3. It must be a *producing* class; for, if it is not, *i.e.,* if it has no immediate share in the production of values, it may at best destroy, being unable to produce, create, organize.

4. It must be a class that is *not bound by private property,* for a class whose material existence is based on private property will naturally be inclined to increase its property, not to abolish private property, as is demanded by communism.

5. This class must be one which has been *welded together* by the conditions of its existence and its common labor, its members working side by side. Otherwise, it will be incapable of desiring - not to mention constructing - a society that is the embodiment of the social labor of comrades. Furthermore, such a class could not wage an *organized* struggle or create a new state power.

In the following table, the presence or absence of these characteristics in the various classes and groups is indicated by a + or - sign.

Class Properties	Peasantry	Lumpen proletariat	Proletariat
1. Economic exploitation	+	-	+
2. Political oppression	+	+	+
3. Poverty	+	+	+
4. Productivity	+	-	+
5. Freedom from private property	-	+	+
6. Condition of union in production, and common labor	-	-	+

In other words, the peasantry-for instance-lack several elements necessary to make them a communist class: they are bound down by *property,*and it will take many years to train them to a new view, which can only be done by having the state power in the hands of the proletariat; also, the peasantry are not held together in production, in *social* labor and common action; on the contrary, the peasant's entire joy is in his own bit of land; he is accustomed to *individual* management, not to cooperation with others. The *lumpenproletariat,* however, is barred chiefly by the circumstance that it performs no productive work; it can tear down, but has no habit of building up. Its ideology is often represented by the anarchists, concerning whom a wag once said that their whole program consists of two paragraphs. *Para.* 1. There shall be no order at all; *Para.* 2. No one shall be obliged to comply with the preceding paragraph.

We have thus seen how the conditions of material existence determine the psychology and ideology of classes in groups; the proletariat shows: hatred against capital and its state power, revolutionary spirit, the habit of organized action, a psychology of comradeship, a productive and constructive conception of things, a rejection of the traditional, a negative attitude on the "sacredness of private property", that pillar of bourgeois society, etc.; in the peasantry: love of private property, preventing them from favoring innovation; individualism, exclusiveness, suspicion of everything lying outside the village; in the *luvnpenproletariat:* shiftlessness , lack of discipline hatred of the old, but impotence to construct or organize anything new, an individualistic declassed "personality", whose actions are based only on foolish caprices. In each of the above classes, we find the ideology that corresponds to its psychology: in the proletariat, revolutionary communism; in the peasantry, a property ideology; in the*lumpen proletariat,* a vacillating and hysterical anarchism. Obviously, once such psychological and theological nucleus is present, it will set the fundamental note for the entire psychology and ideology of the class or group concerned.

In the old discussions between Marxists and Social-Revolutionaries, the latter usually formulated the question from the point of view of philanthropy, "ethics", "compassion" for the "weaker brother", and similar rubbish of a ruling class intellectual nature. For most of these "ideologists", the question of class was an ethical question of the intellectual, with his qualms of conscience, who, in his desire to overthrow absolutism, which was an obstacle in his path, sought support in the peasant (so long as the latter did not set fire to the estates of the intellectual's aunties and uncles), whose confidence he wished to gain, thus compensating for his own guilt by his noble-minded assistance. The Marxists, however, were not concerned with lacrimose sentiments or philanthropy, but with a precise study of class peculiarities, with *finding out* what class would lead in the impending struggle for socialism.

A good study (although conservative and apologetic, supporting the Black Hundred) of the psychology of the peasant is to be found in the book of the evangelical pastor A. L'Houet (*Zur Psychologie des Bauerntums,* 2nd ed., Tübingen, 1920). This learned Christian dominie esteems Germany's peasantry "above all as its supply of bodily, mental, moral, and religious health, as the Reich's war-hoard" (p.4; L'Houet means *cannon-fodder*). The pastor, who finds among the earmarks of the firmly rooted peasantry: its "homogeneous mass", its exclusiveness to the outside world, its fidelity to tradition, etc., gives an excellent description of the class psychology of the peasantry but he is inspired with feelings of rapture with those of its qualities that we regard as the "idiotism of country life" (Marx). For instance, L'Houet praises the *inertia* of the peasantry, its aversion to innovation. "As contrasted with this outspoken preference for everything that is new, the peasant unmistakably belongs to a world that reveres the old, that retains the ancient themes of life, continues to spin the old thread, to roll the old stones. With the disadvantage that he 'remains behind the times', 'does not keep abreast of the times but with the great advantage that all the achievements of his life, by reason of this one-sidedness, are characterized by reliability, solidity tried and true methods" (p.16). This inertia is found everywhere in the preservation of the original settlement, of the old home, of the old farm-names, baptismal names, costumes, the old dialect, the old folk poetry, the old mechanism of the soul, the old faces! In all, we find the same old conservative sense." (p.16). Herr L'Houet is delighted with the fact that peasant dwellings in 1871 were practically the same as in the Stone Age. He rejoices in the hereditary simplicity and poverty of the psyche, in the fact "that the number of life problems faced at any moment, in a religious, moral, artistic sense or whatever other sense - is not very large, that each generation hands down the same supply of these things to the next" (p.29). He is pleased to find that these limitations, this "idiotism" - not the fault but the misfortune of the peasantry - is not destroyed by steam and electricity, for this "principle of the past" is the basis of a simple grandiose existence in the ancient sense" (!!). *"Solidity"*, thrift and avarice,*lust for possession,* etc., are of course also highly esteemed by our dominie (as on p.6, for instance). These examples fully express the character of the class psychology and class ideology of landlords and their priests, who cherish and nurse precisely those qualities of the peasantry that prevent it from "advancing with the times".

The class psychology of the *country nobility (i.e.,* the feudal landholders) is characterized by the same outspoken conservative and reactionary spirit, which no other class possesses to the same degree. This is not hard to understand; the feudal landholders, as we know, are the representatives of feudal society, which has now passed away in almost all countries. Fidelity to tradition, to the "established forms of worship of the aristocratic family (its excellences, its fame, its worth"), symbolically expressed in the "ancestral tree"; "merit and service" the estate, the honor appropriate to "noble station", contempt for those of lower station, the attempt to limit sexual and all other intercourse to those of like station only; these are the characteristic traits of this once ruling class (*cf.* G. Simmel: *Soziologie*, p.737 *et seq.*).

The psychology and ideology in the classes of bourgeois society, i.e., the urban classes, are far more mobile. The bourgeoisie, particularly when it was a rising class, not directly threatened by the proletarian by no means presented the conservatism of the nobility. Its characteristic traits were: *individualism,* a result of the competitive struggle, and *rationalism,*a result of economic calculation, these conditions being the basis of the life of this class. The *liberal* psychology (various "liberties"), and ideology were based on the "initiative of the entrepreneur". Very interesting observations are made by Werner Sombart and Max Weber, particularly on the economic psychology of the bourgeoisie and the various stages in its development. Thus Sombart traces the rise of the entrepreneur psychology, which arose necessarily from the fusing of three psychological types: that of the conqueror, of the organizer, of the trader; from the conqueror, it takes the ability to make plans, to carry them out; the conqueror has "toughness and persistence . . . elasticity, mental energy, high tension, an indomitable will"; the organizer must be able to "control men and things in such manner as to obtain the desired profit without any reduction"; the trader, the merchant, is capable of trading and profiting by trade (Sombart: *Der Bourgeois,* München and Leipzig, 1913, p.70 *et seq.*). The bourgeoisie was characterized at the period of its highest development by a combination of these three traits. We have already discussed the psychology of the proletariat, as our whole book is concerned with the proletariat.

It is obvious that the psychology and ideology of the classes *will change, depending on the alterations in the "'social being" of* the corresponding classes, as has been repeatedly stated in the preceding chapters. One thing should still be mentioned: *the psychology" of the intermediate classes also constitutes an intermediate stage, while that of the mixed groups is a mixed psychology, etc.* This also explains the fact that the bourgeoisie and the peasantry, for example, are constantly "vacillating" between proletariat and bourgeoisie, for "two souls - alas! - dwell in their breast", etc. As Marx puts the matter in his *Der Achtzehnte Brumaire des Louis Bonaparte* (Hamburg 1885, p.33): "Over the various forms of property, over the social conditions of existence, there rises an entire superstructure of various peculiarly constituted feelings, illusions, modes of thought, and views of life. The entire class creates these out of its material foundations, as well as out of the corresponding social relations."

d. The "Class in Itself", and the "Class for Itself"

Class psychology and class ideology, the consciousness of the class not only as to its momentary interests, but also as to permanent and universal interests, are a result of the position of the class in production, which by no means signifies that this position of the class will *at once* produce in it a consciousness of its general and basic interests. On the contrary, it may be said that this is rarely the case. For, in the first place, the process of production itself, in actual life, goes through a number of stages of evolution, and the contradictions in the economic structure do not become apparent until a later period of evolution; in the second place, a class does not descend full-grown from heaven, but grows in a crude elemental manner from a number of other social groups (transition classes, intermediate and other classes, strata, social combinations); in the third place, a certain time usually passes before a class becomes conscious of itself through experience in battle, of its special and peculiar interests, aspirations, social "ideals" and desires, which emphatically distinguish it from all the other classes in the given society; in the fourth place, we must not forget the systematic psychological and ideological manipulation conducted by the ruling class with the aid of its state machinery for the purpose of destroying the incipient class consciousness of the oppressed classes, and to imbue them with the ideology of the ruling class, or at least to influence them somewhat with this ideology. The result is that a class discharging a definite function in the process of production may already exist as an aggregate of persons before it exists as a self-conscious class; we have a class, but no class consciousness. It exists as a factor in production, as a specific aggregate of production relations; it does not yet exist as a social, independent *force* that knows what it wants, that feels a mission, that is *conscious* of its peculiar position, of the hostility of its interests to those of the other classes. As designations for these different stages in the process of class evolution, Marx makes use of two expressions: he calls class *"an sich"* (*in itself*), *a class* not yet conscious of itself as such; he calls class *"für sich"* (*for itself*), a class already conscious of its social role.

This has been splendidly explained by Marx in *The Poverty of Philosophy,* in the case of working class evolution:

"It is under the form of these combinations that the first attempts at association among themselves have always been made by the workers. The great industry masses together in a single place a crowd of people unknown to each other. Competition divides their interests. But the maintenance of their wages, this common interest which they have against their employer, unites them in the same idea of resistance - *combination.* (*Combination* here means workers' combination, *N.B.*) Thus combination has always a double end, that of eliminating competition among themselves while enabling them to make a general competition against the capitalist. If the first object of resistance has been merely to maintain wages, in proportion as the capitalists in their turn have combined with the idea of repression, the combinations, at first isolated, have formed in groups, and, in face of constantly united capital, the maintenance of the association became more important and necessary for them than the maintenance of wages. This is so true that the English economists are all astonished at seeing the workers sacrifice a good part of their wages on behalf of the associations which, in the eyes of these economists, were only established in support of wages. In this struggle - a veritable civil war - are united and established all the elements necessary for a future battle. Once arrived at that point, association takes on a political character.

"The economic conditions have in the first place transformed the mass of the people of the country into wage workers. The domination of capital has created for this mass of people a common situation with common interests. Thus this mass is already a class, as opposed *to capital,* but *not yet for itself.* In the struggle, of which we have only noted some phases, this mass unites, it is constituted *as a class for itself.* The interests which it defends are the *interests of its class."* (*The Poverty of Philosophy,* Chicago, 1920, pp.188, 189, my italics, *N. B.*)

e. Forms of a Relative Solidarity of Interests

From what has been said above, it is clear that under certain circumstances a *relative* class solidarity becomes possible; two principal forms may be distinguished.

In the first place, we have the form of solidarity in which the permanent interest of one class coincides with the temporary interest of another class, while this temporary interest may contradict the general class interest.

In the second place, we may have a form of solidarity in which this contradiction is lacking, and in which we may yet have a coincidence between the permanent interests of one class and the temporary interests of another class, or between temporary interests of both classes.

The first form may be illustrated by an example from the imperialist war of 1914-1918, namely, the attitude of the working classes at the *beginning* of this war. It is well known that in most of the great advanced capitalist countries, the workers, contrary to their internationalist class interests, rushed to the defense of their "fatherlands". Their "fatherlands" were of course only the state organizations of the bourgeoisie, *i.e., class* organizations of capital. We therefore find the working class defending the organizations of its employers, which had come into conflict with each other for the division of markets, sources of raw materials, spheres of investments for their funds; this was certainly a sacrifice of the workers' own class interests, due to a condition of *relative solidarity* between the proletariat and the bourgeoisie in the nations of financial capitalism. We may understand this condition by imagining the entire system of world economy to be a countless number of intersecting threads - the production relations - meeting at several points in big, thick knots: the great capitalist countries, where live the "national" groups of the bourgeoisie, organized as a state authority. They remind us of the huge enterprises, the gigantic trusts, operative in world economy. The more powerful such a state becomes, the more mercilessly will it exploit its economic periphery: the colonies, spheres of influence, semi-colonies, etc. As capitalist society develops, the condition of the working class should become poorer. But the predatory states of the bourgeoisie, which hoodwink the workers in The "spheres of influence", were feeding "their own" workers and making them take an interest in the exploitation of the colonies. This condition brought about a relative material interest between the imperialist bourgeoisie and the proletariat; these production relations gave rise to a corresponding psychology and ideology, resulting in a recognition of the duty to defend one's country. The course of reasoning was simple: if "our" industry (which happens not to be "ours", but that of our employers) develops, wages will increase; but industry expands by obtaining markets, and spheres for the investment of capital; consequently the working class has an interest in the colonial policy of the bourgeoisie, must defend the "nation's industry", must fight for the nation's "place in the sun". All the other things followed naturally: laudation of one's mighty fatherland, the great nation, etc., and the endless high-sounding rhetoric about humanity, civilization, democracy, unselfishness, etc., so prevalent in the first stage of the World War. This was the ideology of "labor imperialism", leading the working class to sacrifice permanent and general interests for the crumbs thrown to it by the bourgeoisie as the latter squeezed the last drop out of the colonial laborers, semi-laborers, etc., etc. Ultimately, the course of the war and of the post-war period showed the working class that it had lost the game, that the permanent interests of the class are more important than its temporary interests. There ensued the process of a swift "revolutionizing" of minds.

The late Professor Tugan-Baranovsky, a "pseudo-Marxist", for a time a White Minister, in the early stage of the Russian revolution (for pure "ethics"; he always reproved Marx for his lack of ethics, his permitting himself to be carried away by class hatred, which is, of course, quite vicious) - this Tugan-Baranovsky takes up the cudgels against Marx in the following terms: Marx does not see the solidarity of interests, denies its presence in capitalist society; yet "all social classes are equally interested in the preservation of the political independence of the state, insofar as the latter has an ideal worth in their eyes. In the economic field, the state not only serves to establish class rule, but also to advance economic progress, enhancing the total national wealth, which is in accord with the interests of all classes of society. In addition, we have the cultural mission of the state, which is interested in the advance of education, and in raising the mental level of the population, if only for the reason that political and economic power cannot be separated from the advance of culture." (*Theoretische Grundlagen des Marxismus*, p.114.)

Herr Cunow (*ibid.*, vol. ii, pp.78, 79) quotes and supports this passage from Tugan, asserting, however, that Tugan here confuses social interests with the interests of the state. In reality, Cunow is confusing the revolutionary standpoint of Marx with the traitor standpoint of the Scheidemanns. The Tugan-Cunow reasoning is truly childish. We are told that the state *is not only* concerned with oppression, but also concerned with it; therefore, all classes have *an* interest in the state. By this method anything might be proved. Since,. the trusts are not *only* concerned with exploitation, *"but* also" (!) arer concerned with production, they are of general utility. Since the detective bureaus in America *not only* twist the arms of revolutionary proletarians, *"but also"* catch thieves, all classes have an interest to them, etc. It is with stuff of this kind that Herr Cunow fills the two volumes of his study on

Marxian sociology!

Cunow, however, excels all the distorters of Marxism with cynical impudence:

"According to the Marxian theory of society," we read (vol. ii, p.77 *et seq.,* of Cunow's work), "any such general will as so excellently served the purposes of the older social philosophy, does not exist; for society is not a unified thing with perfectly uniform interests (?! society!), but it is divided into classes (not so bad; but what is Cunow going to do with the state? Whose will is expressed by the state? *N.B.*). To be sure, there are also general social interests, for, since a living and working together in society is impossible without a certain order, all the members of society - with the exception of those who question the existence of society at all - are interested in maintaining this order; but, since they have different *ideals of order,* depending on their different positions within the social order, they have not the same interest in the various rules of this order, which they regard from various points of view, depending on the class angle of their vision." To put the matter in plain words; men may think that it is the bourgeoisie that is interested in preserving the capitalist order, while the proletariat is interested in overthrowing this order; but nothing could be further from the truth. The wise Cunow sets us right on this subject: since life is impossible without order, all have an interest in maintaining capitalism. But since the workers have a different "ideal of order", let them "criticize the various rules of the order" - so much Cunow will permit. But don't dare go beyond that, for then you will be one of the persons who "question the existence of society at all". This is Marxism as revised and supplemented by Cunow !

We may also take as an example that period in the evolution of the working class when it lived in a so called "patriarchal" relation with the entrepreneurs in each specific industry; in view of the general weakness of social institutions, the workers had an interest in the success of the enterprise. The workers and their "benefactors", their employers, afford an excellent illustration of a relative solidarity of interests at the expense of the general class interests.

A certain analogy is afforded by the community of interests between *slaves* and *slaveholders* in antiquity, so long as there were still "slaves of the slaves" (the Roman *vicarii*). The slaves who held slaves were themselves slave-owners, their interests thus coincided, to this extent, with the slaveholders of the "first degree". In the present-day agricultural cooperatives in Western Europe we often find the peasantry working hand in hand with the great landlords and the capitalist estate owners. The peasants unite with the others in order to dispose of their agricultural products; being *sellers,* they are opposed to the urban population; they desire high *prices* as much as does the wealthy estate-owner.

We are now already leaving the outlines of the first form of solidarity, since in this case a true agricultural bourgeoisie, recruited from the peasantry, differs in no respect from the hereditary agricultural bourgeoisie.

The best examples of the *second* form of relative class solidarity, namely, where this relative solidarity is not in contradiction with the permanent interests of the classes involved, are found in cases of class attacks against the common enemy, which are quite possible at a certain stage of evolution. For example, in the first phase of the French Revolution, the feudal system was opposed by *different* classes, both in economy as well as in politics: the bourgeoisie, the petty bourgeoisie, the proletariat, all these groups being interested in overthrowing feudalism. Of course, this general *bloc* later disintegrated, and the petty bourgeoisie, in spite of its struggles against the great bourgeoisie, which had become counter-revolutionary, simultaneously fought the incipient proletarian movement ruthlessly. Here we have a temporary class solidarity at variance with the general and permanent interests of the classes.

f. Class Struggle and Class Peace

Various gradations of interest give rise to various forms of struggle. As already shown, not every interest of a section of a main class is for that reason the class interest. If the interest *of* the workers of a single factory contradicts the interests of the remaining sections of the working class, we have not a class interest, but a group interest. But even when we are dealing with the interest of a group of workers which does not collide with the interests of other groups, the groups may yet fail to be united, class interest being absent in the consciousness of the classes; strictly speaking, there is yet no class struggle: the beginnings of a class interest, the germs of a class struggle, are present. A *class interest arises when. it places one class in opposition to another. The class struggle arises when it throws one class into active conflict with the other.* Class struggle, therefore, in the true sense, develops only at a specific stage in the evolution of class society. In other phases of social evolution it reveals itself as a *germ-form* (individual sections of the class are fighting; the struggle has not yet advanced to embrace the class as a principle, uniting the entire class), or as a concealed, "latent" form (open conflict does not ensue; "stolid resistance" is offered; the ruling class is forced to pay attention to this resistance). "Freeman and slave, patrician and plebeian, baron and serf, guild member and apprentice, in short, oppressors` and oppressed all were opposed in like manner to each other, waged ¢! an uninterrupted, now hidden, now open battle, a battle that always terminated in a revolutionary transformation of the whole society or with a common destruction of the struggling classes" *(The Communist Manifesto).* It will be useful to consider a few more examples.

Let us suppose, in a slaveholding society, that an insurrection is taking place in a latifundium belonging to a great landowner; there is plundering, damage to things and persons, etc. We may Fl not call this a class struggle in the proper sense of the word: it is the elemental fury of a small section of the slave class. The class as a whole is calm; a small band wages a bitter struggle, but remains isolated, includes but few in its numbers. The class *as such* does not come into action; one class is here not opposing another. Quite different is the case when the rebellious slaves, led by Spartacus, fought a real civil war for their liberation; here the slave *masses* were carried away: this is class struggle.

Or, let us consider the example of a movement for higher wages among the wage workers of a factory. If all the other workers in the country remain calm, we have only the promise of a class struggle, for the class as yet is not kindled. Let us consider, however, the case of a "strike wave". This is class struggle: one class stands opposed to the other. We are no longer dealing with the interests of the group impelling another group, but with the interests of a class impelling another class.

The example of the peasant serf is also interesting. Among, these serfs, there was a vague, sullen discontent; this feeling may break out, but since the class as a whole continues to be held down, it does not do so; the slaves, in terror, do not fight, but "mutter". This is the "concealed" form of the struggle, mentioned by Marx. Class struggle therefore means a struggle in which *one class has entered into action against the other class.* From this arises the extremely important principle that *"every class struggle is a political struggle"* (Marx). Indeed, when the oppressed class rises as a class power to oppose the oppressing class, this signifies that the oppressed class is undermining the bases of the existing order. And since the organization of *power* of the existing order is the *state* organization of the commanding class, it is obvious that each action of the oppressed class is directly aimed against the state mechanism, even though the participants in the struggle of the oppressed class may not at first be fully conscious of their hostility to the state power. Each such action is therefore necessarily political in character.

An interesting error of the I.W.W., in the United States, and of revolutionary syndicalists in general, may be detected by applying this principle. The I.W.W. reject the political struggle entirely, for they naively understand it to be synonymous with the parliamentary struggle. But if the I.W.W. should organize a general strike, or only a strike of railroad workers, miners and metal workers, it is obvious that this strike would have an immense *political* value, because it would have succeeded in organizing the most important armies of the proletariat, in terrifying the bourgeoisie as a class, in threatening to cut a breach in the machinery of the organized bourgeoisie; and therefore, because this strike would be directed, in reality, against the state power of the bourgeoisie.

This transformation of the individual episodes of conflict into the class struggle, in the case of the proletariat is excellently shown by Marx in the *Communist Manifesto.* "Now and then the workers are victorious, but only for a time. The real fruit of their battles lies, not in the immediate result, but in the expanding unison of the workers. This unison is helped on by the improved means of communication that are created by modern industry, and that place the workers of different localities in contact with one another. It was just this contact that was needed to centralize the numerous local struggles, of the same character, into *one national struggle between classes, but every class struggle is a political struggle:"* (*Communist Manifesto,*.Chicago, 1912, pp.24, 25.) Marx defines this transformation of the various conflicts into a class, *i.e.,* political conflict, as follows: *"Nota bene ad* political movement: The*political movement* of the working class has of course, the final object of conquering the *political power* for that class, which requires, of course, a previous organization of the*working class* to a certain point, which organization is conditioned by its own economic struggle. On the other hand, any movement in which the working class is opposed as a class to its rulers, seeking to compel them by *pressure from without, is a political movement"* Briefe an Sorge, p.240, also quoted by Cunow, *ibid.,* vol. ii, p.59) the italicized passages are in English in Marx's letter; both Marx and Engels, owing to their long stay in England, interlarded their letters with English words. *Translator).*

Herr Cunow, in quoting this passage, interprets it as follows: "at a certain stage in evolution, various social classes develop out of the economic process as a whole, with their special economic interests, in accordance with their role in this process, and attempt to put through these interests in the political life" (*ibid.*, vol. ii, p.59). This commentary is not quite correct, for Cunow suppresses the most important point, the point to which Marx gives chief emphasis: the opposition of one class to the other in principle, when each struggle is a portion of the process of the general struggle for power and for domination in society.

In an exceptionally impudent article: *Die Marx'sclae Geschichtsauffassung* (*PreussicheJlahrbücher*, 1920, Vol. 182, no. 2, p.157 *et seq.*), Professor Hans Delbrück "criticizes" the theory of the class struggle, simultaneously displaying a truly titanic ignorance in matters of Marxism. On p.165 he maintains that Marx failed to distinguish classes from castes; on p.156 he states that there was no "destruction" of the two classes in ancient Rome, while he admits the decline of the Roman Empire to be an undeniable fact. First there were civil wars, after which neither the victors nor the vanquished slaves were capable of leading society onward. On p.167 he says that feudalism never existed in England! On p.169 he "refutes" Marx with the fact that the peasants sometimes join hands with the Junkers (*cf.* our own remarks in large type), etc. But the gem of his "objections" is the following example. Delbrück quotes an ancient text discovered by the well-known Egyptologist, Ehrmann, in which we' read of the ancient Egyptian revolution, in which the slaves managed to seize power. This text is interesting in that it might have been written by Merezhkovsky or any other White Guard gentleman in his rage against the Bolsheviks; It depicts the most frightful atrocities. Herr Delbrück calls our attention to this horrible example of the class struggle? But this worthy and truly German professor falls quite unwittingly into his own trap when he adds the words that this condition lasted for "three hundred years" (p.171). Any fool would know that there can be no possibility of maintaining life for three hundred years in a state of absolute anarchy and without production. Things, therefore, cannot have been quite so bad, and Delbrück's argument, an appeal to the *emotions* of the terrified bourgeois, is simply ridiculous.

Amusing objections to the Marxian theory are also raised by Mr. J. Delevsky (*The Social Antagonisms and the Class Struggle in History,* Petersburg, 1910, in Russian); his chief objection is the following. After quoting this passage from Engels: It was Marx,; himself who had first discovered the complete law of motion of history the law according to which all historical struggles, whether proceeding on the political, religious, philosophical, or any other ideological ground, are in fact only the more or less distinct expression of the struggles between social classes" (Marx: *Der Achtzehnte Brumaire des Louis Bonaparte,* Hamburg, 1885, Engels' preface to the 2nd ed.), Mr. Delevsky states that he agrees with Sombart's opinion that the principle of the class struggle must be replaced by the principle of the *struggle between nations.* The objection of Plekhanov, who said that nothing need be added here, since the class struggle is a conception connected with the internal processes of society and not with the relations between societies, is considered insufficient by Mr. Delevsky. "Either - or", writes Mr. Delevsky, "either history is based on two principles or on one. If on two principles - that of the class struggle and that of the struggle between nations - what is the law which is formulated in the second principle? . . But if " we have only the principle of the class struggle, what sense is there in distinguishing the struggle within society from the struggle between societies? " Or, perhaps the societies, nations, states, are likewise classes?" (p.92), This statement is truly delightful. Let us look into the matter; two fundamental situations are possible: either we dealing with a society (for instance, the world-wide economy of the present day) divided into the state organizations of the "national" sections of the bourgeoisie, or with the rather *loose, different* societies (for instance, if war is waged between different peoples, one of which - let us say - has suddenly intruded from very remote regions, as has happened repeatedly in the course of history: the conquest of Mexico by the Spaniards is an example). In this *first case,* the struggle between the bourgeoisies is a special form of capitalist competition. No one but Delevsky could even imagine that the theory of the class struggle would exclude, for instance, capitalist competition, which is a form of the antagonisms within the class, which have never succeeded in altering the bases of the given structure of production. While the Marxian theory recognizes the possibility of a relative clarity between classes, it also recognizes the possibility of a relative antagonism within the classes. It is hard to see how this refutes the theory of the class struggle. *Second case.* This is a methodological question. The theory of the evolution of society is the theory of an evolution of an *abstract* society, and it is quite true that this theory does not need to concern itself with the relations between societies; it analyzes the nature of society *in general,* ascertaining the laws of evolution of this "society in general". But if we leave these questions in favor of more concrete questions, i.e., among others, the question of the relations between the various societies, we shall again obtain special laws, which in their turn are also not in contradiction with the Marxian theory; not for the reason that the different societies are different classes (this assumption of Mr. Delevsky is simply wrong), but because "expansion" itself has economic causes, since - let us say - conquest inevitably is transformed into a regrouping of class forces; because in such cases the higher mode of production "below" always carries off the victory, etc. Nothing in this invalidates in any way the theory of the class struggle.

We have therefore seen that the oppressed classes do not always wage a class struggle in the proper sense of the word, which by no means signifies - as we have also seen - that such comparatively peaceful epochs are filled with nothing but peace and harmony. It merely signifies that the class struggle is proceeding in a concealed or incipient farm. It will *later* become a class struggle in the true sense of the word. Let us not forget that dialectics conceives everything as in course of *motion*, evolution. Even if the class struggle be absent, it is *evolving,* it "grows". Such is the case with the oppressed classes. As for the ruling classes, they are waging the class struggle *unceasingly.* For the existence of the state organization proves that the ruling class has constituted itself as a class *for itself,* as a state power. This implies a complete consciousness of the fundamental interests of this class, which wages war with the classes whose interests oppose it (war against the immediate danger as well as against possible dangers), for which purpose it makes use of all the instruments of the state machinery.

g. The Class Struggle and the State Power

We have already considered the problem of the state as a superstructure determined by the economic basis (see first part of "The Superstructure and its Outlines," chapter vi, *d,* of this work). We must now approach this question from another angle, namely, that of the class struggle. We must again emphatically point out that the state organization is *exclusively a class organization*; it is the class which "has constituted its state power", it is the "concentrated" and organized social authority of the class (Marx). The oppressed class, the bearer of the new mode of production, in the course of the struggle, as we have seen - becomes transformed from a class in *itself* into a class *for itself;* in this struggle, it creates its fighting organizations, which to an increasing degree build up organizations that carry with them the entire mass of the given class. When revolution, civil war, etc., is at hand, these organizations break through the enemy's front and constitute the first cells of the new state mechanism in open or concealed form. For example, in the French Revolution: "The `people's' or Jacobin groups - the former Societies of Friends of the Constitution, were at first bourgeois and now became democratic, Montagnards, Sansculottes, advocates of equality and unity . . . . They were founded for the purpose of popular enlightenment, for propaganda rather than for action; but circumstances forced them into political action, to participate directly in the administration (when the petty bourgeoisie came to the helm. *N.B.*). By the Decree of 14th Frimaire, the Jacobins in all of France became the electors and the purifiers of the officialdom."[2] "Taking everything into consideration . . . it was precisely the Jacobin clubs that now maintained unity and saved the country."[3] In the English Revolution, the revolutionary "Army Council" provided the men for the State Council. During the Russlan revolution the fighting organizations of the workers and soldiers - the soviets - and the extreme revolutionary party - the communists - became the fundamental organizations of the new state.

Two types of arguments are used in objecting to the class conception of the state authority.

The first type is of the following kind: the peculiarity of the 6tate is its centralized administration; therefore, the anarchists tell us, any centralized administration is a state authority. Therefore, even the most advanced communist society, if it has a systematic economy, will also be a state. This reasoning is based entirely on the naive bourgeois error: bourgeois science, instead of perceiving special relations, perceives relations between *things,* or *technical* relations. But it is obvious that the "essence" of the state is not in the *thing* but in the social relation; not in the centralized administration as such, but in the class *envelope* of the centralized administration. As capital is not a thing (as is, for instance, a machine), but a social relation between workers and employers, a relation expressed by means of a thing, so centralization *per se* by no means necessarily signifies a state organization; it does not become a state organization until it expresses a class relation.

The second objection to the class theory of the state has already been considered, in part. This objection is still more ridiculous, being based on the conception that the state discharges a number of generally useful functions (for example, the modern capitalist state builds electrical power stations, hospitals, railroads, etc.). This argument unites most pathetically in one group: the Social-Democrat Cunow, the Right Social-Revolutionary J. Delevsky, the conservative Delbrück, and even the Babylonian king Hammurabi! But this honorable company is much mistaken. For the existence of generally useful functions on the part of the state does not alter the pure class character of the state authority. The ruling class is obliged to resort to all kinds of "generally useful" enterprises in order to maintain its ability to exploit the masses, extend its field of exploitation, and secure the "normal" working of this exploitation. Capitalism can of course not develop properly without an extensive railroad system, without trade schools (if there are no skilled laborers, no scientific institutes, there will be no improvement in capitalist technique, etc., etc.). In all these measures, the state power of the capitalists is guided by its class interests. We have already given the trusts as an example; the trust also guides production, without which society. cannot exist, but it guides production in the direction of its class advantage. Or, to take the example of some ancient despotic state of great landlords, such as that of the Egyptian Pharaohs, whose huge constructions for regulating the course of rivers were of general utility. The Pharaonic state did not, however, maintain these constructions for the purpose of averting hardship for the starving, or subserving the general weal, but merely because they were a necessary condition for the process of production, which was simultaneously a *process of exploitation*. Class advantage was the basic impulse in activity; such measures may not be taken, therefore, as a proof of the incorrectness of the class point of view.

Another group of generally useful measures is called forth by the oppression of the "lower classes", for example, the labor protection legislation in capitalist countries. Many hair-splitting scholars (like the Russian pseudo-sociologist, Takhtarev) therefore do not consider the state as a pure class organization, for it is based ultimately on a compromise. A moment's thought will correct this view. Does the capitalist, for instance, cease to be "pure capitalist", because his fear of strikes makes him see advantage *to himself* of making concessions? Likewise, the state may make concessions to other classes, as the employer, in the above example, makes concessions to the workers. But does not signify that the state ceases to be a pure class state, an organization of a class bloc, *i.e.,* becoming a truly and generally useful organization.

Naturally, Herr Cunow does not understand this either. It is a pleasant sight to behold the impudent Professor Hans Delbrück, whom we have already mentioned, poking fun at these crack-brained distorters of Marxism: "The difference between us social-politically thinking persons, and you, is only a difference of degree. You have only to take a few steps more on the path you have begun, gentlemen, and your Marxian nebula will soon be dissipated" (Hans Delbrück; *op. cit.,* p.172).

h. Class, Party, Leaders

A class is a group of persons connected by reason of their common situation in production, and therefore also by their common situation in distribution, in other words, by common interests l (class interests). But it would be absurd to suppose that every class is a thoroughly unified whole, all parts being of equal importance, with Tom, Dick, and Harry all on the same level. In the modern working class, for instance, there is no doubt much inequality in brain-power and ability. Even the "being" of the various parts of the working class is unequal. This is due to the fact that, first, complete uniformity of the economic units is absent, and second, the working class does not step down full-grown from heaven, but is being constantly recruited, from the peasantry, the artisan class, the urban petty bourgeoisie, *i.e.,* from other groups of capitalist society.

A worker in a huge, splendidly equipped plant is a different person from the worker in a small shop, the cause of the difference in this case being the difference in the establishments, as well as between the entire resulting modes of work. Proletarian "age" must also be considered as an element, for a peasant who has just taken a job in a factory is different from a worker who has been in a factory since childhood.

The difference in "being" is also reflected in consciousness. The proletariat is *unequal* in its consciousness as it is unequal in its position. It is *more or less* a unit as compared with the other classes, but not with regard to its own various parts.

The working class, therefore, *as to their class consciousness, i.e.,* their permanent, general, not their personal, not their guild or group interests, but as to the interests of the *class as a whole, is* divided into *a number of groups and sub-groups, as a single chain consists of a number of links of varying strength.*

This *inequality of the class is* the reason for the existence of the party. If the working class were perfectly and absolutely uniform, it could at any moment come out in its full strength; its struggles might be led by persons chosen *in rotation;* a permanent organization of leadership would be superfluous and unnecessary. As a matter of actual fact, the struggle of the working class is inevitable; this struggle must be guided; this guidance is the more necessary, since the opponent is powerful and cunning, and fighting him is a serious matter. We naturally expect to find the entire class led by that section of it that is most advanced, best schooled, most united: the *party.*

The party is not the class; in fact, it may be but a small part of the class, as the head is but a small part of the body. But it would be absurd to attempt to find an opposition between the party and the class. The party is simply the thing that best expresses the interests of the class. We may *distinguish* between class and party, as we distinguish between the head and the entire body, but cannot discuss *them as opposites,* just as we cannot cut off a man's head, unless we wish to shorten his life.

On what does the result of the struggle depend under these conditions? It depends on a proper relation between the various parts of the working class, particularly on a proper mutual relation between those in the party and those outside of it. On the one hand guidance and leadership are necessary; on the other, instruction and conviction. No leadership is possible which does not instruct and convince. On the one hand, the party must be held together and organized separately as a *part* of the class, on the other hand, it must secure closer and closer contact with the non-party masses and draw a greater and greater section of these` masses into its organization. The mental growth of the class will therefore find its expression in the growth of the party of this class, and, conversely, the decline of the class will be reflected in the decline of the party, or the decline of its influence on the non-party elements.

We have already seen that the lack of uniformity within the; class makes necessary the existence of the *party* of this class. But the capitalist conditions of "being" and the low cultural level not only of the working class, but of the other classes also, produce a situation in which even the *vanguard* of the proletariat, *i.e.,* its party, also lacks internal uniformity. The party is more or less uniform as compared with the *other* sections of the working class, but not within itself. The same observations may here be made as in the case of the class. Let us assume - as we did before - that the party is entirely uniform in class-consciousness, experience, executive ability, etc., which is the complete reverse of the truth. Leaders would be unnecessary; the functions of the "leaders" might be performed in rotation by all the members, without detriment to the cause.

But in reality no such perfect uniformity exists even in the vanguard, and this makes necessary the formation of more or less stable groups of individual "leaders". Good leaders are leaders because they best express the proper tendencies of the party. And as it is absurd to represent party and class as opposed to each other, so it is absurd to represent the party as opposed to its leaders. To be sure, we have done this, when we opposed the working class to the Social-Democratic leaders, or the masses of organized workers to their leaders. But we did this - and still do it - in order to *destroy* the Social-Democracy, to *destroy* the influence of the bourgeoisie, operating through these *social-traitor* leaders. But it would be absurd to attempt to transfer these methods for the destruction of a hostile organization to ourselves, and represent this process as an expression of our peculiar form of revolution. The same situation may also be found in other classes; when, in modern England, the bourgeoisie ruled through party of Lloyd George, Lloyd George's party was ruling through the persons of its leaders.

The above will show the absurdity, among other things, of all the criticisms raised against the dictatorship of the Bolshevik Party in Russia, a dictatorship which is represented by the enemies of the revolution as *opposed to* the dictatorship of the working class. It is clear from the above that the class must necessarily rule through its head, *i.e.,* the party; it can rule in no other way. And if its head, *i.e.,* the party, is destroyed, the class itself and the class *in itself, is* also destroyed, being transformed from a conscious and independent social force into a simple factor of production and nothing more.

Herr Heinrich Cunow regards the matter differently. "A party .does not ask him who wishes to join it: Do you belong to a certain class? Not even the Social-Democratic party. He who accepts the party's principles, demands, and its platform, in all essentials, may become a member. This platform not only includes certain economic planks (interest demands), *but also,* like the platforms of other parties, certain *political and philosophical views lying outside the economic sphere of interests* (concluding italics are mine, *N.B.*). To be sure, the basis of most parties is a certain class grouping; but in its structure each party is simultaneously an ideological formation, the representative of *a specific political thought-complex,*and many persons join a party not because they have the same special class demands as the party, but because they are attracted by " this thought-complex." (*Die Marx'sche Geschichts-, Gesellschafts- und Staatstheorie,* Berlin, 1921, vol. ii, p.68.) These observations by the now head-theoretician of the Social-Democracy are extremely instructive. Herr Cunow gaily opposes the political and philosophical conceptions in the party platform to the *economic demands* of this platform. But how could you, Citizen Cunow! What has become of your Marxism? The platform is the highest expression of the *consciousness* in all the "thought-complexes". The "political and philosophical conceptions" are not made of whole cloth but grow up from the life conditions of these classes. They are not only not opposed to these life conditions, but, on the contrary, are their expression, and insofar as we are discussing the demands of the platform, it is obvious that the philosophical and political portion of this platform serves as the envelope for its economic portion.

We may observe this fact even in Herr Cunow's party, the German Social-Democracy. Absorbing more and more non-workers, receding further and further from the working class, by supporting chiefly the aristocracy of skilled labor in that class, the German Social-Democracy has also changed the mental-political thought-complex of its "platform", which has become much more moderate in its demands; in its ideology, it therefore favors the well - groomed-pardon the word - castrated "Marxism" of Herr Cunow, chooses Herr Bernstein an old betrayer of Marxism) as interpreter of its program, and makes Herr Vorländer (an idealist Kantian) its official philosopher.

i. The Classes as an Instrument of Social Transformation

If we consider society as a certain system developing objectively, we find that transitions from one class system (from one "social formation of classes") to another is accomplished through a bitter *class* struggle. In this objective process of social changes the classes constitute the basic apparatus of transmission for reshaping the entire body of the living conditions of society. The structure of society changes *through* men and not outside of men; the production relations are as much a product of human struggle and of human activity as are flax or linen (Marx). But if we seek among; the countless individual wills running in all directions, but ultimately yielding a certain social resultant, to find the basic tendency, we shall obtain certain uniform "bundles of wills": "the class wills". These are most sharply differentiated in revolution, *i.e.*, in an upheaval of society during a transition from one class form to another.

But hidden behind the law of cause and effect in the evolution of the class will and the various permutations and combinations in the clash of the opposed class wills - differing from each other - is the profounder causality of the objective evolution, a causality that determines the phenomena of the will at every stage in evolution.

Furthermore, the phenomena of the will are *limited* by external conditions, *i.e.*, each alteration in these conditions, proceeding under the reverse influence of the human will, is limited by the preceding stage in these conditions. Thus, the class struggle and the class will constitute an active transmission apparatus in the transition from one social structure to another.

The new class, in this process, serves as the organizer and bearer of the new social and economic order. A class which is not the bearer of a new mode of production cannot "transform" society. On the contrary, the class power which embodies the growing and ever advancing conditions of production, is also the fundamental living lever of social transformation. Thus, the bourgeoisie, when it was the bearer of new conditions of production and a new economic structure, shunted society from its old feudal track to that of bourgeois evolution; similarly, the proletariat, the bearer and organizer of the socialistic class formulation will shift society - no longer capable of living on the basis - from the bourgeois track to that of socialism.

j. The Classless Society of the Future

Here we encounter a question that has been but little discussed in Marxian literature. We have seen that the class rules through the party, the party through its leaders; each class and each party therefore having its staff of officers. This staff is technically necessary, for we have seen that it is the result of the lack of uniformity within the class and the inequality of the party members, Each class therefore has its organizers. Viewing the evolution of society from this point of view, we may reasonably ask the following question. Is - in general - the communist classless society, of which Marxists speak, a possibility?

It is. We know that the classes themselves have risen organically as Engels described, from the division of labor, from the organizational functions that had become technically necessary for the further evolution of society. Obviously, in the society of the future, such organizational work will also be necessary. One might object that the society of the future will not involve private property, or the formation of such private property, and it is precisely this private property that constitutes this basis of the class.

But this argument need not remain unanswered. Professor Robert Michels, in his very interesting book, *Zur Soziologie des Parteiwesens in der modernen Demokratie* (Leipzig 1910, p.370) says: "Doubts again arise on this point, however, whose consistent application would lead to an outright denial of the possibility of a classless state (the author should not have said `state' but `society' - *N.B.*) Their administration of boundless capital (*i.e.,* means of production - *N.B.*) assigns at least as much power to the administrators as would possession of their own private property. " Viewed from this point of view, the entire evolution of society seems to be nothing more than a substitution of one group of leaders for another. Accordingly, Vilfredo Pareto speaks of a "theory of the circulation of élites" (*théorie de la circulation des élites*). If this view is a correct one,

Michels must also be correct in his conclusion, i.e., socialists may be victorious, but not socialism. An example will show Michels' error. When the bourgeoisie is in power, it is by reason of the power - as we know - not of all the members of the class, but of its leaders. Yet it is evident that this condition does not result in a class stratification *within* the bourgeoisie. The landlords in Russia ruled their high officials, constituting an entire staff, an entire stratum, but this stratum did not set itself up as a class against the other landlords. The reason was that these other landlords did not have a lower standard of living than that of the former; furthermore, their cultural level was about the same, on the whole, and the rulers were constantly recruited from this class.

Engels was therefore right when he said that the classes up to a certain moment are an outgrowth of the insufficient evolution of the productive forces; administration is necessary, but there is not sufficient bread for all, so to speak. Parallel with the growth, of the socially necessary organizational functions, we therefore have also a growth of private property. But communist society' is a society with highly developed, increased productive forces. Consequently, it can have no economic basis for the creation of its peculiar ruling class. For - even assuming the power of the administrators to be stable, as does Michels - this power will be then power of specialists over machines, not over men. How could they, in fact, realize this power with regard to men? Michels neglects the fundamental decisive fact that each administratively dominant position has hitherto been an envelope for economic exploitation. This economic exploitation may not be subdivided. But there will not even exist a stable, close corporation, dominating the machines, for the fundamental basis for the formation of monopoly groups will disappear; what constitutes an eternal category in Michels presentation, namely, the "incompetence of the masses" will disappear, for this incompetence is by no means a necessary attribute of every system; it likewise is a product of the economic and technical conditions, expressing themselves in the general cultural being and in the educational conditions. We may state that in the society of the future there will be a colossal overproduction of organizers, which will nullify the *stability* of the ruling groups.

But the question of the *transition period* from capitalism to socialism, i.e., the period of the proletarian dictatorship, is far more difficult. The working class achieves victory, although it is not and cannot be a unified mass. It attains victory while the productive forces are going down and the great masses are materially insecure. There will inevitably result a *tendency* to "degeneration", *i.e.*, the excretion of a leading stratum in the form of a class-germ. This tendency will be retarded by two opposing tendencies; first, by the *growth of the productive forces*; second, by the abolition of the *educational monopoly*. The increasing production of technologists and of organizers in general, out of the working class itself, will undermine this possible new class alignment. The outcome of the struggle will depend on which tendencies turn out to be the stronger.

The working class, having in its possession so fine an instrument as the Marxian theory, must be mindful of this fact: by its hands an order of society will be put through and ultimately established, differing in principle from all the preceding formations; namely, from the primitive communist horde by the fact that it will be a society of highly cultivated persons, conscious of themselves and others; and from the class forms of society by the fact that for he first time the conditions for a human existence will be realized, not only for individual groups, but for the entire aggregate of humanity, a mass which will have ceased to be a mass, and will become a single, harmoniously constructed human society.

BIBLIOGRAPHY

An exhaustive study of the classes will be found in Professor Solntsev's book, *The Social Classes* (in Russian); Marx and

401

Engels: *The Communist Manifesto*; Karl Marx: *The Poverty of Philosophy*; Karl Marx: *Capital*;Karl Marx: *historical writings*; Friedrich Engels: *The Conditions of the Working Class in England*;Friedrich Engels: *Feuerbach* (English translation, Chicago, 1906); Friedrich Engels: *Origin of the Family, Private Property, and the State*; Karl Kautsky: *Die Agrarfrage*; Karl Kautsky: *Widersprüche der Klasseninteressen während der grossen französischen Revolution; N.* Roshkov: *Karl Marx and the Class Struggle,* in the Collection, *To the Memory of Marx* (in Russian); A. Bogdanov: *Empiriomonism* (in Russian), vol. iii; Victor Chernov (Social-Revolutionist): *The Peasant and the Worker as Economic Categories* (in Russian); J. Delevsky ,.(Social-Revolutionist): *Social Antagonisms and the Class Struggle* (in Russian); H. Cunow: *Die Marxsche Geschichts-, Gesellschafts- und Staatstheorie.*

NOTES

[1]*Social Classes: The Principal Factors in the Evolution of the Class Problem and the Principal Theories,* Tomsk, 1919 (in Russian), pp.268 *et seq.*

[2]*Aulard: Histoire politique de la révolution française,* Paris, 1901, pp.386, 387.

[3]*Ibid.,* p.350.